CW00731548

Liberators

In the autumn of 1944, Belgium was liberated at lightning speed. Yet Allied troops continued to dominate much of Belgian society until late 1945. Peter Schrijvers' revisionist account reveals that, during that time, strong currents of discontent began to build beneath the waves of gratitude and admiration. Chronic shortages of food and coal, rampant venereal disease, and deteriorating discipline led the Belgian population to lament "from the liberators, oh Lord, liberate us". Despite all this, however, the countries and cultures that the Anglo-American troops represented still exerted substantial attraction and influence, causing them to have a lingering impact on Belgian society in ways that would set the tone for the remainder of the turbulent twentieth century. Using newly discovered material from the Belgian state security archives as well as testimonies of the liberated, this book vividly reconstructs the largely unknown history of Belgium's liberation era.

Peter Schrijvers is Senior Lecturer at the University of New South Wales in Sydney. He is the author of *The Crash of Ruin: American Combat Soldiers in Europe during World War II* (1998), *The GI War against Japan: American Soldiers in Asia and the Pacific during World War II* (2002) and *The Unknown Dead: Civilians in the Battle of the Bulge* (2005).

Studies in the Social and Cultural History of Modern Warfare

General Editor
Jay Winter, *Yale University*

Advisory Editors
Omer Bartov, *Brown University*
Carol Gluck, *Columbia University*
David M. Kennedy, *Stanford University*
Paul Kennedy, *Yale University*
Antoine Prost, *Université de Paris-Sorbonne*
Emmanuel Sivan, *Hebrew University of Jerusalem*
Robert Wohl, *University of California, Los Angeles*

In recent years the field of modern history has been enriched by the exploration of two parallel histories. These are the social and cultural history of armed conflict, and the impact of military events on social and cultural history.

Studies in the Social and Cultural History of Modern Warfare presents the fruits of this growing area of research, reflecting both the colonization of military history by cultural historians and the reciprocal interest of military historians in social and cultural history, to the benefit of both. The series offers the latest scholarship in European and non-European events from the 1850s to the present day.

For a list of titles in the series, please see end of book.

Liberators

The Allies and Belgian Society, 1944–1945

Peter Schrijvers

CAMBRIDGE
UNIVERSITY PRESS

CAMBRIDGE UNIVERSITY PRESS
Cambridge, New York, Melbourne, Madrid, Cape Town, Singapore, São Paulo, Delhi

Cambridge University Press
The Edinburgh Building, Cambridge CB2 8RU, UK

Published in the United States of America by Cambridge University Press, New York

www.cambridge.org
Information on this title: www.cambridge.org/9780521735575

© Peter Schrijvers 2009

This publication is in copyright. Subject to statutory exception and to the provisions of relevant collective licensing agreements, no reproduction of any part may take place without the written permission of Cambridge University Press.

First published 2009

Printed in the United Kingdom at the University Press, Cambridge

A catalogue record for this publication is available from the British Library

Library of Congress Cataloguing in Publication data
Schrijvers, Peter, 1963–
Liberators : the allies and Belgian society, 1944–1945 / Peter Schrijvers.
p. cm. – (Studies in the social and cultural history of modern warfare)
Includes bibliographical references.
ISBN 978-0-521-51482-8 (hardback) – ISBN 978-0-521-73557-5 (pbk.)
1. World War, 1939–1945 – Belgium. 2. World War, 1939–1945 – Social aspects – Belgium. 3. Belgium – History – German occupation, 1940–1945. I. Title. II. Series.
D802.B4S37 2009
943.53′493–dc22
2009015142

ISBN 978-0-521-51482-8 hardback
ISBN 978-0-521-73557-5 paperback

Cambridge University Press has no responsibility for the persistence or accuracy of URLs for external or third-party internet websites referred to in this publication, and does not guarantee that any content on such websites is, or will remain, accurate or appropriate.

For Elle

Si je désire une eau d'Europe, c'est la flache
Noire et froide où vers le crépuscule embaumé
Un enfant accroupi plein de tristesse, lâche
Un bateau frêle comme un papillon de mai.

If there is one water in Europe I want, it is the
Black cold pool where into the scented twilight
A child squatting full of sadness, launches
A boat as fragile as a butterfly in May.

Arthur Rimbaud, *Le Bateau ivre*
(English translation by Oliver Bernard)

Contents

Plates

Maps

Acknowledgments

This book could not have been written without the variety of rich materials at the Center for Historical Research and Documentation on War and Contemporary Society (CEGESOMA) in Brussels. Among the many experts at the center, special thanks are due to Dirk Luyten and Dirk Martin. Thanks also to the center's librarians Hilde Keppens, Isabelle Sampieri, and Kathleen Vandenberghe.

Luc Lievyns of the Institute for Social History (AMSAB) in Ghent, Patricia Quaghebeur of the Documentation and Research Center for Religion, Culture, and Society (KADOC) in Leuven, and Raf Van Laere of the Provincial Archives and Documentation Center Limburg (PAD) in Hasselt have been most instrumental in facilitating access to numerous useful collections. Advocaat-Generaal L. De Vidts was kind enough to give permission to conduct research in the archives of the Belgian military tribunals that have found a home at CEGESOMA.

The list of those who have directly or indirectly contributed to this book during many years of research and writing is much longer than I can acknowledge here. For comments, suggestions, and feedback I am grateful to, among others, Martin Conway at the University of Oxford, Bruno De Wever at the University of Ghent, J. Robert Lilly at Northern Kentucky University, Benoît Majerus at the Université libre de Bruxelles, Mark Van den Wijngaert at the Catholic University of Brussels, Louis Vos at the Catholic University of Leuven, and my colleagues at the University of New South Wales in Sydney.

A special word of thanks goes to three people who in the course of my professional career have proven unstintingly helpful and encouraging: Luc De Vos, my energetic mentor at the Royal Military Academy in Brussels; Allan R. Millett, my formidable graduate adviser at The Ohio State University in Columbus; and Philippe Burrin, my inspirational colleague at the Graduate Institute of International and Development Studies in Geneva.

A book like this requires much time and financial support, even more so when one has to travel back and forth from Down Under. Both were provided generously by the Australian Research Council in the form of a Discovery Grant for a period of three years. A fellowship from the research group American Studies at the University of Antwerp enabled me to take out time from teaching for almost half a year. For the latter I am particularly grateful to Luc Herman and to Vice Dean for Research Dirk Van Dyck. I would also like to acknowledge the financial support provided by the University of New South Wales in the form of a research grant from the Faculty of Arts and Social Sciences.

As an historian and author who writes in a language that is not his own, I owe a very special word of gratitude to two people who have acted as guardians of the English language and, in this world of bottom lines, have done so pro bono and with indestructible good cheer. Caroline Finch, in Belgium better known as Martin's mum, kindly agreed to spend a winter in Norfolk on yet another of my manuscripts. I have been drawing on my sister Karin's linguistic expertise from the time of my very first book, as indeed I have been drawing on her advice in all kinds of matters long before I started writing.

At Cambridge University Press I would like to thank my editor, Michael Watson, for his encouragement and efficiency. Thanks also to Liz Davey, Joanna Garbutt, Helen Waterhouse, David Watson, and the anonymous readers.

To my family I can only say that I wish I could have seen more of them in the past few years. Australia is hauntingly beautiful, but it is also dauntingly far away. It is my privilege and good fortune to have parents who imbued all four of their children with the belief that passion and interest should know no borders. It explains why I have written this book with my parents, brother, and sisters looking over my shoulder.

Finally, this book is dedicated to my wife, Elle, for whom the maelstrom of history has come to signify a life of globetrotting and discontinuity. It takes a person of total Zen to accept it all with such admirable calm and lightness of being.

Note on Belgian place names

Belgian place names have been anglicized throughout the book (for example, Antwerp instead of Antwerpen). However, in instances where anglicizing the names of Flemish places might be misunderstood to mean that they are located in the French-speaking part of the country, the original Dutch-language names have been left unchanged. Thus Leuven is used instead of Louvain and the prefix "Sint" is not translated into "Saint."

Abbreviations

AA:	Archival collection CEGESOMA
AB:	Unpublished primary source CEGESOMA
AS:	Armée Secrète
AWOL:	Absent Without Leave
BT:	Smith Simpson, ed. "Belgium in Transition." *The Annals of the American Academy of Political and Social Science* 247 (September 1946)
CA:	Civil Affairs
CAC:	Conseiller en Affaires Civiles
CEGESOMA:	Centre d'Études et de Documentation Guerre et Sociétés Contemporaines – Studie-en Documentatiecentrum Oorlog en Hedendaagse Maatschappij, Brussels, Belgium
CEPAG:	Commission Belge pour l'Étude des Problèmes d'Après-Guerre
FFI:	Forces Françaises de l'Intérieur
FI:	Front de l'Indépendence
FR:	Fortnightly report
HBVL:	Het Belang van Limburg
JAG/ETO:	Judge Advocate General/European Theater of Operations
MP:	Military Police
MR:	Monthly report
OMA:	Office of Mutual Aid or Office de l'Aide Mutuelle/ Dienst voor Onderlinge Hulpverleening
OWI:	Office of War Information
PA:	Partisans Armés
POW:	Prisoner of War
RAF:	Royal Air Force
SE:	Haut Commissariat à la Sécurité de l'État/Hoog Commissariaat voor 's Lands Veiligheid

SHAEF:	Supreme Headquarters of the Allied Expeditionary Force
SHAEFB:	Supreme Headquarters of the Allied Expeditionary Force Mission to Belgium and Luxembourg
UNRRA:	United Nations Relief and Rehabilitation Administration
USAAF:	United States Army Air Forces
VNV:	Vlaamsch Nationaal Verbond
WR:	Weekly report

Introduction

Eighteen days of *Blitzkrieg* in May 1940 sufficed for Germany to sweep away Belgian independence for a second time in a generation. As the soldiers disarmed, the refugees returned from France, and the government settled down in London, control of the small country that more than eight million people called home was taken over by Militärbefehlshaber General Alexander von Falkenhausen. It was the onset of more than four long years of hunger, want, humiliation, and fear. Occupied Belgium was forced to put its industrial production at the disposal of the German war effort while receiving little in return. Growing scarcity gave rise to an increasingly strict regimen of rationing and a black market in which prices in 1943 were eighteen times higher than at the start of the occupation. In the cities and industrial areas ever more people were going hungry. In October 1942 the German authorities caused another shock wave when they announced that henceforth Belgians could be shipped off to Germany as forced laborers. Despite loud protests and mass evasion, almost 200,000 Belgians failed to escape this fate. Some 3,200 would never return from the German factories, mostly as a result of Allied bombardments. Meanwhile, the racist and totalitarian regime continued to perfect the mechanisms aimed at removing anyone labeled misfit or opponent. Of the approximately 56,000 Jews registered by the Germans in Belgium, some 25,000 (including almost 4,200 children) were put on convoys to camps in the east. No more than 5 percent of the deportees survived the ordeal. A multitude of military and Nazi security forces also chased down anyone involved in the resistance. The hunt accelerated in July 1944, when the military governor was replaced by civilian Reichskommissar and Nazi faithful Josef Grohé, who unleashed collaborating militias. Of the 30,000 members of the resistance caught by the Germans during the occupation, a total of 15,000 were executed or sent to their deaths in prisons and camps.[1]

[1] Van den Wijngaert et al., *België*, 49–50, 69, 82–4, 103, 108, 167, 169, and 293.

The summer of 1944 was one of hope as well as terror. After weeks of bitter fighting following the long-awaited Allied invasion on June 6, the liberating armies in August at last broke free from their shackles in the Norman hedgerow country. The speed with which they now pursued the Germans in the direction of Paris and Belgium was astounding. On August 25, Allied troops took control of the French capital and crossed the Seine. On September 2, Belgians were stunned to hear the BBC announce that the first liberators had already set foot on their own soil near Tournai. The whirlwind advance of the Allies beat anything the Germans had demonstrated in May 1940. At dusk on September 3, British spearheads from Hainaut were already finding their way into the Belgian capital. The day after, they rushed headlong into the crucial port of Antwerp. With that they had effectively cleaved through the heart of Belgium and sliced the small country in two. British, Canadian, and Polish troops fanned out west of the main axis to push the German XVth Army out of Belgium. British troops also continued their rapid advance east of Antwerp and Brussels towards Leuven and Diest, the Kempen, and northern Limburg. Meanwhile, American troops rushed to pursue what remained of the mauled VIIth Army east of the main axis, capturing close to 30,000 Germans in the Mons pocket, reaching Liège and Hasselt on September 7, and setting first foot on German soil five days later. If the Germans had taken only eighteen days to inflict a humiliating defeat on Belgium, the Allies had needed no more than ten days of combat to chase the tormentors from most of the country. The Germans did manage to put up a fight north of Antwerp and the Albert Canal until October, and in a pocket around Knokke in northern West Flanders province until early November. But such resistance could not lessen among troops and civilians a sense of immense relief about the comparatively minimal losses and damage with which the liberation of Belgium had been accomplished at lightning speed.[2]

All this, as much as the satisfaction of having regained their freedom, explains why Belgians across most of the country received their liberators amidst chaotic scenes of joy and gratitude so intense they would impress many an Allied commander and soldier for the rest of their lives. It probably also goes a long way towards explaining why much of the literature on the liberation of Belgium has traditionally focused on the stunning military feats of the Allies and why the memories of the liberated are often content to linger on the initial euphoria and the clichés of chewing gum

[2] Ibid., 267–71 and www.60jaar.be/nl/liberation/history/history2.html. Last accessed on June 8, 2005.

and chocolate. They would almost have us believe that, after the cheers and kisses in September 1944, the Allied armies packed up, moved on to Nazi Germany, and vanished from Belgium altogether, allowing the country to get back to normal all by itself. The reality was, however, that as long as the campaign against neighboring Germany continued, there remained a mass presence of Allied troops in Belgium. Indeed, even when Germany was defeated in May 1945, pulling out troops and equipment took time, so that even by the spring of 1946 a significant number of Allied soldiers remained on Belgian soil.[3]

That this presence of a large body of foreign troops, on the heels of a traumatic enemy occupation of more than four years, was likely to pose complex legal, political, and social challenges had, of course, been uppermost in the minds of those involved in planning the liberation of Belgium. On May 16, 1944, representatives of the Belgian, British, and American governments concluded an agreement on the civil administration and jurisdiction in Belgian territory liberated by an Allied Expeditionary Force. The agreement stipulated that during military operations in Belgium, the Commander-in-Chief of the Allied forces would exercise "supreme" responsibility and authority. As soon as this military phase had passed, however, the Belgian government would be allowed to resume full control over the civil administration and to enact laws, as long as this did not in any way prejudice the use by Allied forces of ports, airfields, lines of communications, and other facilities vital for the prosecution of the war. It was agreed also that the Allied Commander-in-Chief would have the power to requisition billets and supplies and make use of lands, buildings, transportation, and other services for military needs. The terms of the agreement made it clear that the jurisdiction over all members of the Allied soldiers belonged exclusively to Allied service authorities and courts, although the local police forces were allowed to arrest and detain soldiers who committed offenses against Belgian law until they could be handed over to the appropriate Allied service authority. On the other hand, however, Belgian courts were given jurisdiction over civilians alleged to have committed offenses against the persons, property, and security of the Allied forces, albeit on the important condition that these ensured speedy trials. Another

[3] Apart from some excellent local research (Sulbout on Liège, for example, and the seminar papers on Walloon Brabant written by students under the supervision of Professor Jacques Lory), notable exceptions in the general literature are studies by Conway (mainly limited to the Allied presence insofar as it impacts the Belgian political scene), De Vos (a brief synthesis on the presence of American troops), Hardenne (a brief synthesis of Allied–civilian relations without notes about the sources), and Pauwels (an excellent work on the smaller contingent of Canadian forces). On the Allied troop presence as late as 1946, see de Pinchart, *Office d'Aide Mutuelle*, 7, 8, and 16.

important decision that would do much to smooth relations between liberators and liberated was the establishment of claims commissions. These were to be created by the respective Allies with a view to treating claims for compensation in cases of damage or injury to civilians committed by Allied forces, with the important exception of those resulting from operations against the enemy.

On September 8, 1944, in the wake of the Allied armies, Belgian Prime Minister Hubert Pierlot and his government returned to Brussels after more than four years of exile in London, making Belgium the first liberated country with a restored constitutional government. Two days later, British Major-General George Erskine arrived in the Belgian capital. He and his American adjunct, Colonel John Sherman, formally established the Supreme Headquarters of the Allied Expeditionary Force Mission to Belgium, which took control of Allied affairs at the national level. The Allied Mission included a Civil Affairs staff that was to handle all problems of national scope. At the same time, British and American forces created Civil Affairs detachments at provincial and local levels, which were to act as their eyes and ears, to encourage good relations, to coordinate efforts with the local administration, and to aid the Belgians wherever possible by providing food, medical supplies, and transportation.[4]

The Civil Affairs agreement of May 1944 had assigned an important role also to the so-called Mission Militaire Belge. This Mission was appointed by the Belgian government in London and was to act as a liaison between the Allied military command and Belgian authorities. The first of its three sections consisted of a purely military liaison staff. The second concerned itself with matters pertaining to civil affairs and administrative and economic reconstruction. The third section was by far the most powerful as it comprised the Haut Commissariat à la Sécurité de l'État, which the Belgian government had already called into being as early as July 1943 with an eye to ensuring law and order as soon as the national territory had been liberated. The logical choice for the person to head the Haut Commissariat was Walter Ganshof van der Meersch. After all, in his capacity of Auditeur Général, van der Meersch was already in control of Belgium's military tribunals, the very tribunals that not only were to hear the cases against suspected Nazi collaborators, but also the charges against civilians presumed to have committed offences against the Allied forces. As Haut Commissaire, van der

[4] Delbrück, "International Law and Military Forces Abroad," 86; Donnison, *Civil Affairs*, 37–40, 111–19, and 469–71; and De Vos, "US Forces," 181–3.

Meersch had officers stationed in all of the nine provinces, where they served as his and the Belgian government's eyes and ears.[5]

This book combines the highly confidential sources of the Supreme Headquarters of the Allied Expeditionary Force Mission to Belgium, the Haut Commissariat à la Sécurité de l'État, and the Belgian military tribunals with the countless written and visual testimonies of the liberated and the myriad densely textured histories put together by local and amateur researchers. In doing so, the book goes beyond the euphoria of the first days to reveal in great detail the largely unknown history of Belgium's liberation era. The structure for this history consists of six chapters and an epilogue that each have a distinct theme.

The first two chapters describe how the humiliating retreat of the once invincible Germans and the often clumsy interventions of the Belgian resistance in open warfare set the tone for the wholehearted embrace of the Allied armies and their astounding might.

A third chapter analyzes the carnivalesque reception and celebrations as well as the first Belgian impressions of the Anglo-American liberators and the exciting new worlds they represented (the small contingent of Polish liberators are outside the scope of this book). The fourth chapter focuses on the dark side of the first days of liberation, when people, in often horrific rituals of branding and cleansing, set out to exorcize anyone and anything reminding them of Germany's failed and loathed New Order.

Chapter Five demonstrates how the initial perceptions of the Allies evolved and matured as the population had increasing opportunities to get to know the liberators better in 1944 and 1945. It pays particular attention to the means by which the Allies attempted to breed trust as governors in uniform and how, as ambassadors in uniform, they came to showcase their respective countries, the latter above all in terms of material abundance and the popular culture of film and music.

But if Chapter Five confirms the waves of admiration that continue to form the basic texture of today's dominant popular memory of the liberators, a sizeable Chapter Six provides this book with a significant revisionist twist by laying bare strong yet largely forgotten currents of discontent. These formed not only a permanent nagging concern for Allied and Belgian authorities alike, but during the winter of 1944–5 in effect threatened to undermine the legitimacy of the Allied presence in the eyes of the liberated, and in the summer of 1945 again did much to harm relations between troops and civilians.

[5] Laureys, "Le Personnel du HCSE: Un profil socioprofessionel," 267–8.

Finally, despite the strong currents of discontent that the mass presence of Allied troops gave rise to in 1944–5, the countries and cultures they represented did not fail to exert substantial attraction and influence. The epilogue considers the lingering impact of the Anglo-Americans on Belgian society beyond their immediate presence as liberators. And it does so by reflecting on the growing cult of abundance, the erosion of traditional authority, and the emergence of an American world order, all of which would set the tone for the remainder of the turbulent twentieth century.

Part I

The big void

1 The sun sets

The German troops steamrolling the Low Countries in May 1940 had so impressed the population that in one powerful drawing that month, a political cartoonist had likened them to a giant futuristic robot clanking its way through the gently rolling countryside. During the tortuous years that followed the shock invasion, the Nazi occupiers had proved themselves as zealous and efficient as they were unforgiving. In the late summer of 1944, however, these images of the Germans as haughty and invincible, built up over a period of more than four years, were wiped away in less than four weeks.[1]

The end is near

Sure enough, the last spasms of the occupiers' power stretched into the final weeks before the liberation. The dreaded call-ups for forced labor in Germany, for example, continued unabated throughout much of the summer of 1944. And even on the last day of August, German agents were staging raids in Brussels to get hold of young men who had refused to report to the occupying authorities and gone underground. Even so, the portents of the Nazi regime's imminent demise were becoming unmistakably clear that same summer. People carefully tracked the advances of the Anglo-Americans from Normandy and the Soviets from the east. They strained their necks to catch glimpses of the ever-growing formations of bombers on their way to the Nazi homeland. And they prayed in their basements each time the intensifying Allied air raids threatened to pound railroads and bridges close to their own homes.[2]

By the middle of August 1944, public life in much of Belgium was grinding to a halt. Retreating German convoys poured in from France and monopolized the roads. Enemy troops requisitioned schools and

[1] Leo Jordaan created the cartoon, which appeared as "De Robot" in *De Groene Amsterdammer.*

[2] Neckers, *Bevrijding*, 24; and Balace, "Bruxelles," 59.

other large buildings to get much-needed rest. Allied fighter-bombers, on their part, pounced on any vehicle on the move, thus adding to the chaos and congestion. By the end of August, textile factories in Verviers, for example, were forced to close their doors because raw materials stopped getting through. Provisioning became a growing problem for consumers in communities large and small. In the town of Leopoldsburg not a single bakery remained open early in September, and even milk was hard to come by. People in the capital stood in line for ever scarcer bread and vegetables, seeking shelter against houses each time German anti-aircraft batteries opened up and shrapnel rained down. On the first day of September, the telephone and telegraph lines in Verviers went dead. The town's newspaper stopped appearing the following day. During the next few days, Verviers discontinued its mail service and brought its trams to a halt. In Bruges on September 3, 1944, German authorities ordered all cafés closed at 6 p.m. with a curfew setting in two hours later.[3]

The Germans showed signs of increasing nervousness. For fear of the resistance lobbing hand grenades at them, the *Feldgendarme* in Comines thought it wise to put bars on their headquarters' windows early in August. A month later, German authorities in Brussels decided it was safer to have all Belgian policemen and gendarmes hand in their arms. Similar disarmaments took place across the country, and Germans everywhere were now frisking men they thought looked even remotely suspicious. To ensure that the population in the capital would remain docile, the occupier arrested several high-ranking officials and declared them hostages. On September 4, the German Kommandantur in the Flemish city of Ghent put up posters to announce a curfew as well as a ban on gatherings in the streets of more than two people. In contrast to the many *Bekanntmachungen* that had preceded it during four long years of occupation, this announcement was no longer printed in stern black letters. It had been scribbled in pencil and in a hurry.[4]

Getting ready

The Germans had serious reasons to be in a hurry. The devastating effect that the Allied juggernaut was having on the enemy first became clear to the Belgians in the form of endless hospital trains pulling into their stations from France. Packed together like sardines, casualties of

[3] Wynants, *Verviers*, 1–8; Bours, *Limburg*, 91; Banneux, "Souvenirs," August 28–September 3, 1944, AB 712; and Warnier, *Brugge bevrijd*, 12.

[4] Vierstraete et al., "Comines-Warneton," 492 and 506; Balace, "Bruxelles," 61–2; and Marchal, *Gent*, 19.

close combat and the pursuing fighter-bombers (*Jabos* as the Germans called the dreaded aircraft) arrived in carriages and boxcars that had Red Cross symbols painted on roofs and sides. The numbers soon exceeded hospital capacity, and in response the Germans requisitioned large buildings everywhere. In Lovenjoel near Leuven even the fragile women inhabiting a spacious mental home had to be evacuated to make room. Early in September, the fire-brigade siren in Duffel woke the Belgian Red Cross personnel in the dead of night. Agitated German soldiers ordered the sleep-drunk nurses to the local station. A long train screeched to a halt. The Red Cross staff gasped and gagged when the heavy doors of the boxcars were thrown open. Soldiers lay heaped together on a thin layer of straw. Some were thrashing about and screaming with pain, others barely seemed to be breathing. Puss seeped from filthy casts and bandages. Fearful of imminent *Jabo* attacks, the Germans on the platform barked at the nurses to transport their comrades to a nearby convent. The staff scurried to obey. They loaded the unfortunates into decrepit trucks and horse wagons. Some of the wounded had to make the trip on push carts. One of the nurses cried as she listened to the soldiers moan and beg with each jolt on the long cobblestone road.[5]

German authorities in Belgium meanwhile were readying more trains to facilitate their own retreat. Administrative personnel began pouring out of Brussels on August 29. The last train reserved for noncombatant personnel pulled out of the capital's station two days later, its carriages filled with hundreds of administrative officers, clerks, and telephone operators. Gauleiter Grohé, head of the Zivilverwaltung, called it quits on August 30. Richard Jungclaus, commander of the Wehrmacht, SS, and police, followed suit almost immediately. But he did not do so before drawing up a statement in which he urged the Belgian population to form a united front against both "the terrorists" (the occupier's preferred name for the resistance) and "the armies of the slaves of American imperialism."[6]

In cities and towns across Belgium similar scenes were repeated as more administrative personnel loaded files and office furniture onto trains and trucks. Hospitals too eventually had to be evacuated. In Leuven alone the Kriegslazarett housed more than 1,000 wounded soldiers. Those with light wounds left on foot. The others boarded green buses that had come all the way from Paris. Fearful collaborators from the Dutch- and French-speaking parts of the country joined the chaotic exodus or hurriedly organized their own convoys destined for Germany. Some of the enemy had been stationed in Belgium too long to bear the thought of leaving. The police in Leuven reported the case of a German

[5] De Vos, *Bevrijding*, 43; and Schilders, "Duffel," AB 122.
[6] Balace, "Bruxelles," 59–60.

soldier who had shot his Belgian "mistress" with his pistol and had then taken his own life.[7]

The preparations for the retreat were accompanied by destruction of all kinds. At the end of August, in full summer, fire brigades everywhere rushed to quell chimney fires as Germans and collaborators tried to burn stacks of incriminating documents. In Herstal on September 4, frantic Germans could be seen burning files and correspondence in one of the public parks. That same day, snippets of singed paper were raining down on the inhabitants of Brussels. The day before, German police forces in the basement of the landmark Palais de Justice had doused their archives with gasoline and set them on fire. Alerted by the billowing smoke, people rushed to the scene. Inhabitants of all walks of life were soon forming chains to rescue the building's art and library. Photographs show men carrying heavy leather-bound volumes and a woman hugging a bust of the country's beloved Queen Astrid. Flames meanwhile licked their way to the famous dome and caused it to collapse.[8]

The Germans did not just get rid of sensitive documents. They also made sure to prevent any military equipment from falling into the enemy's hands. They set fire to stacks of ammunition in streets and on sidewalks, causing serious damage to many a home. In the vicinity of Ghent, the occupier set the barracks and fuel stocks of the airport at Sint-Denijs-Westrem ablaze and then did the same with the large ammunition dumps in Zwijnaarde, where the explosions lasted deep into the night for more than nine hours. On September 3, two horrific explosions made the earth tremble in Ronse. Not long after, pieces of wood, leaves, and dirt began to fall from a clear, blue sky. They drifted in from where the Germans had blown up a large stock of V1s. The explosions obliterated the nearby wood and castle, shattering windows and tiles within a radius of more than three miles.[9]

While the Germans destroyed what they did not want others to get hold of, they simply took whatever it was they needed. Hospitals, civilian as well as military, were emptied of as much medical equipment as possible. From Liège's Saint-Laurent hospital, for example, the Germans took all the medical instruments and medicines they could find as well as all of the bed linen. What the retreating soldiers needed most, however,

[7] Aerts *et al.*, *Leuven*, 24 and 27.

[8] De Vos, *Bevrijding*, 79–80; *Herstal 1944*, 65. On the fire in the *Palais de Justice*, see Balace, "Bruxelles," 72; Taghon, *België 44*, 60; and J. S., "Bruxelles, septembre 1944: C'est la Liberté," *Pourquoi Pas?*, September 5, 1984, 13–14.

[9] For the German orders to destroy anything that the enemy might find useful militarily see, for example, "Kommandanturbefehl betr. Verhalten bei Absetzbewegungen," August 24, 1944, AA 525; Deseyne, *Zonnebeke*, 92; Marchal, *Gent*, 10; and De Tollenaere, "Oorlogsdagboek," 86, 90, and 93, AB 1734.

was transportation. Combat and *Jabos* in France were wreaking such havoc with their motorized vehicles that soon nothing much remained of the clanking German robot that had stamped through the Low Countries four years earlier. As early as June 1944, the Germans had confiscated some 15,000 bicycles across Belgium. Now, with the retreat from Belgium in full swing, Germans were requisitioning bicycles everywhere. They searched homes and halted cyclists in the streets. During two days at the end of August, the occupier cordoned off major roads leading into Brussels and proceeded to seize hundreds of bicycles from unsuspecting civilians. People were soon resorting to all kinds of tricks to hang on to their highly valued last means of transportation. They stopped using bicycles for visits and shopping and hauling things. They hid them beneath the hay in barns, dug holes and buried them protected by burlap sacks and straw, or dismantled them, hiding key parts in cellars and attics.[10]

The Germans were just as eager to get their hands on horses and wagons. "For the retreat," an order from the Oberfeldkommandantur in Mons read, "each horse and all means of civilian transportation should be put to good use." A traveling funfair in Zonnebeke quickly broke up its tents as soon as they learned that in nearby villages the sturdy wagons of colleagues had already been impounded. Farmers everywhere tried as best they could to hide the horses they so desperately depended on for their livelihoods. In the small village of Opitter, for example, farmers smoothly cooperated to bring horses together in a field shielded from the main road by a dense wood. Even pushcarts and wheelbarrows that remained in view ran the risk of disappearing.[11]

Food and drink too were being requisitioned by soldiers preparing to push off. Germans entered homes demanding "schnapps". The theft of rabbits, chickens, and hogs was so rampant that farmers in many places had to hide them in makeshift cages in the woods. Germans in Leuven could be seen leaving homes loaded with sugar, flour, and jars with jam and pickled preserves. For the Belgians who had suffered from shortages for four long years, German convoys laden with booty at times proved too much of a temptation. In Braine-le-Château an enemy officer had to fire his machine gun into the air to scare away looters from vehicles left unattended for just a brief moment.[12]

[10] Kaiser, "Croix-Rouge," 8; De Vos, *Bevrijding*, 79; and Gemeentebestuur Mechelen, "Oorlog 1940–1944," 20, AB 81.

[11] "Kommandanturbefehl betr. Verhalten bei Absetzbewegungen," August 24, 1944, AA 525; Deseyne, *Zonnebeke*, 89; interview Jan Vangeloven by author, December 9, 2005; and Gemeentebestuur Mechelen, "Oorlog 1940–1944," 20, AB 81.

[12] *HBVL*, September 4–5, 2004 and October 26, 1944, 2; Aelbrecht and Maghe, "Braine," 24 and 26; and Aerts *et al.*, *Leuven*, 26–7.

Robots to rabble

As the German retreat unfolded, stunned bystanders watched how the enemy metamorphosed from a onetime army of robots into rabble. The first waves of retreating forces in late August continued to look formidable enough as sleek tanks and columns of half-tracks and mechanized artillery rumbled through the streets. The soldiers looked determined, and people sensed that to betray any *Schadenfreude* was to invite trouble. Most hid their glee behind the curtains of upstairs windows as they spied the enemy's every move. An inhabitant of Braine-le-Château was smart enough to attach a small mirror to the outside of his window. That allowed him to take in the spectacle of retreating Germans on the road from Tubize without having to show even a glimpse of himself. Some found it impossible to contain their excitement and took risks. When early in September German troops began to pull out of his neighborhood in Antwerp, Robert Donnet sneaked onto his balcony and swiftly stole a picture of the historic moment he had been counting down to for so long. He made sure to record carefully not only the day on which he took the photograph but even the exact time: 3.05 p.m.[13]

The novelty of Germans on the run would soon wear off, but not the astonishment at the steadily deteriorating condition of the enemy troops. For the occupied Belgians, who had become convinced of the German army's superiority by its high degree of mechanization and motorization, nothing proved more eye-opening than the rapidly worsening state of enemy transportation. Vehicles that had been pushed to the limit regularly broke down, throwing orderly columns of tanks, half-tracks, and mechanized artillery into disarray, and frustrating their crews. Not a few tanks could be seen screeching by on just one tread. When a mechanized cannon lost a tread in Waremme, its crew jumped out cursing and kicking the vehicle. They took out some belongings and tinkered with the engine. Onlookers thought they were trying to fix the problem, until the Germans suddenly yelled "*Achtung! Achtung!*", dived for cover, and blew up the vehicle. The explosion left several houses badly damaged.[14]

In the wake of the mechanized vehicles followed an amalgam of trucks and cars that looked less and less military. German soldiers whisked by in anything from buses and family cars to fire trucks. Many had been requisitioned in France. An inhabitant of Hasselt saw soldiers roll by in a wobbly ice-cream van from Lille and in a rusty truck that had once

[13] Maerten, "Brabant Wallon," 123–4; Aelbrecht and Maghe, "Braine," 22–3; and Taghon, *België 44*, 68–9.

[14] Laby, *Waremme*, 197.

Plate 1.1 The German retreat in Sint-Niklaas. (CEGESOMA, Brussels, picture number 28550)

belonged to a laundry in Amiens. Some pushed on with one or more tires shredded to pieces. *Jabos* remained a constant source of fear. In the hope of keeping them at bay, many vehicles had Red Cross flags attached to their roofs even though they carried no wounded. In towns and cities, cars camouflaged with leaves and branches presented a silly sight. Soldiers hiding under mattresses in the backs of open trucks looked no less ridiculous.[15]

Many a German would have been satisfied hitching a ride on any form of motorized transport, no matter how undignified. But this became increasingly impossible. Belgians near the border with France saw large numbers of the enemy head home in sturdy wooden wagons pulled by horses, oxen, and even cows. The soldiers had equipment and ammunition piled high and their convoys reminded a thirteen-year-old boy of "a circus." French civilians drove the wagons or followed them on foot. Some did so in the hope of eventually recovering their prized possessions. Others had been forced to join and decided to flee not long after they arrived in Belgium.[16]

[15] Coenegrachts, *Hasselt*, 31.

[16] De Tollenaere, "Oorlogsdagboek," 84, AB 1734; Deweer, *Oudenaarde*, 143; and Marchal, *Gent*, 9.

Plate 1.2 The German retreat in Brussels. (Collection Lambrecht, CEGESOMA, Brussels, picture number 29334)

The image that stuck most vividly in the minds of Belgians was that of the enemy on bicycles which had neither tires nor inner tubes and rattled by on the rims. More and more soldiers trudged by on horseback too. On the morning of September 6, people in Warneton awoke to find the streets thick with droppings. Though the smell was "pestilential," it "made hearts leap," because everyone realized this could only mean that the Germans were finished. Perhaps nothing captured the spectacular demise of the German military better than the worsening condition of the noble animals. One inhabitant of Warneton described the horses as "mere skeletons." On the Boulevard Masson in Mons an emaciated horse collapsed in front of a handful of onlookers and had to be put out of its misery.[17]

Humiliation

Whatever opinion the Belgians had held of the German troops, throughout the invasion and occupation they had never failed to be impressed by

[17] Vierstraete *et al.*, "Comines-Warneton," 513; and Taghon, *België 44*, 39.

Plate 1.3 The German retreat in Braine-le-Comte. (Collection M. Collin, CEGESOMA, Brussels, picture number 28529)

their discipline. The retreat now shattered that image too. With troops in flux and authorities packing up, frustrated soldiers could get away with abuse of power much more easily. Two members of the Hitlerjugend on September 2 dragged a man from his home in Antwerp and forced him to drive to Wilrijk in a truck to haul ammunition for their unit. The boys joined him in the cabin and, through the open windows, from time to time fired salvos at civilians as if in a game. Many Belgians were rounded up to perform tasks facilitating the retreat and any last-ditch defense. The young men of Lommel were called upon to dig foxholes and clear trees and brush so often that most eventually decided to disappear into the woods, where they remained in hiding for several days and nights.[18]

The Germans became increasingly unpredictable, turning violent without warning. To cover the retreat from Ghent early in September, soldiers in armored vehicles with their machine guns sprayed any window behind which they suspected movement or light. Much of the violence was still more indiscriminate. On September 6, one of the Germans in a truck passing through the Walloon village of Bolland threw a hand grenade into a courtyard for no apparent reason. As the laughter from the truck receded, Louis Chaineux looked helplessly at his mangled legs. A neighbor managed to get him to a hospital in Verviers, where he died. An almost identical scene had played out in Strijpen some days earlier. In this Flemish village, grenade fragments severely wounded Albert De Zutter's sister and instantly killed his wife. They caused his seven-year-old daughter to die in hospital two days later. Random violence caused the deaths of scores of civilians across Belgium during the German retreat. In Verviers, for example, Wehrmacht and SS are estimated to have killed six people and wounded fifteen others between September 2 and 8.[19]

As discipline deteriorated, so did the personal appearance of the enemy. Four long years of occupation had made the Germans synonymous with impeccable grooming and rigid military bearing. As the retreat turned into a rout, the scenes unfolding in the streets left Belgians incredulous. German soldiers were unkempt, unshaven, and disheveled. They had dark circles under their eyes. Some were drunk. Many limped as their hobnailed boots were coming apart. In Veldhoven a German suffered the humiliation of having to trade food with a villager in return for footwear. A burly soldier trudged through the streets of Hasselt in full uniform but with his bare feet in a pair of white tennis shoes. The master race had fallen more than a few pegs. With intense satisfaction onlookers compared what they saw now with the cocksure soldiers who in May 1940 had routed Belgian troops and their British and French allies. "Here and there some soldiers wander the streets, begging for bread," seven-year-old Frieda Hendrickx later recalled of the very young and very old German soldiers in Eisden on September 14. "They are all dejected. Some cry like a child."[20]

[18] Gorsele, *Antwerpen*, 71; and *HBVL*, September 2, 2004, 14.

[19] Marchal, *Gent*, 11; Dechaineux, "Herve," 159–60; Commissie voor Oorlogsmisdaden, *Oost-en West-Vlaanderen*, 23–4; and Wynants, "Verviers," 11.

[20] Rijmen, *Ham*, 52; Coenegrachts, *Hasselt*, 31; and Janssen *et al.*, "Maasland," 74.

During the final days of the retreat, German forces showed themselves ever more disorderly and motley. Messages written on walls in paint or chalk tried to bring together units that had disintegrated. Wooden and cardboard signs on trees were put up in an attempt to rally disparate elements into makeshift combat groups. Civilians in Brussels picked up all kinds of equipment – even officers' sabers – as troops discarded anything now deemed useless. Inhabitants of Veldwezelt, a village close to the German border, looked on as enemy soldiers swarmed through fields and meadows because roads could no longer hold their numbers.[21]

Often the fleeing enemy was a far cry from the image of the Nazi posters' blond and muscular Aryan. Foreign soldiers had volunteered to serve in the German military or had been forced to join. They came from all over Europe and even from beyond. Most shocking to the onlookers was the presence among the Germans of soldiers whom they invariably described as "Mongols" or "Tartars." Little did they know that the strange men with their slender build and jet-black hair were former Soviet soldiers from the Asiatic republics who had joined the German ranks. "At one point we ran into a platoon of Mongols," recalled a flabbergasted teenage boy of some of the last enemy who passed through Antwerp. "We had never before laid eyes on such creatures as we had only seen them on the little cards that came with chocolate bars before the war."[22]

Amidst the chaos not a few enemy soldiers decided that now was the time to end the war for themselves. In the small village of Comines alone, people found one German hiding in a beet field and two others in the attic of a barn. For those who did not call Germany home, desertion made even more sense. In Nivelles on September 3, some forty soldiers from the Ukraine simply raised their hands and allowed the town to claim them as prisoners. A few days later an Alsatian slipped away from a convoy that briefly halted in Herve. He rushed into a home, changed into civilian clothes, and sat himself down to wait for the Allies to arrive.[23]

For those who watched Germans continue the war until its bitter end, the experience became just as surreal. A truck full of wounded screeched to a halt at a small German cemetery in Comines, leaving soldiers just enough time to rush and dig graves for two comrades who had died on the road. As there was no such place in Thirimont, the crew of a half-track

[21] Banneux, "Souvenirs," August 28–September 3, 1944, AB 712; and *HBVL*, September 3, 2004, 6.

[22] Emiel Thiron, AB 1591.

[23] Vierstraete *et al.*, "Comines-Warneton," 507; Blanco-Rincon and Dusausoit, "Nivelles," 15; and Dechaineux, "Herve," 149.

decided that for the two corpses they had on board a hastily dug hole at the foot of the monument for the village's Great War dead would have to do. Inhabitants of Nivelles noticed that in a convoy of horses and bicycles there were two trucks. Both vehicles turned out to be transporting corpses "stacked like herrings." None of their hounded comrades took the time to stop and bury them.[24]

Some soldiers sang to keep up their spirits amidst the horror. As they moved through Mechelen on their way to the *Reich*, a column of Germans performed 'Heimat deine Sterne' in melancholy tones. Many anesthetized themselves with alcohol. Fleeing troops in Brussels could be seen taking long swigs from bottles of cognac and champagne. A fourteen-year-old boy in Antwerp watched how a dozen SS troops parked their half-track next to a sleazy café. They were soon lost in "a kind of dance orgy." Stripped to the waist, they swayed to the blaring sound of a gramophone in the company of scantily dressed women, until booming cannon told them to be on the move again. Still others sought solace in quieter surroundings. In Bellegem three of the last German stragglers stopped at the church. One went inside and took his time. The other two did not move until he reappeared. For some there could no longer be any solace. A boy soldier in Braine-l'Alleud had gone mad. All alone and desperate, he rushed along the road from Tubize without even catching his breath. In his cramped fist he clenched a grenade as if it was the only thing in the world that would keep him from more harm.[25]

Humility

As the sun set on the Nazi regime in Belgium, the Germans began to shed their old skin of occupier. The masters who had once been all-powerful now had no choice but to accept the role of extras in what increasingly looked like a huge carnivalesque procession. "The road from Ghent to Antwerp," an inhabitant of Sint-Niklaas noted, "has become an attraction for the people of our town who mockingly watch what is a humiliating spectacle for the Germans." What made this carnival surreal, however, was the leaden silence. Thousands of people flocked to Antwerp's main avenues as they sensed that the last Germans were on their way out. But although engines sputtered and wagons rattled, the hush among soldiers and spectators was almost complete. "The

[24] Vierstraete *et al.*, "Comines-Warneton," 493; Roba and Leotard, *Walcourt-Beaumont*, 100; and Blanco-Rincon and Dusausoit, "Nivelles," 12.

[25] Alfons Claes, AB 1591; Banneux, "Souvenirs," August 28–September 3, 1944, AB 712; Gorsele, *Antwerpen*, 66; Vanbossele, *Kortrijk*, 57; and Aelbrecht and Maghe, "Braine," 67.

people are calm and dignified, but with a quiet cheerfulness," one of the onlookers wrote in his diary, "though sometimes mad and barking *Feldgendarme* waving a pistol startle them and make them recoil." A woman on the Place Meiser in Brussels, who watched the Germans file through from several roads, later recalled a silence that was "total, heavy, and oppressive." "One would not have thought it surprising," she commented, "if the air had exploded."[26]

During the last days of the retreat, German soldiers sensed it was pointless to resist even insults. With tens of thousands of bicycles taken from their owners across the country, often at gunpoint, a soldier in Brussels whose bicycle had only one tire left on September 3 thought nothing of commandeering one more bicycle from a silent onlooker. But this time the Belgian refused to hand over his bike and stood his ground. The startled soldier decided not to insist and simply resumed his trip on the rattling rim. Such small acts of defiance began to be repeated among bystanders across the country. A German in Oostham impounded a bicycle and pushed off, but the girl who owned the bike jumped on the back and refused to let go until the soldier gave up and jumped off. In Waremme on September 6, Marie Beauduin responded with similar bravado. Though she failed to recover her bike, she did manage to snatch the bicycle bags. In them were 500 posters announcing the arrival of the Allies and the reinstatement of prewar Belgian authorities. Ms. Beauduin had been on her way to police headquarters from the printer's. Just a few weeks earlier, discovery of her load might have cost the woman her life.[27]

Still more astonishing were the gestures of goodwill the Germans seemed increasingly eager to display in the final stages. At first, soldiers still had the audacity to charge bystanders money for the quality liquor, tobacco, and coffee that only Germans had been able to obtain during the occupation. But gradually the Germans could be seen giving things away to the Belgians. People who had known nothing but want as a result of the occupation remembered this as one of the more remarkable moments of the retreat. They also thought it to be one of the most puzzling moments. Did the Germans get rid of things to lighten their load? But why then did soldiers in Ghent on September 4 take time to distribute food and coal to civilians from trucks they had already decided to abandon? Surely the Germans in Walcourt did not hand out oranges, the rarest of wartime

[26] Van Bouchaute and De Meester, *Sint-Niklaas*, 39; Neckers, *Bevrijding*, 36; Greeve, "Oorlogsdagboek," 171, AB 2166; and Banneux, "Souvenirs," August 28–September 3, 1944, AB 712.

[27] Banneux, "Souvenirs," September 3, 1944, AB 712; Rijmen, *Ham*, 69; and Laby, *Waremme*, 207–8.

fruit, because these were slowing them down? Perhaps they were giving away to civilians what they did not want the pursuing enemy to have? That might have been the case with the very young soldier in Vrasene who stepped out of a column, walked straight towards a girl in the crowd and, without saying a word, handed her a pair of old motorcycle goggles. Or might such gestures indeed have been an awkward and belated way of saying sorry? German soldiers on the run in Antwerp stopped long enough to put candy in the hands of seven-year-old Liliane Wolters. They also told her not to think of them as bad people.[28]

Whatever the exact reasons for the Germans' sudden generosity, it was clear to onlookers that the enemy's humility went hand in hand with his demise. One of the mauled units that halted in Kortrijk just days before the arrival of the Allies was entirely dependent on horse-drawn wagons for transport. The wooden vehicles were crammed with casualties and the drivers sat slumped and nodding. Soldiers on foot were pale and unshaven. Most wore bloodied bandages and steadied themselves by holding on to the horse collars. At the head of the convoy, a razor-thin officer with graying hair sat high on a light-colored horse, like a Don Quixote tired of fighting against the odds. "Ghent?" he asked instead of demanding. "Just continue straight on," bystanders replied in German with a thick Flemish accent. The soldiers made use of the pause to fill their canteens with fresh water. The officer reached into his pocket, leaned down from his horse, and insisted the Belgians take cigarettes from a silver case.[29]

Chaos and looting

But with the Germans fading from sight, such moments of civility became rare as the occupied refused to rely on the occupier's generosity much longer. More than four years of scarcity and want now pushed people to grab whatever they could find as a gaping power vacuum opened up before them. For a while soldiers made some weak attempts to halt the rolling tide of plunder. Germans who started handing out food from their own depots in Quaregnon came to regret their initiative as things got out of hand in no time. They were soon beating off a crowd of rioting people and ended up firing shots that wounded some. At dusk on September 3, inhabitants stormed the large German depots near the capital's railroad station of Tour et Taxis while there were still some

[28] Marchal, *Gent*, 24; Roba and Leotard, *Walcourt-Beaumont*, 97; De Roey and Van Hee, *Bevrijding*, 75; and Liliane Wolters, AB 1591.
[29] Vanbossele, *Kortrijk*, 58.

soldiers present. In the melee that followed, rifles cracked and stocks of ammunition blew up in a tremendous roar that left some thirty civilians dead.[30]

The last remaining Germans could not be bothered for long as the tide of plunder washed across the length and breadth of Belgium. In some places police forces and resistance fighters intervened to try and stop the looting. In Herstal they had endless trouble restoring order when more than 200 people stormed the enemy's main depots in the center of town. Gendarmes in Waremme were called out to seal off the building that had housed the local *Kommandantur* for fear that looters would make off with everything, including valuable German documents.[31]

But the Belgian authorities were no more successful in halting the plunder than the fading Germans. In several instances, police and gendarmes were afraid to act too repressively. Many had become compromised by exercising their jobs under German occupation and feared incurring the wrath of the resistance or the population at large. At the same time, however, they often proved powerless even when determined to put a stop to the rampage. A report from the Haut Commissariat à la Sécurité de l'État (SE) drawn up just days after the liberation of Charleroi, for example, noted that the police in this city had tried their best to stop the pillaging, but that one had to take into account that here, as in many other places, they had been disarmed by the Germans in the final days of the occupation. It appears that, in fact, in some places the authorities were part of the problem. In Kortrijk, for example, during the looting of the town's refrigerated warehouses, policemen, resistance fighters, and civilians could be seen "working together in unison stealing like crows."[32]

People were soon picking clean any office, warehouse, depot, entrepôt, or freight train that had belonged to the enemy. That some of the buildings they sacked had formerly been those of Jews or labor unions or other targeted people and organizations rarely dawned on the frenzied crowds. Many looters nevertheless remained cool-headed enough to focus on the essentials to take home. Food was top priority, of course, but so was anything that would keep people warm in the winter to come. Inhabitants of Herstal who stormed the depots in the town center were most desperate to get at the sugar, cans of meat, and biscuits stored there. "For days on end," a teenager in Moerbeke remembered, "people threatened to kill each other over a bag of flour." Droves of people flocked to a huge coal

[30] Auquier, *Quaregnon*, 49–50; and Balace, "Bruxelles," 69.
[31] *Herstal 1944*, 75; and Laby, *Waremme*, 189.
[32] De Vos, *Bevrijding*, 87; Report F. Scaillet, September 7, 1944, Folder 972, AA 1311; and Vanbossele, *Kortrijk*, 55.

storage in Deurne. Within hours everyone in the vicinity was walking around with blackened hands and faces; people did not stop digging until a wall collapsed and killed someone. Others in Deurne grabbed pushcarts and hurried to the nearest German barracks, where they piled their vehicles high with wood ripped out with bare hands.[33]

That the enemy appeared to have drowned in luxuries while the occupied had lacked everything was soon causing indignant crowds to want more. According to a municipal report drawn up shortly after the liberation, people in Mechelen hauled everything from pickled fish to stationery, toiletries, and perfumery from the main depots; emptied a freight train of its load of food and tobacco; and gladly impounded the contents of a warehouse that had been "filled to the rafters with Cognac."[34]

But the looting frenzy went far beyond an interest in essentials and luxuries. People were literally taking away anything that was not too hot or heavy, including that which seemed utterly frivolous and absurd. A man in Beveren looked on as fellow citizens trudged by loaded like mules. "What have you?" he commented. "Aluminum locker parts, toothpaste, breadboards … useless, but it had belonged to the Germans, so steal it they did." Perhaps that was indeed part of the reason. Perhaps the apparently senseless plunder was a way of getting even with an enemy who had bled the occupied dry, a way of claiming back what, directly or indirectly, could all be said to have been their own possessions and thus their own identities. But it was much more than that. After years of war in which everything had been lacking, in short supply, or of low ersatz quality, people from a society that had previously enjoyed a decent standard of living desperately felt a need to compensate for being poor. They were hopelessly impatient now to take things home, to own stuff, to consume. If satisfying vital needs remained the most urgent concern, abundance became a fascination. In the city of Ghent the systematic plunder of German depots and offices commenced in earnest on September 2 and continued unabated the next day. "Anything that could be taken disappeared," a local chronicler noted, "plates, coffeepots and milk jugs, car tires and pillows, bags filled with anthracite, mirrors, beds, lockers, scales, refrigerators, typewriters, forks, knives, spoons, and so on." "I came home with two chairs," a teenager who had taken part in the looting in Moerbeke noted somewhat sheepishly, apparently stumped by why he had done so.[35]

[33] De Vos, *Bevrijding*, 87; *Herstal 1944*, 75; De Roey and Van Hee, *Bevrijding*, 60; Gorsele, *Antwerpen*, 56; and Theo Van Oosterwyck, AB 1591.

[34] Gemeentebestuur Mechelen, "Oorlog 1940–1944," 18, AB 81.

[35] Guido Kips, AB 1591; Marchal, *Gent*, 10 and 12; and De Roey and Van Hee, *Bevrijding*, 60.

Few people in those heady days had time to stop and analyze their behavior. Most rushed to join the others with fervor, afraid that, after four years of deprivation, they would miss out once again. The frenzy inevitably spiraled out of control on occasion. In the port of Antwerp, with its myriad giant warehouses, men, women, and children in one location could be seen dragging away club chairs; in another, rolls of fabric, paintings, and heavy boxes filled with disinfectant powder. When dozens of men emerged from a refrigerated warehouse with huge slabs of beef and pork slung over their shoulders, those less fortunate tried to close in and cut away pieces. This led to brawls all over the place and, when the last of the meat had gone, frustrated people turned destructive, ripping phones from the walls and smashing the cold stores to pieces until a pungent ammonia stink drove them off. As the Allied forces were soon to find out, it would take much more than a few days and the departure of the Germans for the frenzied scramble for food and things to die down.[36]

Amidst the scenes of chaos and looting, meanwhile, the Germans slowly faded away like ghosts. Sometime during the final stages of the retreat, people simply stopped noticing them. A photo taken on a crossroads in Mons early in September is less interesting for the five young Wehrmacht soldiers talking to each other than for the careless young boy strolling by in the background with his hands in the pockets of his shorts as if the Germans no longer exist. Around the same time, three boys of a similar age left Niel to walk in the direction of where rumors said the Canadian liberators were about to arrive any moment. The friends were armed with a camera and film that had been put away for four years for this very occasion. Along the way they noticed a German helmet in a ditch. When they tried to pick it up, a young soldier rose up from his hiding place. He offered the boys his rifle. They let the soldier be and hurried to resume their way. "After all," one of the boys later explained, "it was the Canadian tanks we were after." The Belgians were ready for a new world to enter their lives.[37]

[36] Greeve, "Oorlogsdagboek," 172, AB 2166; and Van Cauwenbergh, *Antwerpen*, 16 and 22–3.

[37] For the photograph, see Huet, "Mons," 90; De Roey and Van Hee, *Bevrijding*, 72–3.

2 Shadow fighters

The Allies whom the boys from Niel were about to meet that morning in September would strike them as many times larger than life. Most Belgians were to have a similar experience when first laying eyes on the long-awaited liberators. What made the Anglo-Americans such impressive soldiers instantly was the stark contrast they formed not only with the rabble of retreating Germans. The Allied troops also towered over the local resistance fighters, who in many ways appeared clumsy and inept when finally emerging from the shadows shortly before the autumn of 1944.

The stuff of legend

After the defeat in May 1940, the large majority of Belgians had felt powerless to do anything but make the best of what promised to be a long, if not permanent, occupation. From the very beginning, however, small groups from a broad spectrum of political convictions joined the active resistance against the Nazi German occupier. The numbers of the maquis grew steadily over the years. In 1942 the introduction of forced labor in German industries made countless young Belgians go underground and join up. The Nazi defeat at Stalingrad in 1943 and the Allied landings in Normandy in 1944 convinced many others that risking their lives in the fight against the occupier would no longer be useless.

Though the Belgian resistance failed to make the Germans loose their grip on the country, they did significantly contribute to the final victory through numerous courageous acts that cost many their lives. More than 600 titles of the clandestine press formed a counterweight to Nazi German propaganda. Intelligence services smuggled tens of thousands of documents with valuable political, economic, and military information to the Allies in London. Specialized cells whisked hundreds of downed Allied pilots out of the country so that they could resume battle. Perhaps most importantly, and certainly most visibly, many resistance groups engaged in sabotage. Such acts began to be committed on a large scale from the autumn of 1943 and continued unabated until the liberation. The focus on railroads and the electricity grid caused serious delays to the movement of troops as well as the production and transport of equipment. In the first quarter of 1944 alone, the resistance committed 633 acts of sabotage against the railroad network and managed to cause 87 interruptions in the flow of electricity.[1]

Despite such growing activity, however, the resistance in Belgium remained a small minority. The total number of resistance fighters is estimated never to have been much higher than 200,000, which means that these men and women never formed more than 2 to 3 percent of the population aged between sixteen and sixty-five. Nevertheless, on the eve of liberation most people thought highly of the resistance. In the final months of the occupation, Paul Struye, a keen Belgian observer of public opinion, noted that "the population shows real pride in sensing that an armed force has spontaneously risen in their midst, and the exploits of the 'White Army,' real or imaginary, which flatter and seduce the popular imagination, have by now become part of the stuff of legend." The problem was that the "White Army" was also by definition a secret army, an army that had been forced to operate by stealth and in the shadows. No one really knew how many members it counted, who they were, and what their strength was. "A dense mystery reigns," Struye admitted, "regarding its organization and its leaders." Such mystery gave rise to rumors and exaggerations. And it caused many Belgians on the eve of the liberation to have expectations about the resistance that were unrealistically high. "People expect to see them engage in action openly," the observer continued, "as soon as the Allies approach the Belgian frontier."[2]

A motley crew

All this almost inevitably contributed to a sense of disappointment when the endgame was finally set in motion. Not that the resistance failed to make itself useful in the days before the Allies appeared. But the problem for the resistance's public relations was that now, as in years past, its members continued to make their most vital contributions while hidden from sight. Nothing made them more valuable in the final days, for example, than their actions across the country to prevent key infrastructure from being blown up by the retreating Germans.

[1] Van den Wijngaert *et al.*, *België*, 209, 215–16, 253–4, and 260–2.

[2] On resistance numbers, see Colignon and Gotovitch, "Sang," 102; and Van den Wijngaert *et al.*, *België*, 215. For the public opinion analysis, see Struye, "Sentiment public," 276–7.

The resistance saved vital power plants and innumerable bridges from destruction. More importantly still, they safeguarded the crucial sluices at Nieuwpoort near the coast as well as the ports of Bruges, Ghent, and Antwerp, the latter regarded by the Allies as the key logistical hub for their advance in Western Europe. All this, however, was accomplished mainly by sabotaging telephone lines, cutting cables, engineering power outages, and removing explosives; not the kinds of exploits that thrust the maquis into the limelight. On September 9, when liberation seemed only a matter of hours away, some twenty strange men suddenly arrived in the village of Soiron. They wore overalls and carried weapons. People hid from the Germans who had arrived so unexpectedly, and the worried mayor, who knew a smattering of the enemy's language, rushed to the scene to see what they could possibly want. The armed men replied in French and put the mayor at ease. Neither the villagers nor the mayor had realized that this was what Belgian resistance fighters looked like in the flesh.[3]

A further problem was that on those occasions when the resistance did engage in direct action against the enemy shortly before the Allies arrived, they very often showed themselves to be woefully ineffectual in the full glare of onlookers. Indeed, the resistance seemed strangely out of place where it appeared in the open to fight a regular war with German troops. Their very apparel demonstrated in stark and often unflattering terms what it meant to be part of an unconventional army. Some forces projected at least a semblance of uniformity with the recognizable berets and white overalls. Most, however, in the best case wore no more than brassards indicating their allegiance. Other than that they appeared to be wearing whatever they fancied. Among a group of the resistance in Brussels captured on film, a young fighter looks into the camera with his shirt collar wide open and goggles around his neck, while behind him follows a more mature member in a civilian suit sporting a tie with an impeccable knot. A photo taken on a road near Berzée similarly shows a member of Groupe G wearing a civilian jacket and tie – as well as a flat-rimmed hat and shorts. Not a few reasoned that a genuine military outfit would identify them most clearly as members of the maquis and thus donned a musty Belgian uniform from before the occupation.[4]

The resistance quickly betrayed itself to be a motley crew. In large part because in the final days before the liberation many newcomers

[3] De Vos, *Bevrijding*, 53, 58, and 60–1; and Balace, "Charleroi-Namur," 39. On Antwerp, see Marquet, "Port d'Anvers," 189–90. For the Soiron incident, see *Pepinster*, 14.

[4] The photos can be seen in Taghon, *België 44*, 61 and 137. On the confusion the Belgian uniform caused when the Allies arrived see, for example, Major Cattoir, CAC report, Mons, September 9, 1944, Folder 972, AA 1311.

Plate 2.1 The resistance in Antwerp. (CEGESOMA, Brussels, picture number 27984)

quickly swelled the ranks of those who had been in the resistance for the long haul. In the rural community of Bottelare in East Flanders province, for example, 35 people out of a population of close to 1,400 claimed to be part of the local unit of the Armée Secrète (AS) at the end of the war. Yet the number of members who had been active throughout the war was significantly lower, as only eight people from Bottelare had in fact been part of the "hard core." Two of those, including the leader, had been arrested and would never return from the concentration camps. Not surprisingly, such exaggerated claims of membership did much to harm the image of the resistance in the collective memory of Bottelare, leaving the old guard who had been risking their lives since 1940 and 1941 particularly embittered.[5]

Those who joined the resistance late in 1944 did so for numerous reasons that ranged from sheer exhilaration to naked opportunism. For most of them there were not even overalls or brassards. Many were young and impetuous. Indeed, the leftist Front de l'Indépendence (FI) in the city of Verviers on September 7 posted notices that consciously targeted youth who until then "had been isolated from the Belgian army

[5] Duportail, "Bottelare," 135, 138–41, and 144–6.

of partisans." "Young people," its posters cried unabashedly, "join us, the Country needs you, the moment of vengeance has arrived." During the final days of the war, close to 60 percent of Hainaut province's armed resistance (as opposed to its intelligence services or pilot escape lines) were younger than twenty.[6]

In the streets the situation soon appeared a chaotic free-for-all. Belgian resistance fighters of all ages and various groups and subgroups staked their claims. French resistance fighters crossed into Belgium waving Forces Françaises de l'Intérieur (FFI) flags and joined the battle. Here and there the local resistance could be seen fighting side by side with a deserter in German uniform or Russian POWs who had escaped forced labor in the mines. A photo taken in Ghent on September 6 shows a priest who has taken up station on the King Albert bridge. He wears his trademark black hat and robe. He has pulled a white vest over his cassock. He also displays a brassard and a holster with a gun.[7]

The priest was fortunate. Not all of the many who rushed into the open in the early days of September 1944 had been equipped with weapons by their organizations. As a result there was, as the Allied authorities later noted in a report, a "general scramble for arms." Some just had to pick them up from among the mass of equipment left behind by the Germans in buildings and beside roads. A photo of the resistance in Bruges shows a man in a Belgian army uniform with a German cartridge belt around his hip and a Mauser rifle slung over his shoulder. For some it was much harder to obtain weapons. The resistance in Zonnebeke made the rounds of farmers who were thought to possess weapons for the protection of their cattle and food stocks. On the outskirts of Ghent, meanwhile, some units of the AS engaged in skirmishes with the Germans for the express purpose of obtaining more arms. In Oudenaarde at least one member of the same organization was killed while groping for a rifle in an abandoned enemy half-track.[8]

Amateur soldiers

The Belgian resistance were not well prepared for regular battle with even the tail end of the mauled German military. They were hopelessly

[6] For a photo of the FI poster, see Ruwet, *Verviers*, 89. On Hainaut, see Dauphin, "La Belgique libérée," 71.

[7] On the FFI, see Taghon, *België 44*, 23, and SHAEFB, FR No. 9, January 23, 1945, WO 202/689, AA 1230. For examples of deserters and Russians fighting alongside the resistance, see Janssen *et al.*, "Maasland," 103; and Wollants and Bouveroux, *Russische partizanen*, 155–61. Marchal, *Gent*, 98.

[8] SHAEFB, FR No. 2, October 17, 1944, WO 202/682, AA 1230; Taghon, *België 44*, 108; Deseyne, *Zonnebeke*, 101; Van Poucke, "Liberté," 57; and Deweer, *Oudenaarde*, 85.

divided politically and lacked an umbrella organization like the FFI. This hampered coordination on the ground as well as communication with the Allied authorities in London. Indeed, it took the Belgian government until September 1944 to officially recognize some of the organizations that it considered politically suspicious, not in the least those on the far left. Even local units could be quite fragmented as several lacked firm structures. In Essen, for example, a small rural community on the border with Holland, a population of some 7,300 had spawned two resistance groups. Not only did these groups operate independently of each other, but within each unit at least two leaders had emerged who each more or less followed their own agenda. The situation would soon be causing an "impression of chaos and uncontrolled actions" that did much to discredit the resistance in the village's collective memory until long after the war. Ironically, matters for the resistance in Belgium were further complicated by the very success of the Allied advance once it shook off the shackles of the Normandy *bocage* in August 1944. So rushed was the march towards Belgium late that summer that many of the drops of weapons, radio equipment, and agents that London had promised to the resistance for the liberation phase never materialized.[9]

With or without those reinforcements, however, a major weakness of the resistance was always going to be the lack of any serious instruction in open rather than secret warfare. In a small country under tight occupation such training had of necessity been limited even for the old guard. For the late recruits, soon mockingly known as "the September resistance," it was utterly impossible. "I was given a rifle and ammunition," recalled a boy of seventeen who joined the FI at the end of the war, "and after some fifteen minutes of fire practice I was dragged along to help liberate Reet." "Fortunately," he added, "the ammunition didn't fit the rifle." Others were less fortunate. Because one of his fighters showed himself clumsy with his Sten gun when they prepared to move out onto the streets of Waremme, the leader quickly thrust a pistol into the man's hands. No sooner had they stepped outside then the pistol went off, the bullet ricocheting against a wall and everyone holding their breath for fear that German stragglers might have been alerted. A similar incident killed a member of the Nivelles resistance even as he boarded the truck that was to take him to the nearby woods for an attack against the enemy rearguard.[10]

[9] De Vos, *Bevrijding*, 50–1; Wouters, "Essen," 133 and 157–9; and Van Poucke, "Liberté," 41.

[10] De Roey and Van Hee, *Bevrijding*, 80–1; Laby, *Waremme*, 212; and Blanco-Rincon and Dusausoit, "Nivelles," 15–16.

Plate 2.2 The *Armée Secrète* and a German prisoner in Mont-sur-Marchienne. (CEGESOMA, Brussels, picture number 28007)

In interviews after the war, many of the villagers of Braine-l'Alleud questioned the behavior of the resistance during the liberation because they "went about their business as amateurs." Eager to engage with the enemy and prove their courage in whatever way they could, local fighters fumbled and stumbled. In a tiny village in the Herve area the resistance took two deserters prisoner but wounded one in the process. Spooked and fearing reprisals, they could think of nothing else than to blindfold the two and release them again not far from the village. As Belgians across the country would learn in the waning days of the war, there was no place, and even less mercy, for poorly armed amateurs in pitched battles with what was left of German troops who had gained experience over many years. In the late afternoon of September 6, as the racket of approaching Allied troops could be heard, resistance fighters in Ghent decided to try and gain control of the Desmet bridge. The first ones to near the bridge were picked off by German snipers. The others panicked and fled to a nearby café. There the snipers kept them pinned down until the next day, killing several more who made the mistake of exposing themselves. By dawn, eleven of the resistance lay dead in reckless sacrifice for a bridge that seemed further away than ever.[11]

[11] Aelbrecht and Maghe, "Braine," 68; Dechaineux, "Herve," 159; and Marchal, *Gent*, 80–1.

In a matter of days similar brazen actions left scores of resistance fighters dead, often for no clear purpose: 3 in Sint-Andries, 4 in Wevelgem, 6 in Dadizele, 12 in Waterloo, and 33 in Wodecq, just to name a few. But the worst tragedy for the Belgian resistance undoubtedly took place in and near Forêt, a village just west of Verviers. As in many other places across the country, the resistance of this area in the first days of September had flocked to its assembly point in response to coded orders sent out from London. But the orders were not followed by the promised drops of additional military equipment, leaving a densely packed group of local fighters very conspicuous but only lightly armed. It was a recipe for disaster.[12]

For Forêt the assembly point was the local château and its farms. In the Demonceau farm, 100 fighters were crowding each other, many impatient, some impetuous. On Sunday, September 3, a patrol came back with five German prisoners. Later that Sunday, the maquis killed the occupants of an enemy truck and scrambled to hide the bodies and vehicle. The following day, two Belgian collaborators and a Polish national suspected of being an informer were brought in. As if all this reckless activity of the past two days had not been enough to alert the Germans to their presence, the resistance on Tuesday went out again, capturing three of four Germans guarding an aqueduct over the Vesdre River. Almost simultaneously, another band of the maquis attacked a mobile enemy kitchen in nearby Prayon. In the skirmish that ensued, the maquis killed one German. They then tried to tow the kitchen to Forêt behind their own vehicle. German troops pursued them, however, forcing them to abandon not only the kitchen, but their own vehicle too.

Inevitably, later that Tuesday, an irritated enemy decided it was time to clear the area from *Terroristen*. Between them, the 100 fighters in the Demonceau farm possessed no more than four machine guns, eight captured Mauser rifles, and some pistols and grenades. Three-quarters of an hour later, five local fighters had been mown down, and their comrades were beating a hasty retreat. It was only the beginning of the nightmare. More German troops were sent in, including at least one fully armed battalion of several hundred men. When the enemy finally called off the hunt, 36 fighters lay dead in Forêt and another 22 or 23 in nearby Île Monsin, bringing the total maquis slaughtered in the area to at least 63.[13]

[12] De Vos, *Bevrijding*, 84.
[13] Marquet, "Forêt-Trooz," 106–8; and Colignon, "Fontainebleau," 115.

Reprisals

Though hard to imagine, still worse scenarios played out in other towns and villages across Belgium. As they were being attacked by forces that did not wear regular military uniforms, frustrated Germans on more than one occasion stopped discriminating between partisans and innocents. Just hours before the Allies were to liberate Waremme on September 7, six members of the AS, supported by four gendarmes, took up positions in shops and on balconies in the town center. They were determined to make life difficult for any of the last Germans still trying to make their way home. Sure enough, shortly after, a convoy of three enemy vehicles halted at the town crossroads. As the soldiers got out to look for directions, the maquis opened fire. But things did not go as planned. The person operating the Sten gun was so inexperienced that his salvos raked only the walls above the Germans' heads. In another shop, one of the local fighters was prevented from opening fire at all as the owner pulled him away, afraid that the ripostes would ruin his business. The Germans scurried to their convoy, gunned the engines, and tore away. On the way out they furiously fired at doors and windows. They also fired a burst just above the heads of Maurice Bourguignon and his granddaughter, both of whom stood paralyzed on the sidewalk. But a fuming Guillaume Stouvenakers was quick on his feet and rushed to confront the reckless maquis. "Are you insane or what?" he demanded to know. "You will succeed in having this town burned down and all of us killed."[14]

The town of Waremme was spared such a fate. More than thirty miles to the southeast, however, several rural communities near Verviers were less fortunate. In response to a coded message aired by the BBC, several hundred members of the AS on September 4 left Verviers to take up positions south of the city, at the château of Sohan and its farm. The trip itself looked very disorganized. Many of the fighters were extremely young, some wore casual sports outfits, others were joined at least part of the way by mothers and girlfriends. Only one of every ten men was armed as the promised drops had not arrived from England. A report drawn up by the SE shortly after the liberation noted that the mobilization of the resistance in Verviers had taken place "in the total absence of common sense and for all in the city to see."

The scenario that followed was in many ways similar to that unfolding in Forêt on the same day. Ill-conceived raids in the morning of September 5 led to a total of seven German prisoners. One managed to escape, however, and by noon already, well-armed German troops went on the attack. The maquis ran out of ammunition almost immediately

[14] Laby, *Waremme*, 220–1.

and had to abandon Sohan, leaving two dead comrades behind. Angry and frustrated, the Germans set the château ablaze. They beat up and then killed the band's priest, a Jesuit who had decided to stay behind with the hamlet's inhabitants. Still not satisfied, the soldiers also executed an old man, a woman, a six-year-old girl, and two other civilians.

At about the same time, German troops were taking similar reprisals at Amay, a village much further west, near the city of Huy. Without asking questions, they torched one farm and executed seven people. They covered their victims with straw and set them alight. A woman who was beaten and forced to drag away the charred corpses managed to get away alive to tell what happened in gory detail. A man who miraculously survived both the execution and the pyre could not be moved to speak a word. He had seen his thirteen-year-old son die at the farm and had lost his speech as well as his memory of that fateful day.[15]

Out of place

The horror stories piled up and traveled fast. Foolhardy attempts by the resistance to fight it out in the open with the Germans caused civilians to get increasingly worried and upset. Most of the time the men of the maquis could not even hope to win such battles. Yet they continued to engage with the enemy, serving only one purpose, it seemed to many Belgians, and that was to make the retreating soldiers more trigger-happy and unpredictable than they already were. The Germans had been harassed by partisans from as far away as France and were getting ever more irritated. Often, the very first question they hurled at civilians when halting somewhere was if anyone had seen partisans around. Many a German convoy had soldiers on the roofs and hoods of vehicles nervously pointing their guns at houses and sidewalks. Others took more stringent measures to dissuade the partisans from striking. In Harzé, where the maquis was known to be active in the surrounding forests, SS troops dragged more than forty men from their homes and locked them up in the local school. Then they forced a number of women onto their vehicles as human shields and pushed off again. The women from Harzé were safely released not much later. But most of the eighty civilians who lost their lives in the Mons pocket, for example, did so as hostages or human shields meant to protect against partisans taking ill-advised action.[16]

[15] Wynants, *Verviers*, 9–11; and Commissie voor Oorlogsmisdaden, *Hoei-Namen*, 15–17. The SE report is dated September 22, 1944, Folder 979, AA 1311.

[16] On the German fear of partisans see, for example, Deseyne, *Zonnebeke*, 90; and excerpt from Father Falco Nijs' diary in Marchal, *Gent*, 11. For the Harzé incident, see Henry, *Aywaille*, 104–5. Huet, "Mons," 97.

Not surprisingly, in this tense climate of fear and suspicion, even German troops tired of fighting considered the partisans the last persons on earth to surrender to. When some 300 exhausted German soldiers stacked their rifles against each other and fell to the ground to rest in a square in Comines, local leaders of the AS took the risk of approaching their commander to see if they could get him to surrender. The officer remained calm and polite. But he indicated that, although he was indeed contemplating surrender, the partisans would never be able to offer sufficient guarantees regarding the safety of his men after they had put down their weapons. Not much later, the troops wearily climbed back into their trucks to continue the war they considered lost. A similar situation occurred in the Flemish part of the country, where a combat group of 350 soldiers sought to get some much-needed rest in the convent and school of Sint-Martens-Latem. The parish priest quickly established a rapport with one of the unit's commanding officers, who was a devout Catholic. He convinced the German officer to listen to BBC broadcasts that told him British troops were about to arrive any time now. The priest, eager to save his flock from battle, suggested the unit might do well to surrender then and there. He even managed to arrange talks with the local resistance commander. After some tense negotiations, a compromise was finally reached. The German officers refused to surrender to the partisans. But they did agree to surrender to the British as soon as these arrived. The Germans then marched to the school playground and got organized. Weapons in hand, they bided their time, their eyes on the road from where they knew the regular troops would come to take them prisoner.[17]

Onlookers could not help but wonder. If the resistance could not win battles and on occasion failed to take prisoner even Germans who were ready to surrender, what did they think they were doing out in the open at all, except risking their own lives and that of innocents? On September 8, one day before the liberation, two German soldiers were gunned down in a street of Andrimont, a village just northeast of Verviers. The Germans swiftly exacted revenge, torching four farms and executing six farmers in the same street. No one ever claimed responsibility for the killings that triggered such horrific retaliation. But when interviewed half a century later, most of Andrimont's inhabitants had little doubt that the maquis was to blame. And the family of the victims wondered out loud why the resistance had been so eager to kill two harmless Germans

[17] Vierstraete *et al.*, "Comines-Warneton," 495. On Sint-Martens-Latem, see excerpt from Father Verhegge's parish journal in Marchal, *Gent*, 49; and photo in Taghon, *België 44*, 78.

but were nowhere to be seen when the villagers were in real trouble. Numerous interviews with people who had lived through the war in the French-speaking part of Brabant province, just south of Brussels, generally painted a picture of the resistance that was "not very flattering." Many blamed the deluge of "resistance fighters of the last hour." And they did not hesitate to describe those who sought the spotlight in the streets in September 1944 as "clumsy" and "irresponsible," sometimes even as "selfish" and "cowardly."[18]

To criticize the resistance openly during the days of the liberation, however, was politically incorrect and at times outright dangerous. When it was finally able to reappear early in September 1944, the regional newspaper for Limburg province enthusiastically joined the chorus of praise for the patriots who had risked their lives so that people would one day taste freedom again. But on September 17, the newspaper indirectly and unwittingly did criticize the resistance for their more reckless actions of the past weeks. In this particular edition, *Het Belang van Limburg* detailed the German retaliation against innocent civilians, with murders in Opglabbeek, Lanaken, and several other places. Then it went on to note that in Rekem, Mechelen-aan-de-Maas, and Eisden there had fortunately not been any such tragedies. The absence of German atrocities in this particular region, the newspaper remarked, was "Probably thanks to the White Brigade that was careful enough to remain passive until the arrival of the Americans." They may have been sincere words of gratitude, but they were far from a compliment.[19]

By the time the din of the approaching Allies could be heard in the distance, many Belgians were fed up with scenes that must have reminded some of the Keystone Kops. In Brussels dilapidated vehicles with multiple hastily applied distinguishing marks could be seen crisscrossing the city in all directions but without apparent purpose. Men in ragtag outfits enthusiastically brandished a few antiquated arms, while others in the capital angrily aimed their guns at an enemy who was no longer there.[20]

For three long days, the resistance in Liège's Saint-Denis district had been waiting impatiently for the moment of action. That moment

[18] Meunier, *Dison et Andrimont*, 60–75; and Maerten, "Brabant Wallon," 141.

[19] *HBVL*, September 17, 1944, 1. Half a century later, a history of the liberation of Chaudfontaine would make a similar comment. Noting that the rapid American advance had given the resistance little opportunity for action, the authors expressed relief at the fact that the fighters had at least abstained from rash last-minute action that could have led to reprisals: "For that alone we owe them our gratitude." Lognard-Poncin and Michel, *Chaudfontaine*, 59.

[20] Balace, "Bruxelles," 78–9.

finally came on September 7, when rumor had it that the Americans were on their way. Some twenty men wearing brassards hurried into a cellar. They emerged with what for the most part were old hunting rifles. Shop owners applauded the maquis when they appeared in the street. But then, suddenly, a group of just as many German soldiers rushed by on bicycles. They noticed the armed men and opened fire. The maquis wanted to return fire but couldn't. Humidity had spoiled the cartridges and made the rifles malfunction. All the men could do was run and hide in the nearest shops. But now the owners, fearing retaliation, were less enthusiastic. Denied entrance with their weapons, the fighters quickly tossed their rifles onto the street and then vanished from sight.[21]

It would have been slapstick had it not been so dangerous. People strained their necks to catch a first glimpse of the real soldiers who were soon to step into the big void.

[21] Jour, *Libération Liège*, 28.

Part II

Liberation!

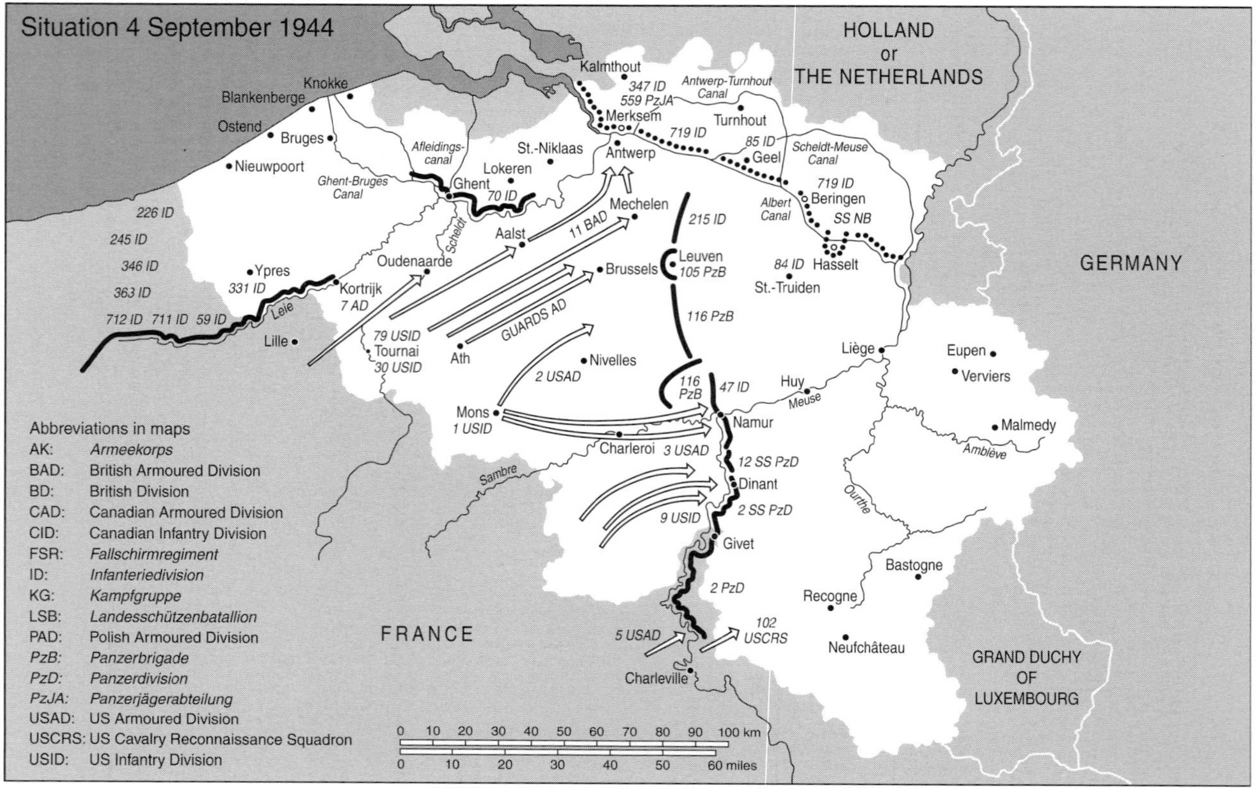

Map 1 The liberation of Belgium, 4 September 1944 (Map Peter Taghon)

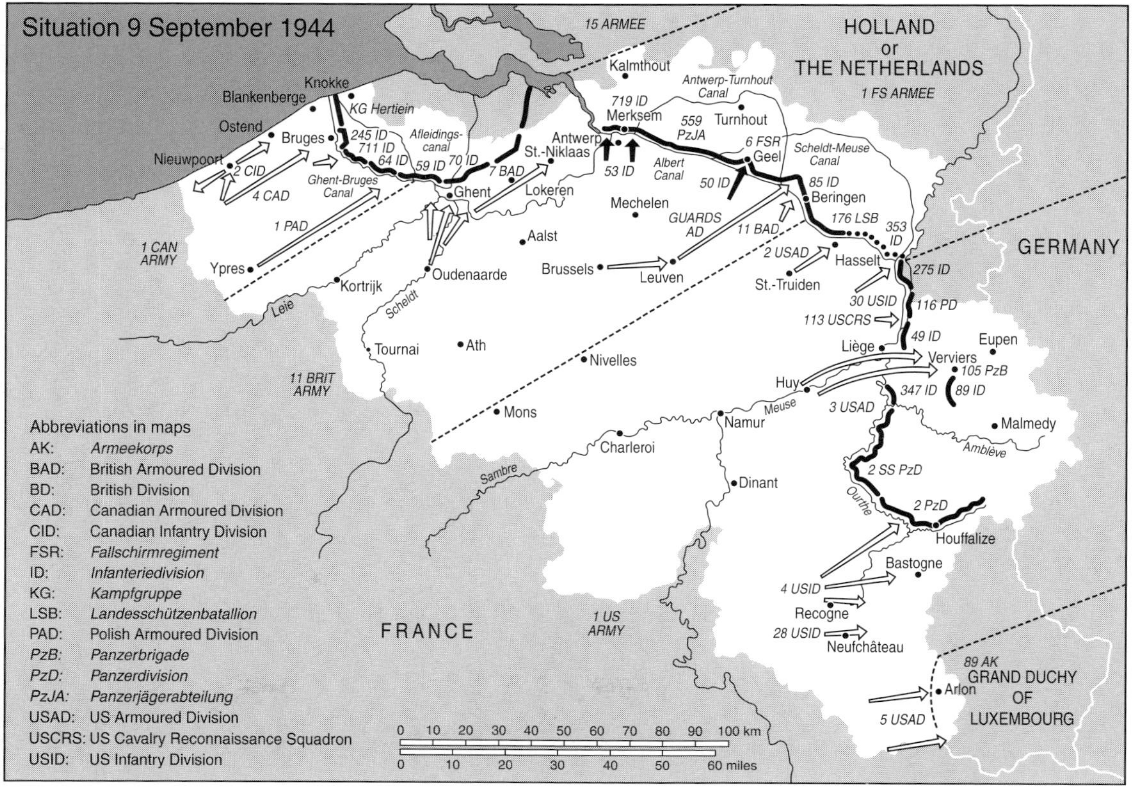

Map 2 The liberation of Belgium, 9 September 1944 (Map Peter Taghon)

3 Embracing the new

BBC Radio

Long before they were straining their necks to see the liberators in the flesh, many Belgians had been cocking their ears to learn about their whereabouts. During the occupation, it was radio, and the BBC broadcasts from London in particular, that kept Belgians informed of how the Allies were faring. As early as September 1940, Radio Belgium had been launched as one of a series of international broadcasts by the BBC. This enabled both Dutch- and French-speaking Belgians to tune in to the BBC at certain times each day to hear programs even in their own language. For the remainder of the war, however, Belgians would do so at great risk as the Germans declared listening to BBC programs illegal in July 1940. Violators risked serious punishments including forced labor.

But the Nazi regime itself considered radio too valuable a propaganda tool to declare the very possession of a set illegal. That, of course, continued to make radio the ideal means of obtaining information about the war from a source other than Berlin. Underground newspapers, for example, could be printed and distributed only on a very small scale, and to have them in the home was a dangerous undertaking. It was less risky to tune in to the regular broadcasts of the BBC, hidden away in a place that muffled the sound, and ready to change stations at a moment's notice.[1]

It was not always easy to keep up with the BBC news on a regular basis. Many lacked a good reception for the London broadcasts, while others lacked the courage to tune in day after day. Still, already by the end of 1940, German police reports indicated that the Belgians were listening to the BBC in large numbers and that others were kept abreast of the Allied news by word of mouth. That way people learned of Nazi setbacks

[1] Hogge, "Propagande," 9, 14–15, and 18.

and excesses, and of Britain's steely determination to continue to resist the criminal regime. The result was, the German reports concluded, that "this information strongly influences the population's attitude regarding the forces of occupation."[2]

As the German war fortunes took a turn for the worse, tuning in to the BBC became more rewarding but not necessarily easier. The power outages caused by Allied bombardments and maquis sabotage in 1944 regularly silenced radios in large parts of the country. And when the Germans in the spring of 1944 feared an invasion from the Atlantic, they ordered all inhabitants of Belgium's coastal area to hand in their radio sets. But four years of occupation had made people cunning and ingenious if nothing else. Those who could switched to crystal receivers whenever the power broke down, while those at the coast in April 1944 made sure to hand in only old sets, keeping their ears glued to radios carefully hidden away. Word of mouth, meanwhile, ensured that the BBC message was spread even among those who could or would not listen to it firsthand. "Radio London," a Flemish newspaper would comment a few days after the liberation, "continues to be the center of attention as it has been throughout the occupation. People are convinced that it is the only reliable source of information."[3]

Fluid maps

During the occupation people used this unique source of information to guide them as they impatiently mapped the advances of the Allies on fronts east and west. Many carried elaborate drawings of the advances in their heads courtesy of the BBC. Others were quick to retrieve detailed maps of Europe from drawers and attics as the tide turned. Even a small village like Braine-le-Château was soon teeming with armchair strategists tracking the Allied advances with pins and small colored flags. "Ever since the Normandy landings a map of Western Europe adorned a wall," a teenager from Moerbeke remembered. "My father placed colored pins next to strange place names. Each day there were more pins. The allies were on their way." A remarkable photo, taken rather recklessly in a living room in Pepinster with the aid of a self-timer, shows two young men sitting on chairs. One has his ear against a large radio and is manipulating the dial, the other has a map on his lap and is diligently tracing the BBC news on Allied movements. For the brothers,

[2] Ibid., 15–16.

[3] Neckers, *Bevrijding*, 23; De Vos, *Bevrijding*, 83; and "Eere aan de BBC," *HBVL*, September 12, 1944, 2.

who lived in a building that had almost entirely been requisitioned by the Germans since the start of the war, obtaining a daily dose of hope involved unending risk.[4]

If the invasion of Normandy was a crucial turning point, for some Belgians the liberation of Paris was a cause of advance celebrations in the privacy of their homes. "Each hour brings new surprises," a man intently listening to the BBC in Antwerp wrote in his journal on August 24. "Yesterday afternoon we learned that the Parisians, after four days of insurrection, have liberated themselves." When London beamed the news into the living room of the Baiverlin family in the tiny village of Wegnez, twelve-year-old Henri watched with astonishment as tears streamed down his father's face. "He mumbled something," the boy later recalled, "like 'Paris is a beautiful city, a great city.'" A boy in the Belgian capital, one year Henri's junior, smacked his lips that same day as his mother baked a rice cake and with jam decorated the top with the words "Long Live the Allies!" And as he went out into the garden and saw his aged neighbor overcome with emotion at the news from Paris, he too would never forget thinking that day "that old people cry too."[5]

Allied flags

Belgians everywhere seemed to be spending much of the last weeks before the liberation fascinated not only by maps but also by flags. Potent rallying symbols of identity and allegiance, the occupier early on had made sure to ban all Belgian and Allied flags. Now, with the German grip visibly weakening, people could hold back no longer. They rushed to fashion the long-forbidden flags in private acts of defiance and resistance that were repeated across the country within the relative safety of homes.

In the run-up to the liberation, substances suited for dying cloth became almost impossible to find in the Belgian capital. The same was true for almost every town and village in the country. "No dye can be found in any of the shops," a man from Eisden cheered in his journal. "We will certainly have enough flags in our village." Those who were well-off could afford to buy quality cloth in the specialized shops. But most Belgians gladly sacrificed some old bed sheets, cutting them up in three pieces, dying them black, yellow, and red, then stitching them

[4] Aelbrecht and Maghe, "Braine," 24; De Roey and Van Hees, *Bevrijding*, 60; and *Pepinster*, 23.

[5] *Pepinster*, 6; and J. S., "Bruxelles, septembre 1944: C'est la Liberté," *Pourquoi Pas?*, September 5, 1984, 11.

back together. With quality dye hard to come by, the national colors were only pale versions of the prewar ones, but that did not stop people from regarding their flags with pride, using a hot iron for a finishing touch.[6]

There were finishing touches to be added also to many foreign flags that now reflected the newly forged family of Allied nations. Those of friendly neighbors like Holland were easy enough to fabricate, though France's newly potent Cross of Lorraine took some research to get right. As a sign of the globe's rapidly shifting power relations, however, Belgians everywhere now found themselves poring over encyclopedias to learn more about the exact patterns and colors of flags of the English-speaking world. The Union Jack's design was complicated enough, but cutting a maple leaf from a sheet took real skill, and producing the exact number of stars on an American banner could tax the patience of even the most sincere well-wisher.[7]

The hardest thing to figure out, however, was what to do with the Soviet flag. Since Stalingrad no one had harbored any doubt about the importance of the Russians in the Allied family, and many were keen to show their flag too as an expression of gratitude and respect. But if in some parts of the country a more radical labor class did not hesitate to show the Soviet flag as it was, sensitivities elsewhere, especially in the less industrialized and fervently Catholic Flanders, dictated a more pragmatic approach. Some agreed to fashion an all-red flag but could not bring themselves to add the dreaded hammer and sickle. They were glad to replace the loaded symbols with the more neutral USSR or URSS. For at least one family in Brussels the issue sufficed to cause a rift: mother refused to waste cloth on a Soviet flag to be hung from the window; father shrugged his shoulders, carved the Soviet symbols from wood, and displayed them on the balcony.[8]

At first, flags were being dyed and sewn in secrecy. Women would keep the children at arm's length while men in some places kept guard at the door. But as the German retreat accelerated, flags began to be fabricated more openly and daringly. Those in the cities with money to spare hardly made a secret of why they urgently needed colored cloth from the department stores. *Volk en Staat*, the newspaper of the Flemish separatist and collaborationist movement VNV, lambasted people for the unabashed manner in which they were purchasing cloth in the national colors. Indeed, Belgian nationalism was being commercialized again as margarine brands began producing little paper flags in black, yellow,

[6] Balace, "Bruxelles," 64; and Janssen *et al.*, "Maasland," 72.

[7] See, for example, Aelbrecht and Maghe, "Braine," 26 and 35.

[8] J. S., "Bruxelles, septembre 1944: C'est la Liberté," *Pourquoi Pas?*, September 5, 1984, 11.

and red proudly displaying brand names like *Adi* and *Solo*. Somehow the flags made their way to newsvendors and into the hands of Belgians even as some of the last German troops could still be seen in the streets.[9]

People scrambled to get their hands on Belgian and Allied flags because these stood to serve more than one vital purpose. Nothing was more effective, of course, in demonstrating one's allegiance to the newly victorious side in the long war than to drape the façade of one's home in clearly distinguishable colors. At the same time, however, flags also were proud markers of a regained freedom, allowing even citizens who were not part of the active resistance to participate in reclaiming what the Germans had taken from them.

Most were satisfied to reclaim their own homes through the display of improvised flags at window sills and balconies. But others armed themselves with flags determined to recapture public spaces from the enemy too. The best way to accomplish this, of course, was to plant the flag on that building which towered over all others. Four young men in Oudenaarde went to collect the Belgian flag from the parish dean and then made the daring climb all the way to the top of the Sint-Walburga spire. In Antwerp a resistance fighter and three other inhabitants sat perched on the city's cathedral spire, tore the giant swastika flag from its mast and, egged on by loud roars from the crowds, replaced it with the Belgian flag. All the while angry rifle fire could be heard as Germans desperately tried to prevent the men from completing the ritual takeover.[10]

Belgian and Allied flags on numerous occasions caused the enemy to erupt in anger and even to take lives. City workers in Bruges came under fire when they began digging holes in the market square to plant flag poles even before the enemy had completely withdrawn. German soldiers enraged by the display of a Belgian flag on a building near a bridge in Berchem opened up with their anti-aircraft battery, killing five people inside and wounding many more. The fifteen-year-old boy who climbed Robermont's church spire with a Belgian flag never made it to the top. Petrified onlookers in surrounding villages watched as German rifle fire caused the dark speck to tumble back to earth.[11]

No man's land

With the exception of those areas where German troops battled it out with the Allies, most communities experienced the surreal time that elapsed between the final departure of the occupier and the long-awaited

[9] For the *Volk en Staat* article, see Neckers, *Bevrijding*, 35.
[10] Deweer, *Oudenaarde*, 144; and Gorsele, *Antwerpen*, 50.
[11] Warnier, *Brugge*, 12; Van de Velde, "Anvers," 39; and Rogister, *Chênée*, 48.

arrival of the liberators in a very similar fashion. Often the last Germans to leave a city or town were personnel from the *Kommandantur*, a handful of *Feldgendarme*, and some nervous troops responsible for destruction aimed at delaying the rapidly approaching Allies. In Verviers reckless inhabitants booed them as they too finally abandoned the city.[12]

In many places the enemy's last act was marked by thunderous noise and clouds of debris. Bruges shook in the early morning hours as the Germans made thorough work of the destruction of more than thirty canal and river bridges in and around the famous tourist destination, causing great damage to buildings and the city gates. Inhabitants of the historic university city of Leuven protected their ears as roaring explosions caused bridge after bridge over the Dijle River to crumble at intervals of ten minutes. Fifty buildings went down with the bridges, while hundreds of others were damaged. Russian *Hilfswillige* were left in charge of the final destructions in Namur. They were in a hurry and made sure to use plenty of explosives. The detonations took out all of the key bridges, but they also destroyed eighty buildings while damaging another 145 homes.[13]

The silence that followed was complete. So complete, in fact, that many would remember this as one of the most salient features of the no-man's-land in which they now found themselves. "September 9," recalled a villager from Cornesse of the day of liberation, "commenced and lingered on in what was the most absolute silence. No more noise of guns, no aircraft, no more traffic or very little." People were left in limbo, a strange state of being neither occupied nor truly freed. "Saturday we cleaned house as usual," a fourteen-year-old from Sint-Pieters-Leeuw explained, "but other than that there was no activity besides preparing food. We stood on the sidewalk or by the window and watched." A woman in Ukkel's maternity ward had a hard time getting the care she needed as nurses congregated on the building's roof to scan the horizon for the Allies.[14]

More and more people began to come together on sidewalks and streets as the calm seemed to hold. "There is a pleasant atmosphere," a man observing fellow citizens on Antwerp's avenues jotted in his diary, "people make small talk and the sound of playing children drowns out the quiet murmur." More people than ever were tuning in to the BBC, hoping to find out how close the Allies might be, some now doing so quite openly. But the Allies were moving so fast that the news from London about what was happening in Belgium was inevitably vague. Close to

[12] Wynants, *Verviers*, 27.

[13] Warnier, *Brugge bevrijd*, 14; Aerts *et al.*, *Leuven*, 30–1; and Balace, "Charleroi-Namur," 27.

[14] *Pepinster*, 13; Wilfried Verleyen, AB 1591; and Offergeld, *Bruxelles*, 34.

midnight on September 2, 1944, the BBC announced that Tournai, a Belgian city near the French border, had been liberated. The following day, BBC broadcasts commenced with the Belgian national anthem and the announcement that Allied troops were crossing into Belgium in large numbers and were heading towards Brussels. On September 5, the first broadcast of a free Belgian national radio told people: "To those who are enjoying the happiness of being liberated there is nothing more that we can say to increase their joy. To the others, who are still waiting for the blessed hour, we say: hang on just a little longer, just a little bit longer; your friends, our great allies, will be there soon."[15]

How soon that would be exactly for a particular village or town, however, was anybody's guess. And in the absence of sufficient information, rumors began to fly, rumors that ate away at everyone's nerves but that were particularly stressful for those who had emerged from their hiding places pale and wan: young men who had evaded forced labor, Jews who had escaped deportation, and all manner of men and women wanted by German authorities for myriad reasons. "All kinds of crazy stories are circulating!" Father Nijs on September 7 noted in the journal he was keeping in Ghent. "They say 15,000 Germans are on their way from Eekloo by way of Nevele." None of that was true. Nor was it true that the Germans were about to return to the village of Felenne to burn it down. But the rumor sufficed to force the villagers to flee to the nearest forest, where they would remain until the arrival of the Americans. Fifty years later, all those who remembered the morning of Tuesday, September 5, at Braine-le-Château still spoke with anguish of the moment when they barricaded themselves in their homes to await the seventy German tanks that rumor had falsely claimed were on the way.[16]

Weeks of tension and fear had strained the nerves. They had left people exhausted and utterly incapable of waiting much longer to catch sight of the Allies who would bring the relief and security they so desperately craved. According to Georges Dejardin's journal, inhabitants of Felenne and vicinity had been announcing the arrival of the Allies as early as the last day of August, yet the first liberators would not actually set foot in the village until six days later. The village priest of Embourg could no longer stand the tension and decided to gather some reliable intelligence himself. He picked up the phone and called some of his flock who lived on the main road further south. To his astonishment the lines

[15] De Tollenaere, "Oorlogsdagboek," 86–7, AB 1734; Balace, "Bruxelles," 62; and Radiodiffusion Nationale Belge Namur, transcript September 5, 1944, AA 82.

[16] Nijs journal excerpt in Marchal, *Gent*, 107; Dejardin, "Journal," September 4, 1944, AB 89; and Aelbrecht and Maghe, "Braine," 32.

appeared to be still intact. In no time parishioners were feeding him the information he had wanted to hear: Americans were passing their homes and they were on the way to where he lived. In Zepperen on September 8 the air was rife with nervous rumors that the Allies were about to arrive any minute now. The town clerk signaled to the sexton that it was time. The bells of Zepperen tolled to announce deliverance before anyone in the village had in fact seen a single liberator.[17]

There they are

The final countdown to the arrival of the Allied soldiers made the atmosphere electric. Exhilaration and fear shot through the crowds in alternate bursts, while flashes of disbelief repeatedly punctured the tense anticipation. People had been waiting for this moment for so long that now many were at the end of their tether. Nowhere was the jumble of emotions more explosive than among the impatient throngs in the Belgian capital. And perhaps no one managed to capture the giddy atmosphere in Brussels better than Paule Banneux in her diary. For several days the young woman had been out on the streets, carried back and forth on waves of emotion fanned by the enemy retreat and rumors of imminent liberation. Close to midnight on Sunday, September 3, people massed together in the streets. Word had it that British troops had already penetrated certain parts of the city. But no one dared to go and have a look as shots continued to ring out. Nervous and disappointed, people withdrew to their homes again. Many went to bed without getting undressed.

Very early on Monday morning, Paule's mother yelled that the British had been seen on the Place Dailly. "I'm coming!" Paule yelled back as she hurried to put the finishing touches to her hair. "No," Paule's mother muttered as she rushed to the door, "I'm not waiting." Paule arrived at the spot not long after her mother. Many onlookers were still dressed in pajamas and nightgowns and had simply put on a coat. "There he is!" someone suddenly yelled. A lone English soldier on a motorcycle made his way onto the square. What followed was mayhem. "It is not he who brings his vehicle to a halt, it seems," Paule recounted, "but the crowd, which surges forward, stops him, smothers him, embraces him, removes his helmet, rubs his hair, caresses his uniform."[18]

For many the moment of liberation was an almost religious experience, the result of some divine intervention defying the longest of odds. It

[17] Dejardin, "Journal," September 1, 1944, AB 89; Lognard-Poncin and Michel, *Chaudfontaine*, 39; and Celis *et al.*, *Zepperen*, 280.
[18] Banneux, "Souvenirs," AB 712.

Plate 3.1 British troops liberate Antwerp. (CEGESOMA, Brussels, picture number 28768)

inevitably transformed those who offered Belgians the sweetest of freedom into characters many times larger than life. Descriptions of the very first Allied soldiers to enter Belgian villages, towns, and cities not rarely convey an image of Olympians. Perhaps because they looked so much more impressive than the dirty, disheveled Germans of the retreat or the motley men of the resistance who had emerged from the shadows pale and thin. The Americans in particular impressed many as men who were exceptionally tall, with an onlooker in Waremme even recalling the GI in the first tank's turret as "a worthy competitor of Gargantua." But even among the British, with their generally more slender physique, onlookers preferred to fasten their eyes on the most impressive soldiers. No one in Braine-l'Alleud, for example, would ever forget that the first liberator to arrive on the scene apparently happened to be a British captain who was "endlessly tall." Indeed, villagers went on record insisting that he measured exactly two meters and four centimeters.

Whatever their exact height, all of the first Allied arrivals impressed with their attractive appearance. The Americans, when they smiled, which they did remarkably often, flashed "teeth of a whiteness that sparkled." People long afterwards remembered the first British liberators in

Antwerp as "robust" and "healthy" men with a "deep tan." Nor were the Allied liberators merely physically superior, they appeared to be so morally as well. Because here were soldiers who, in sharp contrast with the German occupier of four years, were friendly and cordial, soldiers who did not stop smiling and showed the crowds that they loved them.[19]

Those sterling first impressions of the Allied soldiers were perhaps inevitable also because they as individuals personified freedom and thus in those first exhilarating moments could simply not be allowed to look like mere mortals. "It is only after a short while," Paule Banneux noted as she scrutinized the lone British soldier on his motorcycle on the Place Dailly in Brussels, "that I come to realize how dirty he is, terribly dirty and ugly." "But," she added, "for the crowd he is a god."[20]

A new world

Whether godlike or mortal, these soldiers did appear to have arrived from a wholly new world. Not only did they enjoy physical and moral advantages, they also possessed that one quality which had been in short supply for so long on the continent: optimism. "They had such confidence," beamed a man who watched the Americans arrive in Liège, "that it was a joy to behold." That confidence seemed particularly justified when measured by the staggering extent to which the Allied forces were motorized and mechanized. Indeed, the most striking feature of their momentous arrival was the tremendous rumble. Those who cheered the British in Brussels were "in rapture over the war material that rolled by without barely an interruption," much of it with "the metallic noise of trucks, tanks, pontoons, and so on." "On the main road," an inhabitant of a village in Limburg remarked on the passage of the Americans, "there is a roar that is deafening."[21]

To onlookers who had watched the Germans withdraw on horses and bicycles for weeks, there now seemed literally no end to the Allied motorized convoys. On September 7, an inhabitant of Genval recorded in his journal the arrival of the first liberators: "An American armored

[19] Bosse and Van Gucht, *Braine-l'Alleud*, 15; and Aelbrecht and Maghe, "Braine," 73. On the Americans see, for example, Laby, *Waremme*, 227 and 222. On the Brits see, for example, Jérôme Storme, AB 1591; and Greeve, "Oorlogsdagboek," 173, AB 2166. On the perceived moral qualities of the Allies, see Leblon, "Américanophilie et anglophilie," 19–20.

[20] Banneux, "Souvenirs," September 4, 1944, AB 712. There is evidence from other countries too of the liberation by the Allies as a quasi-religious experience. For Holland see, for example, Horn, "More than Cigarettes," 159.

[21] Roger Laroche, transcript interview No. 427, AA 1450; Gheude, *Libération*, 190; and Janssen *et al.*, "Maasland," 102.

column rolls by on the Avenue Gevaert; this lasts from half past nine in the morning until a quarter to one in the afternoon, they say it is fifteen kilometers long." Henri Baiverlin was twelve years old when the GIs arrived in the village of Wegnez two days later. "For about three days," he recalled, "it was an uninterrupted passage. The American might rolled by on our roads and we were proud to have as allies these men who brought us the smile of freedom."[22]

Perhaps the German military had looked robot-like in 1940, but even then the Germans had made extensive use of horses, and the memory of those days had receded anyway. During the four years of occupation, Belgians had not seen the enemy in action, and what they saw of the retreat from behind their curtains convinced them that the Germans no longer embodied the military cutting edge. It was the Allies who now claimed superiority, and in the eyes of the liberated they did so with a sweet vengeance. Forgotten were the drab gray *Kübelwagens*, for example, now that the exciting British Bren Gun Carriers could be seen maneuvering through the smallest of streets. British troops astounded observers also with the size of their tanks. Some in Antwerp province described them as "dangerous colossi"; others maintained they were "as tall as houses." "A monster toad on treads," Father Van Herck remarked of the first British tank to arrive in Kontich-Waarloos.[23]

But it was the American equipment that impressed like nothing else. Months later even Churchill would admit to Eisenhower that "no one who studies war can fail to be impressed by the admirable speed and flexibility of the American Armies." Indeed, much of the equipment of the British was American made and acquired as a result of Lend Lease aid, from the ubiquitous jeep to the Sherman tank, though few Belgians were aware of this. Neither did the Belgians know that German tanks continued to strike the fear of God in American soldiers, who knew their own standard tank to be hugely inferior. Belgians would not have believed this anyway, even if the GIs had told them so themselves. As Limburg's newspaper reappeared, part of the province beyond the Albert canal remained in the hands of the Germans. "But we have admired the powerful equipment of the Americans with our own eyes," an editorial said confidently, "in comparison with which the German equipment is child's play. With such tanks and armored vehicles, manned by such strong guys … the last part of Limburg will soon also be liberated."[24]

[22] Boulet, "Journal," AB 1298; and *Pepinster*, 8.

[23] The Antwerp observers are Greeve, "Oorlogsdagboek," 173, AB 2166; and Guido Kips, AB 1591. *Oorlog en bevrijding te Kontich-Waarloos*, 70.

[24] Churchill is quoted in Reynolds, "Churchill," 48. *HBVL*, September 12, 1944, 2.

The optimism of the liberators proved to be contagious. Onlookers easily came to share the Allies' confidence as a result not only of the continuous rumble of convoys, but also of the myriad aspects of their equipment that spoke of technological sophistication. Where once, years ago, the German Stuka had impressed, people now watched in awe as British Typhoons were called in to aid troops with devastating rocket fire. The Germans had built pontoons the old-fashioned way, with flat-bottomed boats, but Belgians now gaped in amazement as the Allies had Bailey bridges of British design unfold across rivers with prefabricated steel panels and all.[25]

Even the details of uniforms and weapons seemed to indicate that the future belonged to the Allies, and perhaps especially to the Americans. A small boy in Ottignies during the first hours of liberation watched the GIs' every move without so much as blinking. "The Americans moved about with ease," the young villager observed with a sharp eye for detail. "Their uniform was made of a lighter fabric that allowed them more comfort and freedom of movement. Their shoes were made of soft leather and without the hobnails of the German boots, and the soldiers gave me the impression that they were dancing while they marched. Their helmets were rounder and as a result appeared less aggressive. They carried only light packs and what also caught my attention was that their rifle was shorter in comparison with the long and heavy Mauser." Like the GIs in Ottignies, Allied soldiers across Belgium were about to dance their way into the hearts of many.[26]

Publicity caravans

People even liked the smell that the Allies brought with them from overseas. "I have," said a man from Bruges who was eight in 1944, "a very distinct olfactory-memory of the liberation and the Canadian soldiers." And many of his contemporaries readily agreed. Not that the liberators necessarily smelled fresh and clean. Like all soldiers they exuded that pungent mixture of sweat, leather, and grease. But as the Belgians touched, embraced, and kissed the liberators, they detected many new odors that caused these men to appear most intriguing and exotic. Particularly so because many of the unusual odors told people that these were soldiers who had access to tantalizing luxuries.[27]

[25] On the Typhoons, see Father Nijs in Marchal, *Gent*, 151. The Bailey bridges are mentioned in numerous journals and memoirs.

[26] Debroux, "Histoire d'un gamin," AB 2240.

[27] Warnier, *Brugge en september '44*, vol. II, 128–9.

The Allied soldiers stepped into a society that for more than four years had known only shortages and want. Imports had been replaced by lower-quality ersatz products or had not been replaced at all. Agricultural and industrial production had been on a war footing and an unforgiving occupier had siphoned off anything of use to Nazi Germany. Strict rationing had been in place for years and food lines had grown longer with the reversal of German fortunes. Now some odors made memories come flooding back, while others were so new they could not be compared with anything the occupied had ever known before.

"All these GIs," remembered an inhabitant of Waremme, "had a particular odor, impossible to identify, an odor that we were not familiar with." Perhaps that was because this particular inhabitant was only ten at the time of the liberation and did not remember many of the smells that his parents had grown up with. The smell of genuine tobacco, for example, or of real coffee, real chocolate, real soap, and real bread. Barely five years old, a boy in his parents' bakery in Peer stared wide-eyed as English soldiers ritually moved brushes in tiny circles over a paste inside a small round container. More than sixty years later he would still vividly remember the distinct smell of their toothpaste. Adults, on the other hand, at the most unexpected moments had to fight back tears as smells brusquely reminded them of a life before war. That is what happened, for example, to a woman in Brussels before the first Allies had even arrived. "Suddenly," she recalled, "we smelled an odor. An odor of gasoline! We knew that the English were there. And before we even saw them, we smelled them, because the ersatz fuel that the German vehicles used had a completely different odor. Only the Allies could have such fuel. My God, how good it smelled!"[28]

There were many Allied odors bringing about such exhilarating effects. "How tall these men were," an inhabitant of Bruges recalled, "how kind, and how good they smelled of wheat bread." Nothing, however, caused such good feelings as the smell of real tobacco. For men especially, smoking had been one of the most appreciated of the few pastimes left to them. But cigarettes and cigars of real tobacco had all but disappeared. People had resorted to substitute tobacco made from chicory and even beet leaves that most agreed smelled like straw when lit. One of the first things that Father Nijs wrote in his journal on September 6, the day he saw the first liberators end four long years of occupation in Ghent, was that the British soldiers "smoke cigarettes that have a smell so sweet."[29]

[28] Laby, *Waremme*, 222; interview Urbain Schrijvers by author, December 16, 2005; and Offergeld, *Bruxelles*, 44.

[29] Neckers, *Bevrijding*, 21; Marchal, *Gent*, 99; and Jacquemyns, "Société belge," 366–7.

But the Allies were nothing if not generous. And not for a moment did they consider keeping all of those sweet-smelling goods to themselves. Not that this was a sacrifice to them, for their quartermasters worked overtime and things like cigarettes and chocolate were as easily replaced as bullets. People in Belgium did not know that, however, and the effect of the instant generosity of the Allies was immeasurable. Within moments of their arrival, Allied convoys in the eyes of bystanders turned into carnival processions. There was no end to the British vehicles racing through Comines on September 7. Yet for as long as the villagers on the sidewalks cheered, load after load of soldiers in a seemingly blasé manner tossed the kind of quality cigarettes at them that for years had cost a fortune on the black market. Likewise, no matter how hard they tried, people in Waremme could not understand where the Americans were getting so many Camels and Chesterfields from that they could afford to hand them out in street after street without so much as a pause.[30]

Onlookers who during the past days had suffered the humiliation of having to plunder German depots to satisfy their needs and wants could hardly process the sudden change taking place in their lives. A historian of the French liberation has noted that the first US convoys had the impact of "a publicity caravan," instantly selling the liberated on America's "youth, power, and wealth." It was no different in Belgium. Children in Liège, for example, could be seen running after American convoys from which GIs would "scatter onto the sidewalks badges, cartridge cases, cans, and even coins showing the US eagle." As well as the more traditional offerings of peacetime publicity, of course, like fruit and candy and even chocolate and the ceaselessly amazing chewing gum.[31]

The Allies from day one of the liberation stood for an abundance that made people's heads spin. Sometimes quite literally so. A twelve-year-old in the village of Villers-le-Bouillet received enough chocolate from GIs to allow him to pass up other food. "That this chocolate also had stimulating side effects," the boy later recalled nostalgically, "and that it gave you heart palpitations at night could not lessen the fun."[32]

Euphoria

And fun there was in those first hours and days of liberation. Though to call it fun, or even happiness, was an understatement. People in the earliest stage of liberation moved about in a state of utter euphoria. "It

30 Vierstraete *et al.*, "Comines-Warneton," 505; and Laby, *Waremme*, 222.
31 Kaspi, *Libération France*, 473; and Jour, *Libération Liège*, 55.
32 Juul Blondé, AB 1591.

feels," the first broadcast by a free Belgian national radio cried out on September 5, "like the first breath of fresh air filling the lungs of someone who had been buried alive." It was, an inhabitant of Pepinster exalted, the "sensation of being born a second time." No metaphor would do to describe the intensity of the feeling. People responded to the new sensation in a frantic, almost manic manner. They stopped working and found it impossible to stay at home. People roamed the streets, wanted to be with others, yearned for conversation with complete strangers. An inhabitant of Virton noted that immediately after the liberation the town was packed with people and that many even forgot to eat that day. On the day that Liège was liberated, Georges Willot, an ecstatic fifteen-year-old, in his diary kept track of the mad events not hour by hour, but literally minute by glorious minute. "People cry with emotion," a villager from Ploegsteert wrote in his diary. "It is an explosion of joy. We are all drunk with the freedom that has at last been regained." "It was," as one witness tried to sum it all up, "an almost savage joy."[33]

Much of that savage joy was directed at the liberators themselves. As soon as the Germans were gone, people had grabbed paint and whitewash, and now Allied soldiers everywhere were being greeted by huge letters on the streets that said "WELCOME!" In some communities elaborate constructions of saplings, branches, and welcoming banners had been built spanning the roads at main entrances. Photos of the liberation of Antwerp show people packed in avenues and squares, a forest of hands and arms outstretched in desperate attempts to touch the soldiers in the convoys. In a photo of a square in Brussels, thousands can be seen standing side by side with their hands up, all without exception greeting the British troops with the powerful V sign. Elsewhere in the capital, Allied troops moved through walls of sound produced by masses of spectators engaged, as if hypnotized, in ceaseless ovations.[34]

Growing waves of ecstatic people pressed in on the liberators, slowing the convoys down, on occasion even forcing them to a complete standstill. Spectators climbed onto trucks and tanks, begging the Allies for autographs as if they were famous Hollywood stars. Soldiers obliged, scribbling their names on notebooks, money bills, flags, and even arms and legs held out for that particular purpose. Parents scrambled to lift children and babies into the air, hoping to have a liberator touch their offspring, as if in a ritual designed to guarantee the future generation good fortune. As soon as he caught sight of the first GIs in Liège, Herman Bovi

[33] Radiodiffusion Nationale Belge Namur, transcript September 5, 1944, AA 82; *Pepinster*, 11; Sabus, *1944*, 41; "Journal de guerre et de libération," *La Libre Belgique*, September 8, 1994; and Combaluzier and Lepage, "Villers-la-Ville," 22.

[34] Van de Velde, "Anvers," 37; and *Libération: Ayant comme but de rendre un vibrant hommage*, 134.

Plate 3.2 British troops liberate Brussels. (CEGESOMA, Brussels, picture number 29237)

grabbed his child by the hand and rushed to the scene. “I took my small daughter with me,” he explained, “because I wanted her to remember.” A young boy in Ottignies would certainly never forget the way his mother reacted to the arrival of the first liberators in a reconnaissance vehicle. She quickly made sure to check if they were indeed Americans, as some claimed, and not Germans. Satisfied that they were, she turned to her children and those of the neighbors. “You have been saved, children!” she whispered, tears running down her face. “You have been saved!”[35]

So euphoric was the reception by the Belgians that it caught the liberators off guard. With the kind permission of Belgium’s Queen Elizabeth, Sir Brian Horrocks hurried to establish his headquarters in the park of the royal château at Laken, where a strong fence at last offered “some protection against the ecstatic crowds.” “We had,” the British general commented, “become specialists in matters of liberation, what with all the towns and villages that we had passed through since the Seine. But everyone agreed that the welcome provided us by the citizens of Brussels was without comparison.”[36]

[35] Jour, *Villes libérées: Liège*, 52; and Debroux, “Histoire d’un gamin,” 83, AB 2240.
[36] Horrocks is quoted in Balace, “Bruxelles,” 76 and 79.

Plate 3.3 A British liberator in Leuven. (CEGESOMA, Brussels, picture number 29576)

Allied troops readily agreed that this was the case in much of the country. People had to be rushed off with sprained ankles and broken arms or legs as they fell from vehicles or were squashed by traffic. A young man in Chênée had much of his foot ripped off when he was seized by a tank. As she tried to climb a tank with flowers in her hands, a woman in Oudenaarde was hit in the chest by a burst from a machine gun accidentally going off. In Brussels, but also in Ghent, Leuven, Charleroi, and many other cities and towns, Belgian policemen and gendarmes had to call in reinforcements to help control the crowds and get the Allied forces moving again. Commenting on the chaotic scenes of liberation, an American intelligence report dryly stated: "Civil Affairs coming into Belgium found their welcome more warm hearted than in France; and there was no doubt of the warmth of the sentiment of this somewhat emotional people."[37]

[37] Rogister, *Chênée*, 47; Deweer, *Oudenaarde*, 93; and Coles and Weinberg, *Civil Affairs*, 805.

Crush

More emotional even than the Belgian men were their wives and daughters. A photo of Scottish infantrymen on the road to Harelbeke shows among the onlookers two old women in coal-black dresses. One leans on a cane. The other sits on a chair. Both laconically observe the soldiers as if they are part of a religious procession. But the Allies would find the younger women of Belgium less restrained, to say the least. Girls in Arlon ripped the buttons off GIs' uniforms for souvenirs. A photo taken during the liberation of Diest shows a group of women whooping with laughter as they drag a soldier of the Welsh Guards out of his Cromwell tank. Women who tried to do the same in the Rue Féronstrée in Liège caused an American soldier to lose his balance and become crushed under the treads of his own vehicle.[38]

Belgium, to a large extent Catholic and rural, had entered the war as a society quite conservative in matters of sexual morals. But one can be forgiven for not suspecting this when glancing over the photos of the liberation. Teenage girls in Leuven can be seen scrambling onto half-tracks passionately pressing their lips onto those of anonymous Grenadier Guards merely passing through. Young women in Braine-l'Alleud intimately press their bodies against GIs who have arrived just earlier that day. One proudly stares into the camera as a soldier firmly holds her shoulder with his hand; another has a satisfied smile as an American bends over her from his vehicle, his arms folded around her and pressed against her breasts. That most of these men were sweaty and caked with dust did not seem to matter much. "The girls stormed those tanks," a man from Hasselt recalled of the American arrival, "and the kissing went on and on." Having spent two nights in Oudergem without much sleep, the Irish Guards finally decided to establish their headquarters in the château Dietrich so that its fence could serve as a "protective barrier against young Belgian girls."[39]

Some contemporaries, and indeed some historians, have suggested that women and girls from urban working classes, and especially those from the industrial areas in the Walloons, behaved much more licentiously than others. Elsewhere in Belgium the social control imposed by the Catholic church and traditional rural communities supposedly did much to contain such behavior. But close examination of clothing and

[38] Vanbossele, *Kortrijk*, 145; Triffaux and Triffaux, *Arlon*, 54; Taghon, *België 44*, 174; and "Dans l'allégresse mais aussi dans le sang: Libération 44," No. 11, *Vers l'Avenir*, September 20, 1974.

[39] Aerts *et al.*, *Leuven*, 48; Bosse and Van Gucht, *Braine-l'Alleud*, 38; *HBVL*, August 30, 2004, 6; and Balace, "Bruxelles," 76.

surroundings in photos of the liberation undoubtedly show women of all classes fraternizing with Allied soldiers in rather uninhibited ways. And commentators early on were pointing to the same phenomenon. "Young girls were kissing the husky American boys as if they were old acquaintances they had not seen in years," noted Limburg's newspaper. If there was any concern about this, *Het Belang van Limburg* made sure not to show it at this early stage, giving the women of the Catholic and rural province the benefit of the doubt. "But," *Gazet van Antwerpen* lamented in the neighboring province, "what does amaze us, and strikes us as painful, is the behavior of so many so-called well-raised girls, who hover around giggling, imposing themselves on the new soldiers flirting."[40]

If Belgian women were even more emotional about the Allies than men, this was, of course, because they had more reason and opportunity to be so. The liberators were, after all, almost all male. Belgian men, on the other hand, especially the Walloons, were kept in Germany as POWs, while many others remained on enemy territory as deportees and as voluntary or forced laborers. Even when compared with the Belgian men who were still at hand, however, the young, tanned, well-fed, smartly uniformed Allies with their exotic accents could not but unleash passions that had lain dormant for too long. When asked if she had been in love with the American soldiers who arrived in her village half a century ago, a woman from Céroux-Mousty, who had been twenty at the time, was so flustered by the question that she tripped over her words. "Ah no, I don't think so," she responded rather firmly at first. But then she thought again. "I don't remember. I don't remember," she insisted, "they were good looking, in any case. They were young. They were young, they were good-looking. Yes, they were good-looking young people." "Yes," she concluded evasively, "we were happy."[41]

Gratitude

Perhaps kissing and touching was not a bad way of expressing one's happiness and gratitude most clearly to soldiers whose language one often barely knew at all. There was something ironic about this inability to communicate with the liberators. It was they, after all, who brought with them the freedom of expression that Belgians now embraced with

[40] On female licentiousness and class distinction, see Van Cauwenbergh, *Antwerpen*, 51, and De Vos, *Bevrijding*, 72 and 90. *HBVL*, September 12, 1944, 1. *Gazet van Antwerpen* quoted in Van Cauwenbergh, *Antwerpen*, 52.

[41] Marie-Claire Dandois, transcript interview No. 414, AA 1450.

such vengeance. Many commented on what a luxury it was finally to be able again to talk to neighbors, colleagues, even complete strangers, without having to worry about what one said and how loudly, something that in the Nazi police state had been unthinkable. In fact, people began exercising their long-suppressed right of expression in numerous ways from the first moment the Allied convoys rolled past. Graffiti appeared almost instantly, for example, as onlookers everywhere grabbed chalk to scribble messages on tanks and trucks. Almost any photo of the liberation will reveal vehicles covered with chalked words and symbols. Most bystanders were happy to write no more than their name or town, or the date of liberation. Others scribbled insults to the collaborators or to Hitler himself, seemingly innocent acts that just days earlier could have had the gravest of consequences. It was a liberating experience. As was the sight of ordinary citizens donning outfits previously prohibited by the occupier. Children wearing part of their fathers' army uniforms, for example, or boys and girls in Scout outfits that most had outgrown during the long ban. But the most powerful indication of the new atmosphere of expression was the return of a free press. Despite an acute shortage of paper, *La Gazette de Liège* was already being distributed on the left bank of the Meuse on September 8 while enemy fire could still be heard on the right bank. In a matter of days Belgian newspapers of all stripes were making a comeback, with people standing in line to buy copies of no more than two pages printed on dirty gray paper.[42]

It was frustrating then not to be able to express one's feelings to the very liberators who had created this new atmosphere of openness. With banners overhead announcing "Welcome to Our Allies" and "Honor and Glory to Our Liberators," it was easy for the Allies to assume that Belgians were widely familiar with English. In fact, most were not and probably got the banners right with the help of a dictionary and some luck. Most people in the Walloons spoke only French, and if the Flemish spoke a second language at all it was most often French. Younger Belgians knew a smattering of English from school and the more educated classes might have picked up some too. But very few Belgians were truly fluent in English. A study of the liberation of Villers-la-Ville, for example, shows that in this community of 1,200 only one elderly lady knew English well. People like her became much sought after as translators from the earliest hours of the liberation. In fact, some had already been in demand during the occupation. As soon as an Allied

[42] On the Liège newspaper, see Stéphany, "Belgique," 7; and René Henoumont, "Mon dernier soldat allemand," *Pourquoi Pas?*, September 5, 1984, 17–18. On the Scouts, see Neckers, *Bevrijding*, 60.

liberation appeared to be on the cards, some girls in Braine-l'Alleud, for example, had made sure to take lessons from a woman in town who was English herself. Once the liberation was a fact, key roles were also being played across Belgium by those who had fled to Britain during the Great War and had learned the language well during long years of exile.[43]

With British and North American liberators flooding the streets, Belgians suddenly felt an urgent need to catch up on their English. In no time smart entrepreneurs in the larger towns were offering courses in the language of victory. Newspapers also pitched in to facilitate communication with the Allies. Almost from the very start, Limburg's newspaper, for example, was running a column teaching people how to engage in basic conversation and how to master the tricky pronunciation. But all this would take sustained effort and there was too little time to spare during those first giddy days. Which is why the liberated invented hundreds of ways to show their gratitude without the help of foreign words.[44]

For people who had been focused on their stomachs during four years of grating scarcity no gesture of goodwill seemed more potent, of course, than the gift of food. In the countryside especially, where food had been less of a problem than in urban areas, Belgians lined the roads eager to hand to the liberators the fruits of the season. In September that meant apples above all, and women could be seen with baskets full of them. Grapes too were part of the offerings. "We did not know what to do to make them feel welcome," a man from Marchin recalled. So he started to hand out grapes from his backyard greenhouse until there was not a single bunch left. Bystanders quickly developed a keen eye for what it was the Allies seemed to appreciate most. Tomatoes probably were the biggest hit. Civilians near Kortrijk handed Scottish soldiers small baskets full of them, while elsewhere Belgians were surprised to see Americans munch on tomatoes as if they were apples. Fresh milk and eggs too were in high demand and farmers did what they could to respond to the need.[45]

The soldiers, used to being generous with army items, did not think much of it. But in some cases people were making real sacrifices to please

[43] Combaluzier and Lepage, "Villers-la-Ville," 24; and Aelbrecht and Maghe, "Braine," 75. On the role of Belgians who learned English in Britain during the First World War see, for example, Van Braeckel, *Barrier*, 14.

[44] On the business of English language courses see, for example, Aerts *et al.*, *Leuven*, 46. *HBVL* began publishing an English language column as early as September 13, 1944, barely six days after the provincial capital had been liberated.

[45] Chapelle, *Marchin*, 16; and Vanbossele, *Kortrijk*, 118.

the liberators. In cities like Brussels and Liège, for example, civilians could be seen running out to soldiers from their kitchens with plates of hot food prepared from the tightest of rations. At a small farm on the road to Menen, an elderly woman offered British troops some freshly made coffee. As the soldiers gulped down the bitter brew, the old lady confided to the slightly embarrassed soldiers that she had saved some of the last beans in 1940 for whenever it was that the liberation would come. But it did not matter to people that they were making offerings to soldiers who seemed to have everything. Only generosity befitted this special occasion, because Belgians desperately wanted to show their liberators how grateful they were. But also because they believed that with the abrupt end of war had arrived the instant end of scarcity. They could afford to be generous because the Allies, it quickly seemed clear, were not the kind of troops who would hesitate to be generous to them.[46]

It was sufficient cause for celebration not only with gifts of food but also with plenty of toasts. Those toasts started early. Combat soldiers in the vicinity of Chaudfontaine were stunned. They were in the middle of a firefight, indeed one of their comrades was down, yet apparently unconcerned villagers were lining the road with bottles of potent local gin as well as glasses in their hands. The Americans had to yell at the villagers to run for cover. As the skirmishes died down, drink flowed even more easily. In Rosée the owners of the village's cafés reasoned that the best thing to do to demonstrate to the GIs how much they were appreciated was to let the beer flow freely. And free, of course, of charge. That decision turned out to be so costly, however, that the municipal council later had to appeal to the provincial authorities to have some of the costs defrayed. After all, the council argued, the kind gesture had been "in the public interest."[47]

There were, of course, more constructive ways to show gratitude to the liberators. Some newspapers quickly taught Belgians how to say in correct English that they had warm water ready for them to freshen up or would be glad to do some mending. Civilians in Houffalize skipped the small gestures. They went out to fell some trees, hammered and sawed away, and then presented the Americans with a new bridge that replaced the one the Germans had blown up and was strong enough to carry a Sherman tank.[48]

[46] Buchet, "Liège," 144; and Banneux, "Souvenirs," September 4, 1944, AB 712. For Menen, see Decuypere, "Comines-Warneton," 535.

[47] Lognard-Poncin and Michel, *Chaudfontaine*, 39; and Challe, "Florennes," 26, AB 1381.

[48] See, for example, *HBVL* language tips on October 8, 1944, 2. For Houffalize, see Schrijvers, *Unknown Dead*, 125.

But there were plenty of sad occasions too that called for more solemn ways to show appreciation to the Allies. A burst from a German machine gun in Beaumont hit Dominick Gatto of the 47th Infantry in the chest, killing him instantly. Villagers rushed to collect the American soldier's body in the street. They placed the dead soldier on a bier and his helmet on top of his folded raincoat at his feet. Veterans of the Great War and members of the resistance volunteered to form a guard of honor. Villagers filed past all day to pay their respects. When his comrades came to get him the following day, Private Gatto lay hidden under a mountain of flowers.[49]

Carnival

Such sad and solemn moments, however, did nothing to slow the euphoric celebrations sweeping the country. The days of liberation were like "a spectacular open-air party." After the drab, gray days of German uniforms, Belgium suddenly seemed awash with festive colors. While flowers hid Private Gatto's body, they rained down on his more fortunate comrades as they marched on. So many brightly colored petals covered the streets in places that it reminded Belgians of religious processions from before the war. Civilians raided their gardens and with the flowers of late summer formed bouquets which, attached to the camouflage netting, transformed armored vehicles into carnival floats. Women and girls wore skirts and dresses, hats and berets, and ribbons in the national colors as well as the red, white, and blue of the Brits and Americans. Some had even dyed their hair in the colors of the Allies. But it was the sea of flags that washed away the gray of war most firmly. Flags appeared by the hundreds of thousands. Some were giant and could be seen unfurling from church steeples and factory smokestacks. The flag at Olmen's church steeple had been custom-made by the sisters of the local convent and was a unique patchwork of Belgium's national colors, the Union Jack, and the Stars and Stripes. Some of the homes in Ghent had Belgian and Allied flags painted onto their façades. "In a few minutes," an inhabitant of Liège noted, "the city became red, yellow, and black, taking one by surprise as if an old gray film had gone through a bath of colors. Everywhere there was blue, white, and red."[50]

[49] Roba and Leotard, *Walcourt-Beaumont*, 133–4.

[50] The party and procession references are in Deseyne, *Zonnebeke*, 93. For Olmen, see Zusters van Vorselaar, "Dagboek," 8, AB 711. On Ghent and Liège, see Marchal, *Gent*, 24; and René Henoumont, "Mon dernier soldat allemand," *Pourquoi Pas?*, September 5, 1984, 17.

And with the colors came a cacophony of sounds, abruptly detonating the awkward silence of no man's land. This land now belonged to the Belgians again and they wanted it to be known. The liberation was a time of endless clapping and cheering, of laughter and hysterical cries. And through it all sounded the elated tolling of church bells. Or rather what remained of those bells. Because the Germans in 1943, to everyone's consternation, had begun removing the heavy bells to melt their valuable metals into instruments of war. On the eve of the Normandy invasion, more than 4,000 Belgian bells had been trucked away for demolition in Nazi Germany. Only the most historic ones as well as the smaller bells of convents and carillons had been spared. Now, however, the remaining bells were working overtime. In some places the start had been hesitant. In Virton, for example, the Carmelites were already tolling their convent bell on the evening of liberation, whereas the town priest thought it safer to toll the church bell the following morning, after he had made sure that the Allies were still there. Once they were on a roll, however, the bells refused to stop. Other communities used sirens to spread the same message of intense joy. On the steps of Peer's town hall, men took turns cranking a siren on a tripod to make absolutely certain that the message would not get lost.[51]

If ever there was a moment to celebrate with music this was it. And people could hardly wait to get started. Even while the Canadians were still battling the Germans in Moerbrugge on September 9, "fragments of music and gaiety" could be heard in between the rifle and mortar fire. They drifted in from Oostkamp, on the other side of the canal which was in a wholly different mood as it had already been liberated. For fear that it might alert the enemy, American troops in Mons rushed to silence the carillon that was merrily but somewhat prematurely bouncing the Belgian national anthem across rooftops. But as security increased, so did the level of music. In Limburg's capital, Hasselt, carillons and bands could be heard playing over and over again not only the country's own national anthem, but the entire repertoire of British, American, French, and Dutch anthems. From a building in Liège's Place Saint-Lambert jubilant members of the Socialist Party had large speakers blare the fighting song of the "Internationale."[52]

But the liberation was a carnival above all, and more popular still than anthems of all kinds were the songs that sounded happy and made fun

[51] On the church bells, see De Vos, *Bevrijding*, 89. On Virton and Peer, see Sabus, *1944*, 41; and interview with Urbain Schrijvers by author, December 16, 2005.

[52] Warnier, *Brugge bevrijd*, 19; *Libération: Ayant comme but de rendre un vibrant hommage*, 139; "Hasselt ademt weer vrij!" *HBVL*, September 12, 1944, 2; and René Henoumont, "Mon dernier soldat allemand," *Pourquoi Pas?*, September 5, 1984, 19.

of things. Among them, of course, the British classic "It's a Long Way to Tipperary" and, inevitably, "We're Gonna Hang Out the Washing on the Siegfried Line." "After 1,589 days Tuinwijk is liberated," a man in a suburb of Eisden finally ended the long countdown in his diary. With intense emotion he listened to the songs blared out by an old gramophone that a neighbor had brought out into the street. "It is a joy," he wrote, "that one will never be able to forget." Catholic, socialist, and liberal parties in Nivelles in a highly symbolic gesture decided that the most appropriate way to celebrate the unique occasion was to send their rival brass bands onto the streets as one. In Brussels, a spectator remembered, people sang and danced and there was not a square or an avenue without a party.[53]

The liberators were swept up by it all. A photo taken in Verviers shows American foot soldiers pushed forward by a raucous crowd that has forced them to fall in behind a local brass band. Some of the helmeted GIs stare into the camera not entirely sure of what is happening to them. One particularly flabbergasted soldier is without his helmet. Somehow the American has ended up wearing a funny hat at an even funnier angle.[54]

Captured bliss

These were moments, like all parties, that begged to be captured on film. Although it had been almost impossible during the occupation to buy cameras or film, photos of the liberation abound for cities and villages alike. Like their best bottle of wine or valuable real coffee, people who had possessed a camera before the war had safely stored it away together with some last rolls of film with an eye to this special occasion. There are essentially two main categories of snapshots documenting the liberation. Those in the first category capture the energy and movement of the initial moments and are often chaotic and blurry. They show the actual arrival of the Allies with vehicles rushing by and bystanders hailing, touching, and storming the soldiers. A second category of photos is taken later in the day when liberation was secured and soldiers had time to halt and fraternize with civilians. This was also when the Allies were happy to pose for photos with their overjoyed admirers.

Many of the staged photos often involve just one or a few soldiers surrounded by a crowd of civilians proudly staring into the camera to

[53] Janssen *et al.*, "Maasland," 83; Blanco-Rincon and Dusausoit, "Nivelles," 19; and Offergeld, *Bruxelles*, 43.

[54] Ruwet, *Verviers*, 105.

have this blissful moment captured for posterity. The crowds are made up of family and neighbors and the larger community. On the Place Sainte-Anne in Comines, for example, a British liberator poses for the camera with at least thirty admirers, from children to a very old woman. On a square in Virton a single GI does the same with no fewer than forty inhabitants from all walks of life squeezed into the picture. It did not matter whether one knew the person one was standing next to at that particular moment in time. Perhaps it was inevitable that money and status would remain distributed unevenly for ever, but freedom was everyone's birthright in equal measure, and so everyone could partake in the liberation on a similar footing. "People cried," recalled an eleven-year-old from Brussels, "and congratulated each other." An historian has described France's moment of liberation as "a brief flare up of utopia and fraternity." It was no different in Belgium. Or that is at least how people experienced it or wanted to remember it. "We were all each other's friends, that day," remarked a man from the Limburg countryside. "When we welcomed the Americans," affirmed an inhabitant of a village in Walloon Brabant, "… there were no more classes, everyone was equal and everyone was happy."[55]

There was one category of people, however, whom Belgians overwhelmingly agreed were more deserving of the regained freedom than all others. Those were the children, of course, the next generation that everyone hoped would be the first in the twentieth century to grow up without war. Not surprisingly, they were given pride of place in many of the liberation's photographs. In some, a young Brit, Canuck, or GI, visibly ill at ease, is holding an infant in his arms, flanked by proud and insistent parents. In many others, adults have removed themselves from the scene entirely, allowing only children to pose with the Allied soldiers. Perhaps one of the most powerful of these is a photo taken in Sint-Martens-Voeren of two American soldiers surrounded by a boy and some thirty girls, none of them older than ten. The children are dressed for the occasion. The girls wear cute frocks and have ribbons in their carefully combed hair. Most look somewhat uneasy and shy. But all have varying degrees of smiles on their cheeky faces. They do not so much look into the camera as beyond it, no doubt to where their parents are, who are telling them to stand still, encouraging them to smile. And one can only imagine the parents' immense satisfaction at seeing their

[55] Vierstraete *et al.*, "Comines-Warneton," 496; Sabus, *1944*, 61; J. S., "Bruxelles, septembre 1944: C'est la Liberté," *Pourquoi Pas?*, September 5, 1984, 14; *HBVL*, September 3, 2004, 6; and Brigode, "Grez-Doiceau," 27. On France, see Brossat, *Libération*, 21.

Plate 3.4 American liberators in Nivelles. (Photo Sanspoux, CEGESOMA, Brussels, picture number 29657)

children so happy in the company of the guarantors of both their present peace and future freedom.[56]

There would never be more reason for children and adults alike to feel happy, to have fun, to celebrate. In Waremme, like everywhere else in Belgium, on the evening of liberation cafés were jam-packed with people drinking, singing, and dancing. Still in Waremme that same evening, people quickly improvised the first ball held in the *Maison du Peuple* since the start of the war in 1940. "During that crazy night of September 7, 1944," commented Hubert Laby, who was eight at the time, "each inhabitant of Waremme is convinced that a new era has opened up."[57]

[56] For the photo taken in Sint-Martens-Voeren, see Vierstraete *et al.*, *Fourons libérés*, 6.
[57] Laby, *Waremme*, 236.

4 Exorcizing the old

No matter how wild the partying, with an almost primitive instinct people sensed that liberation would never usher in a truly new era as long as the old order was allowed to fester like a malicious cancer capable of poisoning all over again. The euphoric atmosphere of the liberation had a dark side too. And in some strange, surreal manner that dark quality manifested itself side by side with the colorful, festive celebrations. If during the first hours and days the joy was savage, so was the anger. Anger at a foreign regime that had brought hunger, fear, deportation, and death. Anger above all, however, at the even more reprehensible, and more dangerous, contamination from within: the fellow citizens who had been the enemy's accomplices.

Wrapped in the flag

It was vital in those first hours and days of regime change to make it crystal clear that one was firmly on the side of the new powers to be. Ordinary citizens did so by elaborately festooning their homes with Belgian and Allied flags. Prewar local authorities were less certain about how to proceed to establish their credibility. The occupier had forced many to make way for New Order sycophants. Now the occupier was gone. But so was the Belgian king, whom the enemy had taken to Germany as a prisoner shortly after D-Day. And so was the Belgian government, eagerly awaiting its return from exile in London since 1940. Some notables, however, instantly grasped that the new road to power was on the coattails of the mighty Allies pouring into the vacuum.

As soon as the Allied troops arrived, these officials rushed to be seen and identified with the liberators. For some it meant jumping on the bandwagon quite literally. A photo taken in Kruishoutem shows a British armored car in a street lined with people. It is a reconnaissance vehicle and so the liberation must be in a very early stage. Yet on top of the small vehicle, in full view of the spectators, can be seen the prewar mayor in civilian outfit, accompanied by at least five gendarmes in uniform. The

Plate 4.1 The end of the Nazi New Order in Antwerp. (CEGESOMA, Brussels, picture number 28941)

mayor without effort finds the camera and waves, instantly reestablishing his credentials as the consummate politician.[1]

For the notables of Nivelles the day of liberation was one of more strenuous activity. Already early in the morning of September 5, the prewar mayor and aldermen, town clerk, heads of the police and fire brigade, as well as several judges were awaiting the Americans, whom they knew to be close. When finally the first vehicles of the 113th Cavalry Squadron rolled into town, little time was wasted. Several notables in full uniform and regalia made sure to clamber into the first available jeep. The mayor and a local interpreter hurried to hoist themselves and a Belgian flag onto a Greyhound scoutscar. A GI wearing dark sunglasses shook the mayor's hand and a photographer obliged. Then the mayor held on as best he could as the crew took off to the nearest square. There they allowed him to pitch his first speech of the new era, his feet firmly planted on the khaki American platform.[2]

[1] Marchal, *Gent*, 27.

[2] Blanco-Rincon and Dusausoit, "Nivelles," 19, and photo illustration inserted between pages 21 and 22. Another photo of the Nivelles events can be found in Taghon, *België 44*, 149. Photos of similar scenes can be seen in Vierstraete *et al.*, "Comines-Warneton," 528; and Roba and Leotard, *Walcourt-Beaumont*, 116.

Neutralized

Those Belgians who could not credibly drape themselves in Allied flags, however, were in serious trouble. It is remarkable that the anger at the collapsing Nazi regime was not so much vented on its soldiers. Most had been forgotten, it seemed, before the retreat was even completed. Indeed, long before the German withdrawal had started, early in 1944, Paul Struye, the astute political observer, had noted, "When one thinks of 'vengeance,' one has in mind the enemy's collaborators more than the enemy himself."[3]

In September 1944, Allied troops, aided by the resistance, marched thousands of captured German soldiers to prison pens in full view of Belgian bystanders. There were incidents, for sure. Boy Scouts on the Grand Place in Mons, for example, hurled insults at POWs packed together like sardines in American trucks, and many POWs across Belgium had to endure being spat on. Yet there never emerged a veritable swell of hatred against the captured enemy and there are very few recorded instances of serious physical violence committed against them by the population.[4]

One of the reasons undoubtedly is that the Allied troops made it very clear early on that they would not tolerate any abuse of POWs. Soldiers are notoriously allergic to civilians interfering in the business of men in uniform – whether friend or foe – and the liberators were no different. On September 6, after bitter fighting had brought much destruction upon the community of Eine, British soldiers made sure to intervene with a firm hand to protect wounded Germans against some very angry inhabitants. That same day, in Sclayn, the brother of a martyred resistance fighter walked up to a German POW seated on the hood of an American vehicle and punched him in the face. "The GIs," recalled an onlooker, "did not appreciate it."[5]

Neither did the resistance fighters. Interestingly, no matter how afraid the Germans had been to surrender to them, once captured they seemed to have found the Belgian resistance on the whole quite restrained. Although here too there were incidents, some of them serious, the resistance played a key part in keeping civilians away from the POWs. A photo of a single German prisoner somewhere in Ghent shows a gendarme and two members of the resistance calming down an agitated crowd. There are quite a few photos of German POWs in surprisingly

[3] Struye, "Sentiment public," 247.

[4] On Mons, see photo in Taghon, *België 44*, 47. On the relative absence of violence against German POWs, see also Balace, "Hoquets," 90.

[5] Deweer, *Oudenaarde*, 95; and Vandenbroucke, *Andenne*, 93.

relaxed poses with the Belgian maquis. One of them shows a group at a resistance refuge in Saint-Marcoult. Though the men of the AS proudly display their arms, none of the Germans appear particularly worried as they look into the camera. Most seem resigned and glad that it is all over. One German even flashes a smile.[6]

Despite occasional incidents it seems doubtful that, even without protection from Allied troops and the resistance, the Germans would have had to fear a serious popular backlash. An incident in Waremme hints at why this may have been the case. On the day of liberation, a veteran of the Great War failed to restrain himself when suddenly coming face to face with a disheveled and slightly wounded POW. The Belgian taunted the German, spat at his face, then began to slap him. But cooler heads swiftly intervened. They reasoned with the veteran and finally managed to have him admit that this was merely a soldier who could be blamed for nothing more than having done his duty.[7]

Indeed, once these soldiers had completed their duty and morphed into POWs without rifles, there suddenly seemed little about them that was dangerous. Which probably helps to explain why even in places like Oudenaarde and Mons, where the fighting had been exceptionally fierce, civilians thought nothing of volunteering their services to help take care of the enemy wounded. Or why the inhabitants of Beaumont responded as they did on the day of liberation. When the resistance rounded up German stragglers and locked them up in the building that housed the local brass band, the crowd at first responded aggressively. As soon as they laid eyes on the POWs, however, and realized how dirty and exhausted they were, they hurried home to fetch them food.[8]

Savage times

One would be hard pressed to find evidence of Belgians willing to provide similar comforts to any of the collaborators rounded up during the first days of liberation. For the collaborators were not soldiers, but traitors. They had not done their duty; they had violated trust. And by refusing their duty as Belgian nationals, they had committed the mortal sin of undermining unity in the face of a vital external threat. That in turn

[6] Marchal, *Gent*, 97; and Taghon, *België 44*, 55. For similar photos, see Meunier, *Dison et Andrimont*, 94; and Ruwet, *Verviers*, 100.

[7] Laby, *Waremme*, 234.

[8] On medical care, see Deweer, *Oudenaarde*, 145; and Absil, *Gilly*, 141. Another example is in Deseyne, *Zonnebeke*, 96. On Beaumont, see Roba and Leotard, *Walcourt-Beaumont*, 129.

had made foreign occupation so much harder to bear. Collaboration had insidiously eroded the comfort of solidarity in the toughest of times. Belgians who feared for their safety and lives were made to suffer more by neighbors who were informers. People whose stomachs rumbled were made to feel worse by fellow citizens enjoying extras and perks. Worse, perhaps, collaborators more than any German propaganda had sown doubt regarding the chances of Allied victory and had thus allowed even hope to be sapped.[9]

That popular anger at the traitors risked boiling over during the liberation had become clear even while the Germans were still in control. Assassinations by the resistance during the occupation cost the lives of some 850 collaborators, with the rate of killings rapidly increasing during the last months of the war. This had told those who believed they had good reason to be afraid to flee the country. Most did so during the summer of 1944. With the help of their own organizations and the occupier, an estimated 15,000 Flemish and 8,000 Walloon collaborators managed an orderly escape to Germany before the liberation. That this would cause the popular dragnet in September 1944 to catch the small fry rather than the big fish was an irony that failed to register amidst an all-consuming hatred.[10]

What would become known in Belgium as the "street repression" began like a veritable hunt. Mobs in Liège closed in on the homes of suspects like beaters on a bush, chasing their prey from ground to upper floors and then into attics, from where people in the streets could see them climb onto the roofs in desperation. Even those not actively engaged in the hunt found it hard to restrain themselves. A boy stood by as two women were dragged from their home in Brussels. "And then," the shaken eleven-year-old remembered, "the crowd yelled and screamed. With hate and rage. I barely understood it all. My father also yelled. A man ordinarily so calm. I pulled him by the sleeve, slightly embarrassed."[11]

The arrests were as arbitrary as the violence appeared blind and uncontrolled. Paule Banneux, the young woman who had earlier on September 4 watched joy engulf a British liberator on the Place Dailly in Brussels, later that same Monday saw rage vented on collaborators who were being marched to a military barracks in the same square. "The

[9] On this issue see also "Local Revenge and National Renewal" in Conway, "Justice," 18–20.

[10] Van den Wijngaert *et al.*, *België*, 261; De Vos, *Bevrijding*, 81; and Balace, "Hoquets," 108–9.

[11] René Henoumont, "Mon dernier soldat allemand," and J. S., "Bruxelles, septembre 1944: C'est la Liberté," *Pourquoi Pas?*, September 5, 1984, 19 and 14.

crowd is tempestuous," she wrote in her journal, "and if the men of the resistance who led the operation had not paid attention, the detainees would have been lynched. Even so, from time to time a man managed to cut loose from the crowd and hurl himself at the traitors, smashing one or the other with his fist."[12]

These were savage hours and days when many lashed out at presumed traitors with no other thought in mind than to inflict as much humiliation and pain as possible. People were forced to run the gauntlet so that they could be spat and scratched and kicked at and beaten with fists, clubs, belts, and whips. Photos show scene after scene of collaborators being marched through streets or carried off in trucks, their faces bruised, swollen, bleeding. Still other photos show women made to strip naked in public and forced to demonstrate the Hitler salute. There is scattered evidence to suggest a pattern of rape, but until today a strong taboo has shrouded it all in much silence. Much silence too surrounds the lynching and summary executions, with people in interviews half a century after the war willing only to hint at what happened or denying that anything of the kind ever took place at all. Still, we know for sure that in Limburg province alone, for example, during the first hours of liberation, street justice led to five people being executed in Tongeren and three others in Wellen left dead with a bullet in the neck.[13]

A degree of control

Yet, if the anger that existed side by side with the joyous celebrations was savage, what is most remarkable is that it was not totally out of control. Despite some references to the liberation by contemporaries and historians as anarchy and revolution, it was never really that. Each lynching or summary execution was, of course, one too many. But, compared with the number of collaborators killed during the occupation, and taking into account the seething anger now unleashed in the streets, the number of killings remained rather limited. That number, it has to be admitted, was never established with anything resembling certainty. Still, one Flemish historian has estimated the total number to have been no more than 100, while one of his Walloon colleagues for September and October 1944 has put the number at fifty, half of which occurred in Limburg.[14]

[12] Banneux, "Souvenirs," AB 712.

[13] Some shocking photos taken in Huy and Liège will suffice and can be found in Taghon, *België 44*, 230; and Jour, *Libération Liège*, 40. Examples of the silence surrounding certain deaths can be found in Maerten, "Brabant Wallon," 135; and Balace, "Hoquets," 106. On the Limburg killings as well as the issue of rape, see ibid., 91–6 and 89–90.

[14] De Vos, *Bevrijding*, 99–100; and Balace, "Hoquets," 76, 84, and 130–1.

The violence remained relatively controlled in the first place because Allied troops moved too fast for Belgium to remain no man's land for long. The liberators almost instantly filled the vacuum that the Germans left in their wake, thus slamming the small window of opportunity for anarchy and revolution firmly shut. But the resistance also played a significant role in containing the violence aimed at collaborators. It is true that the involvement of the resistance in the street repression did much to discredit them in the eyes of the public, an opinion that became even more pronounced in the postwar era. Resistance fighters were responsible for most of the arrests, had no way of ascertaining guilt or innocence, and freely engaged in excessive violence. What was worse, many of them were known to belong to the much-maligned "September resistance" and often seemed to participate in the hunt for collaborators for want of anything better to do.[15]

On the other hand, however, by getting involved while most prewar Belgian powers had not yet been able to reassert their authority, the more organized elements of the resistance did much to protect countless suspected collaborators from more serious harm. As Paule Banneux noted on September 4 when describing "the tempestuous crowd" on the Place Dailly in Brussels, "if the men of the resistance who led the operation had not paid attention, the detainees would have been lynched." Contemporary accounts attest to this quite often, which is not surprising in a climate where police and gendarmes were poorly armed and often discredited because of their role during the occupation. Indeed, no matter how hard and filthy life may have been in the makeshift prisons with their self-appointed and highly unpredictable guards, several historians have emphasized that the very act of rounding up thousands of suspects and carting them off to those pens undoubtedly saved many from a much worse fate in the streets.[16]

A measure of purpose

There was not only a degree of control to the violence perpetrated by the crowds, but also a measure of purpose. The public display of pain and humiliation left countless people traumatized: the victims, of course, but also many spectators, especially, it seems, those who were children at the time. Yet, somehow, despite its savageness, the violence was never entirely mindless, never geared solely towards inflicting suffering for its

[15] An example of local research demonstrating the negative impact on public opinion of the resistance's involvement in the street repression is Duportail, "Bottelare," 145–6.

[16] On the constructive role of the resistance, see Balace, "Hoquets," 108 and 114; De Vos, *Bevrijding*, 96–7; and Conway, "Justice," 12 and 14–15.

own sake, although there was plenty of that. In fact, much of the violence acted out during the first hours and days of liberation rather took on the appearance of a mass exorcism.[17]

Most exorcisms, across space and time, rely heavily on formula and ritual. And, consciously or not, Belgians in 1944 applied this principle no differently at the end of four years of uninvited occupation. A closer look at the street repression reveals not just frenzied violence, but ritualized forms of purification with symbolic meanings, a set of measures aimed at protecting and ridding the community from further contamination by what had proved to be a false and diabolical New Order.

Branding

There was, in a sense, a remarkable logic to the apparently savage chaos, a logic, one has to bear in mind, that could be acted out only because authorities like the Allies and the resistance, who generally demonstrated that they were in control, licensed it to a large degree. One of the first measures, for example, was to make the collaborators clearly identifiable for all to see. They had become pollutants as a result of their close proximity to the occupier. But, unlike German soldiers, these fellow Belgians were not instantly recognizable to everyone on account of a foreign language or uniform. In fact, Belgians who had once worn the enemy's military or paramilitary uniform had now long shed that poisonous skin, if they had not disappeared altogether.

It was urgent therefore to mark the collaborators as contaminants so as to set them apart from the healthy body of society. The process of marking the doors and façades of suspects' homes with swastikas and slogans started days before the liberators arrived. There was something almost biblical about the smears of tar and black paint on their homes, as if meant to prevent the plague or leprosy from spreading. Once the rounding up had started, it was also common to see people forced to march through the streets holding signs with all kinds of warnings, sometimes simply proclaiming "I Am A Traitor." In other communities the tainted were preceded by a man tolling a bell to alert the inhabitants to their presence. Some of the ceremonies were aimed at maximum humiliation, often through ancient practices that proved dormant rather than dead. Some, for example, were covered with tar to reveal their dark crime of

[17] I have found very useful philosopher Alain Brossat's work, which employs the concept of exorcism to analyze the liberation of France in the Second World War: *Libération*, 37–9 and 44–5.

treason. There are several recorded instances also of traitors branded in the most literal sense, that is with the help of a red-hot iron.[18]

The most common and shocking of all marks, however, and that which holds the most notorious iconic meaning until this very day, was the shaved head. There are a few documented cases, indeed some photographs, of men subjected to the so-called shearing. But, by all accounts, the overwhelming majority of shearing victims were women, because for them, more so even than for men, shearing was known to be the ultimate humiliation. It was a humiliation inflicted on them for a variety of forms of collaboration, but one that most were forced to undergo because they had chosen to sleep with the enemy, the ultimate contamination in the eyes of any male-dominated society. Shearing seemed to befit these women perfectly because in centuries past this very punishment had been meted out to prostitutes infected with venereal diseases. In fact, shearing had already been resurrected in Belgium during the liberation from German rule in 1918. The shearing rituals of 1944, however, more than ever, were numerous and infused with symbolism. Young and old women in Wavre were made to swallow their hair, and with it their pride. Somewhere in Brussels, twenty-five women with bald heads and drained faces were made to pose for a group photo. Those in the back are standing. Those in the front row sit on their knees. The two women in the middle hold a giant framed portrait of Adolf Hitler.[19]

In the midst of these vicious exorcisms, some took great care to juxtapose the diabolized women with the repossessed nation and the newly sanctioned authorities. Much of the shearing and displaying of bald women took place in front of town halls and in Durbuy even on the church steps. Shearings in Bruges were arranged to take place in the shadow of a monument symbolizing two of the city's fourteenth-century freedom fighters. On the balcony of Tielt's town hall three timid women can be seen. They remain largely hidden behind a massive balustrade draped with giant Allied flags. But their roughly shaved heads and the dark swastikas painted on their foreheads are there for all to see.[20]

[18] In Ghent, the homes of collaborators were being marked at least five days before the liberation. Marchal, *Gent*, 8. For an example of the public parading of traitors with signs and bells, see Aerts *et al.*, *Leuven*, 51; and Maerten, "Brabant Wallon," 135. For examples of the tarring and branding of suspects, see Balace, "Hoquets," 106 and 87.

[19] On the shearing of men and women in general and the Wavre case in particular, see Balace, "Hoquets," 87 and 88. On the historical antecedents of shearing, see interview with Laurence Van Ypersele in "Le Corps des femmes comme champ de bataille," *L'Extra du Soir*, August 31, 2004, 12. Offergeld, *Bruxelles*, 49.

[20] For Durbuy, see Balace, "Hoquets," 88–9. Warnier, *Brugge bevrijd*, 27; and Ravyts and Struyve, *Het Tieltse*, 392.

There is plenty of evidence, in fact, that directly implicates various authorities in the shearings. It is no secret that the resistance played a large role in this particular ritual. Nor did the gendarmes refrain from participating. Indeed, in several cases the shearings took place on their premises and at their hands. But perhaps more surprising is the complicity on the part of the Allied troops. Some historians have documented the unease and disgust that the shearings caused among liberators. But a French historian has carefully analyzed the many Allied photos, official and private, that exist of the shearings. And she asks why these troops took photos rather than put an end to the humiliation. Indeed, she wonders why the official captions do not even express disapproval. A Signal Corps photo of a shearing staged on a bandstand next to the church in Lanaken reveals several GIs among the Belgian spectators. In fact, it shows an American on the platform inspecting the work of a shearer from up close. In Belgium, as in France, many more such photos were taken by Anglo-American troops. Surely these soldiers were sufficiently armed to have dared call a halt to any shearing had they really wanted to? Or did the Allies instinctively grasp that steam would have to be let off anyway, and that there were worse safety valves than a ritualized form of exorcism?[21]

It is interesting to note in this regard that, in contrast with France, historians have not managed to map these incidents in detail for Belgium, so we do not have a clear indication of their number. It is equally interesting that in postwar memoirs and interviews most Belgians take great pains to disassociate themselves from the shearings and denounce them. It leaves one wondering who the many civilian photographers of the shearings may have been at the time. And it begs the question of where the countless elated spectators have gone that can be seen in black and white.[22]

Cleansing

Meanwhile, however, the problem remained of what to do with the sheared and smeared traitors. The Allies could be counted on to march

[21] For examples of the complicity of gendarmes, see Ciney, photo No. 29190, CEGESOMA; Deseyne, *Zonnebeke*, 96–7; and photo in De Roey and Van Hee, *Bevrijding*, 51. On the disapproval of shearings among Allied soldiers, see Schrijvers, *Crash of Ruin*, 205–6; and Pauwels, *Canadezen*, 123–6. For the Lanaken photo, see Taghon, *België 44*, 230. On the Allied photos taken in France, see Laurens, "La Femme au Turban," 158–74. Balace notes that many such Allied photos exist for Belgium too: "Hoquets," 89. Maerten mentions the case of a GI in Grez-Doiceau who actually conducted the shearing himself in the gendarmerie courtyard: "Brabant Wallon," 135.

[22] On the absence of clear statistics on shearings in Belgium, see Balace, "Hoquets," 88.

all of the German POWs to the nearest barbed-wire stockade before shipping them back home. Clearly, the safest way of dealing with the traitors too was to remove them from the street altogether. This the resistance and the populace handled in a swift and systematic manner. Allied sources estimated that the Belgians arrested about 80,000 suspects in the early stages of the liberation. That some 30,000 of these would be released again by February 1945 shows how many had been rounded up in the furor for no good reason. The most potent images of the roundup show spectators gaping at men and women thrown together behind the solid bars of cages that had formerly housed the wild animals of Antwerp's zoo.[23]

The arrests were part of a much larger sweep aimed at cleansing Belgian society from all that remained of the diabolical New Order. In his first speech after the liberation, Prime Minister Pierlot promised people that "The government would see to it that any trace of the enemy occupation would be removed." Media of all stripes employed a language of purification, urging people to take an active part in exorcising the demons of the past. "And we, Belgians, what will we do now?" asked *Pourquoi Pas?* in a special liberation issue on September 8. "First," the weekly answered its own question, "disinfect, remove the stench wherever the Germans have passed, clean the offices, the apartments, the club chairs where they have sat with their customary conceit and insolence; the task will not be easy as these gentlemen and their henchmen have invaded everything, soiled everything; but if everyone does his part, it should not take too long."[24]

Not that people needed much urging. Efforts at purification were underway even before the first newspapers reappeared, in some places even before the Allies had arrived. Among the first and most favorite targets were the homes of suspected collaborators. In a ritual repeated thousands of times across the country, mobs kicked in doors and proceeded to destroy as much as possible in a blind rage. A frenzied mob in a house in Tielt managed to smash even the marble mantlepieces and wainscot. But nothing cleansed more rapidly and thoroughly than fire, of course, and in no time plumes of smoke could be seen rising everywhere. In some communities entire homes were set on fire. Most often, however, the ritual consisted of tossing smashed furniture and possessions out of the window and onto the sidewalk in a big pile that was then torched, all

[23] SHAEFB, Final Report No. 21, 28, July 21, 1945, AA 1798/9.

[24] Pierlot is quoted in *HBVL*, September 12, 1944, 1. The *Pourquoi Pas?* special issue was reprinted in *Pourquoi Pas?*, September 5, 1984, 6–7. For similar language of purification see, for example, "Discipline," *Le Soir*, September 16, 1944, 1; and *HBVL*, "Een nieuw België opbouwen," January 25, 1945, 1.

Plate 4.2 The furniture and possessions of suspected collaborators are set on fire in the streets of Brussels. (CEGESOMA, Brussels, picture number 29072)

to the acclaim of elated bystanders. Gangs in Oudenaarde moved from home to home preceded by people playing the accordion. Nothing was spared. Somewhere in Antwerp even a cage with a parrot was thrown onto the fire from the home of a man who was a member of the Waffen SS. If onlookers on occasion expressed any regret, it was because they saw valuable food disappear into the fire too.[25]

In ritual humiliations people forced the collaborators to take part in the cleansing themselves. On Tielt's market square they were made to remove weeds from between the cobblestones. In Waterloo they were told to scrub the sidewalks. In Ghent photos were taken of a notorious collaborator and his two sons cleaning the prison toilets; the photos were then sold to the public with the proceeds going to the local resistance. On September 5, while the first British liberators were rolling through Londerzeel, two collaborators were handed brushes and ordered to remove German slogans painted on a public wall: "The village at that moment became a sea of people pouring in from all sides. They cried

[25] Ravyts and Struyve, *Het Tieltse*, 397; Deweer, *Oudenaarde*, 145; and Van Cauwenbergh, *Antwerpen*, 60.

Plate 4.3 Cleansing Brussels of all that is German. (Collection Lambrecht, CEGESOMA, Brussels, picture number 29459)

and whistled. Stark was the contrast whenever tanks or vehicles passed and the jeering suddenly turned into cheering."[26]

In this Dr. Jeckyll and Mr. Hyde mood, civilians were retaking possession of public spaces even while others were still hailing the liberators. German words and slogans were blotted out with black paint. Enemy posters and signs were torn off, thrown onto piles, and set ablaze. People shredded Nazi flags large and small and insisted that the Allied soldiers accept pieces. They ripped poles from streets and squares with their bare hands, smashing the occupier's traffic signs to smithereens. And they did so, remarked someone in Brussels, "with an almost demonic joy."[27]

Gradually, as the rage burned itself out, the fury of the exorcism made way for a more carnivalesque reversal of the once so oppressive Nazi order. In rituals reminiscent of the symbolic burning of winter, straw effigies of German soldiers or Adolf Hitler were torched, not rarely to the accompaniment of merry music. In many parts of Brussels elaborate

[26] Ravyts and Struyve, *Het Tieltse*, 395; Catoire and de Bellefroid, "Waterloo," vol. II, 7; Marchal, *Gent*, 93; and Vermaesen, *Londerzeel*, 43 and 46.
[27] Banneux, "Souvenirs," September 4, 1944, AB 712.

Plate 4.4 Inhabitants of Brussels symbolically announce Hitler's demise. (Collection Lambrecht, CEGESOMA, Brussels, picture number 29440)

processions were put together staging the funeral of Hitler. In Vorst, for example, the courageous actor who played Hitler was pelted with dirt by the onlookers each time he dared show signs of coming to life again.[28]

The Allies were offered key roles in some of these theatrical catharses. In the church square in Wegnez an American soldier was given the honor of setting fire to a straw doll in a Wehrmacht uniform while an orchestra struck up a tune. In Ieper a luxury funeral carriage took the once almighty German Führer to his grave behind a happy brass band. The carriage was pulled not by the customary horses, but by an American jeep.[29]

With these rites of passage and the symbolic burial of the past, some form of closure had begun and people could start looking to the future. That future held the intense promise of a new era in which the New World of the Anglo-Americans would have greater significance for the Belgians than ever before.

[28] De Sany-Norro, *Forest-Vorst*, 29. Brossat speaks of the "rites of inversion" that inevitably go hand in hand with any carnival: *Libération*, 144 and 147.

[29] *Pepinster*, 8; and Quaghebeur and Verbeke, *Ieper*, 150.

Part III

Liberators

5 Waves of admiration

It took time for the tumultuous atmosphere of liberation to ebb away. In October 1944 a theater in Antwerp was making people laugh with skits, songs, and dance in a production titled *Good Riddance!* The makers billed it as a revue of "disinfection." In a report that same month, the Supreme Headquarters of the Allied Expeditionary Force (SHAEF) Mission to Belgium noted that "there is still evidence of a holiday spirit and a reluctance to get down to work." Limburg's newspaper in November urged people who had still not removed their faded, rain-soaked flags to finally do so. "Homes decorated by flags offer a nice spectacle," it said. "But, like a fun fair or a holiday, it cannot last."[1]

The waves of admiration for the liberators, however, would last. Indeed, they continued to ripple and reverberate as long as the mass of Allied troops remained present throughout 1944 and 1945, a long stretch of time that allowed the Belgian population to get to know the Anglo-American soldiers better in various capacities.

Strangers in khakis

Saying thanks

On Sunday, September 10, 1944, about a week after the liberation, the inhabitants of Braine-l'Alleud were all dressed up and packed together in the market square for an elaborate patriotic celebration. All of the town's authorities were present as well as the local organizations, the resistance, and the wives and children of the deportees. Yet, as the mayor commenced his speech, a British convoy happened to make its way across the crowded square. This caused a loud gasp of excitement, and formalities were instantly abandoned as people stampeded towards the liberators, hailing them once again as they had done many times before.[2]

[1] Neckers, *Bevrijding*, 74; SHAEFB, FR No. 1, 1, October 3, 1944, WO 202/681, AA 1230; and *HBVL*, November 4, 1944, 2.

[2] Aelbrecht and Maghe, "Braine," 89–90.

People were more than happy to show their gratitude to Allied soldiers who remained perfect strangers. But the spontaneous and improvised gestures of the early days gradually made way for more organized ways of paying tribute. These in the first place concerned soldiers who had given their lives for the cause of freedom. Civilians had rushed Sergeant Major Harvey Revill to a hospital in Bruges after a German sniper had hit him in the abdomen. When the Canadian died there, his Belgian caretakers made sure that he received full honors in an impressive funeral service in the Sint-Salvator cathedral. The community of Olsene paid similar respects to Sergeant Arthur Orchard, who was killed on their soil. Though accompanied by his comrades-in-arms, all six of the British Hussar's pall bearers were people from Olsene, and the local cemetery could barely hold the tightly packed inhabitants, which included the mayor, town clerk, notary, head of police, and every other official imaginable. Scenes like this could be seen all over Belgium, especially in November, when All Saints and Armistice Day brought together entire communities to commemorate fallen Allied soldiers in local cemeteries. A photo of one such commemoration in Rijkevorsel shows hundreds of people lining several dozen British graves. All of the graves are in perfect condition and each is decorated with an impressive flower arrangement. Men, women, and children stand in respectful silence, many with their hands folded.[3]

Wounded soldiers too were given much attention. Remembering what it was that the liberators had liked most when they first arrived, local authorities and businesses in Limburg cooperated with veteran and resistance organizations to collect and buy fresh fruit and eggs for the Allies in the local hospitals. The initiative was such a resounding success that by Christmas 1944 a total of thirty-two tons of fruit had been handed out as gifts. A similar initiative was set up by miners to cheer up the American wounded in the Liège sector, while an organization in the city devoted itself entirely to raising money for the purchase of candy and musical instruments to donate to the wounded men.[4]

Soldiers who had remained unscathed, meanwhile, became the object of formal ceremonies across the country. Some of those had already been improvised on the very day of liberation. Corporal C. L. Calas of the 5th Royal Tank Regiment probably did not know what was happening to him in Oudenaarde on September 5 when overjoyed people whisked him off to the city hall, where the mayor, aldermen, and countless other notables were present to greet him as their first liberator. Before any of the notables were allowed to touch a pen, the British soldier was made to

[3] Warnier, *Brugge en september '44*, vol. I, 72–3; *Bijdragen Zulte*, 17; De Roey and Van Hee, *Bevrijding*, 25.

[4] *HBVL*, December 20, 24, and 28, 1944; and Sulbout, "Liège," 29–30 and 101–8.

sign a guest book created for the memorable occasion. In the final luxury edition, taken special care of by the city archivist, the corporal stood forever recorded as "the representative of the long-awaited liberating armies."[5]

As the dangers of battle receded, such ceremonies became more numerous and elaborate, involving all kinds of authorities. In Heide it was the village priest who invited a Canadian delegation to the presbytery for an official celebration early in October. The crowd cheered as the priest said a few words of thanks from the balcony. But, a local newspaper reported, "The joy soared when Martha Hens, the smallest child, held by the priest, received a heartfelt kiss from a Canadian officer." Meanwhile, at the start of the new opera season, the joy in Brussels could no longer be contained. The official opening night in the Théâtre Royal de la Monnaie was scheduled for October 1 with a performance of *Carmen*. But the organizers offered a special performance of *La Muette de Portici* the evening before. Both pieces were highly symbolic of the love of freedom and both had been banned by the Germans. *La Muette de Portici* on September 30 did not fail to stir the emotions of the audience, which included Belgian ministers and Allied military authorities, and gone was the usual restraint of the opera crowd when the evening concluded with a tribute to the Allied armies. When Anglo-American troops appeared on stage and their national hymns resounded, people jumped up from their seats and sang along exaltedly. "The audience," a newspaper reported, "gave off shivers and in expressing their gratitude to our allies the acclamations were close to delirious."[6]

The gratitude expressed to the soldiers was extended to their nations as the Belgians and their authorities thought up all kinds of gestures of appreciation. On September 12 the mayor of Bruges decided to waste no time and cable his thanks to the man who had been directly responsible for the troops liberating his city: "The municipality of Bruges, delivered and preserved today by the splendid conduct of the brave Canadian troops, presents to the Right Honorable William Lyon McKenzie-King, Prime Minister of Canada, the homage of all her gratitude and admiration." Despite the country suffering from shortages of all kinds, SHAEF late in November reported it was arranging "the transport of toys, as a Christmas gift from the Belgian people to the children of England."[7]

It was when the renowned military leaders of the Allied nations visited Belgium in person, however, that intense gratitude gave rise to the most

[5] Deweer, *Oudenaarde*, 160–1.
[6] Neys *et al.*, *Kalmthout*, 20; and Duchenne, "Bruxelles," 16–17.
[7] The cable is quoted in Warnier, *Brugge bevrijd*, 27. SHAEFB, FR No. 5, 15, November 28, 1944, WO 202/685, AA 1230.

emotional of scenes. Montgomery arrived in Brussels just days after the liberation to see crowds lean from windows, pack balconies, and jam the famous *Grand Place*. He appeared on the city hall's balcony to the delirious chanting of "Monty! Monty! Monty!" that mingled with the roaring echo of "For He's a Jolly Good Fellow." The Belgians had to wait until November to catch a glimpse of another of the near mythical heroes of the war. The atmosphere in parliament was electric when Eisenhower was their guest of honor just prior to Armistice Day. Each mention of the name Churchill or Roosevelt in the speeches of Belgian politicians was greeted with a roaring applause from the assembly. More than once they spontaneously broke into a standing ovation directed at Eisenhower, obliging the general to return the tribute with a military salute. When finally Eisenhower himself rose to take the platform, the full assembly jumped to their feet welcoming the American hero "with an ovation that did not end."[8]

Sizing up

There was no end either to the intense scrutiny to which Belgians subjected the Allies. As the soldiers settled down there was more time to size them up and soon they represented the major attraction in many a town and village. "Sunday afternoons," a woman from Lier recalled of a hastily built Royal Air Force (RAF) base, "there was something like a procession of people strolling to and from the airfield. Everyone wanted to see this from up close." Under the Germans, things military had been shrouded in secrecy and danger. Now, suddenly, the Allies proved amazingly lenient with the curious. A boy from Marchin saw his father set off on foot to have a closer look at the Americans, who were said to have established large depots in Huy, nearly six miles north of the village. The 332nd US Engineer Regiment was the first unit to bed down in Walcourt after the liberation. As they are setting up their kitchens in a farm courtyard, a photo shows droves of inhabitants seven rows deep watching the GIs' every move. The unit's history later estimated they had drawn at least 500 spellbound spectators in just this one tiny village.[9]

Each liberator was, in the words of historian David Reynolds, "both a person and a symbol." That made it easy for Allied soldiers to make momentous and lasting impressions, perhaps even more so with the young. "Sometimes," a boy from Bruges recalled of the Canadians, "they handed you a chocolate bar just like that. Just like that. I worshipped

[8] *Le Soir*, September 8, 1944, 1, and November 11, 1944, 1.

[9] Maria Selderslaghs, AB 1591; Chapelle, *Marchin*, 15; and Roba and Leotard, *Walcourt-Beaumont*, 183 and 185–6.

Plate 5.1 Civilians approach American soldiers in Liège. (CEGESOMA, picture number 142704)

those men." But if all Allies possessed symbolic powers, none did more so than the American soldiers. Perhaps simply because they were more exotic. The British, after all, were neighbors of a kind, despite the channel separating them from Belgium. *Het Belang van Limburg* alluded to that early on. As the newspaper for a province liberated by the British in the north and the Americans in the south, it was well positioned to make comparisons. "We dreamed of your arrival, England! We dreamed of your arrival!" was the emotional conclusion to a front-page article on September 19 offering homage to "Good Old England." Still, the newspaper had made sure to thank the Americans at least a week earlier. Because, it explained, they were the ones who had liberated the provincial capital where the newspaper was published. But, the article confessed, self-servingly or not, there was something else too: "Precisely because they came from so far we thought of them most and perhaps longed most that they would be the ones bringing us deliverance."[10]

Belgians could be forgiven for mistaking a Canadian for a Brit. Indeed, some Canadians tried to put a halt to the confusion by writing "Canada"

[10] Reynolds made the comment with regard to the GIs in Great Britain. *Rich Relations*, 427. Warnier, *Brugge en september, '44*, vol. II, 129. "Dank aan het goede oude Engeland," *HBVL*, September 19, 1944, 1; and "Amerika dank!" *HBVL*, September 13, 1944, 1.

on their vehicles in chalk. But even in the early stages of liberation there was no way Belgians could mistake a GI for a Tommy or Canuck. In Antwerp a priest who saw only British soldiers in September and October characterized them in his journal as "reserved" and "dignified," but also as "friendly" and "pleasant." And he acknowledged that they had "conquered a place in each heart." But an entry on October 20 shows how much he was blown away by his first encounter with Americans (three young flyboys). "Totally different from the English," he concluded, "lighthearted, cheerful, childish-naïve, and genial: but extremely loud, uninhibited, and fairly rough-hewn; physically impressive like Hercules and tall like giants."[11]

A major divide in space and history had made most Americans distinct enough to be instantly recognizable. But color too did much to distinguish the GIs. Belgians were baffled by the sight of countless blacks in American uniforms. Their country had ruled millions of blacks in the Congo for decades, but that heart of darkness was far from home. Few if any Africans lived in Belgium, and government and church portrayals of the colonial subjects had created shadowy images of primitive people in dire need of a massive civilizing effort. Belgian reactions to the first black GIs might just as well have been those of Europe's medieval explorers first setting foot on the African continent. Half a century after the liberation, a hairdresser from Embourg still relished in great detail his surprise at feeling the frizzy black hair for the first time. Wide-eyed children in Pairay were surprised at how "dirty" the faces of the African-Americans were. "For us," one of them acknowledged, "everything was new and bizarre." That was not just the case with village children, however. On its front page on October 20, 1944, *Le Soir*, the quality Belgian newspaper, printed a large picture of black Americans in military uniform to allow everyone to have a closer look at this intriguing phenomenon.[12]

It was quite a revelation to see the image of dark primitives in need of civilization exploded by black liberators in neat uniforms driving jeeps. But the GIs revealed a lifestyle that was significantly different in more than one way. In another ironic reversal of roles, Europeans now stood in awe of the many trinkets Americans, white and black, offered as tokens of goodwill and friendship. Decadent luxuries like apricots and pineapple and grapefruit emerged from simple cans. Powders changed into milk or coffee or egg in an instant. Tablets made even the most suspect water safe to drink. Belgians, like many Europeans, came to see

[11] Pauwels, *Canadezen*, 60–1; and Greeve, "Oorlogsdagboek," 175, 185, and 190, AB 2166.
[12] Lognard-Poncin and Michel, *Chaudfontaine*, 29; and Jour, *Villes libérées: Liège*, 50.

the GIs, in the words of historian Judith Keene, as the New Men from a New World, the men who brought with them the magic of modernity.[13]

And with that modernity came a particular brand of freedom. A freedom that was not just political but that could be felt in a deeply personal way. A freedom that somehow affected not just the way one looked at the world, but quite literally the way one moved in it. Very early on, Belgians sensed that GIs were the incarnation of this new kind of freedom. No Allied soldiers looked as youthful as the GIs. Indeed, Belgians time and again characterized the American soldiers as men who at heart very much appeared to have remained children. Compared with their British comrades, for example, discipline clearly was not the forte of the easygoing GIs. They were reluctant soldiers, marveled a socialist newspaper, who disliked formal parades and much preferred "to drag their feet while chewing gum." They had that puzzling attitude, *La Gazette de Liège* noted, that was "at the same time relaxed and orderly." Here, the Liège newspaper pointed out, was a mighty military that managed to function well "in a spirit of cordiality between officer and simple soldier," an army where during leisure hours "commanders mingled with their men like comrades." In that way, remarked *La Wallonie* as early as September 15, 1944, "The 'Boys from Uncle Sam' are themselves the carriers of the great ideas of democracy, of liberty."[14]

Comparing and contrasting

No matter what the differences between the various liberating armies, all of the Anglo-Americans were bound to compare well with the have-beens and wannabes of the ruined continent. The German face of defeat was utterly humiliating, of course. A seven-year-old girl from Eisden much later recalled "the rows of captured Germans with their hands in the air" in September 1944. "Some of them cried," she noted. "That made quite an impression on the child that I then was: boys were not supposed to cry." Let alone men who had once claimed the right to rule all of Europe and much of the world. Now Belgians watched the self-proclaimed master race await their fate in more than 1,000 hectares of barbed-wire fields across the country. In Overijse alone, the largest such camp in all of Europe, more than 80,000 disheveled Germans could be seen spread out over 150 hectares.[15]

[13] Judith Keene, "GI Joe and the G-Man: Public and Private Memories of the Korean War," paper presented in the "War and Memory" forum at The Centre for Peace and Conflict Studies, University of Sydney, August 4, 2006.

[14] The socialist newspaper is quoted in Janssen *et al.*, "Maasland," 126; the French-language newspaper quotes are from Sulbout, "Liège," 25.

[15] Janssen *et al.*, "Maasland," 101; and *La Réparation par l'Office d'Aide Mutuelle*, 185.

But already long before the liberation, the Germans had defeated themselves by imposing on Europe an authoritarian regime of such terror and exploitation that most of those who by the late 1930s had doubted the wisdom of democracy were soon looking back at it with bitter nostalgia. If in 1940 German soldiers had managed to impress Belgians with their rigid order and discipline, the newly liberated now were all too happy to be rid of these attributes. "What is striking, in comparison with the Germans," a priest in Antwerp noted as soon as the British troops had arrived, "is the total absence of barked commands." People were "thrilled," a Flemish newspaper wrote, to be able to listen to an American military band "with all manner of brass instruments and drums" instead of "the cadenced German marches." The Walloons *L'Éventail* agreed metaphorically. The German, it admitted, had shown he could sing well, but always in tune with his comrades. The Allied soldier, on the other hand, "sings, hums, happily intones that stanza which pleases him and takes his fancy at any given moment."[16]

But how well too did the Anglo-Americans compare with anything the Belgians themselves had to offer as the dust settled on the collapsed New Order. The armed forces had proved ineffectual in May 1940 and many of the French-speaking soldiers would remain prisoners in Germany until 1945. The resistance had behaved with utmost courage during the occupation. Indeed, once the Allied troops arrived, the resistance often fought bravely on their side, as in the Mons pocket and north and east of Antwerp, just to name a few examples. And they performed countless valuable tasks, from intelligence gathering to guarding key infrastructure. In doing so, no less than 1,000 resistance fighters sacrificed their lives between September 2 and 12, 1944. But if the resistance had stirred the imagination during the occupation, it failed to do so during the liberation. Few people were in a position to witness the resistance's most successful contributions on the front lines with the Allies. What many did witness, however, were the resistance's botched attempts to dislodge the Germans before the Allies were able to bring to bear their full strength, only to see them suffer the ignominious fate of needing rescue by Allied troops. On September 4 alone, for example, a panicky resistance in and around Brussels had to call on the Allies to come to their aid several times. The maquis in Waterloo prior to the arrival of British troops occupied key public buildings and proudly hoisted the Belgian tricolor. But as soon as they spotted some German tanks, they rushed to get help from armored vehicles of the Guards Division. As the Germans abandoned Nivelles, resistance fighters chased after them in

[16] Greeve, "Oorlogsdagboek," 175, AB 2166; *HBVL*, October 31, 1944, 2; and Leblon, "Américanophilie et anglophilie," 20–1.

the surrounding woods, but encountered such heavy counterfire they had to plead for help from American tanks. And there were many more such incidents across the country that caused the resistance to be perceived as ineffectual and largely powerless.[17]

What made them appear outright ridiculous, and indeed caused many Belgians to feel ashamed, were the notorious "September Resistance." In just a few weeks they caused irremediable damage to the image and reputation of countless courageous members who had been quietly part of the resistance for many years. In his diary, an outraged Father Greeve in Antwerp dismissed the "hundreds, perhaps thousands of ragged young guys," brandishing guns without apparent purpose, as "heroes from an operetta." "They make us blush," he wrote, "in front of the English liberators." But no matter how much he admired the original resistance, even they, he had to admit, cut a poor figure next to the Allied troops. As he watched them lay flowers at a Great War monument during an official ceremony on November 1, he noted the absence of uniform outfits and headgear and the fact that only half of them carried weapons. But it was not just that. Compared with the Allied soldiers, there was also "the sallow complexion, the sunken cheeks, all signs of 4½ years of hunger, cold, and deprivation."[18]

No wonder then that it was the Allied soldiers and not the resistance fighters who were all the rage during the liberation. A photo taken in a street in the village of Comines shows two English soldiers. One of them looks into the camera with a cocky smile as a local woman happily leans on his shoulder with both arms. The caption identifies a man with a bike in between both soldiers as a resistance fighter. The man manages to flash a grin. In his arms he is holding a Sten gun. But no girl. Such scenes repeated themselves across Belgium and before long a fashion of fascination was modeling itself after the Allied uniforms. *Variétés Magazine* in November 1944 advised female readers "to be dressed from head to toe and in all accessories in accordance to a certain allied military influence." These included, among others, berets, large pockets, tartan designs, and the very short coats that imitated military vests and were known as *canadiennes*. The most prized items by far, however, were the nylon stockings of American origin that were fast replacing the silk ones. In addition to all that, the fashion magazine assured, it was always bon ton to add to one's outfit some military insignia. Indeed, by the beginning of 1945 SHAEF was urging Belgian security forces to

[17] Colignon and Gotovitch, "Sang," 112–13; Huet, "Mons," 97–8; De Vos, *Bevrijding*, 84; Catoire and de Bellefroid, "Waterloo," vol. I, 8–14; and Blanco-Rincon and Dusausoit, "Nivelles," 15–16.

[18] Greeve, "Oorlogsdagboek," 175, 183, and 199–200, AB 2166.

crack down on shops across the country engaged in "the manufacture and sale of such insignia."[19]

Governors *pro tempore*

The presence of Allied troops in liberated Belgium involved not just fun and fashion. It concerned also the serious business of government. The nature of that business and, more importantly, the sensitive delineation of Belgian and Allied powers, had been dealt with in a number of Civil Affairs (CA) agreements signed in London before the liberation. Aware of the vital importance of clear communication on matters of future government to a people that had carried the burden of foreign occupation for four years, both Belgian and Allied authorities in the days following the liberation hurried to clarify the arrangements in the newly established press. Immediately after his return from exile in Britain, Prime Minister Pierlot called on the Belgians to make sure to show the obeisance due to the Allied Supreme Headquarters under existing Belgian legislative agreements. In his own message to the Belgian people, General Eisenhower, the Allied Supreme Commander himself, took pains to clarify that such obeisance was essentially required to allow him to fulfill his main responsibility, namely the execution of the war. It was up to the Belgians themselves, he was keen to emphasize, to install their own civil administration and to ensure the security of the Allied armies by respecting the law and public order.[20]

At the local level, Allied government became most clearly and directly visible in the form of CA detachments. Such missions were installed in cities and towns that were of administrative and economic importance. Many a village would never host a CA detachment and thus have no permanent Allied presence. But CA missions could just as well be set up in smaller localities that had some particular importance because of industrial activities, the presence of a railway station or depots, and so on. Historian Jacques Wynants has likened the presence of those Allied detachments to that of the *Feldkommandanture* during the German occupation, albeit "in more pleasant circumstances."[21]

The nature of those circumstances can be illustrated by taking a closer look at the arrival and initial activity of the CA mission in the Nivelles district of Walloon Brabant, which was fairly typical of missions in other

[19] Vierstraete *et al.*, "Comines-Warneton," 525; Leblon, "Américanophilie et anglophilie," 20–1; and SHAEFB, FR No. 8, 7, January 9, 1945, WO 202/688, AA 1230. See also Colignon and Gotovitch, "Sang," 104.

[20] See, for example, publication of both proclamations in *HBVL*, September 12, 1944, 2.

[21] Transcript interview Jacques Wynants, MS421, AA 1593.

mid-sized communities. A detachment of seven CA staff arrived on September 6, the day after the liberation of Nivelles and its nearly 12,000 inhabitants by the 2nd US Armored Division. One of the first steps they took was to appoint a local to their office as permanent interpreter. The CA team functioned as a liaison between the Allied military authority and the local civil authorities. One of its first and main concerns was issuing letters of safe-conduct, night permits, and identity cards in order to ensure that civilian circulation would in no way obstruct or endanger the movement of Allied troops.

But the CA staff in Nivelles clearly were aware also that creating a general atmosphere of goodwill would do much to benefit the Allied war effort. That is probably why they did not hesitate to get involved in matters that were not an immediate Allied concern but nevertheless crucially important to the community. On September 16, for example, the CA commander called all principals into his office to discuss the speedy reopening of schools. When they pointed out that there were no textbooks available for the new school year, the CA commander dispatched trucks to Brussels and Namur to fetch them without delay. The commander also agreed to act as a godfather for the local Scouts organization, and he made sure to have a load of vitamin-rich food trucked in for the weaker children. Not long after, one of Nivelles' children fell seriously ill and a local doctor said he urgently needed special medicines that to the best of his knowledge could be obtained only in Paris. The CA commander instantly arranged for a special permit, a jeep, and sufficient quantities of fuel. The medicines arrived in Nivelles that same evening, saving the child's life.[22]

Bringing calm

Like the team in Nivelles, CA and other Allied authorities across the country had their work cut out in more than one way where it concerned the population. Although their main concern would always be the protection and facilitation of military operations against Nazi Germany, the Allies soon found themselves deeply involved in various matters, some only tangentially related to the prime mission. Circumstances in Belgium forced them to. At the national level it took time for the government to find its feet after many years of exile in London. Prewar local authorities, on the other hand, were out of the loop or in disarray, while those that had functioned during the occupation were under suspicion and in need of purging. "For four years the Belgians have had their

[22] Blanco-Rincon and Dusausoit, "Nivelles," 52–4.

country run for the benefit of the Germans," SHAEF summed up the situation early in October 1944. "The apathy and lack of initiative is noticeable in the machinery of government."[23]

One of the first priorities for the Allied authorities was to bring calm. After years of intense turmoil, Belgians were in desperate need not only of peace, but peace of mind. SHAEF listed "law and order" as one of the "most important and almost primitive requisites" for the stabilization of the country. The Allied role in this would prove to be crucial as Belgium's own security forces were a shambles in the autumn of 1944. The Germans had preferred to rely on their own extensive security apparatus and had largely neglected the Belgian forces. Indeed, shortly before the liberation they had thought it safer to disarm many of the police and gendarmes altogether. On top of that, once the Allies arrived, Belgian authorities began purging the local forces of many of those who had obtained their posts during the occupation. The result was that in the newly liberated Belgium, police and gendarmerie lacked men, weapons, and means of transport.[24]

In Brussels, Ghent, Bruges, Liège, and Hainaut, the gendarmes at the end of September 1944 were at no more than 70 to 80 percent of their normal strength. In Antwerp they were more than 40 percent short of the required manpower. To make matters worse, the gendarmes who did walk the streets often had no weapons with which to wield any authority. In urban areas like Antwerp, Arlon, Brussels, and Bruges, fewer than six out of ten gendarmes were armed. More than half of all gendarmes in Ghent were without weapons, while in Namur 65 percent of the corps remained unarmed.[25]

The police were in even worse shape. Of all the forces in the country, only 36 percent were in possession of a firearm in September 1944. SE officers reported that in Antwerp province there were about two policemen per 1,000 inhabitants and in the densely populated cities of Antwerp and Mechelen no more than three. With the exception of the provincial capital, few municipalities in Namur could count on more than one policeman, while the role of the police in West Flanders province was said to be "nil" beyond the cities. In Luxembourg province not even the cities had "police forces worthy of the name."[26]

[23] Chief of SHAEF Mission to Belgium, General-Major Erskine, in SHAEFB, FR No. 1, 1, October 3, 1944, WO 202/681, AA 1230.

[24] SHAEFB, FR No. 3, 1, October 31, 1944, WO 202/683, AA 1230.

[25] Dauphin, "La Belgique libérée," 104–6.

[26] Laureys, "Maintien de l'ordre," 6, and "Het bevrijde België," 34; and Van Ypersele, "La Belgique libérée," 8–9.

The resistance made grateful use of the vacuum to enhance their own power. They had risked much for their country and expected their courage and sacrifice to be translated into political leverage. At the national level this immediately proved difficult as the government in exile as early as September 8 put itself back in the saddle with a firm helping hand from the Allied forces. SE officers were sent out straightaway to act as its eyes and ears and they would prove very suspicious of the resistance and its leftist elements in particular. Moreover, the Allied liberation had happened so fast that it had not provided the shadow army with much of a moment in the sun to be exploited. What could be exploited to establish their credentials as a post-liberation force, however, was the lack of security provided by local authorities.

Indeed, SE intelligence noted that in parts of the country police and gendarme action was "hampered and even openly obstructed" by the resistance. The gendarmes were "afraid to confront the resistance" who, like much of the population, did not hold the security forces in high esteem. Like the local prewar authorities, however, the resistance were quick to grasp that the best way to establish their credentials was to convince the new Allied powers of their enduring value. That was not too difficult as the Allies proved quite satisfied with the help they had received from the resistance during the lightning liberation. There was not only the stunning coup the resistance had pulled off in the vital port of Antwerp. British military sources, for example, lauded the resistance also for their help during the advance on Brussels, while an American report concluded, "All military authorities will admit that the Belgian Resistance groups have offered them much more aid during the days of Liberation than have similar groups in France." Indeed, after the liberation, Allied troops across the country did not hesitate to employ thousands of resistance fighters to guard German POWs, key infrastructure like bridges, power plants, railroads and factories, and even Belgium's border with Holland.[27]

The Belgians themselves, however, became increasingly convinced that, where law and order were concerned, the resistance were part of the problem rather than the solution. In the wake of the liberation, complaints about abuses committed by the resistance rapidly multiplied. This was not entirely surprising. While the weakness of police and gendarmes allowed the sway of various resistance groups to inflate, many of these

[27] On the relation with police and gendarmes, see Dauphin, "La Belgique libérée," 57; and Van Ypersele, "La Belgique libérée," 6. The Allied military sources are mentioned in Taghon, *België 44*, 54–5; and Gotovitch, "Communistes," 55. The total number of resistance fighters performing guard duty for the Allies and in prisons holding collaborators in the autumn of 1944 is estimated at 10,000. Lagrou, "Résistance," 131.

groups lacked sufficiently strong central commands to keep that power in check. Intoxicated by their newfound authority, local commanders and their bands began to act as if they were above the law. Some were intoxicated by more than power. Police in the Brussels suburb of Sint-Joost-ten-Node, for example, reported that on September 4, elements of the resistance had broken into cafés (supposedly owned by collaborators) and stolen wine, beer, and champagne as well as money. Local authorities responded with growing anxiety. "The mayor," the SE reported from Mons on September 9, "is awaiting clear orders. He is perplexed by the multiplicity of groups, the rights they are demanding etc." On September 19, the mayor of Lier sounded the alarm in a letter to the Antwerp governor: "Members of the White Brigade and the Front of Independence are closing down groceries and tobacco shops and carting off their stocks. All our attempts to make the resistance organizations abide by the law are failing." In Liège that same month authorities were pointing to the armed resistance as "the prime danger to public order."[28]

In such circumstances the resistance were proving poor substitutes for police and gendarmes. People complained that the resistance threw up road checks at will and then proceeded to harass passersby arbitrarily. Indeed, they inadvertently caused casualties among comrades and bystanders alike as many proved clumsy with firearms. In mid-October 1944 bereaved inhabitants flocked to the church in Hamont to say farewell to a nine-year-old. The boy had been killed by a bullet in the chest when a young resistance fighter tried to show off his pistol. For a people that had suffered hunger for many years, however, nothing made sympathy for the resistance dwindle more rapidly than the illegal means by which they were seizing food. They requisitioned provisions in the name of operational necessity or as punishment for collaboration. They checked traffic and pedestrians at will, confiscating food they claimed had been procured illegally on the black market. Or they just took what they wanted without explanation. A report in the SE files on Hainaut province, dated September 13, noted that "the requisitioning of flour, wheat, meat, and even cattle and hogs causes much dissatisfaction among the rest of the population which deplores that the partisans are much better fed than they are and are clearly abusing the fact that they

[28] Report police Sint-Joost-ten-Node, October 4, 1944, Folder 951, AA 1311; and SE report, "Mission à Mons," September 9, 1944, Folder 972, AA 1311. The mayor of Lier is quoted in De Zaeger, *Lier*, 120. Liège is mentioned in Van Ypersele, "La Belgique libérée," 10. Mons is the capital of the heavily industrialized Hainaut province where the leftist resistance was particularly strong. Many contemporary sources would single out the FI and its *Partisans Armés* as the most lawless forces. But research has shown that none of the resistance groups was without such elements. Balace, "Hoquets," 129–30.

are the only ones who are armed." A month later, gendarmes in Dudzele near Bruges reported that people were fed up with the resistance stealing chickens, ducks, and sheep, supposedly with the Canadians' permission. "The members of the resistance groups have gone so far," the report claimed, "as to refuse to make statements to the Gendarmerie."[29]

In a matter of weeks after the liberation, problems with law and order were making patience with the Belgian authorities wear thin. In Limburg, where some elements of the resistance would eventually join gangs engaged in outright banditry, the province's newspaper demanded to know: "Has liberated Belgium become a lawless republic and is there no longer any government?" Indeed, the prewar national government that had returned from London was proving weak and out of touch with a people that had experienced the hardships of occupation. Local authorities, meanwhile, remained ineffectual as they were being purged and reconfigured. "The only ones," in the words of historian Laurence Van Ypersele describing the immediate post-liberation period, "to hold effective power, in practice and with sufficient legitimacy in the eyes of the liberated populations, are the allied armies."[30]

By the end of September 1944, those Allied armies too were becoming weary of the resistance's continuing recalcitrance. Although they were using the resistance as military auxiliaries in several capacities, they understood that other elements were posing a significant threat to law and order in the streets. The American CA detachment in Tongeren had given the gendarmes the authority to conduct night patrols and provided them with brassards for that specific purpose. But neither the gendarmes nor the mayor of Tongeren in a special meeting managed to convince the leftist Partisans Armés (PA) to accept that arrangement. "They want to act independently," a gendarmerie report said, "and refuse to recognize the established authority." The disgruntled American commander of the CA mission in Charleroi summoned local authorities to his office. He expressed serious worry about the incidence of aggression, vandalism, theft, and other crimes committed in the name of the resistance and demanded to know why they were failing to clamp down on this. The point the American officer drove home was that all this threatened not only the security of the inhabitants but, in the final analysis, also that of the Allied troops.[31]

[29] On Hamont, Hainaut, and Dudzele, see *HBVL*, October 14, 1944, 1; Dauphin, "La Belgique libérée," 60; and report gendarmerie Brugge, October 17, 1944, Folder 958, AA 1311. On the nature of the abuses more generally, see Balace, "Hoquets," 129–30.

[30] "Kolen, eten en ... orde," *HBVL*, October 22, 1944, 1; and Van Ypersele, "La Belgique libérée," 1.

[31] Report gendarmerie Tongeren, October 10, 1944, Folder 986, AA 1311; and Hasquin, *Charleroi*, 47.

British military authorities were coming to the same conclusion in their sector. On September 29, an SE officer responsible for West Flanders reported that, "As they are increasingly being called upon by the civilian authorities, the Civil Affairs officers are beginning to get worried." He added that, two days earlier, the British general responsible for the province had suggested bringing in Belgian soldiers to have them wield authority in the streets rather than the unruly resistance. British troops in the first half of October set up road blocks in Antwerp. They checked 1,890 vehicles in 35 hours. Of the resistance behind the steering wheel, 54 were in violation for using Allied fuel, 233 for not having a license, and 64 "for irregular possession of the vehicle." Though SHAEF noted that no charges would be pressed, the random security check once again revealed the extent to which the resistance were ignoring the law, and British authorities in Antwerp would continue to raise alarm over instances of "pillage, abuse of authority, illegal requisitioning, looting, etc."[32]

Sensing that the onus of bringing calm to the streets was on them, not only to satisfy the population, but increasingly also to safeguard their own troops, the Allies decided there were two measures they could take. The first was to employ their own troops. But that was out of the question as the battle with Nazi Germany took absolute precedence. The Allies possessed much more firepower than manpower. A logical decision therefore was to rearm Belgium's regular security forces as rapidly as possible. "With the various armed factions in Belgium," SHAEF noted on October 3, "it became necessary to ensure that the Gendarmerie, as the most stable element in the country, were adequately armed." Indeed, a week earlier, 916 arms of various types had been handed over to the gendarmes from Allied stocks. And five days after that, 5,000 Sten guns and ammunition had been flown in from England and dropped over Belgium by parachute.[33]

It was only the beginning of a more systematic Allied campaign to help contain the irregular armed forces out on the streets. But the next logical step, disarmament of the resistance, would prove to be politically highly sensitive. General Eisenhower, in an official statement on October 3, paid tribute to the Belgian resistance but at the same time called on them to put down their arms. The AS that same week announced that it would heed the call and disarm. Other groups made similar promises but dragged their feet as they wanted more guarantees in terms of jobs for their members in the Belgian military. The FI, however, the leftist

[32] Ct. Ruzette to Col. Gregoire, September 29, 1944, Folder 958, AA 1311; SHAEFB, FR No. 2, 17, October 17, 1944, WO 202/682, AA 1230; and Van Ypersele, "La Belgique libérée," 12.

[33] SHAEFB, FR No. 1, 12, October 3, 1944, WO 202/681, AA 1230.

resistance group led by the communists, flatly refused to cooperate. This prompted British General Erskine, head of the SHAEF mission in Belgium, to go on national radio on October 27 to repeat Eisenhower's appeal. In this broadcast, Erskine too thanked the "various Belgian underground movements" for their "courage and initiative." But he then went on to emphasize that "It is not their business, as armed bodies or individual armed men, to interfere in the civil or commercial life of the country." Yet, despite these calls, by the end of October, 70,000 resistance fighters – 25,000 of whom belonged to the FI – had still not disarmed. The Belgian government for its part could count on no more than 8,000 gendarmes who, despite some Allied transfers, remained poorly armed. In such circumstances the government remained reluctant to lock horns, no matter how keen it was to have the resistance, and especially their leftist elements, eliminated as a threat to its authority.[34]

But the Allies, worried about a destabilization that might affect their lines of communication in the war against Germany, were showing increasing impatience with the spineless approach to disarmament. "This is a matter," an irritated SHAEF noted on October 17, "which has been considerably exercising the Belgian government, and their handling of it has so far been weak and vacillating." Two weeks later, Eisenhower's chief of staff bluntly put an ultimatum to Prime Minister Pierlot, stating that armed civilians would no longer be tolerated on the Allied lines of communication. However, it was only when the Allies offered the government the firm assurance that they would, if necessary, militarily intervene to help enforce disarmament that Prime Minister Pierlot finally dared put his own ultimatum to the resistance.[35]

That ultimatum, early in November, caused the FI, egged on by a Communist Party that hoped to increase its political leverage, to hold protest marches in Brussels and several other cities. The unrest culminated in a large march on Brussels on November 25. When some elements broke through the cordon sealing off the capital's political heart and neutral zone, the gendarmes were forced to use violence, leaving several dozen protesters wounded. But the violence in the capital also left the resistance, and the communists in particular, badly discredited in the eyes of public opinion. It was the final straw for General Erskine too. Though SHAEF reported that Allied troops had been "held in readiness," they had during the turbulent November days "not been involved actively in any disturbances." Now, however, General Erskine

[34] SHAEFB, FR No. 3, Annexure 1 to General Summary, 1, October 31, 1944, WO 202/683, AA 1230; and Van den Wijngaert *et al.*, *België*, 278.

[35] SHAEFB, FR No. 2, 15, October 17, 1944, WO 202/682, AA 1230; and Van den Wijngaert *et al.*, *België*, 278–9.

issued a clear threat to the leaders of the Communist Party and the FI that next time he would not hesitate to call out his own troops to quash the resistance.[36]

The events of November 25 broke the backbone of the recalcitrant underground. "The political situation," General Erskine summed up on 12 December, "after a sharp rise in temperature has settled down and reached a degree of stability which it has not had since the liberation of Belgium." "But it must be made absolutely clear to all concerned," he warned, "that political ambitions cannot be fought out in the street across our lines of communication. If this happens, or there is a serious threat, the military forces become involved." That no longer proved necessary, however, as in the course of the winter the various resistance groups quietly faded away. Disarmament, which had proved a major headache in October and November, now proceeded at a rapid pace. Gendarmes generally took the lead, stockpiling the weapons in their headquarters before transferring them to Allied depots. The Allies made good on their promise to help enforce disarmament where necessary. On November 30 the SE reported that in West Flanders British CA units had played "a very active role in collecting arms," especially in places like Bruges, Zeebrugge, Ieper, Izegem, and Roeselare, where groups like the PA had remained reluctant to cooperate. Intelligence gathering and house searches by British troops, supported by the gendarmes, had led to the discovery of major arms caches. It had, the report remarked, "given rise to major relief across the province." SE officers in other parts of the country also reported that many, predominantly leftist, resistance groups had eventually handed over their arms to Allied troops rather than the gendarmes. On December 12, SHAEF mentioned that "there has been a steady stream of arms coming in during the last fortnight." Indeed, two weeks after the resistance had created havoc in the capital, a total of nearly 30,000 weapons, 3½ million small-arms rounds, and 16,458 grenades were counted in Allied depots. SHAEF's final inventory in July 1945 revealed that gendarmes and Allied troops had collected a total of 41,727 firearms of all kinds.[37]

[36] Some contemporaries interpreted the November events as the harbinger of a coup. But the same SHAEF report provided a more level-headed assessment when it stated that "The period under review has been upset by political events of a nuisance value out of proportion to their real significance." SHAEFB, FR No. 5, 11 and 1, November 28, 1944, WO 202/685, AA 1230; and Van den Wijngaert *et al.*, *België*, 279.

[37] SHAEFB, FR No. 6, 1, December 12, 1944, WO 202/686, AA 1230; SE, "Note sur le désarmement des mouvements de résistance en Flandre Occidentale," November 30, 1944, Folder 892, AA 1311; Van Ypersele, "La Belgique libérée," 9, 13, and 14; and SHAEFB, FR No. 6, 12, December 12, 1944, WO 202/686, AA 1230.

In some places the Allies continued to rely on elements of the resistance for auxiliary tasks long after the crisis of November 1944. But by the end of winter, these groups too were gradually being disbanded. Employed by SHAEF to guard bridges, armed members of the AS in the Rekem sector, for example, were replaced by Belgian soldiers in February 1945. A month later, SHAEF ordered Canadian troops in the Turnhout area to stop employing the resistance for border control or to have them absorbed as part of the regular Belgian border authorities. Belgium's gendarmes and police, meanwhile, continued to grow stronger as they now received weapons not only from Allied stocks, but also from those seized from the resistance. 21 Army Group in March 1945 "handed over 4,000 serviceable rifles and 1,000 unserviceable ones for repair by Belgian armourers, all taken from the arms collected from resistance movements." SHAEF estimated, however, that this still left the gendarmes some 13,000 arms short. In SHAEF's final report in July 1945, gendarmerie and police were said to have received from Allied and resistance stocks a total of 8 armored cars, 17,112 rifles, 7,348 automatics, and 200 revolvers.[38]

Building trust

The Allies went a long way towards breeding a climate of trust by bringing calm to Belgian streets. But they also made a conscious effort to engage in various other activities aimed at building confidence in foreign troops among a population badly traumatized by forceful occupation. Some consisted merely of prompt responses to emergency situations. Aware that the equipment of local fire brigades had become outdated and dilapidated, for example, Allied troops were keen to provide assistance wherever they could. In just a few weeks in the autumn of 1944, Americans decisively intervened in two fires in Limburg province. In Sint-Truiden the American fire brigade on the nearby air-base rushed to assist their Belgian colleagues in fighting the blaze at a pharmacy in town. African-American soldiers in Koersel, meanwhile, took huge risks attempting to save as many of the contents as possible from a home that had caught fire. When the regional newspaper caught wind of what had happened, it not only thanked "the many negro soldiers" in a separate article, but also placed an English translation next to it for their benefit.[39]

[38] On Rekem and Turnhout, see gendarmerie Tongeren, MR February 8, 1945, Folder 1103, AA 1311; and SHAEFB, FR No. 12, 9, March 6, 1945, WO 202/692, AA 1230. On rearmament, see SHAEFB, FR No. 11, 11, February 20, 1945, WO 202/691, AA 1230; and Final Report No. 21, 14, July 21, 1945, AA 1798/9.

[39] *HBVL*, November 8, 1944, 2, and October 31, 1944, 2.

Local commanders also made certain that their troops were involved in the many public activities that the population was now free to engage in for the first time in years. In Liège, for example, local and GI brass bands were soon marching through the city's streets together, and eventually Belgian policemen and American MPs could also be seen performing side by side on an open-air bandstand on Sunday afternoons.[40]

The population appreciated the participation of Allied troops in more solemn public events at least as much, if not more. And the liberators were quick to grasp the importance of this in cultivating continued goodwill. Scottish troops who liberated Nevele on September 7, for example, two days later already found themselves part of a political procession winding its way to the town hall to formally install the acting mayor. Much more numerous, however, were the patriotic commemorations. Such ceremonies had been prohibited during the German occupation and now Belgians hurried to honor the many soldiers, resistance fighters, and civilians who had paid with their lives in the struggle for freedom since May 1940. In Brussels, for example, there was "a veritable explosion" of ceremonies, with many taking place in September 1944 and again on All Saints Day, Armistice Day, and Dynasty Day in November. By the end of 1944 there had been no fewer than 236 patriotic ceremonies large and small across Greater Brussels. These ranged from laying flowers at monuments to funeral processions for the more recent victims, and they were repeated in cities, towns, and villages across the country. Occasion enough then for the Allies to participate in emotionally charged commemorations that enabled them to send strong messages of solidarity with, and respect for, the people they had liberated.[41]

In the first weeks following the liberation it was the funeral processions for members of the resistance killed in the final battles that attracted some of the largest crowds. Photographs of the funeral of three of the resistance in Tongeren show hundreds of people lining the streets. Hundreds more form part of the procession that is composed of all kinds of officials and inhabitants carrying wreaths. Two representatives of the US Army can be seen marching behind a gendarme and two nurses, with in their wake a large contingent of the resistance in their trademark overalls. A photograph of a similar procession in Herve shows a detachment of no fewer than thirty American soldiers solemnly marching behind their flag in full view of a reverent crowd.[42]

[40] Sulbout, "Liège," 101–8.

[41] Janssens and Van Maldeghem, *Nevele*, 11; and Brigode, "Commémorations," 3, 7–8, and 54.

[42] Rutten, *Tongeren*, 36; and Dechaineux, "Herve," 152.

Many of the ceremonies honoring patriotism in the autumn of 1944 tended to crystallize around the monuments of the Great War. Often too the veterans of that war led the way as the younger generation of soldiers were either still imprisoned or poorly organized. Again the Allies were very much aware of the symbolic importance of these events and of the opportunity they offered to strengthen a community of shared values and interests. Tournai had barely been liberated, for example, when, after the *Te Deum* on September 4, officials and inhabitants in procession walked to the monument dedicated to the dead of the Great War. There, a captain of the US Army, according to one of the people present, "declared himself happy to pay tribute to the Belgian soldiers of 1914–18 who had fought with the American army."[43]

A close reading of Limburg's newspaper for November 1944 reveals that both the British in the north and the Americans in the south undertook sustained efforts to send detachments to commemorations in even the smallest of villages. After the ceremony in Eigenbilzen on November 11, for example, "there was some heartfelt celebrating and fraternizing in the veterans' club house in a truly Anglo-Belgian atmosphere." The church service for the war victims of Sint-Huibrechts-Lille was attended by "a large group of English soldiers under command of their major." The Belgian villagers returned the honor after the service and in procession headed for the local military cemetery to pay tribute to the slain English soldiers.[44]

It was equally important for many of the inhabitants of the predominantly Catholic country to see Allied soldiers participate in religious celebrations. When GIs attended church services in Visé, for example, the local priest early in November 1944 was quick to note that "Everybody is struck by the respect they show in church." During the German occupation many of the age-old Catholic processions had been prohibited from taking to the streets. Locals must have expressed much approval then when Canadian soldiers insisted on carrying the statue of Our Lady in the procession of Antwerp's parish of Sint-Paul. English soldiers who volunteered to do the same in Heist during the afternoon procession on Sunday, September 24, must have made just as big an impression, though the exigencies of war forced them to pack their bags before they had time even to finish the church service.[45]

Allied soldiers did not have to be Catholic, or even religious, to be eager to participate in the celebrations on December 6 surrounding

[43] Devolder, *Tournai*, 51.
[44] *HBVL*, November 19, 1944, 2, and October 27, 1944, 2.
[45] Waterval and Lensen, *Basse-Meuse*, 230; Van Cauwenbergh, *Antwerpen*, 55; and Patteet, *Heist*, 406.

Saint Nicholas, revered in Belgium as the patron of children. They provided the occasion for many an Allied unit to spoil the neighborhood's children and, in doing so, to win the hearts of their parents too. British and American troops in Limburg competed trying to please the children. GIs in Hoeselt had the holy man with the white beard and red robe arrive in a jeep. Tommies in Peer hosted a party for eighty children and their mothers, treating all of them to cookies and hot chocolate. They were outdone by British comrades in Kwaadmechelen who invited a total of 270 children to meet Saint Nicholas and made sure that all of the guests received "sandwiches, chocolate, candy, beef tea, apples, and other treats."[46]

Troops were happy to repeat the good times when some weeks later they hosted parties across the province to celebrate Christmas and New Year. *Het Belang van Limburg* thanked English soldiers in Wijchmaal for having shared with local children "the treats they had received for themselves on the occasion of Christmas." On January 12, 1945, GIs possibly broke a national record when they had some 1,000 children attend a belated Christmas party in Opglabbeek. The New Year's charm offensive was not limited to children alone. British soldiers in Helchteren sent out a convoy to pick up some 200 elderly inhabitants. They treated them all to a sumptuous lunch, topped off with chocolates and cigarettes and a parting gift for every man and woman present. An emotional mayor thanked officers and enlisted men "for the generosity and kindness they showed to our people time and again."[47]

And there were many other informal occasions for the Allies to cultivate continued goodwill towards their authority. Still in Limburg, the American military in Sint-Truiden, for example, threw its weight behind a large concert with the promise that all proceeds would go to the Belgian Red Cross and a hospital for tuberculosis patients. British troops, on the other hand, had the not inconsiderable advantage of being well versed in the art of football. Communities and organizations vied to have excellent British teams from the air force and army challenge their own players. And if these occasions were used to raise money, the proceeds might benefit either side. The inhabitants of Hasselt, for example, eagerly awaited the arrival of the English regimental team that had already played first-rate clubs in Anderlecht and Eindhoven. They were all too glad to pay for the tickets, knowing that the money would go to the families of the English players' fallen comrades.[48]

[46] *HBVL*, December 15, 1944, 2; December 13, 1944, 2; and December 16, 1944, 2.
[47] *HBVL*, January 12, 1945, 2; December 28, 1944, 2; and January 10, 1945, 2.
[48] *HBVL*, November 16, 1944, 2; and December 9, 1944, 2.

Providing work

But it was through work rather than play that the Allied forces made the largest contribution to building a community of shared interests. By the time of the liberation in September 1944, many Belgians found themselves out of work because transport had come to a standstill and factories had been forced to shut their gates. SHAEF, however, had high hopes for Belgium, one of Europe's pioneer industrializing countries. It called the country's economic position "enviable" because of its "highly variegated industry," which as a result of the lightning liberation had remained "practically entirely intact." What was lacking, it pointed out, were raw materials. Belgium possessed coal in abundance, but other than that had always been a mass importer of raw materials. Now, however, production in the mines had plummeted during the chaos of liberation and, with the war still raging in Europe, Belgium could not hope to attain the level of imports needed to get its industries humming with activity again. "At present," SHAEF warned on October 3, 1944, "Belgium is like a large and most efficient factory with all the doors closed."[49]

By the end of 1944 the dire consequences of this could be felt throughout the country. In November the number of people officially registered as unemployed stood at more than 225,000. This was a troubling statistic for a country of no more than eight million inhabitants, especially when taking into account that many women abstained from work outdoors, while countless able-bodied men were still dispersed abroad for a variety of reasons. Still more worrisome was that the trend appeared to be getting worse, with the number of unemployed rising to over 240,000 in December 1944.[50]

If there were any lifelines in terms of jobs in those somber autumn months, they were thrown by the Allied armies. At the end of September 1944, General Erskine in a letter to the Belgian government listed as one of SHAEF's top priorities, "The organization of labour for military purposes." Before the end of that month, a major conference had hammered out an agreement to come into effect on October 15. Under that agreement, the Belgian government became responsible, as part of its contribution to the war effort, for the procurement, administration, and pay of all civilian labor required by British and US forces. At the most basic level

[49] SHAEFB, FR No. 3, 18, October 31, 1944, WO 202/683; No. 4, Annexure 1 to General Summary, 2–3, November 14, 1944, WO 202/684; and No. 1, 1, October 3, 1944, WO 202/681, AA 1230.

[50] From here on, all statistics on Belgian unemployment are from the Institut d'Éducation et de Documentation Nationales, "Chronique," 177; all those on Allied employment are from de Pinchart, *Office d'Aide Mutuelle*, 16.

this meant that Allied forces would turn to the municipal authorities with their requests for labor, and that these authorities would then take care of time cards, family allowances, social insurance, holiday pay, and so on, later to be reimbursed by the Belgian government in Brussels.[51]

Even before that agreement came into being, Allied forces had been hiring civilian workers in a variety of capacities, providing a significant boost to many a community. People in Waterloo, for example, recalled that there was very little unemployment immediately after the liberation as a result of the giant British ammunition depots along the major roads leading into Brussels. In Braine-l'Alleud, a town of fewer than 12,000 people, some 300 men were given well-paid jobs loading and unloading British trucks along those same roads. In Nivelles, a nearby community of about the same size, between 200 and 300 unemployed men were absorbed by an RAF base that urgently needed them in maintenance shops and for the loading and unloading of Dakota transport planes.[52]

Allied troops across the country sought civilians for a variety of what SHAEF called "service trades." For their huge air base at Florennes, for example, the Americans hired civilians as clerks, mechanics, chauffeurs, carpenters, painters, plumbers, and so on. The Canadians in Ghent put many civilians to work as nurses in military hospitals. The British in December raised eleven Belgian motor transport companies, recruiting several hundred men, many of whom traveled to France for the purpose of returning abandoned military vehicles to Belgium. Towards the end of 1944, the Allied military very gradually began to put people to work in a number of factories too. Some became involved in the booming business of repairs. As early as September 26, the FN armories at Herstal had signed a massive contract with the American army for the repair of what by August 1945 would be a total of more than 200,000 firearms. The Ford Motor Company plants in Antwerp as well as factories in Liège and Verviers began hiring people for the assembly and repair of countless American trucks and jeeps. Other factories came to life again because of Allied orders that could be filled thanks to emergency allocations of raw materials. By mid-October 1944, for example, the US army was asking Belgian industry to provide them with 80,000 jerrycans a day. In December the Englebert factories in Liège were producing

[51] SHAEFB, FR No. 1, Appendix A to Section I, October 3, 1944, WO 202/681, AA 1230. For the practical arrangements regarding Allied recruitment, see SHAEFB, FR No. 1, Appendix C to Section IV, October 3, 1944, WO 202/681, AA 1230; and "Aanwerving van werkkrachten" in Ministerie van Financiën, *Rondschrijven gemeentebesturen*, 10–11.

[52] Catoire and de Bellefroid, "Waterloo," vol. II, 14; Aelbrecht and Maghe, "Braine," 76; and Blanco-Rincon and Dusausoit, "Nivelles," 54–5.

large numbers of tires, while around Christmas workers were sought in Roeselare to fill massive orders for shoes and gloves and in Diest for underwear for the British military.[53]

All in all, even if at the end of 1944 the unemployment statistics remained bleak, the Allied military had provided the Belgian job front with some significant relief by creating 39,000 jobs in November and employing 65,000 people in December. And these statistics failed to take into account not only the jobs created indirectly by Allied demands to have factories fill orders, but also the employment in small businesses boosted by troops who had plenty of money to spend. Limburg's regional newspaper in the fall of 1944 published articles with language tips aimed at barbers and even watchmakers to help facilitate their brisk business with soldiers, while a job advertisement for a dry cleaner in the province's capital now asked for personnel who could speak English in addition to Dutch and French. The son of a cobbler in the small Limburg village of Veldwezelt on the Dutch border recalled how his father almost abandoned repairing shoes when an apparent fad caused increasing numbers of GIs to pay him handsomely for custom-made leather holsters tied around the leg with strips.[54]

As winter approached, however, Belgians grew more worried about employment as well as provisioning. And an SE report from La Louvière late in November 1944 showed how aware people were of the importance of the Allies regarding the former when it noted that "One finds in all social environments a unanimous wish that, in terms of jobs, the Country will make a substantial contribution to the Allies waging war." Winter proved hard indeed for employment. Extreme cold paralyzed transportation and the German counteroffensive in the Ardennes caused production in the coal mines to falter with a resulting steep drop in the supply of electricity. In those circumstances activity in the factories reached a low ebb, with only the Allied military able from time to time to provide some much needed relief. Roeselare, where unemployment was particularly high early in 1945, saw at least a glimmer of hope, for example, when several factories were asked to produce beds for the Allies. And in one factory in Charleroi in February a fortunate labor force was able to make idle furnaces breathe fire again when the American military put in

[53] For the service trades, see Challe, "Florennes," 30, AB 1381; Pauwels, *Canadezen*, 141; and Donnison, *Civil Affairs*, 422–4. On the jerrycans, see SHAEFB, FR No. 2, 19, October 17, 1944, WO 202/682, AA 1230. On Roeselare and Diest, see SE, WR February 1, 1945, Folder 958, AA 1311; and *HBVL*, December 28, 1944, 2. All other information is from de Pinchart, *Office d'Aide Mutuelle*, 15.

[54] *HBVL*, September 29, 1944, 2; November 26, 1944, 2; November 16, 1944, 2; and September 3, 2004, 6.

Plate 5.2 Belgian workers repair shoes for the American military. (CEGESOMA, picture number 30011)

a request for the production of more than one million cups and plates. The Americans managed to kickstart the production only by using some of the valuable raw materials set aside for the military and providing the factory with everything from coal to sheet iron and borax.[55]

Yet, if during the winter of 1944–5 the Allies could provide only piecemeal work in the factories, they were able to absorb a mass of unemployed people when the giant port of Antwerp finally resumed its activities at the end of November 1944, instantly becoming the key logistical hub in Western Europe. Already in mid-November SHAEF had calculated that "the impending use of the port of Antwerp will provide jobs for more than 15,000 dock laborers." As hiring accelerated in the course of winter, this estimate was shown to have been conservative, so that by the beginning of March 1945 almost 20,000 Belgians were working for the Allies on the Antwerp docks.[56]

[55] La Louvière, WR November 24, 1944, Folder 1054; Roeselare, WR February 1, 1945, Folder 958; and Charleroi, WR February 17, 1945, Folder 1020, AA 1311.

[56] SHAEFB, FR No. 4, 20, November 14, 1944, WO 202/684; and No. 12, 19, March 6, 1945, WO 202/692, AA 1230.

Indeed, employment in Antwerp accounted for much of the increase in the total number of jobs created by the Allies in winter, a number that in January 1945 stood at almost 85,000. Even then, however, official unemployment figures in Belgium had jumped to 290,000 that same month, up 50,000 from December and "an alarming increase" in the words of SHAEF. No wonder then that those Belgians who held well-paid jobs with the Allies counted their blessings and were all too happy to go that extra mile when asked to do so. "There have been," a satisfied SHAEF reported on January 9, "no strikes and few threats of work stoppages. Despite difficult working conditions and low rations, Belgian workers have stuck tenaciously to their jobs. Civilians working for the military stayed on the job through both holidays in response to the government's appeal." Conditions had been particularly hard for the dockers in the Antwerp port. They, SHAEF acknowledged in special tributes later in 1945, had "never faltered in their work." And they had continued "operating [the port] to full capacity in the face of every V1 and V2 the enemy could find to hurl at it" until the German offensive had at last abated early in April 1945.[57]

By the spring of 1945, things were looking up on several fronts, not least on the job front. With the Germans pushed out of the Ardennes by the end of January, and the onset of milder weather in February, the economy began to warm up too. As early as the end of February, unemployment fell from the 290,000 peak of the previous month to just under 236,000. By the end of spring, the number of people out of a job had decreased to fewer than 125,000.

One of the reasons for this spectacular turnaround was that the Allied military's hiring had become particularly vigorous with the onset of spring heralding the start of the final push against Nazi Germany. The number of civilians directly employed by British forces peaked on April 1, 1945, with a total of more than 100,000. For the American military, peak employment stood at 45,000 on May 15. For May this meant an increase in combined Allied hiring of some 65 percent when compared with that of January. To free up their own troops for the final campaign, the Allies were asking civilians to perform myriad vital tasks in the rear. As the thaw set in, thousands of Belgians were being hired for urgent road repairs from Antwerp to the Ardennes. As early as February, for example, Americans reduced unemployment in Tongeren by half with a single request for road works, while some 200 of the 520 jobless laborers in Athus at once found employment clearing rubble for the Americans in Bastogne. But the Allies

[57] SHAEFB, FR No. 11, 18, February 20, 1945, WO 202/691; and No. 8, 22, January 9, 1945, WO 202/688, AA 1230. On Antwerp, see SHAEFB, FR No. 15, 3, April 17, 1945, WO 202/695, AA 1230; and Final Report July 21, 1945, AA 1798/9.

also sought large numbers of chauffeurs for military vehicles as convoys frantically moved to and from Germany. At the German POW camp in Zedelgem they even recruited civilians to take over guard duty from English soldiers urgently needed elsewhere.[58]

There were still more job opportunities popping up in spring. With Allied soldiers flooding into Germany, nearby Belgium was ideally suited to take care of large numbers of exhausted troops. These troops needed rest and relaxation and were eager to spend money that had served no purpose at the front. For GIs the city of Liège, for example, was a major center, and at the end of February 1945 the SE observed, "The morale of American troops is excellent. For them Liège is a place of recreation, a city to rest in. As a result business continues to grow." In nearby Spa, home of the famous health springs and a large number of hotels, the upmarket casino was barely able to handle the GI stampede, but management quickly trained many young men and women as additional staff to keep the roulette wheels turning at all times.[59]

Business also boomed in Eisden, a small Flemish village north of Liège that in March 1945 had the good fortune of being selected as the 19th Corps Recreation Area. Modest by the standards of Liège and Spa, this recreation area for African-American troops until the end of summer would nevertheless host an average of 225 enlisted men and 25 white officers. These men would have a major economic impact on Eisden and its surroundings. The officers created a structure whereby the local hotel, cafés, barber shop, and cinema became integral parts of the recreation complex. Belgian managers and personnel were put on the American payroll, and more people were soon being hired even from other villages, eventually bringing the total number of civilians employed by the US recreation center to between 75 and 90. The center also gave a major boost to small businesses as far away as Lanaken and Dilsen, which were asked to provide everything from workers to tools and paint and furniture.[60]

The most encouraging sign of a reviving economy, however, was the steady increase in industrial production. "A sizeable number of articles are now being manufactured in Belgium for the armed forces," SHAEF noted mid-April, "such as battle-dress, bridge material, tyres and tubes, cotton goods, mess equipment and yeast." Indeed, if the Allies were directly employing some 135,000 Belgians by the end of April, SHAEF

[58] SHAEFB, FR No. 19, 17, June 12, 1945, WO 202/700, AA 1230. Tongeren, WR February 24, 1945, Folder 1103; and Athus, February 16, 1945, Folder 1006, AA 1311. On the chauffeurs and guards, see Malines, WR April 13, 1945, Folder 1066; and Roeselare, April 5, 1945, Folder 1090, AA 1311.

[59] Provincial report, February 24, 1945, Folder 979, and WR March 24, 1945, Folder 1099, AA 1311.

[60] Kohlbacher, "Eisden," 33; and Janssen *et al.*, "Maasland," 163.

estimated that indirectly they were also providing jobs for another 80,000 locals by means of "firms engaged on army contracts."[61]

Allied employment caused troops and civilians to attain a high degree of symbiosis. The American military port commander at one point remarked that each docker in Antwerp took the place of an Allied soldier needed at the front. But the same could be said of every civilian employed by the Allies, and SHAEF was happy to acknowledge this. "Belgium's military contribution has taken the form of maximum co-operation in the scheme of liberated manpower," it stated in its final report in July 1945. "Her contribution has been most useful and been given in a generous and loyal manner."[62]

The Belgians in turn had found the Allies to be most loyal and generous in their employment schemes. Loyal, because no matter how often SHAEF repeated its mantra of the war effort as top priority, the head of its mission in Belgium clearly demonstrated a concern about the well-being of the Belgian population that went beyond purely military interests. "It is not part of the Supreme Commander's responsibilities to rehabilitate the life and industry of the country," General Erskine said at the end of a very dark January in 1945, though he quickly added, "but for obvious reasons this must be done as soon as it is humanly possible." Erskine was very much aware that this meant Belgium should be empowered as soon as possible to produce goods for its own population rather than just foreign troops. "Consequently," Erskine was emphasizing as early as February, "second only to the importation of food is the demand for the importation of raw materials." Concerted efforts by SHAEF and the Belgian government to increase such imports slowly began to bear fruit even before the war in Europe had ended. "The wheels of industry are beginning to move a little more rapidly," Erskine could note early in April, "and this is giving very considerable satisfaction. Ships have arrived on the Belgian Civil Account with cotton, wool and rubber." As soon as the war in Europe was over, ships with raw materials for Belgium's civilian industries began multiplying at a rapid pace, more than doubling the 88,000 tons of May to 196,000 tons in June. This went hand in hand with a further increase in jobs. "Industry has only started to move during the last 2 or 3 months but each week brings an improvement," SHAEF noted in its final report in July 1945. Direct and indirect military employment had helped tide Belgian society over during what would otherwise have been an even

[61] SHAEFB, FR No. 15, 15, April 17, 1945, WO 202/695; and No. 16, Supplement, May 1, 1945, WO 202/697, AA 1230.

[62] De Vos, "US Forces," 191; and SHAEFB, Final Report No. 21, 2, July 21, 1945, AA 1798/9.

rougher period of economic transition. That was illustrated most clearly by statistics at summer's end. By then Allied forces were employing 72,000 Belgians fewer than at spring's end. Yet, not only did industry now rapidly absorb all of these, it also further reduced the already low unemployment of June by more than 10,000.[63]

Still, the Allies had endeared themselves to countless Belgian employees not just with their loyalty, but also with their generosity. As early as September 20, 1944, an advertisement from the national agency for employment encouraged people to sign up for work at Sint-Truiden's American airbase, touting the work conditions as "excellent!" The same was true for other Allied employers. An inhabitant of Zomergem recalled that "working for the Englishman" soon became an expression, and that those who did get such jobs "were envied because they made lots of money." Both military and government authorities repeatedly denied that the liberators were paying better wages than Belgian employers. But continued attempts as late as 1945 by various commissions "to establish more equitable and uniform wage rates for civilian labour supplied to the Allied forces" told a different story.[64]

And the story was not just one of money. "It was quite an experience," remembered one of the civilian employees at the 19th Corps Recreation Area in Eisden, "to have the Americans put trucks at our disposal to take people from the vicinity ... home. Talk about considerate employers." It certainly compared well with Germans rounding up people like cattle and shipping them off to Germany against their will. Perhaps most indicative of the hurt caused by war and occupation was the extent to which food formed an incentive to work for the Allies. Employees talked as much about the hot meals and meat swimming in greasy calories as they did about their fat paychecks. Scores of laborers from Nivelles, recruited for maintenance work on the nearby British air base, happily paid their bosses the biggest compliment of all by visibly gaining weight in a very short time. SHAEF at the end of October 1944 issued strong support for the continuation of serving civilian labor one warm meal a day. Given

[63] SHAEFB, FR No. 9, General Summary, 1, January 23, 1945, WO 202/689; No. 11, General Summary, 1, February 20, 1945, WO 202/691; and No. 14, General Summary, 1, April 3, 1945, WO 202/694, AA 1230. SHAEFB, Final Report No. 21, 2, July 21, 1945, AA 1798/9.

[64] *HBVL*, September 20, 1944, 2. On Zomergem, see Gabij Van de Wiele, AB 1591. The quote on rate adjustments is from SHAEFB, FR No. 7, 21, December 26, 1944, WO 202/687, AA 1230. See also SHAEFB, FR No. 8, 21–2, January 9, 1945, WO 202/688, AA 1230. A Belgian academic analysis at the end of 1945 acknowledged that "through some lack of co-ordination in policy, the remuneration for such [Allied military] jobs was set substantially higher than in industry." Léon-H. Dupriez, "Belgium's Unemployment Problem," in BT, 151.

the food supply situation, it noted, these meals were "of the greatest value to the workmen." Indeed, in March 1945 strikes threatened on several airbases when these began to be turned over to local private contractors and Belgians stopped working for the Allies directly. The unrest had come about, SHAEF noted, because employees feared not only "a reduction in hourly wages," but also an end to "their mid-shift meal."[65]

Ambassadors of hope

Stores of goodwill

The appeal that Allied troops held for the Belgians went beyond the basic concerns of safety and a full stomach. The liberators were admired also as representatives of Anglo-American societies and cultures that had gained tremendously in reputation during the German occupation. Great Britain's prestige in particular had grown by leaps and bounds since the start of the war. Belgians had never been as familiar with the island nation as they had been with France and Holland, the contiguous neighbors whose languages they shared. More importantly, though Britain had played a crucial role in enabling Belgium's independence in the 1830s, and in guaranteeing its neutrality, Belgian public opinion in the late nineteenth century had become deeply suspicious of its hegemonic and imperial policies. Especially when these seemed to be threatening Belgium's own empire in Central Africa. The Boer War in South Africa, for example, as well as Britain's campaign against the excesses of King Leopold II in the Congo, had stirred up ill feelings among many in Belgium. A major turning point in the Anglo-Belgian relationship, of course, had been the Great War, when all of a sudden both countries found themselves fighting side by side in an epic struggle against Germans now portrayed as barbarian Huns. Still, the 1930s had done much to erode the good feelings of the Great War. The appeasement policies of an economically depressed Britain had made it look like the epitome of a discredited parliamentary democracy. And when that appeasement had taken the form of encouraging Nazi Germany to look towards the Belgian colonies as compensation for its imperial losses after the Great War, old fears of perfidious Albion had easily been rekindled. The weak performance of the British Expeditionary Force in May 1940,

[65] Kohlbacher, "Eisden," 34; and Blanco-Rincon and Dusausoit, "Nivelles," 60, note 22. SHAEFB, FR No. 3, 14, October 31, 1944, WO 202/683; and No. 13, 22, March 20, 1945, WO 202/693, AA 1230.

in such stark contrast with the country's admirable intervention in the Great War, had done much to strengthen the perception of a Britain that was no longer great.[66]

After only one year of German occupation, however, public opinion observer Paul Struye noted that, although suspicions regarding the British continued to linger in some circles, these were drowned out by an increasing realization that Britain's interests now clearly coincided with those of Belgium. Nine-tenths of all Belgians, he claimed, were greeting the smallest British success "like a national victory." More importantly still, "the immense majority of the population" was developing a "deep admiration" for the courage of the British. Their refusal to give up despite tremendous setbacks and their decision to continue the fight all by themselves had, Struye wrote, made the British as popular as the Finns in the winter of 1939. Their resilience in response to Germany's ferocious bombing campaigns had further fueled that admiration. The British were now no longer seen as "selfish" and "decadent" but as "strong" and "healthy." In short, they were showing themselves to be "a great people" again. By the spring of 1943, most Belgians, Struye asserted, showed admiration also for the British political system, especially "the dignity with which free discussion continues in the midst of war," something that stood in sharp contrast with the German totalitarian regime. All these newfound qualities of the British people by that time were personified by their political leader, Winston Churchill, who stood for "dynamism" and "indomitable energy." Churchill was now regarded as "the great man of our era," whose decisions "were supposed to have most directly influenced the course of events."[67]

It took President Roosevelt and the US much longer during the occupation to gain a similar prestige. The US had remained largely unknown in Belgium before 1914. It was the massive American campaign to provide relief during the Great War that had caused the huge country to take firmer shape in Belgian consciousness. Many would never forget the wheat, corn, rice, sugar, and lard that had helped alleviate hunger courtesy of the Americans. Belgian schoolchildren after the armistice gladly posed for photographs holding signs expressing gratitude to that faraway people. Yet, despite President Wilson's military and peacemaking roles at the end of the conflict – and a steep rise in American goods, music, and films after the war – the reluctance of the US to accept international responsibility and the crippling depression of the 1930s had caused the giant country to appear irrelevant again.

[66] For a survey of Anglo-Belgian relations until May 1940, see Stengers, "Grande-Bretagne," and Colignon, "Résistance"; 30–1.

[67] Struye, "Sentiment public," 83–5, 131, 169–70, 214–15, and 252.

Economic support for Great Britain and entry in the war at the end of 1941 had changed all that, of course, but even as late as the spring of 1943, the same Belgian observer charting the ascendancy of Britain could note that public opinion was "confused and often disappointed by the little it knows, or thinks it knows, of what is happening in the US." News of strikes on the homefront, "mediocre" performances by GIs in Tunisia, and the American preoccupation with the war against Japan did much, Struye claimed, to contribute to the uncertainty surrounding the giant's potential to make a difference in Europe.[68]

Regardless of the relative merits that Belgians assigned to the British and the Americans, the only time during the occupation when combined Allied prestige was threatened with serious harm was during the bombing campaigns. The population was left in shock, for example, when in the spring of 1943 American bombers aiming for German factories in Mortsel near Antwerp accidentally obliterated nearly one thousand civilians in the blink of an eye. Things became worse in 1944 when systematic air raids against key infrastructure preceded the invasion of Normandy and Allied bombs in a matter of months left some 6,500 civilians dead across Belgium. Although Struye emphasized that people considered this "the unavoidable price for the Liberation that the quasi-unanimity of the country wishes for," he had to admit that many nevertheless found it a very bitter pill to swallow.[69]

But the euphoria of liberation not only washed away that nasty taste, it also laid bare the immense stores of goodwill the Allies had built up during the German occupation. Gone was the least trace of recrimination about historic wrongs, for example, when one of Flanders' Catholic newspapers thanked England on September 19, 1944, as "the only one of our large neighbors that never did us any harm in the past and that always was our protector." In the same article there was not a hint of suspicion about a British empire now portrayed as a beneficent commonwealth of subjects and allies "ready and eager to help." Better still, the newspaper brought back to memory not only Britain's "brave sons" of the Great War, but even "the wars of Napoleon and the glorious battle at Waterloo where you saved Europe from tyranny." Many others, high and low, considered Waterloo too potent a symbol for the newfound friendship between Belgium and England to pass up. Montgomery during his visit to Belgium early in November 1944 made sure to visit the famous battlefield and sign the guest book. That same autumn, with much less

[68] Struye, "Sentiment public," 171 and 216. On the lingering memory of American aid during the Great War see, for example, Lognard-Poncin and Michel, *Chaudfontaine*, 28. Maleux, "Propagande," 57.

[69] De Vos, *Bevrijding*, 102; and Struye, "Sentiment public," 217 and 271.

pomp and ceremony, René Boulet, headmaster of a school in Genval, took several English soldiers on a bike ride across the battlefield. And he was glad to repeat the gesture with others the following spring.[70]

There had been no American troops at Waterloo. But with their heroics in Normandy and reversed *Blitzkrieg* in the late summer of 1944, GIs deftly made up for lost time. They had their own immortal heroes now. As they crossed the Belgian border early in September 1944, in many a community the first sight of what was thought to be an American general inevitably set in motion rumors about the arrival of Patton. By that time too, Franklin Roosevelt was on a par with Winston Churchill. Limburg's newspaper made that very clear in a special tribute to the American president on September 22: "When England stood alone, we did not despair. England was sure to win, but how long would it take before it was ready to engage in the decisive battle? Some spoke of a hundred years war ... Then came Roosevelt. First with his aid to England, then with his Fleet and his Army in direct action. It was he who gave the war a new direction. It was then that we could say: victory is near."[71]

America's material abundance

Roosevelt gave the war a new direction above all by putting at the disposal of the Allied coalition his country's economic strength. The war succeeded where every other stimulus had failed and, before long, the Great Depression was nothing but a bad memory in the US. In the course of the war, much of the Allied as well as the enemy propaganda regarding the US revolved around the role it had announced for itself as the "Arsenal of Democracy." As soon as the US entered the war, British aircraft were dropping leaflets over Belgium extolling the industrial might of the nation that had now at last officially joined the alliance. Great Britain, one of the first such pamphlets said encouragingly, could now count on "munitions, heavy and light arms, airplanes straight from the Ford factories that for the time being have suspended the production of cars." Another leaflet showed a drawing of airplanes and other war materials spilling from Roosevelt's arms as if he were a modern-day Santa Claus. The much more influential British radio broadcasts played on similar themes. Indeed, economic might constituted so potent a feature of the American war contribution that Nazi propagandists in Belgium considered it vital to try and undermine that particular image. As early

[70] "Dank aan het goede oude Engeland," *HBVL*, September 19, 1944, 1; "Montgomery bezoekt Waterloo," *HBVL*, November 8, 1944, 2; and Boulet, "Journal," AB 1298.

[71] "Franklin Roosevelt," *HBVL*, September 22, 1944, 1. On the Patton rumors, see Taghon, *België 44*, 34.

as 1942 the *Brüsseler Zeitung* was highlighting shortages in the US of raw materials like bauxite and rubber, and was pointing to industrial strife and massive budget deficits incurred to finance war production. "The greatest danger for us," an article in the same newspaper reiterated in October 1943, "is that we allow ourselves to be morally impressed by the possibilities of the enemy's war potential."[72]

Continuous hammering on the same theme by supporters and detractors of the US alike ensured, however, that economic might was exactly that which, by the time of the liberation, had become most impressive about America in people's minds. Not the least because it reached back across the Great Depression to tap into older European images of the US as the home of modernity and wealth. Those images had begun to take shape at the end of the nineteenth century and become firmly entrenched during the decade that followed the Great War. They now took on a new life in the big void brought about by the dramatic failure of Germany's professed New Order. By 1944 the sight of giant formations of planes heading for Germany in plain daylight and news of the massive armada disgorging troops and equipment on Normandy's beaches formed irrefutable proof of the power of Fordism. In a local newspaper in Roeselare in June 1944, the collaborationist organization *DeVlag* warned about the dire consequences of an Allied victory and scathingly referred to the GIs as "American billionaires." But when on September 5, 1944, Nivelles was rid of the Germans and the prewar town council was able to meet again for the first time, they hurried to put out an official proclamation. In it, they thanked the Allies for the different strengths they had contributed to make liberation possible. For Great Britain this was its resilience and courage even in the darkest hours, and for the Soviet Union the containment and rollback of the shock invasion. But where the US was concerned, the Nivelles town council did not doubt for a moment that its decisive contribution, apart from hundreds of thousands of fresh troops, had been in the form of "its industrial might."[73]

Belgians had thus been conditioned to think of the GIs as ambassadors of abundance even before they arrived. There was much irony in this, of course, because, as David Reynolds has noted, for a majority of American soldiers the Great Depression had been "*the* formative experience of their previous life." Hard times for many had come to an end only when the military at last provided them with steady employment. But by the autumn of 1944 there was nothing any longer that associated the American liberators with hard times. Their very name – GI for

[72] Maleux, "Propagande," 36 and 71–2; and Stirk, "Anti-Americanism," 72.
[73] *Roeselare Bevrijd*, 15; and Blanco-Rincon and Dusausoit, "Nivelles," 20–1.

Plate 5.3 Belgian workers help unload Allied goods in the port of Antwerp. (CEGESOMA, picture number 81383)

"Government Issue," stamped on military equipment – made them synonymous with the seemingly limitless war supplies provided by a wealthy Uncle Sam. And during their extended stay in Belgium, it was the GIs in particular who would do much to strengthen the initial impressions of abundance generated by liberating Allied convoys resembling publicity caravans.[74]

What would continue to conjure up images of a faraway dreamland like nothing else was the scale and diversity of the food put on display by American troops. GIs thought nothing, for example, of the exotic fruit the military was able to get to them in huge quantities. But the German occupation had caused such fruit to disappear from Belgian shops. And though the Red Cross had on occasion succeeded in providing schools with vitamin-rich oranges, many children failed to recognize the fruit, leaving generous GIs puzzled to see them take bites as if from an apple. Belgians, young and old, also relished the mouthwatering sight of slices of bread that were standard issue in any GI kitchen. People for years had

[74] Reynolds, *Rich Relations*, 29.

filled their stomachs with a soggy grayish bread baked from dough that contained a good measure of flour made from potatoes, peas, beans, and even straw. To be able to taste the GIs' soft white bread, which smelled like cake, was a privilege and a feast that many would remember for the rest of their lives. But the thrill was just as memorable when experiencing the first taste of an endless array of new American products, from peanut butter and ketchup to Mars and donuts. And it was not just the taste that was new and exciting, but also the look and feel of fancy brand-name products in attractive packaging, from the crackers in cellophane to the cheese in cans that came with a smart gadget designed to peel away the lids.[75]

Cans with food were the first things GIs in the rear wanted to get rid of as they had grown sick and tired of the C and K rations in the front lines. They preferred to stand in line for the warm meals dished out by mobile kitchens and in canteens. Belgian personnel employed in the kitchen of the 19th Corps Recreation Area in Eisden in 1945 could see why. Whenever a new batch of African-American soldiers arrived from the front, big slabs of steak (a luxury many Belgians had been dreaming of for years) would be prepared on giant stoves. To ensure that the wood in the stoves would ignite fast, the Americans liberally doused it with gasoline (another scarce commodity for civilians). With many of the new arrivals too exhausted to even touch the meat, Belgian kitchen staff happily fed their families with what otherwise would simply have ended up in garbage cans. The ritual on Sundays was different but no less impressive. Then chicken was on the menu as a special treat. Belgian employees were surprised to see special trucks deliver the meat not only frozen solid, but in quantities the soldiers could again not hope to finish in a single meal. The amazement of the Belgian kitchen staff was complete when one day they were taken to the famous bottling plant of Spa. Now operated by US authorities, the Belgian plant was bottling neither the mineral water nor the lemonade of old, but America's iconic Coca-Cola. The Belgians returned to Eisden with a truck full of the dark drink to quench the GIs' thirst. "It seems a bit laborious," one of the local staff remarked in retrospect. "But the Americans knew that a happy soldier was a good soldier."[76]

Belgians were soon convinced that if the GIs were not happy, no soldiers ever would be. The abundance of American matériel never ceased to amaze. The endless statistics on US war production in the

[75] See, for example, transcript interview Georges Brausch, 5, M348–9, AA 1593; and Jean Pigeon, "Chleuhs à 20 cm, libérateurs à 200 m," *Pourquoi Pas?*, September 5, 1984, 22–3.

[76] Janssen *et al.*, "Maasland," 141; Kohlbacher, "Eisden," 35–6; and Spa, WR March 24, 1945, Folder 1099, AA 1311.

Belgian press bordered on the incredible. One article at the end of September 1944 claimed that since America's entry into the war at the end of 1941, steel production had increased by almost 40 percent to 65 million tons a year, the fleet had tripled in size, annual production of tanks stood at 75,000, and seven times more aircraft were rolling from the factories to a stunning total of 100,000 in 1944 so far.[77]

Everything about this mass of American matériel seemed impressive and sophisticated. The Belgian press devoted entire articles, for example, to the practical design of the American helmet, which was deemed emblematic of the "simple, yet near perfect equipment of the American soldiers." It was the motorized and mechanized aspects of the American military, however, that continued to cause by far the most awe and admiration. Bystanders in the tiny village of Gingelom stared in wonder at the giant flatbed trucks loaded with tanks. The convoy was stuck under the railroad bridge because some turrets had become wedged against the tunnel's ceiling. All the GIs could do to allow the mighty monsters safe passage was deflate their tires. Still, size and robustness were not the only qualities of American transportation. This was vividly illustrated by the vehicle that most easily caught the imagination of civilians young and old: the jeep. In September 1944, when the phenomenon was still new and unusual, Belgian journalists could be seen misspelling the odd-sounding name as "yeep". But there were no more such irreverent mistakes by the time the distinct-looking vehicle was commonplace in cities and rural areas alike and the admiration for its speed and versatility virtually universal.[78]

The jeep is, one newspaper declared, "as fast and as maneuverable as the American cars." Indeed, if the GIs were ambassadors for a society of abundance, the countless jeeps were just as many mobile billboards for the motor industries of Detroit, and by extension for America's roaring consumer culture. Belgium had experienced the first clear glimpses of its seductive power after the Great War, when marketing and products of American brands like Singer, Otis, Columbia, and Ford – to name just a few – had become ubiquitous. Now, at the end of this war, as one Belgian newspaper reported in September 1944, the US would reduce its war industries by no less than 40 percent. Inquisitive subscribers could not but ask themselves what kinds of consumer products these highly efficient industries would be turning to next. A local leftist paper in June 1945 claimed: "The little time that America needs to transform

[77] "De oorlogsproduktie in Amerika," *HBVL*, September 30, 1944, 1.

[78] For articles on the American helmet and jeep see, for example, *HBVL*, November 12, 1944, 2; and September 23, 1944, 2. On Gingelom, see Boffin, *Zuid-West Limburg*, 27.

Plate 5.4 A jeep in Brussels: symbol of Allied technological superiority. (CEGESOMA, picture number 29464)

its civilian and economic life into a huge military power and impressive weapons arsenal! That is the miracle of this war!" To attentive readers it was clear, however, that this transformation could be reversed just as quickly and was bound to send even larger waves of civilian products to the Old World's shores as soon as peace arrived.[79]

After years of want and deprivation, however, many Belgians did not care much where these waves were coming from as long as they made their standard of living improve. Certainly, as long as peacetime conditions had not returned, they were grateful for anything trickling down from the American arsenal of democracy. Big-ticket items like cars were the last of their concerns in these unsettled times and a simple ride hitched in a jeep often sufficed to answer the dreams of many for the time being. The American military allowed civilians at least the pleasure of small luxuries again. After an eternity of wearing socks and stockings of coarse material, working women were not ashamed to spend a week's wages on their first pair of fine nylon stockings made in the USA. Sick of

[79] *HBVL*, September 23, 1944, 2; and "De oorlogsproduktie in Amerika," *HBVL*, September 30, 1944, 1. The socialist paper *Bevrijding: Het blad van de arbeidersjeugd* is quoted in Janssen *et al.*, "Maasland," 125.

tobacco made of clover and rhubarb leaves, men had no qualms begging for American cigarettes with the magic brand names. "I love to smoke American cigarettes," one Flemish newspaper quickly taught its readers to say suggestively in English. Some were not even ashamed to collect Camels and Lucky Strikes left in the gutter half-smoked.[80]

As long as their own industries were not restored to full capacity, Belgians especially welcomed those Allied products that could make the difference between life and death. By the end of September 1944, a serious shortage of medical supplies was making itself felt. A special Belgian commission was created to make an inventory of all key stocks, ensure their fair distribution, and counter the thriving black market in medical supplies. The available stocks proved nowhere adequate, however, to satisfy all of the urgent needs, and so the Belgian government was forced to turn to the Allies for help once more. By the end of April 1945, the Allied military had supplied the Belgian health services with a total of 344 tons of hospital equipment, layettes, surgical instruments, dressings, disinfectants such as DDT, and insulin among many other drugs. By the summer of 1945, the SHAEF mission in Belgium was relieved to note that, in part because of this robust medical assistance, there had been "no important epidemics, in spite of several potentially serious outbreaks, e.g. typhoid fever in the Liège and Tournai areas, [and] typhus fever carried from Germany."[81]

Here too, however, it was the especially rich stocks of the Americans that proved most crucial. The US military pitched in not only with their own supplies, but also with the robust trucks they possessed in abundance. These means of transportation helped carry medical supplies from a variety of American sources to those Belgians who needed them most. By the end of April 1945, for example, of the 350 tons of "assorted medical supplies" delivered by the International Red Cross, 250 tons came from its branch in the US. In addition to clothing, soap, fruit juices, dried milk, and "other comforts," much of the 2,000 tons distributed by the United War Relief of America again consisted of medical supplies.[82]

Still, it was the US military itself that scored the most impressive victory on the medical front as the main source of the new miracle drug penicillin. It was ironic that, although penicillin had been discovered

[80] On nylons and cigarettes see, for example, De Roey and Van Hee, *Bevrijding*, 76 and Janssen *et al.*, "Maasland," 142. The language tip is from "Spreekt Engelsch," *HBVL*, September 17, 1944, 2.

[81] Kaiser, "Croix-Rouge," 8 and 35; SHAEFB, FR No. 16, Supplement, May 1, 1945, WO 202/697, AA 1230; and Final Report No. 21, 28–9, July 21, 1945, AA 1798/9.

[82] SHAEFB, FR No. 16, 17, May 1, 1945, WO 202/696; and No. 16, Supplement, May 1, 1945, WO 202/697, AA 1230; and Grégoire Koulischer, "Belgian-American Relations, 1944–45," in BT, 178.

by the British scientist Dr. Fleming before the war, it was the US pharmaceutical industry that during the war succeeded in producing the powerful antibiotic in sufficient quantities to meet the huge global demand for ways to fight crippling infections. According to SHAEF, the best the British military could do early in January 1945 was "to loan supplies of penicillin, pending arrival from the US of a small consignment for Belgian civil use." When the first American consignment finally arrived later that month, it was only "a small quantity," so small in fact that it was to be distributed across Belgium with extreme care "under control of a board of professors." But as early as the start of April, a relieved SHAEF could note that purchases in the US for Belgium were "mounting rapidly" to about 20,000 vials for that month, so that by the end of May already the allotments of penicillin were considered "adequate to meet all ordinary needs." Belgian hospitals and doctors were well aware that if they wanted to share in the miracle cure it was America's military ambassadors they needed to see.[83]

America's cultural dazzle

Hollywood

The Allies brought with them other miracle cures to make people feel better. On the lighter side, a side many Belgians were keen to explore after many dark years, the liberators, and again the Americans in particular, represented cultural dazzle as much as material abundance. If the Americans plunged Belgians into darkness it was most often a pleasant and comforting one that allowed people to escape at last. "Went to the cinema with mom this afternoon," a teenage girl from Antwerp scribbled in her war diary on August 15, 1944, "a sad film: *Immensee* starring Kristina Söderbaum." Barely two weeks after the liberation, however, on September 21, the same girl was over the moon as she confided to paper that, the following day, she and a friend would go see "the first American movie." The feature film had the much more upbeat title *Little Princess*, a role played by the infectiously glamorous child star Shirley Temple.[84]

The abrupt rupture in movie fare could be felt in theaters across the country in the fall of 1944. American movies had been very popular in Europe and Belgium before the Nazi-German occupation. The Great War had dealt a heavy blow to the European film industry, cutting it off from the giant US market and allowing American movie corporations

[83] SHAEFB, Minutes 10th Meeting, 2, January 15, 1945, WO 202/554; FR No. 9, 18, January 23, 1945, WO 202/689; No. 14, 19, April 3, 1945, WO 202/694; and No. 18, 15, May 29, 1945, AA 1230.

[84] D. Aerts, AB 1591.

to gain strength for an international offensive. In 1912 most films were made in France. By 1928, 90 percent of all films were being produced in the US. In the second half of the 1920s, 70 percent of all films distributed in France and 85 percent of those shown in the Netherlands were of American origin. As late as 1937, no less than 75 percent of the movies screened even in fascist Italy were made in the US. It was Nazi Germany, however, that slammed the door shut for English-language movies. Keenly aware of the propaganda value of motion pictures and determined to make their own film industry the dominant one in Europe, they banned Anglo-American products at home as well as in the occupied territories. Belgium was no exception. By the summer of 1940 all British and American films had been impounded and carted off to local factories to be processed into chemicals useful for the war effort. Although a limited number of carefully selected French films continued to be allowed, Belgian distributors henceforth needed licensing from the Nazi *Propaganda Abteilung* and from one day to another found themselves overseeing a German film invasion.[85]

Yet, regardless of the deserved reputation of film stars like Marika Rökk or Heinz Ruhman, German films shown during the occupation were inevitably associated with the enemy and tainted by an omnipresent and stilted Nazi propaganda. No wonder then that at the end of the long and uninvited German presence, Belgians were yearning for the return of the friendly invasion of carefree entertainment. Just days after the liberation of Liège, René Henoumont's first assignment as a journalist for a socialist newspaper was to track down and review any American movies from the prewar era that had survived and were bound to be screened in the city's theaters soon. Meanwhile, movie theaters in Brussels reopened on September 15, 1944, barely ten days after the arrival of the Allies. *La Dernière Heure* commented that, despite the beautiful weather, this had caused "a veritable rush" for tickets. Long lines of people for one theater became intertwined with queues for movies elsewhere in the capital and occasional "scuffles" highlighted the tense anticipation.[86]

The name of the film did not really matter, one moviegoer in Brussels recalled, as long as the announcement said "English spoken" or "a major American movie." That was fortunate, because few new movies from overseas were to make their appearance as long as there was a war on. The armed services ensured that their troops could relax with the newest productions. But these were often shown in separate theaters (like the

[85] Wagnleitner, *Coca-Colonization*, 230–6; and Van de Vijver, *Cultureel leven*, 58.
[86] René Henoumont, "Mon dernier soldat allemand," *Pourquoi Pas?*, September 5, 1984, 19. The newspaper is quoted in Marechal, "Cinéma et jazz à Bruxelles," vol. A, 22.

Scala or Eldorado in the capital) that were not open to the public and at best admitted only Belgian females lucky enough to be taken there on a date. That many old English-language movies could be shown in Belgium so soon after the liberation was due to the unexpected find in two factories of large numbers of copies that had remained intact despite having been taken there for destruction in 1940. They were dusted off with loving care and brought back into circulation with haste so that, within weeks, Belgians were flocking to the theaters again to reacquaint themselves with once familiar stars like Myrna Loy, Errol Flynn, Johnny Weissmuller, Ginger Rogers, and Shirley Temple.[87]

Of all the films shown in Brussels during the first six months after the liberation, some 72 percent were old ones made before the start of the war in 1940. After more than four years of Nazi occupation, it was hardly surprising that one out of every two movies shown in the capital during the first half year of regained freedom was a comedy. More telling, however, was the turnaround that had taken place regarding the source of this mass entertainment. By February 1945, barely 2.5 percent of the movies that had been screening in Brussels since the liberation were of Soviet origin, while slightly less than 9 percent were French, and another 9 percent British. Almost 79 percent of the movies for which people in the Belgian capital had been queuing impatiently were made in the US. It was 1945 when one such movie, *Gone with the Wind*, finally premiered in Brussels. The box-office hit, based on the runaway best-seller by Margaret Mitchell, was released amidst "an exceptional prestige" that involved a gala event and the announcement that the proceeds would go to a fund for Belgian war victims. No one in Belgium cared that this epic story of passion and adventure blowing in from the US was more than six years old.[88]

Swing time

Getting movie theaters up and running again amidst the ruins of war was not a simple task. But there were forms of entertainment much easier to organize among people eager to have some fun and forget hard times. And again the Americans would provide a major source of inspiration. On the evening of December 10, 1944, an inhabitant of Arendonk noted in his journal that the town was hit by a power outage. "The movie theaters are emptying," he wrote, "the dancing in the cafés continues." As indeed dancing would across the country, often by the light of nothing more than candles and kerosene lamps.[89]

[87] Pierre Thonon, "Au cinéma, la Libération, c'était ... autant en emporte le vent!" *Pourquoi Pas?*, September 5, 1984, 36; Marechal, "Cinéma et jazz à Bruxelles," vol. A, 27; and Radiodiffusion Nationale Belge Namur, transcript October 21, 1944, AA 82.

[88] Marechal, "Cinéma et jazz à Bruxelles," vol. A, 6–7; and Stéphany, "Belgique," 36.

[89] Van Gorp, *Arendonk*, 181.

There had been few opportunities for recreation during the German occupation. People spent most of their days worrying about work and food. And the little leisure that remained could scarcely be called quality time with real tobacco scarce, newspapers censored, and German movies a far cry from the light-hearted Hollywood products. More often than not, moviegoing was restricted to the daytime anyway as curfews prohibited people from leaving their homes between dusk and dawn. Security reasons of all kinds regularly led the totalitarian state to prevent public events – whether sports, religious processions, or fun fairs – from taking place even in broad daylight. If all this had been difficult enough for adults, it had proved extremely hard on teenagers at an age where they should have been socializing and dating. "My youth, and that of many young girls at the time," recalled Julia Vermeulen who lived in Ghent and was eighteen at war's end, "began only really with the Liberation. For four long years all we had done was play games around the table."[90]

What young and old had missed most were the balls, matinees, and thé dansants. In some places music had begun blaring even before the last Germans had well and truly made their exit. As soon as the Allies were there to stay, dances were being organized all over the country at a feverish pace. People were having so much fun in Verviers, for example, that records for September 1944 show significant drops both in library loans and visits to the local hospital's dentist. Politicians, resistance groups, shopkeepers, local organizations, owners of dance halls and cafés, all had good reasons to throw parties, and on weekends especially people happily thronged together to let it all out. In Arendonk, where in December 1944 even a power outage failed to derail the dances, the law was no more successful. Though the town's cafés were not licensed to organize dances, all of them were hiring small bands to meet the demand and increase revenue. Surprise raids by the police on several occasions caused locals and British soldiers to flee into the darkness, but customers thought it part of the fun and resumed partying as if nothing was wrong. In February 1945 an exasperated mayor finally took it upon himself to intervene more forcefully, closing down several rebellious cafés for a whole month.[91]

Some took offense at such flagrant enjoyment at a time when Nazi Germany had still not been defeated. "We live," *La Libre Belgique* complained, "as if the war is over. Everywhere people are busy organizing

[90] Interview with Julia Vermeulen in "Dat RAF-uniform sprak me wel aan," *Het Volk*, August 17, 1994, 11.

[91] Van Gorp, *Arendonk*, 179, and Wynants, *Verviers*, 44.

parties and balls. They are trying to outdo each other and there is an element of competition in all this that is undermining the gravity of the moment." It was especially galling to see people have so much fun while hundreds of thousands of Belgians remained in serious danger in Germany. The very first broadcast by a free national radio on September 5 immediately reminded Belgians that liberation did not mean the end of the war, and that they should keep foremost in their thoughts the POWs, deportees, hostages, and prisoners of the Gestapo. Still, even the close relatives of such unfortunates, who did not need reminding of the continuing gravity of the situation, were in dire need of some fun and relaxation after years of unrelieved tension. In Braine-l'Alleud, for example, the wives of POWs admitted that the much-talked-about dances organized by British troops on weekends posed "a moral conflict." But that was not the same as saying that they refused to attend as a matter of principle.[92]

And so the partying continued unabated, in part because the Allies themselves played a key role in the organization of all kinds of festive events that allowed soldiers to relax at a safe distance from the front lines. The Allies were in a much better position to do so because they had easier access to food and drink and were often in control of the largest buildings in any town or village. In Nivelles, for example, British troops on an almost weekly basis were inviting locals to dances held in schools, the local château, and one of the town's hotels, all of them places they had requisitioned for their own troops.[93]

But the Allies drew Belgians to their dances like moths to a flame because they were offering yet another main ingredient: the right music. Weary of fear and stress, people craved music, not so much for its soothing words as for its pulsing beat. They were tired of listening and obeying; they wanted to move, experience their bodies, feel alive again. What music then could better suit the mood of the times than that which had sprung from ragtime and blues, the melodies and rhythms that black slaves had developed in America to give expression to their deep longing for freedom. Nothing could feel more liberating at the end of four years of authoritarian rule than to dance to the improvisations and deliberate distortions of jazz, the lively rhythm of swing, the emotional excitement of hot, and the nonsense of scat.

These exciting new forms of American music, like the motion pictures made in the US, had already found enthusiastic audiences in the Old World before the war. In fact, it was a Belgian, Robert Goffin, who as

[92] *La Libre Belgique* is quoted in Stéphany, "Belgique," 17–18. Radiodiffusion Nationale Belge Namur, transcript September 5, 1944, AA 82; and Aelbrecht and Maghe, "Braine," 78.

[93] Blanco-Rincon and Dusausoit, "Nivelles," 82–4.

early as 1921 had published one of the first jazz magazines. By the 1930s several European countries were developing their own distinct variations of jazz. But if jazz remained the preserve of an elite of connoisseurs, it was the swing version with its large white bands that made jazz known to a wide and enthusiastic audience on the eve of the war. Then suddenly, however, under the reign of the Nazis, jazz ended up in a dubious gray area. The official position was that jazz was the quintessential product of a degenerate and mongrelized American people and, as such, a threat to the purity of Aryan culture. There were Belgian collaborators with influential posts in the music world who readily toed the Nazi line. They dismissed jazz as the sound of "black Bamboulas" while at the same time warning that it was like "a raging virus" capable of infecting "the health of the nation." The irony was, however, that German soldiers loved to hear the supposedly subversive music. In response, the Nazi propaganda machine in this area proved pragmatic enough to allow diluted forms of jazz and swing that did not sound too blatantly un-Aryan when played on the radio or at dances. This meant that in Belgium jazz remained alive during the occupation in an atmosphere of semi-clandestine activity. The Hot Club in Brussels, for example, stayed in business for German troops with the blessing of the *Propaganda Abteilung*, but only after changing its name to the more neutral sounding Club Rythmique de Belgique. Belgian jazz bands in this club and many others continued to entertain their new patrons with American and British numbers, though they made sure to play it safe by providing them with the camouflage of French titles.[94]

While Belgian musicians gladly accepted such improvisations to remain practiced in the art of jazz, many more of their fellow citizens were turning to American music as a subtle form of protest against the Nazi regime. Some took action and created their own jazz band. Already during the first bleak winter of occupation, Jacques Goundry did so in Nivelles, a town of fewer than 12,000 inhabitants, and he succeeded in keeping the band alive until the liberation. In Andenne, an even smaller place, twenty-year-old Charles Michel in 1943 created a similar band with four young men his age. They called it Les Zazous and by doing so became part of a much wider movement of young people in Europe – Zazous or Petits Swings in occupied France, the Swing Jugend in Germany – who, by dressing and talking and playing music like Americans, were making a statement against the totalitarian regime

[94] On jazz in Europe before and during the war, see Wagnleitner, *Coca-Colonization*, 202–5 and 215. For the Belgian situation, see Van de Vijver, *Cultureel leven*, 67; Marechal, "Cinéma et jazz à Bruxelles," vol. C, 4; and Felix Facq, transcript interview No. 118, AA 1450.

of the Nazis. Many more Belgians, however, signaled resistance simply by pressing their ears against the radio to catch the messages of hope broadcast by the BBC. Messages not only in the form of news, but in the guise of upbeat tunes. On school holidays, for example, teenagers loved to listen to programs broadcast to keep British factory workers happy on the job, and from them learned much more about American music than they ever had before the war. By the time of the liberation, without the help of record sales or live performances, Glenn Miller had become a household name among Belgians, and his brand of swing a symbol of freedom.[95]

What had been a trickle of American music before the war turned into a flood with the arrival of the Allies. For jazz devotees like the band members from Nivelles and Andenne the liberation era was to be the heyday of their amateur careers. When for the liberation ball in Nivelles on September 10, 1944, Goundry's band found itself short of a trumpet player, the American CA commander spared neither time nor energy to help them find a suitable player for the big occasion. In the weeks that followed, Goundry added some gifted British jazz musicians from a nearby RAF base to his group so that before long its name, Jacques Goundry and His English Boys, resembled that of a professional swing band. The career of Les Zazous from Andenne was even more turbulent. Asked to play for local GIs at first, they soon found themselves housed in a military barracks in Namur so that they could perform for American troops at balls, in night clubs, and in casinos. Some of the band members even ended up playing for GIs in Holland and Germany.[96]

But it was not just the jazz aficionados who were having the time of their lives. A much larger audience than ever before was now being exposed to the exciting American music and its British and Continental adaptations. New Anglo-American records, like their movie counterparts, remained scarce for a long time, though in a matter of months Belgian companies were producing jazz records under labels with exciting names like "Hot" and "Victory." But people could now openly tune in to their favorite music on the BBC and the newest tunes could also be brought to them by live performances. And there was never any shortage of bands promising to spoil the crowds with plenty of rhythm and fun. The atmosphere in Brussels in particular was red-hot.

95 Blanco-Rincon and Dusausoit, "Nivelles," 82–4. On the Andenne band, see C. D., "*Les Zazous* ont joué pour les GI's," *Vers l'Avenir*, September 10–11, 1994. On the BBC, see transcript interview Georges Brausch, M348-9, 4–5, AA 1593. On the broader phenomenon of youth protest through American culture see, for example, Beck, "Anti-Nazi Swing Youth"; and Willett, *Americanization*, 86–9.

96 Blanco-Rincon and Dusausoit, "Nivelles," 82–4; and C. D., "*Les Zazous* ont joué pour les GI's," *Vers l'Avenir*, September 10–11, 1994.

On September 24, 1944, a major "Concert de la Libération" was held at the Ancienne Belgique, one of the capital's main performance halls. Judging by *Le Soir*'s review, the event set the tone for things to come. The hall, the newspaper reported, "was filled to the rafters with young people whose roaring enthusiasm did not abate for a single moment." If the jazz band of the British 59th Division received "a delirious reception," all hell broke loose when a famous RAF band appeared on stage and its musicians struck up "some tunes that the banned radio had taught us to know and love." The evening was a guaranteed smash hit when organizers eventually decided to turn the stage into "an immense dance floor."[97]

In the months that followed, jazz and swing musicians in the capital proliferated, with each self-respecting music hall, night club, cabaret, club, café, and even restaurant inviting bands large and small. American military bands mixed with those from the RAF, Royal Marines, and British divisions, and many a Belgian jazz band enjoyed having musicians from both armies jam with them. Soldiers and civilians flocked to popular places with sexy Anglo-American names and music: Harry's Bar, Broadway, and the Canadian Club, for example, but above all the Victory Club, which could accommodate up to 200 people. It was in this heady multicultural atmosphere that some of the postwar icons of Belgian jazz like Bobby Jaspar, René Thomas, and Toots Thielemans would cut their teeth.[98]

But although the epicenter of the new music was located in the capital, shock waves reverberated across the country, affecting provincial outposts and small villages alike. In Braine-l'Alleud, a town of fewer than 12,000 inhabitants, dance hall Eldorado and cafés Bristol and Le Liberator lured customers by dangling the carrots of jazz, swing, and "musique de rythme" in newspaper advertisements. From Hasselt, a provincial town larger than Braine-l'Alleud but further away from Brussels, *Het Belang van Limburg* approvingly reported on December 15, 1944, that the American military band which had performed in the town square had drawn "a great mass of spectators" and that each piece had been greeted with "a deafening applause." By March 1945 the province's newspaper was talking about a "dance fury" that had infected every town and village. Before long, even in so small a place as Arendonk, where the mayor had so much trouble controlling the boisterous music in cafés, people were referring to any small orchestra simply as a "zjas."[99]

[97] Marechal, "Cinéma et jazz à Bruxelles," vol. C, 6 and 9–10.

[98] Marc Danval, "Les Orchestres de l'automne," *Pourquoi Pas?*, September 5, 1984, 44–5; and Marechal, "Cinéma et jazz à Bruxelles," vol. C, 7 and 9–10.

[99] Aelbrecht and Maghe, "Braine," 100–2; *HBVL*, December 15, 1944, 2 and March 22, 1945, 1; and Van Gorp, *Arendonk*, 179.

The cultivation of sound ideas

The liberated Belgians danced to the Allied beat with total abandon. They did not need Hollywood's master illusionists to convince them that what Anglo-Saxon societies stood for was much more appealing than anything the false Nazi prophets had ever promised. "There is," General Erskine acknowledged in mid-October 1944, "a very healthy appetite for British and American news, information, films, and literature." Still, the SHAEF mission in Belgium did not intend to leave anything to chance in this deeply ideological war and showed itself keen to help mold the Allied message wherever it could. "As a means of rubbing out past Nazi efforts and instilling sound ideas in future," Erskine continued, "I hope every endeavor will be made to meet our requirements."[100]

Special responsibility for the cultivation of "sound ideas" fell to two SHAEF branches. The first, the Public Relations branch, was responsible for censorship. It cooperated closely with the Belgian Civil Affairs section of the Mission Militaire Belge that acted as a liaison between SHAEF, the Belgian government, and regional and local authorities. The Civil Affairs section included a division responsible for "information," subdivided into five sections encompassing film, radio, press, publications, and exhibitions. Two days before the first movie theaters were to reopen in the capital, Allied and Belgian authorities banned not only all films and documentaries produced by enemy powers and collaborationist organizations, but also those that might prove insulting to one or more of the Allied powers. No clear definition was provided of what might constitute an "insult," but by the time they arrived in Belgium, new American films had already passed through a first filter anyway. At the end of 1942, the Office of War Information (OWI) in the US had indeed been given the power to ban the export of films highlighting the less attractive side of American society. This affected not only films dealing with racial or labor conflicts, for example, but also westerns and crime movies where law and order failed to come out on top.[101]

Still, Allied and Belgian authorities were more concerned about the newspapers and how they would handle military information. SHAEF sent out directives stipulating in great detail which subjects would have to be cleared with the censors. These included operations and the movement and location of troops. But if much of this involved straightforward concerns about security, SHAEF nevertheless made sure to

[100] SHAEFB, FR No. 2, 3, October 17, 1944, WO 202/682, AA 1230.

[101] Plumet, *Presse quotidienne*, 151–3 and 177; and Marechal, "Cinéma et jazz à Bruxelles," vol. B, 16 and 18–19. On Hollywood films, see Wagnleitner, *Coca-Colonization*, 238.

define "military information" as broadly as possible. Though it had emphasized as early as June 1944 that there was to be "no censorship of opinion," it did add that censors would delete not only rumors and statements deemed "misleading" and "unauthenticated, inaccurate or false," but also "reports likely to injure the morale of the Allied Forces." In a similar vein, Belgian legislation accorded the government special powers for the duration of the state of siege. That state remained in existence until January 1946 and allowed the government to prohibit newspapers from making public anything that could "benefit the enemy or undermine the morale of the armies or the population." Here again the lack of clear definitions resulted in a number of gray areas. Were reports on lack of discipline, misbehavior, or crimes committed by Allied soldiers on Belgian soil, for example, to be construed as harmful to morale or beneficial to the enemy? Whatever the case, the Belgian press in 1944–5 appeared more than willing to apply a rigorous measure of self-censorship. For, even though newspapers for practical reasons were often subjected to scrutiny only after publication, there occurred few if any serious clashes with censors over reports on Allied troops.[102]

The censorship role of SHAEF's Public Relations branch was made relatively easy in the existing climate of trust and goodwill. Allied authorities spent much more time facilitating the spread of information likely to sustain and increase confidence in Britain and the US. This was largely the responsibility of a second SHAEF section, the Psychological Warfare branch. As it was nearly impossible for Belgian newspapers to obtain news from abroad as long as the war lasted, for example, this branch was quick to monopolize the distribution of international news. By early October 1944, it was flying British newspapers in from London daily so that the Belgian press could follow their lead in the coverage of foreign affairs and the conduct of the war. In addition, Psychological Warfare staff, in close cooperation with the press staff of the Belgian Civil Affairs section, were providing local newspapers with numerous articles and photographs on military operations. Many of these efforts were in response to concerns expressed by General Erskine and the British ambassador at the end of September 1944. Worried that before long the Belgian population would be turning its attention to domestic hardships and that this might poison relations, they pointed to favorable coverage of the Allied war effort as an important antidote. For that same purpose, SHAEF's Public Relations branch also sent Belgian journalists to England and Canada early in 1945 to allow them a firsthand look at the countries' home fronts. At around the same time, the American

[102] Plumet, *Presse quotidienne*, 176–83 and 192–3.

OWI played its part in the campaign for hearts and minds by inviting half a dozen Belgian newspapermen over to the US.[103]

On top of that, acute shortages of shipping space and paper could not deter the Allies from making a concerted effort to reach Belgian audiences with their own publications. At the end of November 1944, SHAEF reported that 73,000 copies of a magazine produced by the OWI for Belgium as well as another 38 tons of Allied publications and posters had arrived by sea. Two weeks later, the Allied mission in Belgium was happy to report that the number and circulation of its publications had seen a large increase and that a special effort was being made to supply Belgian schools. Indeed, between the end of 1944 and the spring of the following year, the number of publications put out by SHAEF's Psychological Warfare branch in Belgium rose from slightly more than 700,000 to over 3 million.[104]

SHAEF also tried its hand at exhibitions to impress people with the Allied war effort and the vibrant Anglo-American societies sustaining it. An exhibition was opened in Brussels as early as November 10, 1944, with the purpose of providing the Belgian people with "insight into the work of the RAF and Allied Air Forces since 1940." It was such a success that in February of the following year it reopened in one of Ghent's university buildings, where it averaged more than 8,000 visitors a day in the first week. In April the exhibition traveled to Charleroi, where a total of 92,000 people showed up in just two weeks. Meanwhile, in February 1945, Brussels was made to host an even more ambitious exhibition which set out to provide Belgians with the liberators' version of "World Events since 1939." The undertaking was, SHAEF happily reported, "a success in every way." Officially opened by General Erskine in the presence of the Belgian Prime Minister and the British and American ambassadors, the exhibition lasted eight weeks instead of the initially foreseen four weeks. According to SHAEF's statistics, some 400,000 people came to have a look in the capital at the end of the long winter. When the exhibition reopened in Antwerp's *Grand Bazar* in June 1945, with summer in the air and victory certain, an astonishing 666,000 visitors took in the world according to the Anglo-Americans.[105]

[103] Plumet, *Presse quotidienne*, 6, 153, 177, and 168–9; SHAEFB, FR No. 2, 16, October 17, 1944, WO 202/682, AA 1230; Final Report No. 21, 15, July 21, 1945, AA 1798/9; and Grégoire Koulischer, "Belgian-American Relations, 1944–45," in BT, 178.

[104] SHAEFB, FR No. 5, 8, November 28, 1944, WO 202/685; No. 6, 12, December 12, 1944, WO 202/686; No. 7, Annexure "Publication figures," December 26, 1944, WO 202/687; and No. 16, Supplement, May 1, 1945, WO 202/697, AA 1230.

[105] SHAEFB, FR No. 4, 6, November 14, 1944, WO 202/684; No. 9, 5 and 8, January 23, 1945, WO 202/689; No. 12, 5 and 12, March 6, 1945, WO 202/692; No. 16, 5 and

Still, it was film that clocked up the most impressive statistics in the psychological warfare waged by the Allies to maintain their good standing. If Belgians flocked to the movie theaters to escape, SHAEF made certain they could not look past Erskine's "sound ideas" as propagated in Allied newsreels and documentaries preceding Hollywood's feature films. SHAEF at the end of October 1944 felt encouraged by the fact that so soon after the liberation "fifty percent of all cinemas are showing news-reels." In its final report in the summer of 1945, the Allied mission in Belgium was even more pleased to report that it "estimated that 16,000,000 spectators have seen SHAEF films up to 30th June."[106]

Role models

Even if people in the cinemas were fully conscious of the subtle or not so subtle ways in which messages were being molded in Allied reporting, they could not be expected to care or worry much about it. After four years of blatantly misleading Nazi propaganda, the actions of the Allies spoke a thousand times louder than any of their slogans. The liberation they had brought felt very real, physically and mentally, and did not need complex ideological underpinning. And in the big void created by the collapse of the Nazi regime, Belgians were all too eager to embrace promises of a better future mirroring the vitality of Anglo-American societies.

The liberated Belgium of 1944 did not have the *Stunde Null* experience of a defeated Germany in 1945, but its people had experienced sufficient trauma and its society enough of a setback to accept that inspiration for the time being would have to come from elsewhere. Far removed from the crash of Europe's ruin, America now more than ever before appeared to be the beacon of modernity. "Skyscrapers," admitted Jean-Paul Sartre, one of the leading philosophers of postwar Europe, "were the architecture of the future, just as the cinema was the art and jazz the music of the future." If this was true, then America was the country of the future. Many in Belgium certainly thought so at the end of the second great war imploding the Old World. Describing American plans for partial demobilization after the defeat of Germany, an admiring Flemish newspaper in September 1944 concluded: "America foresees it all and is in time for everything." The following month, journalists from the same newspaper went out onto the streets to ask GIs about their impressions of Belgium. They were happy to report that the small country in its cleanliness and

10, May 1, 1945, WO 202/696, AA 1230; and Final Report No. 21, 14, July 21, 1945, AA 1798/9.

[106] SHAEFB, FR No. 3, 6, October 31, 1944, WO 202/683 and Final Report No. 21, 14, July 21, 1945, AA 1798/9.

industriousness reminded many an American soldier of home. And they were even happier to relay to their readers the ultimate compliment: "Everywhere the American has been thus far people were one hundred years behind America. In Belgium we are only twenty years behind!"[107]

Such a role model warranted closer scrutiny and a better understanding. Belgians had not been particularly well versed in the history of the distant giant, but they were now making valiant efforts to catch up. Their newspapers lent them a hand and the press in turn was helped along by booklets on the US and its history put out by SHAEF's Psychological Warfare branch. Late in November 1944, for example, Belgian journalists had no problem providing detailed analyses of the quintessentially American celebration of Thanksgiving, which most readers had never heard of before. Reports about the manner in which the Americans were waging war also said much about the kind of society they came from. When at the end of October 1944 the press announced that the Americans had declared the French port of Cherbourg operational again, "after barely four months and despite major destruction," this was seen as yet "new evidence of their great talent for organization." That SHAEF was involved in editing military information and accrediting Belgian war correspondents to attend briefings undoubtedly went a long way in marshalling such evidence.[108]

Meanwhile, the OWI's initiative of early 1945 to invite Belgian correspondents to the US, by the spring of 1945 was bearing considerable fruit too. Spread out over several weeks, extensive coverage of the US by the major newspapers' own correspondents was splashed across front pages. The aim had initially been to have the correspondents impress Belgians with America's war effort. But with the war in Europe over by the time the Belgians set out on their tour of the US, their hosts apparently decided that the newspapermen might just as well use the occasion to enlighten their audiences back home about America's giant potential for a future world at peace. Which is why in June 1945 Belgians found themselves reading not just rapt reports about yards "where ships shoot up like mushrooms," but about the cargo that would soon be filling their holds, from the meat processed in Chicago to the fantasies generated by Walt Disney and the film studios of California.[109]

[107] On *Stunde Null*, see Willett, *Americanization*, viii. Sartre is quoted in Duignan and Gann, *Rebirth*, 410. *HBVL*, September 17, 1944, 2; and "Amerikaansche soldaten vertellen," *HBVL*, October 1, 1944, 2.

[108] The booklets are listed in SHAEFB, FR No. 9, Annexure I to Appendix D, January 23, 1945, WO 202/689, AA 1230. On Cherbourg, see *HBVL*, October 31, 1944, 2. On accreditation, see SHAEFB, Final Report No. 21, 15, July 21, 1945, AA 1798/9.

[109] It was *Le Soir* that on June 10, 1945, for article VI in its front-page coverage on the US homefront, used the title "Where the ships shoot up like mushrooms."

Against such an impressive backdrop, the British could hardly be expected to play the role of the Americans' competitors in terms of modernity. Yet, in its own way, Britain had shown it had retained much of the Anglo-Saxon vitality the Belgians were now admiring. For the British this was not so much apparent in their vibrancy and dynamism, but more in their gift for tenacity and endurance, their ability to take it on the chin and grin. Which was why, when newsreels in cinemas in Brussels in September 1944 showed images of the Blitz, and a grave English voice declared that, despite all the pain, London had stood fast, electrified Belgians jumped from their seats, drowning the voice in applause. And audiences were up again and cheering when moments later troops from that same obstinate island could be seen liberating the Belgian capital on screen.[110]

What the British and Americans were projecting each in their own way, on and off screen, was strength. And the Belgians were very much aware that although both peoples were clearly very different, they had one important thing in common, and that was a robust democratic regime hardened by time and many a trial. Gone now were the dark doubts of the depressed 1930s about democracy's viability. Gone also the Nazi sneers of parliamentarians as effete. It was in the united chambers of Congress that the US had declared it would join the war as one of the Allies in 1941. It was no wonder then that during the American elections in November 1944 the Belgian press was paying front-page attention, as it would during the rest of the century, to how the system worked and what the parties stood for. It was in a determined parliament that Churchill had found his resolve bolstered. And it was thus no surprise that Belgians in the Palais des Beaux-Arts in Brussels in December 1945 were keen to listen to anything that Harold Nicolson, a politician and member of the board of governors of the war's legendary BBC, had to say in a lecture on the subject of English democracy.[111]

There was an irony, as well as much relief, to find that the Nazis, so obsessed with strength, had been wrong in thinking that it stemmed from authority. The Anglo-Americans with their overwhelming power had demonstrated conclusively that strength flowed from freedom. A society derived its vitality, as *La Libre Belgique* emphasized on September 12, 1944, not "from submission under the German doctrine to that transcendental and quasi divine abstraction called State (*Reich*)." Quite the opposite. The most vital of societies were those that encouraged their individual members to think and do what was right according to their inner selves.

[110] These scenes were reported by *La Dernière Heure* on September 23, 1944. See Marechal, "Cinéma et jazz à Bruxelles," vol. A, 25.

[111] Nicolson's visit is mentioned in Institut d'Éducation et de Documentation Nationales, "Chronique," 169.

It was the Anglo-Saxon countries, according to the same newspaper, that had succeeded in creating "a good individual-society antinomy by ranking the concern for the common good among the first of individual virtues." And in a sense the Allied soldiers walking the streets of Belgium could be understood to embody that principle. If the American, British, and Canadian troops appeared much less enamored with drill and rank than the Germans, *La Libre Belgique* continued, they had no problem accepting "voluntary discipline and a reasoned compliance with order and law, because at heart they were conscious of and concerned with the common good." It was the soldiers' example, leftist newspaper *Le Peuple* declared, joining the chorus in October 1944, that made Belgians truly understand the principles of the American Declaration of Independence and "what a long democratic tradition meant in terms of free discipline, social solidarity, and egalitarian pride."[112]

The language of victory

Le Peuple concluded its words of praise for the democratic model espoused by the Anglo-Americans with the solemn promise that "all of Belgium had embraced its liberators with a gratitude and confidence that would not weaken." Gaining in force, meanwhile, was a nationwide effort to learn the language of the new role models. For many it proved to be quite a challenge to get their minds around English. The people of Limburg were told by their newspaper not to be discouraged, because many words in Dutch were similar and even identical to English, from *hand*, *lip*, *tong* and *vinger* to *bier* and *sigaret*. But stringing words together so that they made sense to the Allies was, of course, quite another matter. Before long, Belgian newspapers were showing themselves more pragmatic, teaching people to pronounce simple phrases that asked soldiers to repeat what they had said more slowly, if they happened to speak any French, or to wait until they had found someone who could speak English properly.[113]

Still, the incentives to pick up at least a smattering of English were many. Curiosity was one of them, of course, as people wanted to learn more about individual liberators, their hometowns, and their fascinating countries. People at the local level often did not need prompting from SHAEF's Psychological Warfare branch to learn more about the Allies. The Socialist Party in the city of Liège, for example, organized several information evenings on the British and American war effort. In the much smaller town of Nivelles, a local cultural organization

[112] "Les Anglo-Américains et nous," *Le Peuple*, October 21, 1944, 2. *La Libre Belgique*'s article is quoted in Leblon, "Américanophilie et anglophilie," 21.

[113] *HBVL*, September 12 and 17 and October 10, 1944.

had speakers talk about the Walloon language and the architectural challenges of reconstruction, but also on "How to Get to Know the Allies Better." Gatherings like this left people across the country wishing they were better versed in the language of the world's rising stars.[114]

But political and economic necessity spoke much louder than healthy cultural curiosity. To create goodwill and curry favor, for example, mayors even in smaller towns and villages thought it good diplomacy to have speeches in Dutch or French followed by an English version for the benefit of the Allied detachments, no matter how clumsy both translation and pronunciation. Everyone from shopkeepers to barbers and watchmakers stood to gain considerable financial benefit from advertising in newspapers or on doors that they spoke English. Indeed, those who were fortunate enough to know English well could hope to land some of the country's plummiest jobs. The well-paying US military, for example, was always seeking interpreters. And, with basic American salaries already generous, guidelines stipulated that clerks, typists, and technical employees would be awarded a premium of up to 10 percent if they were able to speak and write English fluently.[115]

Many were smart enough to see opportunities in the very demand for English. Within days of the liberation, vendors in the Belgian capital could be seen hawking pocket dictionaries. Individuals who were well versed in English began placing advertisements offering private lessons. Newspapers boosted sales by offering regular language columns. Flemish mail-order companies quickly expanded their offerings of packages for self-study of French and accounting to include English, advertising their move in the press with bold letters. No wonder then that in February 1945 even a priest in Voeren, a small rural community where people spoke Dutch and French, could comment in his journal that "The Americans are surprised to see that the population is learning English so fast."[116]

At ease

Friendship

In the final analysis it was sheer goodwill more than any dictionary or instruction that did most to smooth communication between Belgians and their liberators. When André Grégoire was asked long after the war how the people of Nivelles had been able to talk with American and

[114] Sulbout, "Liège," 101–8; and Blanco-Rincon and Dusausoit, "Nivelles," 88.
[115] For the US military wage scales, see OMA, Emp-2500, 2 and 4, AA 1341.
[116] The priest is quoted in Waterval and Lensen, *Basse-Meuse*, 260.

British soldiers, the man simply replied that "they had scraped all bits of knowledge together." "And I will tell you," he added, "that as in love, when you really like someone, words are of very little importance."[117]

After the harsh Nazi occupation, it was a relief to feel comfortable around so many men in uniform, and admiration and curiosity prompted civilians everywhere to extend invitations to Allied soldiers in their time off. Like stars of the screen, they were in great demand as guests of honor in events across the country. The proprietors of electrical appliance shop Actor in Liège, for example, were quick to organize an evening for American troops, and they had beer flow generously as soldiers and civilians mingled ever more freely. On Christmas Eve 1944, the Association of Bruges Hairdressers asked a contingent of Canadian soldiers to attend their party and, after some heartfelt speeches, the Canucks were given the honor of opening the dance.[118]

Many more soldiers found a home away from home in the intimacy of individual households. When someone floated the idea, for example, of finding families to put up Canadians visiting Brussels for rest and recreation rather than have the soldiers stay in the Maple Leaf Club or other military hotels, the response was overwhelming. Even though the capital was already flooded with Allied troops, in less than two days more than 5,000 families signed up to have one or more Canucks stay with them. Thousands of American and British soldiers were given the same treatment across the country and close contacts inevitably developed over long meals and during evening chats. About a month after the liberation, Limburg's newspaper said it was happy to learn that many in the province were having British and American soldiers over for card games. The Flemish paper pitched in by printing the English terms for whist. In the spring of 1945, Luc Philips was born in the Walloon village of Heusy. His godmother had the very Belgian-sounding name of Rosa Vankrinkelveldt. His godfather was an American soldier from faraway Lima, Ohio.[119]

More remarkable was that for a people raised on colonial images of blacks as primitives, Belgians did not hesitate to extend the hand of friendship also to liberators who were African-American. A photograph taken in Soiron in October 1944 shows three men and four women. One of the women proudly holds a baby boy in a fancy white dress. Another of the women smilingly has her hand on the arm of Johny, a black GI invited to the family's intimate christening ceremony. Long after the war, when calling to mind the soldiers he had had over as guests in

[117] Transcript of interview, M359, 6, AA 1593.
[118] Jour, *Libération Liège*, 66; and Warnier, *Brugge bevrijd*, 78–9.
[119] Pauwels, *Canadezen*, 154; *HBVL*, October 7, 1944, 2; and Lecerf, *Libération*, 179.

Liège, Herman Bovi managed to recall a tall and shy GI named George, two American nurses, "and also a black soldier who played piano with my wife at Christmas." He did not say whether these GIs were there at the same time. But it is highly unlikely. In the armed forces of the US, black and white troops were strictly segregated, and white GIs more often than not preferred to keep it that way while on leave. Anyway, back home in the States, North or South, a white woman playing piano with a black man would have done more than raise an eyebrow.[120]

Romance and marriage

In October 1945, a family in the village of Wegnez received a kind letter from a young woman in Illinois. Letters from her GI husband had told her so many good things about how well they had treated him that she had decided to send them a note of thanks herself. Wives and girlfriends across America might have been more suspicious of the pampering of their men, had they known that in the first weeks of liberation, one of the popular revues in Brussels was called *I Want a Khaki*. And their peace of mind would have been shaken even more had they been aware that a Belgian newspaper as early as October 1944 was listing the following phrases in English with tips for the correct pronunciation: You look handsome. Are you married? Do you have a girlfriend in England/in America? Do you sometimes get a letter from her? Does she love you much? My dreams are all yours.[121]

Indeed, with armies of young men out on the streets, the closest of Allied contacts with civilians inevitably were those with the female population. Belgian women had opportunities to get to know Allied soldiers well in a variety of circumstances. Some did so during dinner conversations in their parents' home, others while doing chores like laundry in return for soap and chocolate. Many, however, found their hearts skipping a beat during one of the many dances organized by the Allies. Away from parental and social control, immersed in the music of swing and crooners, these dances served as pressure cookers for romance. A joke was soon circulating in Belgium about a woman wearing one of the fashionable military insignia on her dress. Pointing at the three bars on the badge, someone says, "Ah, a captain?" "No," the woman replies, "three sublieutenants."[122]

[120] *Pepinster*, 95; and Jour, *Villes libérées: Liège*, 53.
[121] *Pepinster*, 120–1; and Duchenne, "Bruxelles," 24. The language tips are in *HBVL*, October 26, 1944, 2.
[122] For the joke, see Stéphany, "Belgique," 37.

Yet, if some romances barely survived the evening, others would last a lifetime. Six weeks after British troops had liberated Brussels, newspapers were reporting the first wedding between a Tommy and a girl from the Belgian capital. Two months later, a confidential diplomatic report said that "a significant number" of marriages between Canadian soldiers and Belgian women were in the making or had already been performed. By early February 1945, sufficient numbers of women were considering marriage with GIs for SHAEF to become involved. It reported that Belgian authorities had agreed that, in the event of marriage between a member of the US forces and a Belgian subject, the law of the state from which the American citizen came would govern for the purposes of parental consent.[123]

Many parents eventually waved goodbye with high hopes and heavy hearts as their daughters left for the promise of Anglo-American worlds with the liberators they loved and admired. Canadian reports mention a total of 649 Belgian war brides accompanied by 131 children. A rough estimate puts the number of Belgian women tying the knot with British soldiers at 2,000. Although the exact totals for Belgian women marrying soldiers from the large British and American contingents are not known, it is clear that the impact could be felt all the way from the city to the countryside. "Two girls were so smitten," a local history of the British presence in Ham states, "that they said 'I do' to their overseas heroes." One of those girls lived in Kwaadmechelen, a village of slightly fewer than 3,000 inhabitants; the other was from Oostham, population 2,337. In Liège, on the other hand, a city of some 150,000 people during the war and a garrison for large numbers of mainly American troops, a total of 218 women would marry GIs between 1945 and 1949. The largest number would do so in 1945, the year in which Belgian-American unions made up more than 8 percent of all marriages in this Walloon city. Most Liégeoises would follow their husbands to the US. According to one estimate, they were part of a migration of more than 150,000 women from across Europe who between 1944 and 1950 exchanged the tired Old World for the brave new one.[124]

[123] The Canadian report is quoted in Pauwels, *Canadezen*, 75. The SHAEFB report is FR No. 10, 21, February 6, 1945, WO 202/690, AA 1230.

[124] Pauwels, *Canadezen*, 75; De Vos, *Bevrijding*, 91; Rijmen, *Ham*, 80; and Sulbout, "Liège," 67 and 94. The overall estimate for marriages with GIs is in Shukert and Scibetta, *War Brides*, 2.

6 Currents of discontent

In the morning of September 5, 1944, the day after the liberation of Brussels, exciting news spread across the Belgian capital like wildfire. Hitler had committed suicide. A shaken Germany was scrambling to sue for peace. The war was over! So tenacious was the unfounded information, and so disquieting the misplaced enthusiasm it elicited, that authorities hurried to disprove the rumor through loudspeakers on trucks crisscrossing the city.[1]

The war was far from over. Another eight months would pass before Nazi Germany was brought to its knees. And it would take many more months for the tide of Allied troops to ebb away from Belgium. All the while it was by no means merely love and good feelings between the civilian population and the mass of Allied soldiers. Even while much of Belgium was dancing to the mesmerizing beat of the liberators, currents of discontent were gaining significant force beneath the waves of admiration.

Nuisances of war

For the Allies the liberation of Belgium may have been cause for satisfaction and a brief relaxation in discipline, but their foremost goal and concern remained the defeat of Nazi Germany. Bordering the enemy homeland, for the Belgians this meant that for the duration of the campaign their lives were to play out in a rear area within hearing distance of booming cannon. With this came myriad military orders, prohibitions, and limitations. Some were eerily reminiscent of the German occupation. Others were new rules particular to the Allied armies and their objectives. But, after long and exhausting years of war, none could be other than annoying and unpleasant, no matter how necessary they were understood to be.

[1] Balace, "Bruxelles," 77–8.

That the war was far from over, the inhabitants of Arlon experienced five days after the liberation. On September 10, 1944, the CA commander announced that only authorized vehicles could be on the roads. Even civilians on foot or bicycle were not allowed to go beyond a 6-kilometer radius from their homes without a special permit for work or study. The Americans also reminded the population that blackout regulations remained in place, that there was a curfew from nine in the evening to six in the morning, and that there was to be no more photographing of Allied convoys.[2]

Security crackdown

These were some of the standard measures the Allied military issued across Belgium. After their intensive use during the festive days of liberation, for example, cameras gradually disappeared from sight again as SHAEF imposed a "ban on outdoor photography and the carrying of cameras." It was part of a larger security crackdown that in some places also involved a ban on binoculars and by early November caused a total prohibition throughout Belgium on flying carrier pigeons. Made nervous by the proximity of Germany, rumors were rife among Allied troops of Fifth Column activity, the parachuting of German agents, clandestine transmitters, and shots being fired at passing vehicles. Although by mid-November 1944, SHAEF was reporting that "little or no evidence in support is ever produced and where the appropriate authorities have investigated the allegations, they have proved to be without foundation."[3]

SHAEF remained careful, however, and part of its continued vigilance was the censorship of communications between Belgians. Internal postal service for civilian mail for most of Belgium was re-established on October 1, allowing the circulation of postcards, one-page letters, postal checks, and newspapers. Yet, by mid-October, SHAEF had to delay the opening of further postal services because of a shortage "of personnel, equipment and space allotted for the carrying out of the necessary censoring." It took until that time for the Allied authorities even to consider opening "certain telephone communications" for civilians, though in view of doing so they stressed "the necessity for monitoring and the possibility of lines being tapped." Civilian telephone and telegraph services for much of the war remained limited to communication

[2] Triffaux, *Arlon*, 53.

[3] SHAEFB, FR No. 4, Appendix D, November 14, 1944, WO 202/684; and No. 3, 7, October 31, 1944, WO 202/683, AA 1230.

within local sectors. The Allied military did not authorize unrestricted postal, telephone, or telegraph services until the end of April 1945, when the defeat of Germany was just days away.[4]

Curfew regulations also stayed in place for much of the war, although they were gradually relaxed to the point where, already in the course of September 1944, in most places people could stay out until about eleven in the evening. At that time, all cinemas, theaters, restaurants, cafés, dance halls, and other public places were to close their doors and civilians had to be in possession of a special permit if they continued to be out on the street. In some places, on the other hand, Allied authorities ordered shops to stay open in the evening beyond normal times for the benefit of the soldiers. And the Allies further tinkered with time by having everyone in the country turn back their clocks by one hour in the night of September 16 to 17.

Military as well as civilian authorities were especially strict about the compliance with blackout regulations, which generally were in effect from half an hour after sunset to half an hour before sunrise. After four years of such regulations and a deep-seated fear of air raids, however, Belgians did not need reminding of the importance of the safety precautions. Indeed, inhabitants of Roeselare, for example, in January 1945 wanted a much stricter observance of the blackout and complained that the Allied troops themselves were not taking it seriously enough. It would take until April 1945 for the regulations to be relaxed and until May 16, more than a week after the surrender of Nazi Germany, for the Belgian Ministry of the Interior to receive authority from both the British and American military for all blackout restrictions to be lifted.[5]

It took even longer for the traffic restrictions to end. Much of Belgium served as a transit zone for Allied convoys traveling to and from Germany. This meant that the Allies took possession of the country's entire transportation system. Within days of the liberation, newspapers were publishing ordinances prohibiting the use of any motorized vehicle without a special permit, to be issued by Belgian authorities in accordance with Allied restrictions. Civilians were reminded that military traffic had the right of way at all times, that vehicles could not be parked on roadsides, and that people moving about on bicycles should strictly avoid riding next to each other. By December 1944, however, it became apparent to SHAEF that "an abuse of the issue of travel permits was taking place." A new agreement that tightened controls was signed with the Belgian

[4] SHAEFB, FR No. 2, October 17, 1944, 13, WO 202/682; No. 16, 18, May 1, 1945, WO 202/696; and Minutes 12th Meeting, 15, WO 202/554, January 29, 1945, AA 1230.

[5] SE Roeselare, WR January 6, 1945, Folder 1090, AA 1311; and SHAEFB, FR No. 19, 9, June 12, 1945, WO 202/699, AA 1230.

government on December 18 and immediately put into force. Controls were loosened in April 1945, but it would take until June 30 for them to be lifted entirely.[6]

Accommodation and justice

If anything was causing serious inconvenience, however, it was the accommodation of huge numbers of soldiers that continued to pour into the country. It had been agreed between SHAEF and the Belgian government by early October 1944 that, as with civilian labor, any facilities, buildings, and billets required by the Allied military would be procured through the appropriate Belgian authorities, usually the mayors. As part of Belgium's contribution to the war effort, local authorities would have to pay the costs. The Allies would provide them with receipts enabling them to be reimbursed by the government in Brussels. Only where the Belgian authorities failed to procure the necessary accommodation in time, or where operational or security reasons demanded it, would Allied officers have the right of direct requisition.[7]

As a general rule, the policy was to take over, before any others, buildings that had previously been requisitioned by the Germans. This was inconvenient enough for many, but the demands of the Allied war machine were soon proving to be much more taxing and intrusive. The Allies were waging a large-scale campaign and thus needed much more accommodation than the enemy's occupation force before them. Within days of Tielt's liberation, for example, British authorities were urgently asking mayors of the district to present lists of all facilities available for the billeting of troops: rooms for soldiers and officers, workshops for motor repairs, depots and warehouses, dance and meeting halls that could serve as mess halls, buildings that could house offices, and so on. At the request of the military, the mayor of Herstal on September 14 announced that all buildings previously occupied by the Germans, as well as all other available large buildings, would be put at the disposal of American troops. This meant that Herstal had to relinquish the use of more than forty buildings, including all schools, entertainment halls, movie theaters, and a military fort. In Brussels alone, the Americans requisitioned 18 hotels, the British 16, and the Canadians 9. The immense scale of Allied requisitioning and billeting across the country became clear by May 1, 1945, when SHAEF reported that some 30,000 buildings of various types had been procured to house troops, hospitals,

[6] SHAEFB, Final Report No. 21, 11–12, July 21, 1945, AA 1798/9.

[7] SHAEFB, Administrative memorandum No. 6, October 12, 1944, WO 219, AA 1230/2.

garages, workshops, cinemas, leave centers, clubs, and places of entertainment. For the lodgment of troops alone, the Allied military by that time had requisitioned buildings and homes for a total of 2,738,000 nights.[8]

As the heavy and urgent requirements for accommodation increased, grievances among the population became inevitable. If, according to SHAEF, the Belgian people during the first weeks of liberation had accepted those burdens "willingly," by mid-October already it was referring to accommodation as "perhaps the most thorny problem" of its mission. A first problem was that it caused the start of the new school year, considered a priority by both Belgian and Allied authorities, to be delayed for several weeks in many localities. Even when schools eventually resumed, teaching could often proceed only on a part-time basis for the rest of the school year, with several schools across the country switching to a half-day system, in which boys would be taught in the morning, for example, and girls in the afternoon. In Limburg, the Flemish province closest to the German front, so many service units and resting combat troops were being housed in schools by March 1945 that in many municipalities any kind of education was said to have become "utterly impossible." Worried voices could be heard urging the provincial government to try to reach some kind of agreement with the regional military authorities.[9]

But individual families too were finding the billeting of troops in their homes increasingly burdensome. It was one thing, observed the SE in Arlon early in October 1944, to invite Allied soldiers over to have dinner and spend the evening. But it was quite another matter to be ordered to lodge several soldiers day and night, especially given "the abuse that had been made of the requisitioning of billets under the German occupation." British and American billeting officers had to do no more than furnish the mayor of a town or village with an order indicating the number of officers, NCOs, and enlisted men to be given a roof over their heads. The mayor would then have to figure out which homes to designate as billets for what number of soldiers. But some civilians had clearly had enough after four years of occupation. When American troops in Eisden moved on at the end of November and British soldiers arrived in their place, a furniture maker was told to billet another twenty men. When the British

[8] SHAEFB, Final Report No. 21, 21 and Annexure 6 to Appendix F, July 21, 1945, AA 1798/9; Ravyts and Struyve, *Het Tieltse*, 412; *Herstal 1944*, 95; and SHAEFB, FR No. 16, Annexure VIII to Appendix G, May 1, 1945, WO 202/696; and Supplement to No. 16, 9, May 15, 1945, WO 202/697, AA 1230.

[9] SHAEFB, Final Report No. 21, 21, July 21, 1945, AA 1798/9; and FR No. 2, 7, October 17, 1944, WO 202/682, AA 1230; and "Onze scholen moeten heropenen," *HBVL*, March 31, 1945, 1.

discovered that the Belgian had forged the billeting order and lowered the number, they punished him by sending twenty-eight soldiers to his doorstep. By early December 1944, Limburg's newspaper was chiding civilians on its front page for their reluctance to house soldiers, accusing them of selfishness and questioning their patriotism.[10]

The irony was, however, that towards the end of 1944 much tension was arising from the fact that Allied demands regarding accommodation were seen as hampering the execution of Belgium's patriotic duties. Some 80,000 suspected collaborators were awaiting their fate in state prisons and a bewildering array of makeshift jails. Many of those facilities, SHAEF reported, were "packed to four or five times their capacity." Military tribunals in all of the large towns were working overtime to hear the cases. Belgians were clamoring to see justice done without delay. "The people," an SE officer noted in a report on Hainaut province early in October 1944, "have suffered too much during the occupation, they want punishment and they want it without pity." The Allies were well aware of how crucially important this process was to Belgium, both politically and psychologically. But their main concern was the execution of the war. And as reinforcements continued to pour in for the campaign against Germany, they were in urgent need of ever more facilities to lodge them. Unfortunately, many of the buildings that the Allies coveted were already housing either prisoners or tribunals.[11]

"The task of reconciling these two points of view," SHAEF admitted as early as mid-October 1944, "is not easy." To free the prisoners was not an option, SHAEF recognized, as it posed "a great danger to security" and was "against Allied Military interests." Moreover, it would place the Belgian government "in an impossible position vis-à-vis their own people." With no overall agreement in place, a tug-of-war over accommodation erupted between military commanders and local authorities. By the end of October, the Allies had requisitioned many of the military barracks and forts that had been holding large numbers of collaborators. This forced local authorities in Liège, for example, to convert at least seven schools into jails and to cram other facilities with even more prisoners. Authorities in Charleroi complained that, by forcing them to do so, the Americans were making already deplorable hygienic conditions and rampant infectious diseases worse. Tempers flared in Antwerp, where the British military first forced the evacuation of prisoners from

[10] SE Arlon, WR October 7, 1944, Folder 993, AA 1311; SHAEFB, Administrative memorandum No. 6, October 12, 1944, WO 219, AA 1230/2; Janssen *et al.*, "Maasland," 144; and "Patriotisme?" *HBVL*, December 5, 1944, 1.

[11] SHAEFB, FR No. 2, 7, October 17, 1944, WO 202/682, AA 1230. The SE report is quoted in Dauphin, "La Belgique libérée," 135–6.

several of the city's military barracks, then complained that cramped conditions in the remaining jails threatened to cause epidemics that might harm their troops. The Allies eventually raised the issue of health conditions inside congested prisons on a national level. But an equally irritated Minister of Justice retorted that whenever new buildings had been secured and readied to relieve the congestion, it was the Allies themselves who had taken them away again to house their own troops.[12]

Matters came to a boil in November, when trains were arriving with thousands of wounded from the front lines. Army groups were in dire need of buildings in which to install their hospitals, especially in Ghent, Brussels, and Liège. By now, however, all suitable accommodation had already been occupied. The only way to meet the demand was to requisition even the facilities housing the military tribunals responsible for the collaborationists' trials. This proved particularly sensitive. On November 15, for example, a Belgian liaison officer sent a letter to Colonel Watney at SHAEF in Brussels. He alerted him to the fact that the Canadian military in Ghent intended to requisition the city's agricultural college. "The burgomaster offers any other accommodation in town. Could you use your influence," the officer implored, "to the effect that the Canadian authorities do not insist on a requisition which would, for weeks, jeopardize the course of military justice in East Flanders." Colonel Watney, who was responsible for procurement and requisitioning, was receiving similar alarming letters regarding the intentions of American and British authorities from all over the country. On several occasions Prime Minister Pierlot himself personally intervened. The Belgians in matters of accommodation, SHAEF reported later that month, had shown "the greatest co-operation and helpfulness." "There is no doubt, however," they warned, "that there is a limit beyond which we cannot go without seriously impairing our relations with them and that limit has very nearly been reached."[13]

The extent to which military operations and political cleansing were working at cross-purposes was highlighted when, late in November, Belgian authorities tried to transport some 2,500 suspected collaborators

12 SHAEFB, FR No. 2, 7, October 17, 1944, WO 202/698, AA 1230. On Liège and Antwerp, see Van Ypersele, "La Belgique libérée," 16 and 18; and Laureys, "Het bevrijde België," 59 and 74–5. On Charleroi, see "Compte-rendu de l'entretien avec le Major Godefroid," October 5, 1944, Folder 968, AA 1311; and Balace, "Hoquets," 120–3. On the Minister of Justice, see SHAEFB, FR No. 6, 18, December 12, 1944, WO 202/686, AA 1230.

13 SHAEFB, FR No. 5, 12, November 28, 1944, WO 202/685, AA 1230; and CAC Major Cattoir to Colonel Watney, G4 SHAEF, November 15, 1944, Folder 1170, AA 1311. More such letters can be found in, for example, folders 1170, 1172, and 1176.

in two train convoys from Limburg to a facility in Merksplas near Antwerp. The transport was a fiasco in large part because of obstacles thrown up by the Allied military. On the day of departure, British authorities at first refused to make the necessary carriages available, causing serious delays. This made the Belgian guards very nervous as there were too few of them to ensure tight security. The Allies had commandeered large numbers of gendarmes for the regulation of heavy military traffic and the apprehension of German agents rumored to be active in the vicinity. As a result, no more than eighty-five gendarmes were available for the mass transport. Support was provided by some 100 civilian guards, but the gendarmes considered them largely unreliable. Next, on their way to Merksplas, both convoys were constantly being sidetracked to make way for the many military trains. In one such instance, British station guards prohibited the gendarmes from walking around armed for fear that they might harm troops stationed nearby. Then suddenly, in Turnhout, the guards were told they would have to walk their prisoners to Merksplas for the remaining 11 kilometers. Nonstop military traffic further complicated security on the last stretch, forcing the prisoners to string out alongside the road across a distance of two kilometers. By the time a head count could be organized in Merksplas, no fewer than 200 suspected collaborators had vanished into thin air.[14]

Nothing was more sensitive to Belgian public opinion than the obstruction of justice. Some of the dissatisfaction and complaints about the Allied pressures of requisition eased, however, with the arrival of winter, when industry came to a near standstill and empty factories conveniently served to shelter troops and equipment. Yet, with spring in the air, the demands on the population increased again, and with it the strain. While countless troops were arriving for rest and recreation after having weathered the German counteroffensive in the Ardennes, still more soldiers were settling down in Belgium to prepare for the final Allied offensive. "Public opinion and the attitude of the Government," SHAEF's report on accommodation indicated as early as February 20, 1945, "has now shown definite signs of hardening." But, as 30,000 suspected collaborators had been released by February for lack of any serious evidence, the strain had now become more economic in nature. With coal production slowly on the rise and more raw materials expected to arrive, SHAEF noted, "Belgian industry was getting impatient to get under way again." But where the military continued to occupy factories this proved to be impossible.

[14] Report district commander gendarmerie, Limburg province, November 23, 1944, Folder 572, AA 1311.

Verviers at the end of March was a case in point. As a major rest area and thoroughfare for a succession of units, most of its buildings were requisitioned. The judiciary was satisfied because, after having been dispersed across a variety of buildings, the Palais de Justice was about to be returned to them. A few of the town's schools had just been released too. But Verviers' textile industrialists, and their employees, had no reason to rejoice. They were expecting large quantities of wool but nourished little hope that the American military would be abandoning their factories any time soon. Meanwhile, Belgians who did not own their own homes were also feeling the pinch. Steep increases in rent were being reported in spring and inhabitants of Brussels in particular complained bitterly of the cost of housing in what was a mecca for Allied rest and recreation.[15]

When the Allies finally pushed into the heart of Germany, this again generated pressures on accommodation. By mid-May these had taken the form of an estimated 4,000 Belgian POWs and deportees returning home each day. Many of them needed temporary lodging or required instant medical care. And so another tussle started between local authorities and the Allied military for control of certain facilities. Authorities in Arlon, for example, were pleased when the Americans finally decided to evacuate the Léopold barracks. With the town's normal school still an American military hospital, they hoped to use the barracks for Belgians pouring in from Germany. But, early in May, a local SE officer noted that the situation regarding lodgement had become "tense once again." This time in response to news that an American army corps intended to turn Arlon into a rest and recreation center capable of processing 1,000 soldiers every three days. "Very few buildings are at our disposal," the officer remarked impatiently, "and if the repatriation service postpones claiming the Léopold barracks much longer, we risk having the Americans requisition them all over again." As the arrival of POWs and deportees accelerated, the Belgian government some weeks later appealed "for prompt de-requisition of civilian hospitals, sanatoria and other medical installations no longer absolutely necessary to the Allied authorities."[16]

[15] SHAEFB, Final Report No. 21, 21, July 21, 1945, AA 1798/9; and FR No. 11, 14, February 20, 1945, WO 202/691, AA 1230; and SE report, Heusy-Verviers, March 29, 1945, Folder 979, AA 1311. On the cost of housing, see SE Bruxelles, WR April 6, 1945, Folder 1018, AA 1311.

[16] SHAEFB, FR No. 17, 1, May 15, 1945, WO 202/698, AA 1230; Report Lieutenant Anspach to SE, May 5, 1945, Folder 896, AA 1311; and SHAEFB, FR No. 19, 16, June 12, 1945, WO 202/698, AA 1230.

Damages

Mass requisitioning by the Allies caused not only much inconvenience but also widespread damage. As part of the Reverse Lend-Lease agreement with the US, signed on January 30, 1943, and the Mutual Aid agreement concluded with Britain on August 17, 1944, the Belgian government accepted to compensate civilians for damages caused by Allied troops. Together with the payments for civilian labor, supplies, and facilities provided to the Allies, these reparations were seen as part of Belgium's contribution to the war effort. Oversight of the various compensations was assigned to the Office of Mutual Aid (OMA), which created a special Claims Office to investigate damages.[17]

Countless claims for reparation concerned damages caused by Allied troops to the structures and interiors of large apartment buildings, hotels, châteaux, and religious institutions. Schools in particular suffered much as a result of requisitioning. In Antwerp, for example, a city that because of its port activities and role as a center for rest and recreation housed large numbers of troops, many schools reported not only damaged buildings but also wrecked and vandalized teaching materials. In Liège, another major garrison city, the equipment of no fewer than thirty-nine schools was claimed to have been damaged or removed.[18]

Damages tended to be even more significant whenever mechanized vehicles were involved. To create repair shops for tanks, trucks, and artillery, the Allied armies requisitioned numerous industrial facilities, from factories to service stations. Quite often troops ripped out gates and walls to create more space. They also caused tools and equipment to become unusable or vanish. OMA received a total of 1,934 claims for industrial reparations worth 380 million Belgian francs, of which close to 200 million would eventually be reimbursed. Large payments were made also to towns and villages where Allied troops caused major destruction to vital parts of the infrastructure. This was the case, for example, in Brasschaat and Schoten, north and east of Antwerp, where the British military requisitioned long stretches of road to station their armored divisions and the maneuvering tanks tore up surfaces, sidewalks, flowerbeds, and trees.[19]

But the Claims Office had to investigate many more grievances than those related to damage caused by requisition. One of the most spectacular instances, for example, occurred at Houthulst in West Flanders province, where British troops were in control of a large depot

[17] De Pinchart, *Office d'Aide Mutuelle*, 1–2 and 13–14.

[18] *La Réparation par l'Office d'Aide Mutuelle*, 195 and 187; and De Vos, "US Forces," 187.

[19] *La Réparation par l'Office d'Aide Mutuelle*, 184–5 and 187.

of collected German ammunition. By March 1945 enough explosives had been piled up in the open air to fill an estimated 100 boxcars. On the afternoon of Saturday, March 24, something happened that caused three sections of the depot to go up in tremendous explosions. With the damage to Houthulst significant and its inhabitants shaken, British authorities on March 28 decided to avoid further risk by detonating the large quantities of remaining explosives themselves. Although they informed Houthulst and some of the surrounding villages of their intentions that Wednesday, nothing could have prepared the inhabitants for the violence of what should have been four controlled explosions. Indeed, the explosions were much worse than the accident on Saturday. When the dust settled, Houthulst was shown to have become "quasi uninhabitable." Almost all houses were seriously damaged as well as 50,000 roof tiles and two wagonloads of window glass brought in earlier to repair the damage caused on Saturday. Worse, much destruction was now caused also to surrounding villages that had escaped unscathed on Saturday. Windows were shattered as far away as Roeselare and Tielt, places where the first incident had scarcely registered. "The population," one report warned, "is very disgruntled and even embittered about the careless procedures and obvious incompetence of the technicians who are responsible." Indeed, reports on the events were soon flying back and forth, one even reaching the desk of General Erskine, the chief of the Belgian SHAEF mission himself.[20]

Injuries

None of the examined reports on the damage wreaked in and around Houthulst made mention of any serious casualties. But OMA did receive many dossiers on injuries to persons. Most conspicuous were those pertaining to traffic accidents. Just days after the liberation, a serious collision occurred in Verviers between a tank and a tram, leaving one civilian dead and four others wounded. It was the beginning of a wave of accidents across the country between military vehicles and trams, horse-drawn wagons, cyclists, and pedestrians. Most vulnerable of all were the children. On November 16, 1944, the local newspaper reported the death of a seven-year-old girl hit by an army vehicle in Genk when she crossed the road without looking. The soldiers, "badly shaken

[20] SE Roeselare, WR March 29, 1945, Folder 1090; Report Lieutenant Vanden Bavière, March 30, 1945; Capitaine Commandant F. L. Ganshof, "Note sur la catastrophe d'Houthulst," March 30, 1945; and Ganshof to Major General Erskine, April 20, 1945, Folder 1047, AA 1311.

by the incident," had tried in vain to save the girl by rushing her to the nearest hospital. "This tragic accident," the newspaper noted, "has caused understandable commotion in the neighborhood." It was just one of many neighborhoods struck by sadness and consternation as newspapers across the country reported on countless such accidents. On January 4, 1945, with Allied military traffic busier than ever in response to the German counteroffensive in the Ardennes, the commander of the American MP in Liège listed civilian traffic casualties as one of his prime concerns. OMA blamed the many victims on the advanced motorization of the Allied armies, the urgencies of the moment, the rushed training of chauffeurs, and the lack of caution among a population grown used to reduced traffic during the German occupation. By the time the Allies had disappeared from Belgium, OMA reported a total of no less than 14,829 dossiers related to traffic accidents. Slightly fewer than 8,000 of these involved American troops, just over 7,000 were claims against British forces. Of the 480 million Belgian francs claimed, OMA paid some 235 million in reparations to families that money could not console.[21]

The long winter of discontent

As soon as Belgium was liberated, the basic policy became, in the words of SHAEF, that of "helping the Belgians to help the Allies." Most Belgians managed to shrug off the many military impositions as nuisances to be endured for victory. But the Allied command was acutely aware that civilians would be less patient concerning "the three most important and almost primitive requisites." SHAEF had been quick to identify law and order as one of them. But it recognized from the outset that food and coal were the other two. The reason for the Allies' continued presence in Belgium was the defeat of Germany. To accomplish this, the lines of communication needed to be safeguarded at all cost. "The most narrow conception of the object of the Mission," SHAEF therefore reminded itself, "was to prevent disease and unrest in Belgium." Hunger and cold were certain to bring both, putting a severe strain not only on the civilian population, but on their relations with the liberators as well.[22]

[21] Wynants, *Verviers*, 41; Sulbout, "Liège," 116; and *La Réparation par l'Office d'Aide Mutuelle*, 193 and 200–1.

[22] SHAEFB, Final Report No. 21, 1, July 21, 1945, AA 1798/9; and FR No. 3, 1, October 31, 1944, WO 202/683, AA 1230.

Basic needs

The situation was particularly sensitive in a country where people, after long years of harsh and relentless rationing under enemy occupation, had become obsessed with basic needs like keeping their stomachs full and their homes warm. It was this obsession that had driven Belgians to the frenzied plunder of wood and coal as soon as the Germans left in September 1944. With winter not far away, people in Kortrijk from one of the city's depots had made off with 50 tons of coal in less than three hours, while inhabitants of the Belgian capital had snatched even wooden benches from sidewalks and parks.[23]

The procurement of adequate foodstuffs had been a constant headache for all Belgians during the occupation, but even more so for people in the cities and the working classes. If 2,300 calories were considered the minimum daily average for a not-too-active adult in normal times, and if the Allied target for liberated countries was 2,000 calories, for much of the German occupation daily calorie levels for Belgians had remained just below 1,500. Due to the disruption caused by the Normandy landings, however, this figure had seen a further drop, so that by the time the Allies arrived in September 1944, Belgians had been living on less than 1,200 calories per day for three months. No wonder then that in the weeks leading up to the liberation, civilians, afraid that battle would make the harvest impossible, had been descending on fields under cover of darkness to steal as many potatoes as possible to increase their stocks. Few of the German horses gunned down by Allied *Jabos*, meanwhile, had escaped being cut up by men and women eager to take home slabs of precious red meat.[24]

Unfortunately, as soon as the Allies arrived in convoys resembling publicity caravans for a life of plenty, Belgians were convinced they had regained all of President Roosevelt's "Four Freedoms," including that from want. People rushed to slaughter fat chickens or ducks, gladly sharing with their neighbors or the liberators. The acting mayor of Zonnebeke declared rationing lifted for two days, allowing bread and meat to be bought without coupons. Inhabitants of Bruges on the day of the liberation took to the streets singing, "No more soup without bone, no more soup without fat."[25]

Belgians had not suffered starvation under German occupation. But they certainly were the victims of chronic malnutrition and many were

[23] Jacquemyns, "La Société belge," 299, 330, and 369; Vanbossele, *Kortrijk*, 50; and J. S., "Bruxelles, septembre 1944: C'est la Liberté," *Pourquoi Pas?*, September 5, 1984, 13.

[24] Arthur Wauters, "The Return of the Government," in BT, 4; SHAEFB, Final Report No. 21, Annexure XI to Appendix G, July 21, 1945, AA 1798/9; "Des habitants racontent," 22–3; and Taghon, *België 44*, 48.

[25] Deseyne, *Zonnebeke*, 100; and Warnier, *Brugge bevrijd*, 4.

in dire need of more and better food. Although noting that the situation did "not appear to be as bad as was originally feared," SHAEF acknowledged that adolescents and the elderly had suffered "most severely." The organization of Young Christian Workers arranged medical tests for its members shortly after the liberation. It found that 90 percent of those examined suffered from dental caries, that 76 percent were anemic, and that 70 percent of the children showed bone defects due to calcium deficiency. The mortality from tuberculosis, meanwhile, had seen an increase of 50 percent. When school finally resumed in September 1944, a teacher in Braine-l'Alleud noticed that his skinny pupils were neglecting their homework in favor of scouring the fields for potatoes and grains left behind after the harvest.[26]

And there were other problems. General Erskine himself expressed "serious concern" about the impact of low rations on civilian labor. Reports to the SE in Brussels talked of miners descending into the pits with nothing more than water and dry bread. On the question of work resumption in Charleroi's factories, another report signaled, "This will be difficult because the worker is not being provisioned. Bread is scarce, meat is lacking, just like potatoes and milk." "Since food is the fuel for the work people," Erskine warned, "the serious shortages which exist at present will adversely affect labour output, even if they do not lead to internal disorder and discontent."[27]

Food headaches

To acknowledge the many problems surrounding the supply of food was one thing. To correct them, however, was quite another. In September 1944, SHAEF estimated that Belgian wholesalers possessed enough stocks to keep their customers supplied for no more than two or three weeks. Meanwhile, however, food collection services were shown to be completely disorganized. This was made much worse by a transport system in total disarray. Allied air raids and German demolitions on the eve of liberation had left much of the infrastructure in ruins. 358 railroad bridges over roads and waterways, 12 percent of the total in Belgium, had been blown up. The country's dense and vital canal system was largely paralyzed. 31 locks were damaged beyond use, 203 bridges were either completely destroyed or impassable (on the Albert Canal alone, 69 out of 71 bridges were lying in the water), and 830

[26] SHAEFB, FR No. 1, 1 and 14, October 3, 1944, WO 202/681, AA 1230. For the health statistics, see Arthur Wauters, "The Return of the Government," in BT, 4. Aelbrecht and Maghe, "Braine," 105.

[27] Van den Wijngaert *et al.*, "België," 285; and Dauphin, "La Belgique libérée," 57.

barges had been sunk at various points. There were a total of 600 blockages of various kinds and on no section could a canal barge operate unhindered for more than 15 kilometers.[28]

Meanwhile, much of the Belgian transport system that had remained intact was hurriedly being monopolized by an Allied military eager to continue their hot pursuit of the enemy. With their lines of communication stretched to the limit, Allied armies were finding it difficult enough to feed and maintain themselves. They were neither able nor willing, therefore, to take on the responsibility of provisioning millions of needy civilians. "In the early days," SHAEF admitted, "there were no means of rendering any substantial material help to Belgium." The best that Allied troops could do in the first weeks following liberation was to allow ad hoc measures to relieve at least some of the pressure on the population. As food was hard to obtain in urban areas in particular, Allied commanders in several cities quickly decided to make the stocks left in German warehouses available to the population. Enemy stocks in Herstal, for example, instantly allowed American troops in Liège to distribute some sugar, 100 tons of starch, 1,000 tons of rye flour, and 100,000 cans of meat. Because bread was the most urgent requirement, the Allied military in Belgium also handed over as much captured enemy flour and grain as possible.[29]

These distributions, however, amounted to no more than drops in the ocean. CA detachments in the cities tried hard to improve the situation by getting some relief convoys organized amidst the many hectic military priorities. Still in Liège, army trucks managed to provide the population with another 1,900 tons of American foodstuffs, including flour, oats, macaroni, sugar, and canned as well as fresh meat. But this did not stretch very far for more than 150,000 people. On September 13, local newspapers in Charleroi praised the GIs for having driven eight trucks into town with some 3,000 pounds of coffee and 20,000 cans of fish, meat, and milk. But they had to point out to their readers that the quantities were simply insufficient for local authorities to undertake city-wide distribution. SHAEF acknowledged that by the end of September 1944 the Belgians were experiencing "much hardship."[30]

The high expectations of liberation caused disappointment to spread very quickly. Wartime propaganda had painted a picture of Allies rich in resources and this had been borne out by the generosity of the liberators

[28] SHAEFB, Final Report No. 21, 18–19 and 26–7, July 21, 1945, AA 1798/9.

[29] SHAEFB, Final Report No. 21, 1 and 26–7, July 21, 1945, AA 1798/9; and *Herstal 1944*, 95.

[30] Sulbout, "Liège," 44–6; Hasquin, *Charleroi*, 45–6; and SHAEFB, Final Report No. 21, 26–7, July 21, 1945, AA 1798/9.

in the first convoys. For the Belgians, moreover, the tremendous success of the highly efficient American relief effort during the Great War had left an indelible imprint on the collective memory. Now, however, the Allies were suddenly showing themselves incapable of ensuring even a hand-to-mouth existence. Authorities had made certain to warn the population to remain realistic. In the first week of liberation, Belgian Prime Minister Pierlot had called on people to be aware that "a balance will have to be struck between the primordial demands of the supply of the army and the needs of the civilian population." Eisenhower had weighed in with a warning to the Belgians in the press "that ammunition for the war has to be supplied first." Nevertheless, within less than a month after the Allies' arrival, complaints were being aired in different quarters. "People express much amazement," René Boulet, a headmaster in Genval, wrote in his journal on September 21, "about the fact that provisioning has not improved since the liberation, and that quite the opposite is true." A week later, an SE officer concluded a meeting with the governor of Hainaut with a warning regarding public order. "It is indispensable," his report noted, "for the population to be provisioned; in the labor districts, the food situation is almost dramatic." The gendarmerie in its report on Liège on October 6 described the people's state of mind as "generally good." "Nevertheless," it added, "a certain measure of discontent exists and is gaining strength among the population as a result of the lack of coal and the problems of provisioning." By that time too, Lieutenant General Paul Tschoffen, head of CA in the Belgian liaison mission, was using the Belgian press to try to deny rumors that the food shortages were to be blamed on Allied armies requisitioning domestic supplies.[31]

Autumn blues

Matters regarding basic necessities became worse as autumn hardened its grip. The harvests had not been bad, though the threshing of bread grains had been held up for lack of diesel oil. A much more systemic problem was, however, that after its return from London, the Belgian government had instantly dissolved the national organization for food

[31] The messages of Pierlot and Eisenhower can be seen in, for example, *HBVL*, September 12, 1944, 1 and 2 and that of Tschoffen in *HBVL*, October 8, 1944, 1. The complaints are in Boulet, "Journal," AB 1298; "Conférence tenue avec M. le Gouverneur du Hainaut le 28 septembre 1944," Folder 972; and MR gendarmerie Liège, Folder 1057, AA 1311. Between the German invasion of their country and Pearl Harbor, Belgians had been hoping that the US would come to their aid with something akin to the Commission for Relief in Belgium of the Great War. Crombois, "Milieux," 253.

distribution from the German occupation era because it was regarded as tainted. Unfortunately, the government had not deemed it necessary to replace it with anything similar. This left the collection and distribution of food in the hands of what the Allied command referred to as "uncontrolled private enterprise." Indeed, these were not normal circumstances for standard market principles to apply. Much of the agricultural production simply could not be brought to market because the internal transport network was paralyzed. Damage to key infrastructure was further complicated by a critical shortage of rolling stock, barges, and vehicles. In October, an Allied census of road transport revealed the availability of only 3,350 vehicles of 3 tons and more, and only 17,000 vehicles of less capacity. This amounted to no more than 25 percent of the number of trucks available in Belgium before the war. Most, particularly the heavy and newer types, had been removed by the Germans, and what remained was old and in bad repair. To make matters worse, there was a critical shortage of tires. As the Allies monopolized much of the rail and water transport for their military requirements, the need for road transport thus far exceeded the availability of Belgian trucks.[32]

By the end of October, SHAEF could not but acknowledge the ill effects of all this on the distribution of food. On the one hand, there was the official Belgian ration of 1,461 calories per day, which was "of at least minimum sufficiency." On the other hand, however, there was "the plain truth," which was that food was not arriving in the shops in large enough quantities to allow the ration coupons to be honored. That was especially true for the urban centers, where vegetables were expensive and meat and fats were in particularly short supply. Some in the cities had not seen a single gram of butter or margarine in two months. Others were serving "meat balls" in which the meat had been replaced by oats. But bread was not being distributed equally either. People in the urban area of Antwerp, for example, did not even receive the official ration's meager 250 grams per person per day. Civilians could always turn to the black market, which continued to thrive as it had during the German occupation. But that solution was expensive, of course, and could not be afforded by just anyone. *La Dernière Heure* calculated that to feed a single person decently for a month with foodstuffs acquired via rations and black market purchases would cost 1,688 francs. The average monthly salary, meanwhile, ranged somewhere between 900 and 2,500 francs.[33]

32 SHAEFB, FR No. 2, 1 and 9, October 17, 1944, WO 202/682, AA 1230; and Final Report No. 21, 17, 26, and 31, July 21, 1945, AA 1798/9.

33 SHAEFB, FR No. 2, 19, October 17, 1944, WO 202/682 and No. 3, Appendix G, October 31, 1944, AA 1230; and Stéphany, "Belgique," 15. See also Fernand Baudhuin, "Economic Problems of Liberated Belgium," in BT, 27.

In October, with winter on the horizon, Belgian and Allied authorities were facing another serious challenge besides food. The wood and coal looted in September would not last long to fight the cold. Coal should not have been a problem. Belgium was extremely rich in coal and possessed a well-developed system of mines that had suffered virtually no damage by the time of the liberation. "Physically," SHAEF asserted, "Belgium is better prepared to satisfy its own coal requirements than is any other of the liberated countries." Stocks of dug-up coal were extremely low, however. In mid-October the Allies estimated Belgium's pre-winter stockpile to be the lowest since 1918. Meanwhile, the pace of coal production had fallen dramatically. Indeed, it had almost come to a standstill amidst the chaos of September 1944. The average daily production was less than half of what it had been at the end of German occupation and a mere 18 percent of the 1939 level. And there were several reasons why it proved hard to improve production. One of them was a shortage of experienced miners. SHAEF estimated that the retreating Germans had taken between 30,000 and 40,000 foreign miners with them. Lack of transport also made it difficult for sufficient numbers of Belgian miners to be trucked and bused in from across the country. The miners on the job, moreover, were in short supply of the kind of food needed to sustain hard labor. On top of that, an acute shortage of wooden pit-props slowed down the digging of coal even more, prompting the Allies to divert even pulpwood destined for newsprint. Not surprisingly, by November 1944 coal production still stood at only 40 percent of the prewar level. Much of the coal that was dug up, however, suffered the fate of what was harvested in the fields. Lack of transport in the final week of October, for example, made it impossible for some 20 percent of the already low quantities of extracted coal to be shipped out. To make matters worse, the Allies, in contrast with their policy regarding foodstuffs, did requisition considerable quantities of coal for the military effort, thus depriving the civilian population of even more of the much-needed natural fuel. Less than a month after the Allies liberated Brussels, the power in the capital was cut off from early morning to dusk because there was not enough coal to produce sufficient amounts of electricity.[34]

SHAEF admitted at the end of October 1944 that all of this had led to "a mounting exasperation." The mayor of Diest complained to a Belgian liaison officer that the British, in order to haul more ammunition, had

[34] SHAEFB, FR No. 1, 8, October 3, 1944 and No. 2, 11, 17, and 19, October 17, 1944, WO 202/682, AA 1230; SHAEFB, Final Report No. 21, 1, 22–3, and 25, July 21, 1945, AA 1798/9; Fernand Baudhuin, "Economic Problems of Liberated Belgium," in BT, 28; and Institut d'Éducation et de Documentation Nationales, *Chronique*, 177.

requisitioned most of the few civilian trucks that were left. As a result, just four dilapidated trucks remained to make the daily trek to the mines so as to supply this fair-sized town with coal. In Antwerp on October 25, Father Greeve noted in his diary: "Since the liberation there is still the same scarcity of bread that existed during the worst days of occupation. We have also not received a single gram of butter, margarine or fat, no tobacco, no coal, almost no gas, less light. The only thing that people possess in abundance is the freedom to complain." Some made good use also of the newly regained freedom to demonstrate. Early in October more than 200 women took to the streets in Mouscron to demand more food and coal for their children. The mayor later reported that at one point the protesters had threatened to march to the surrounding farms to take what they needed. In Brussels on October 19 several hundred women marched on the political heart of the capital with signs reading "Butter," "Bread," and "Coal."[35]

The female protesters in Brussels blamed the Belgian government for much of their predicament. But they also carried signs in English, which indicated they did not think the Allied authorities should be allowed to go scot-free. The press took offense at the fact that some were blaming the Allies so soon after the liberation. One Flemish newspaper said it understood that people "lived in fear of the coming winter months," but warned that in the midst of preparations for an autumn offensive against Germany, it would be "all too naïve" to expect much help from the Allies. "The problem," it pointed out, "is one of organization, of capable and decisive government." *Le Soir* agreed. It said that Belgians had to rely on themselves and appealed to the government to demonstrate "Total and rapid energy, the energy of war." And it lashed out at those who now could be heard proclaiming that things had not been so bad under the Germans after all: "To compare them with the Allies is shameful. The Allies are our liberators and this word's true meaning should not be forgotten." The Allies, *Le Soir* lectured, had not taken anything from the Belgians. On the contrary, they were doing what they could to help, but could not be expected to take care of everything at the same time.[36]

Amidst the rising polemics, General Erskine thought it urgent to speak to the people directly as head of the Allied mission to Belgium.

[35] SHAEFB, FR No. 3, Appendix G, October 31, 1944, AA 1230; Report CAC Lieutenant J. Crevecoeur, November 2, 1944, Folder 947, AA 1311; Greeve, "Oorlogsdagboek," 190–1, AB 2166; Mayor of Moescron to chief of police arrondissement Kortrijk, October 11, 1944, Folder 958, AA 1311; and Stéphany, "Belgique," 11–12.

[36] "Kolen, eten en ... orde," *HBVL*, October 22, 1944, 1; and "D'une semaine à l'autre," *Le Soir*, October 17, 1944, 1.

The British general began his radio speech on October 27 much in the manner of President Roosevelt in his famous fireside chats to the American nation. "I have seen you all," he commenced, "during the happy days which immediately followed the liberation of your country and during the difficult weeks through which we are living today. I am now quite at home here and I feel I can talk to you as a friend." However, after having thanked the Belgians for their warm reception and the resistance for their courage, Erskine cut straight to "some rather less pleasant things." He reminded listeners that the battlefront was still close to the Belgian border and that the fighting was "very stubborn." The war was not over and there was going to be "a very hard winter." Though he talked about coal too, his emphasis was on "the question of food." Here Erskine assured his listeners that the Allied military authorities were "of course anxious that the Belgian people should be well fed." He also repeated that the Allied armies did "not feed on local resources." Finally, in a move calculated to regain confidence and goodwill, Erskine announced that the Allied military had decided to take from their own stocks 200 tons of food per day for twenty days to help tide the Belgians over beginning on November 1.[37]

Antwerp and import hopes

SHAEF called the public's response to the announcement "most gratifying." But the promised Allied stocks did not stretch far. They were "a nice gesture," *Het Belang van Limburg* commented, but no more than that. It urged its readers to remain realistic about the numbers, pointing out that they would amount to no more than half a kilogram of food per Belgian. If there were to be any significant solution to the food problem, the Belgian government would have to act more decisively. "It is shameful to have to say this," the newspaper continued, "but it is the pure truth. The Germans accomplished what they wanted because they made threats, used the whip, requisitioned with force, and arrested recalcitrants."[38]

The Allied command joined the blame game. The British general in his radio address had been low key about the role of the Belgian government in the food crisis. But in a secret report four days later, SHAEF talked about "a Government which seemed to do everything in the world

[37] SHAEFB, FR No. 3, Annexure 1 to General Summary, October 31, 1944, AA 1230. Erskine delivered the speech in English, but it was followed by a translation in Dutch and French.

[38] SHAEFB, FR No. 3, Appendix G, October 31, 1944, WO 202/683, AA 1230; and "Neen, het kan zoo niet blijven duren!" *HBVL*, November 9, 1944, 1.

save take a firm lead and govern." SHAEF realized, however, that, given the seriousness and urgency of the situation, what was needed were solutions, not accusations. By mid-December 1944, after three months of Allied control, the official food ration, measured in calories per day, continued to be slightly worse than it had been under the Germans before the Normandy invasion. The head of the SHAEF mission agreed that the Belgian food ration, at "only a little more than half of the British civilian ration," was "miserably low," and that it was "vitally important" to reach the target of 2,000 calories per day as soon as possible. "There will never be political peace," Erskine warned in his report, "with empty stomachs and insufficient coal to heat even this meager ration." The best that the Allied military could do, however, was to free up some rail and road traffic to help distribute the godsend of exceptionally large stocks of herring caught by Belgian fishermen in the North Sea. As tension in the press rose and demonstrations in the streets continued, Erskine sounded increasingly concerned. He realized full well that, given the high degree of trust the population had placed in the Allies, the blame would eventually wind up on their doorstep. "It is perfectly clear," he wrote on December 12, "that if reasonable contentment is not provided by some authority, discontentment will prevail to an increasing degree. If this should happen, the discontentment will be directed against the Allied Forces. The result will be internal disorder much more difficult to deal with than the recent minor political explosions."[39]

Putting the blame for the food crisis squarely on the Belgian government had always been somewhat disingenuous. Apart from war's destruction and disorganization there was also the question of imports. Belgium had always relied heavily on imports both of raw materials and foodstuffs. In the years just prior to the war these had averaged more than 2,800,000 tons per month. During the German occupation they had fallen to 600,000 tons. But since the arrival of the Allies, imports for the civilian population had virtually ceased to get through altogether. Erskine himself readily agreed that, in the final analysis, this was the key issue to be resolved. It is why, within weeks of his arrival in Belgium, he had been pinning much hope on the reopening of the port of Antwerp. This, of course, was bound to give military logistics a huge lift. But, Erskine conceded as early as October, earmarking even a small part of the tonnage for the Belgians would

[39] SHAEFB, FR No. 3, Appendix G, October 31, 1944, WO 202/683; No. 5, 1 and 14, November 28, 1944, WO 202/685; and No. 6, 2, December 12, 1944, WO 202/686, AA 1230. On the street demonstrations see, for example, Report CAC Lieutenant J. Crevecoeur on Aarschot, November 4, 1944, Folder 947; and SE Malines, WR December 7, 1944, Folder 1066, AA 1311.

also provide the civilian population with an important psychological boost. As the Scheldt estuary was being cleared from Germans and mines, hope soared. As early as mid-November, SHAEF noted that the prospect of the port's reopening had helped "to raise Belgian civilian morale." Indeed, in December 1944 a newly industrious Antwerp slowly began to deliver on its promise. On December 12, the first of more than 11,000 tons of food imports for the Belgian population that month were being loaded onto barges. Newspapers were happy to announce that, beginning on December 17, the official ration would raise the daily calorific value to almost 1,600. Shortly before Christmas 1944, things were finally beginning to look up.[40]

The Ardennes offensive and hopes dashed

It was not to be. The day before the improved ration was to come into effect, German armies launched a ferocious counteroffensive in the west. And they launched it through the Belgian Ardennes. Indeed, one of Hitler's main objectives was to stall the Anglo-American offensive by seizing the vital port and logistical hub of Antwerp. If the German offensive took the Allied military completely by surprise, it left the civilians stunned. As news slowly seeped through, the Psychological Warfare branch noted that the first reaction of Belgians who did not live in the Ardennes was one of "great calm and confidence." "The vast amount of war material which the people have been watching passing through this country since it was liberated impressed them to such an extent," the Allied report explained, "particularly when comparing it to what the Germans had left to them when they departed from here, that the possibility of a sudden come back by the enemy was completely ruled out of their minds." When it gradually became clear, however, that the Allied troops were indeed being pushed back, there was "a very noticeable deterioration in the morale of the country with a distinct undercurrent of acute nervousness and uneasiness which grew steadily from day to day." There was "a widespread exodus," SHAEF reported, from Liège and Verviers, cities close to the Front. Further to the rear, people in Tienen did not quite know what to think or do. They teetered, an SE report observed shortly before Christmas, between "fear and hope." "The passage of refugees from Liège," the same report noted, "has caused the mood of the people to be somewhat nervous, but English and American troops marching

[40] On the imports, see Lagrou, "US Politics of Stabilization," 217; and Institut d'Éducation et de Documentation Nationales, *Chronique*, 175. SHAEFB, FR No. 3, 1, October 31, 1944, WO 202/683; No. 4, 16, November 14, 1944, WO 202/684; and No. 7, 19, December 26, 1944, WO 202/687, AA 1230.

through the city in the direction of the front have brought some relief." Still further to the rear, SHAEF in Brussels observed that there were "numerous instances" of people making preparations to leave the capital. On December 26, the mayor of Beaumont, aware that it might "cause scandal" to the many refugees and Allied soldiers in his village, called a halt to the organization of all balls and concerts and declared dancing in cafés prohibited until the end of hostilities.[41]

On October 17, General Erskine in a report had warned that "it would not take much to cause a setback which might have serious repercussions." That danger had not yet passed, he had said, "and such stage will not be reached for several months at least." He had gone on to compare the situation to "an early Spring where one hopes there will not be a sudden frost to destroy the promise of a fruitful season." Now, suddenly, a most cruel frost had wiped out all of December's budding optimism in a single week. The Allied forces managed to halt the German attack around Christmas, but it would cost them more than a month to push the stubborn enemy out of the bulge in their lines. The fighting took place in a severe winter that made many roads impassable and by early February had frozen up most of the canals. Some elements of the resistance attempted to stage a comeback, clamoring to be rearmed in order to defend the nation, an offer that SHAEF "politely but firmly refused." In the new climate of fear, SHAEF also hurried to announce that "no persons known to be pro-German and anti-Allied in their outlook" should be released from internment, "whether or not they have committed a punishable crime." Meanwhile, as part of the German offensive, V1s and V2s, which had been affecting Belgian morale since November, began to pound Antwerp and Liège mercilessly. They caused widespread destruction across the country and would eventually leave more than 800 Allied soldiers and 6,000 civilians dead.[42]

The devastating psychological blow was made worse by the fact that people were also soon feeling the pinch where it concerned basic necessities. For quite some time General Erskine appeared to be underestimating the potential impact of the enemy offensive on the food and coal supply in Belgium. "Such a rude reminder that the war is still very close to them," he glibly commented as late as December 26, "may do no harm." But if the suggestion was that a good dose of fear was likely to

[41] SHAEFB, FR No. 7, Annexure II to Appendix D, December 26, 1944, WO 202/687, AA 1230; SE Tienen, WR December 23, 1944, Folder 1102, AA 1311; and Roba and Leotard, *Walcourt-Beaumont*, 193.

[42] SHAEFB, FR No. 2, 1, October 17, 1944, WO 202/682; No. 7, 1, December 26, 1944, WO 202/687; No. 8, 7, January 9, 1945, WO 202/688, AA 1230; and SHAEFB, Final Report No. 21, 20, July 21, 1945, AA 1798/9. On the V1s and V2s, see De Vos, *Bevrijding*, 119 and 122.

distract the population from hunger and cold, the Allies were soon very much deceived.[43]

Battle in the Ardennes cut off one of the main domestic sources of meat and butter. And it complicated food supply further by chasing large numbers of refugees to urban centers west of the Meuse River. The only bright spot was that the Allied military managed to raise imports for the civilian population from 12,000 tons in December to 33,000 tons in January. This, however, was by no means sufficient to compensate for the recent losses in domestic food supply. And a further boost in imports was unlikely any time soon so long as V1s and V2s continued to rain down on Antwerp and hunger too left the dockers discouraged. Meanwhile, frozen canals, slippery roads, and military priorities were making it hard to distribute any kind of food in large enough quantities anyway. "In short," SHAEF stated early in February in a report sounding a wholly different tone, "the low point has been reached when domestic supplies have almost run out while the imports (45,517 tons to 31st January) have hardly begun to flow into consumer channels." In mid-February the official Belgian ration had to be lowered again to the level of calories of the German occupation. With SHAEF at the same time admitting to "a bread crisis" and calling meat supply in several cities "critical," many Belgians knew that in reality even this bleak standard was overly optimistic. SHAEF agreed, recognizing that the rapidly worsening conditions were "fertile soil for unrest."[44]

What added to the unrest was that the surprise attack in the Ardennes also caused a sharp drop in the production of coal. Most of the mines were dangerously close to the combat area. This did little to improve the morale of miners who were now also receiving less food. But the most dramatic impact of events in the Ardennes forests was that the mines were now cut off from their source of pitwood. The Allies had already been calling the supply of coal to civilians "most disappointing" before the Ardennes offensive. Indeed, SHAEF at the end of November had decided to take the drastic step of "according all coal movement a top priority equivalent to that of military stores," even to the detriment of other essential traffic like that of sugar beets. Now, however, with stocks "desperately low" and both production and distribution taking a hammering, SHAEF in the first week of January 1945 was describing the coal situation as "very critical." In response, the Allies rushed to transfer 75,000 tons of coal from stockpiles at mines in Holland. They also made four forestry companies cut trees into pitwood west of the Meuse and

[43] SHAEFB, FR No. 7, 1, December 26, 1944, WO 202/687, AA 1230.
[44] SHAEFB, FR No. 8, 17–18, January 9, 1945, WO 202/688; and No. 10, 2 and 20, February 6, 1945, WO 202/690, AA 1230.

engaged two transport companies to dispatch it to the Belgian mines. Meanwhile, 50,000 additional tons of pitwood were being shipped to Belgium from France and Britain.[45]

But all this was taking too much time to have any effect on the Belgian population when needed most. In January, lack of coal for the power plants caused electricity to be cut off during daylight hours on certain days of the week not just in the capital, but in other areas of the country too. That same month, SHAEF announced that the already low ration of coal would have to be cut by 15 percent. Priority in coal was given to pregnant women, the seriously ill, and families with small children. But even the most vulnerable civilians were finding it difficult to have their rations honored. In desperation, to stave off at least some of the biting cold, people turned to what was known as *terril* (mine waste containing a little coal), *schlamm* (coal dust), and *spriet* (a mixture of coal and wood). For most, however, wood remained the only real alternative. People first turned to anything made of wood in and around their own homes that did not have too much value. Then they were forced to look elsewhere. Trees were being chopped in public woods, farmers had their fence posts pulled up, and fruit growers their orchards cut down. Newspapers warned that the Allied military would regard those caught removing wooden telephone poles as saboteurs. On February 14, 1945, the gendarmerie laconically reported that in several municipalities of West Flanders province "wood thefts had diminished because there were no trees left along the public roads."[46]

"The civilian population," SHAEF concluded early that same month, "is going through its darkest and direst days since liberation." Contrary to General Erskine's erstwhile prediction, the rude reminder of war was now doing much harm to public opinion. A first casualty of the bitter mood was the Belgian government. From the outset, people had regarded Prime Minister Hubert Pierlot as out of touch because he had not experienced the hardships of occupation. Since their return from exile in London, Pierlot and his government had found it increasingly difficult to convince Belgians they were doing enough to improve their lives now that they were liberated. With the winter at its worst, slogans painted on walls were screaming, "Give us butter!", "We demand coal!", and "Down with Pierlot!" The Catholic Prime Minister failed to survive February's frigid political climate. His government was soon replaced

[45] SHAEFB, FR No. 5, 12, November 28, 1944, WO 202/685; and No. 8, 1, January 9, 1945, WO 202/688, AA 1230.

[46] SHAEFB, FR No. 8, 1, January 9, 1945, WO 202/688; and No. 9, 19, January 23, 1945, WO 202/689, AA 1230; and Gendarmerie Brugge, February 14, 1945, Folder 958, AA 1311.

by a new one under the leadership of socialist Achiel Van Acker. This left the Allied command reasonably satisfied. They understood that Belgian popular opinion had moved to the left as a result of the war and that Van Acker's government was "more acceptable to the masses." But they also welcomed, like many Belgians, a prime minister who was regarded as more pragmatic and energetic, particularly in the wake of a government whose efforts in matters of food supply SHAEF considered "neither comprehensive nor heroic."[47]

A worried SHAEF realized, however, that in matters of essential supplies many Belgians were coming to the same conclusion where it concerned the Allied forces. Reports pouring into the headquarters of the SE in Brussels from across the country were full of warnings that Belgians were putting more and more blame for their predicament on the Allies too. In Namur the military setback in the Ardennes and the lack of food imports had "considerably lessened the prestige that the Americans and English had enjoyed," so that relations with the civilians "no longer had the same warmth as in the beginning." People in Brussels could be heard criticizing the Allies "for abandoning the country to itself and its own resources." "There is talk," the gendarmerie reported to the SE from Leuven on January 8, 1945, "of butter and coal being shipped to England. The population is less favorably disposed towards the allied soldiers than before." From Ghent to Zottegem, another report said, inhabitants were openly claiming that the supply situation had been better under the Germans.[48]

On the first day of February, the Confederation of Belgian Workers and the Confederation of Belgian Christian Unions presented the Allied authorities with a joint memorandum on the subject of supplies for the Belgian people. The document stated that workers were suffering as a result of critical shortages in basic necessities and because salaries did not allow them to make up for these on the black market. Everyone realized, it continued, that improvements now depended "almost exclusively" on imports and that these were the responsibility of the Allied authorities. So long as Cherbourg in France had been the only major port available to the Allies, working families had accepted the scarcities. But now, with Antwerp reopened since November, patience was running low. Workers unanimously agreed that soldiers who risked

[47] SHAEFB, FR No. 10, 19–20, February 6, 1945, WO 202/690, AA 1230. On public opinion and the Pierlot government, see Lagrou, "US Politics of Stabilization," 213–14.

[48] Gendarmerie Namur, MR February 8, 1945, Folder 1075; SE Bruxelles, March 5, 1945, Folder 526; and Gendarmerie Leuven, MR January 8, 1945, Folder 1063; Gendarmerie Gand, WR January 19, 1945, Folder 1035; SE Zotteghem, WR February 2, 1945, Folder 1119, AA 1311.

their lives and health at the front had to be cared for first. However, the memorandum stated, "[workers] believe that more extensive imports of food and other products of first necessity for their account might be carried out without endangering the war effort."[49]

"The people," SHAEF summed up on February 6, "are hungry, cold and disgruntled; and all this is finding expression in many ways, none of which are in the least advancing the Allied cause." "There is no doubt," the Allied command continued, "that the economic difficulties have embittered the population and the popularity of both British and Americans has suffered in consequence." Ironically, as the Germans were being pushed out of the Bulge, Allied popularity was further hurt by accumulating evidence of what SHAEF itself called "wanton pillaging by our own troops." SE officers reported that in the Ardennes this was giving rise to "very strong animosity" towards Allied forces and bitter complaints about American soldiers in particular. GIs were said to be "picking up where the Germans had left off." SHAEF at the end of January noted that the damage of this to public relations had spread beyond the region and that news of the "large number" of such incidents "undoubtedly had an effect on Belgian public opinion."[50]

By early February there were enough reasons for General Erskine to decide that it was again necessary for him to be speaking directly to the Belgian people over the radio. But, this time, the tone of his speech was less conciliatory and understanding than it had been early in November. Perhaps because Erskine understood that the current of discontent was now running so deep it could be rechanneled only with firmness. Perhaps also because the British general felt irritated by the sharpness of the rebukes from a people who only five months earlier had given the Allies such an incredibly warm welcome. Erskine first proceeded to tackle the "false rumors" and "futile lies" that could be heard across the country. He listed the details of three months of civilian tonnage unloaded in Antwerp to dismiss as a "falsehood" that the Allies had not imported any food for the Belgians. And in reply to "apparently common gossip," Erskine categorically denied that as much as a single ton of Belgian coal was finding its way to Great Britain. The especially grating comment that the Germans had succeeded where the Allies had failed in terms of bringing coal to the people, Erskine did not deign worthy of a complex

[49] SHAEFB, FR No. 10, Annexure I to General Summary, February 6, 1945, WO 202/690, AA 1230.

[50] SHAEFB, FR No. 9, 6, January 23, 1945, WO 202/689; and No. 10, 8 and 19, February 6, 1945, WO 202/690, AA 1230; and Gendarmerie Verviers, MR February 9, 1945, Folder 1107, AA 1311. On US troops in the Ardennes and their relations with the civilians, see also Schrijvers, *Unknown Dead*.

argument. If, with the front line "on our doorsteps," Montgomery and Bradley would have used trucks to deliver coal "for civilian purposes round the country," the British general commented rather icily, "I should probably not have been speaking to you from Brussels now." People would simply have to accept, Erskine hammered home, that as a result of the combination of winter and war, "It is not always possible to meet all the requirements of Belgium." Instead of discontent, he asked Belgians to show loyal acceptance of Allied decisions "as a demonstration of our complete support of General Eisenhower." And if that was not forthcoming, Erskine chided the Belgians, they should do well to consider that the situation in their country, bad as it might be, was still not "as hard as it is in Poland, Holland and Greece." Finally, before wishing listeners good night, Erskine pointedly noted that he did not believe "there is a single Belgian who would exchange even the hardest conditions of life, and freedom – for German occupation, Gestapo, torture and murder."[51]

Spring and the return of confidence

Labor and the unions in their memorandum of February 1, 1945, had assured the Allies "of the gratitude of the Belgian people who will never forget that they owe them the liberation of their country." Still, they said, Belgians could not help but "wonder whether our Allies are well aware of their distress and the privations they have to put up with. They doubt it." Fortunately for the relations between Allies and Belgians, SHAEF around the same time came to the conclusion "that things cannot get much worse without getting better." The winter was half over. And the war news was encouraging. The Germans had weakened as a result of the failure of their offensive in the West, and the Soviets were signaling that they were stronger than ever. The issue of coal was sure to become less critical with the emergence of spring. Meanwhile, SHAEF was relieved to see a more assertive Belgian government take the lead in improving the supply of food.[52]

The new Belgian government did not pull any punches, however, where it concerned the role of the Allies in this matter. They made it crystal clear that they needed the military to import 80,000 tons of food per month (two and a half times the amount of January) to make the 2,000-calorie ration

[51] General Erskine's speech was broadcast on February 4, 1945. The integral text of the speech is in SHAEFB, FR No. 10, Annexure II to Appendix E, February 6, 1945, WO 202/682, AA 1230.

[52] SHAEFB, FR No. 10, 19 and Annexure I to General Summary, February 6, 1945, WO 202/690, AA 1230.

possible at all. General Erskine on February 20 called these requirements "reasonable." He even pointed out that he understood that, from a political point of view, "The present Government have nothing to lose and everything to gain by being 'tough' with the Allies." Labor and the unions were clearly restless, and some strikes had already occurred in the mines and the port of Antwerp in the course of January. Should things not improve now that the worst of winter and war was on the wane, more strikes could be expected. If that were to be the case, Erskine reasoned, "The government would have to choose between supporting its own people against the Allies or suppressing its own people to help the Allies." He had no doubt, he acknowledged, that "if matters got out of hand because of failure in our programme or lack of sympathy it would back its own people."[53]

It never came to that. As early as February, reports for the SE in Brussels were making clear that trust in the military capabilities of the Allies was becoming fully restored. "The confidence is growing everywhere," a report from Virton said on February 10, "because numerous columns of German prisoners are passing by on the roads, on their way from the front to the rear. All of the sympathies of the population go out to the allied soldiers." "The Allied armies are regaining popularity," an SE officer wrote from Arlon on the last day of March, "and especially the American army to whom the population is grateful for its splendid feats of arms in Germany." Much relief came also from the fact that in March the last of the V weapons were being sighted over Belgium.[54]

The advent of spring caused a détente in relations with the Allies not just because of improving military fortunes. "It cannot be too strongly urged," SHAEF had said early in February, "that every attempt should be made to relieve the coal and food situations when there is no doubt whatsoever that sentiment would alter rapidly in our favor." That is exactly what happened. In the middle of March the food ration suddenly climbed from the new low of 1,464 calories per day to more than 1,700 – the highest it had been since the start of the German occupation in 1940. Reports for the SE indicated that this was not just a theoretical improvement, but one that people were very much experiencing even in the urban areas. The relief was brought about in large measure by a steady increase in imports arriving at the port of Antwerp. Not just under the Allied military import program for Civil Affairs but, beginning in March, also under the national civil import program on the account of the Belgian government. At the same time, the collection and

53 SHAEFB, FR No. 11, 1–2, February 20, 1945, WO 202/691, AA 1230.
54 SE Virton, WR February 10, 1945, Folder 1111; and SE Arlon, WR March 31, 1945, Folder 1005, AA 1311.

distribution of foodstuffs was made somewhat easier when the Allied military for that specific purpose handed over to the Belgian government more than 800 trucks, most of them of the heavy type that could carry up to 6 tons.[55]

Late in March already, the Allied mission in Belgium was happy to observe: "Confidence in an early victory – confidence in the Allies – and confidence in the Belgians' own ability to manage their own affairs is the keynote of present public opinion." The long winter of discontent finally appeared to have run its volatile course.[56]

The arts of cheating

Supply and demand

The long winter had indeed run its course by March 1945. But it left a dark and embarrassing shadow over Belgium that would linger stubbornly for much of the year. On March 21, from the roof of a depot in Tessenderlo a British sniper shot and killed twenty-three-year-old Marcel Schuer while he and some friends were prying open an army crate stuffed with chocolate. The sniper had been put in place in response to an epidemic of theft in Tessenderlo, a problem that refused to go away even after Marcel Schuer's death. The problem occurred not just in Tessenderlo: from the depths of scarcity and want had emerged a nation of thieves and fences.[57]

Observers recognized that this transformation had been set in motion by the special conditions of war, long before the arrival of the Allies and the onset of an unforgiving winter. A Belgian sociologist who during the German occupation examined the living conditions of working-class families in Brussels observed how lying and conning had gradually evolved into acceptable elements of an elaborate mechanism of defense. "Neither working nor praying for one's bread suffices any longer," he noted. "One has to cheat and avoid getting caught." Children in particular were said to have been affected by the erosion of moral principles. They had grown up in a society where smuggling and the black market had become part of everyday life and where evading, cheating, and

[55] SHAEFB, FR No. 10, 8, February 6, 1945, WO 202/690, AA 1230. The Allied Military Import Program continued until the end of July 1945 and by that time had procured almost 672,000 tons of food for the Belgians. Frédéric Osterrieth, "The Battle of Supplies," in BT, 44. On the Allied trucks, see SHAEFB, FR No. 12, 14, March 6, 1945, WO 202/692, AA 1230.

[56] SHAEFB, FR No. 13, 1, March 20, 1945, WO 202/693, AA 1230.

[57] Roden, *Tessenderlo*, 265–6.

lying to German and Belgian authorities had become the norm. The number of delinquents judged by juvenile courts had more than doubled between 1939 and 1943 and a large proportion of the cases involved theft. "The consciences of children," one criminologist said at the end of the war, "were totally confused by the fact that the normal notions of law and morals did not apply to an enemy who sought to destroy their own liberty and conscience." That state of mind had culminated most starkly in the frenzied mass looting during the German retreat. On September 18, 1944, for example, Roeselare's municipal council had to lecture inhabitants that anything obtained from buildings and depots just prior to the liberation could in no way legally be considered theirs. It warned that plunder would not go unpunished and that the fire brigade would soon be making the rounds to recover stolen materials, furniture, and other objects.[58]

The Allies soon found themselves agreeing with the Belgian sociologists and criminologists. At the end of 1944, SHAEF noted that the Belgians had been "tutored through the German occupation in the arts of cheating" and that they now continued to find "habit a strong master." But that was only the self-serving part of the explanation. The harsh reality of the liberation was that until late in 1945 there was almost nothing for Belgians to buy on the regular market. And that applied not just to food and coal, but to almost any basic material or consumer product imaginable. For many long months, imports for the Belgian population under the Allies were much lower than those under the Germans. They were, in fact, almost nonexistent. Civil Affairs imports for the population represented only 2 percent of the total military imports into Belgium as late as February 1945. Even in April 1945, when imports on the account of the Belgian government were increasing, most of the still limited coal production went to the armed forces, priority military contracts, and essential civilian needs. As a result, only a small surplus served Belgium's civil industries. Indeed, as late as March 1945 even the War Materials Committee, responsible for the disposal of captured enemy goods in Belgium, in many cases continued to decide in favor of the urgent needs of the Allied forces.[59]

All this put tremendous strain on the supply side at a time when the population's appetite for materials and goods of all kinds proved voracious. And that appetite was made more problematic by immense

[58] Jacquemyns, *La Société belge*, 370–1; C. Van der Bruggen and Louis C. Picalausa, "Belgian Youth Movements and Problems," in BT, 114–15; and *Roeselare Bevrijd*, 96.

[59] SHAEFB, FR No. 7, 16, December 26, 1944, WO 202/687; No. 10, 2, February 6, 1945, WO 202/690; No. 15, 1, April 17, 1945, WO 202/695; and No. 13, 15, March 20, 1945, WO 202/693, AA 1230.

pressures on demand created by the presence in the small country of huge Allied armies involved in an intensive campaign. The Allies needed much more than buildings for their troops to stay in. Despite the support of a massive logistical system, Allied forces craved almost all of the materials and goods in Belgium that the Germans had not already stripped away. Detailed lists drawn up by Vilvoorde's municipal council between October 1944 and April 1945, for example, show a variety of British units requisitioning anything from stove pipes, toilet bowls, rubber hoses, locks, door handles, saws, paint, and light bulbs to buckets, clocks, pepper mills, coffee sets, teapots, inkpots, plates, knives, tablecloths, club chairs, and champagne glasses.[60]

Procurement in Vilvoorde at least followed the official procedures. The council could therefore hope to be reimbursed by a Belgian government accepting such costs under the Mutual Aid and Reverse Lend Lease agreements. In not a few cases, however, Allied troops dispensed with the administrative niceties and simply took what they needed. OMA received almost 3,000 requests for reimbursements regarding irregular procurements in Belgium worth 100 million francs. After repeated complaints by the Belgian government, SHAEF as late as June 1945 continued to warn that it would no longer tolerate the illegal requisitioning of civilian vehicles by Allied soldiers.[61]

By the end of April 1945, when the mass of troops were to remain in Belgium for several more months, OMA estimated the total value of Belgian supplies already delivered to the Allies at more than one billion Belgian francs. The long list of supplies mentioned, among others, more than 22,000 tons of fruit and vegetables; more than a million pieces of leather and hides; close to 200,000 square meters of textile fabrics; almost half a million pieces of porcelain and glassware; more than 11 million bricks and tiles; tens of thousands of tons of chemicals, cement, industrial metals, paper, and timber; and hundreds of thousands of tools and machine parts. By the end of 1945, the total tonnage of coal taken from the already depleted Belgian stocks to supply the British and American militaries stood at 1,875,566.[62]

The massive drain on Belgium's meager goods and resources was made worse by the buying power of the Allied soldiers. This had already created serious problems in France, especially where it concerned the

[60] Gemeentebestuur Vilvoorde, Folder "Diverse documenten betreffende bezetting en bevrijding, 1940–1945," AA 77.

[61] *La Réparation par l'Office d'Aide Mutuelle*, 194; and SHAEFB, FR No. 14, 13, April 3, 1945, WO 202/694; and No. 19, 12, June 12, 1945, WO 202/699, AA 1230.

[62] SHAEFB, FR No. 16, 15 and Annexure VIII to Appendix G, May 1, 1945, WO 202/696, AA 1230; and de Pinchart, *Office d'Aide Mutuelle*, 15.

Plate 6.1 Allied soldiers buy lace in a shop near the capital's *Grand Place*. (CEGESOMA, Brussels, picture number 30010)

Americans. The situation was hardly surprising when even a simple private (who did not have to pay for food, clothing, or housing) was drawing pay higher than that of a skilled laborer. By at least as early as November 1944, Belgian mayors, at the request of American military authorities, were posting public announcements informing the population that GIs were not allowed to purchase heavily rationed items. These included food (with the exception of fruit and vegetables), clothing and shoes, medical supplies, soap, and petrol. Other than those items, however, Allied soldiers were explicitly allowed to buy anything else that was available. In December 1944 SHAEF admitted that "continued high prices" in Belgium had to be attributed at least "to some extent" to purchases by Allied forces.[63]

63 For France, see Torrent, *La France américaine*, 237. On the purchasing power of Allied troops in Belgium, see Van der Wee and Verbreyt, *Oorlog en monetaire politiek*, 618–22. For examples of public announcements in the American sector, see Stad Sint-Truiden, "Bekendmaking," November 14, 1944, Folder 981, AA 1311; and Sulbout, "Liège," 44–6. SHAEFB, FR No. 6, 19, December 12, 1944, WO 202/686, AA 1230.

SHAEF went on to emphasize, however, that it was the lack of goods, more than anything else, that was "causing the country to run a grave risk of inflation." It was "imperative," the Allied command pointed out, that civilians should be able to use "the fruits of labour" to provide "the needs and necessities of life, commencing with such elementary matters as clothing and footwear." Still, in a country where it took even food and coal shortages a long time to become resolved, this remained wishful thinking for many other products considered necessary but not vital. In a report on the situation in Namur in January 1945, the gendarmerie observed that the large majority of people were no longer able to dress adequately against the cold and that it was "pitiful" to have to watch children in the streets wear shoddy shoes or no shoes at all. The Belgian government by mid-May estimated that it needed shoes and clothing for some 600,000 people. Soap was in such short supply until June that even hospitals and miners had to do without for long periods of time. And the list went on and on. Early in January 1945, for example, SHAEF reported that workers lacked not only clothing and soap, but also tires for the bicycles taking them to the factories and materials to repair the houses they went home to. SHAEF expressed concern that such conditions might begin to jeopardize the military effort. Indeed, striking miners and dockers later that month listed not just pay increases among their key demands, but also better food and the kind of clothing and soap they knew even higher wages would not be able to buy them.[64]

Thieves and fences

As the Belgians had learned during the German occupation, one way of obtaining what foreign troops were withholding was to take it from them. It was true, of course, that the Anglo-American troops were liberators and allies. But amidst the soaring want, Allied pay and supplies were perceived as abundant, if not excessive. And this soon caused any qualms about stealing from friends to be smothered by the reassurance that taking from those who had too much would do no real harm. As Allied soldiers nonchalantly pulled out wads of crumpled bills in shops and bars, for example, the temptation to make some easy money off unsuspecting foreigners proved too strong for many. Less than a month after the arrival of the first liberators, Belgian newspapers were lamenting profiteering practices across the country. There were reports, for example, of soldiers

[64] SHAEFB, FR No. 8, 18–19, January 9, 1945, WO 202/688; No. 13, 1, March 20, 1945, WO 202/693; and No. 17, 17, May 15, 1945, WO 202/698, AA 1230. For Namur, see Gendarmerie Namur, MR February 8, 1945, Folder 1075, AA 1311.

being charged three times the normal prices in cities like Brussels and Liège. In mid-October a committee of Belgian veterans and resistance fighters met in Arlon, the capital of Luxembourg province. There they issued a statement condemning what they called the "plague" of profiteering at the expense of American troops. Though they expressed the hope that "the common sense and traditional honesty of the majority of the Arlon shopkeepers" would prevail, several weeks later the resistance was organizing a "Committee for the Survey of Prices." It had the support of the town's police and commercial association as well as that of the local American authorities. At about the same time, the mayor of Sint-Truiden issued a public announcement demanding fair prices for "these courageous soldiers" and ordering the prices for products and drinks to be displayed clearly and unambiguously. Repeated efforts to crack down on perpetrators show, however, that profiteering was hard to stamp out. In January 1945, for example, an exasperated British CA officer called together Knokke's bar owners and simply dictated the maximum price they could henceforth charge for a glass of beer.[65]

Such were the shortages in the regular market, however, that the Allies' material goods exerted a much stronger temptation than their money. There was little that Belgians could not put to good use one way or another, so that almost anything became fair game early on. Allied troops in Brussels, for example, noted that civilians, even during the first days of liberation, were snatching from their vehicles whatever it was they could lay their hands on, from jerrycans to sleeping bags. US authorities in Limburg as early as mid-November complained about youngsters committing theft of military items, while in Liège children as young as twelve, often encouraged by their parents, joined youth gangs specialized in pilfering American food. SHAEF had Belgian authorities remind the population that looting from downed aircraft, whether German or Allied, was strictly prohibited, and local police and Allied MPs had to guard crash scenes to prevent them from being picked clean of anything useful. In November military authorities in West Flanders decided to deny civilians access to certain beaches after learning that briefcases and other items were being taken from corpses of Allied soldiers washed up from the North Sea.[66]

65 For early newspaper reports on profiteering, see Sulbout, "Liège," 31 and 66; and "Voornaamheid!" *HBVL*, October 10, 1944. Comité de Coordination pour la Province de Luxembourg, "Ordre du Jour," October 16, 1944 and "Important Notice for the Shopkeepers of Arlon," November 7, 1944, Folder 993, AA 1311; Stadsbestuur Sint-Truiden, "Bericht," November 27, 1944, Folder 981, AA 1311; and D'hont, *Knokke*, 40.

66 Balace, "Bruxelles," 67; *HBVL*, November 18, 1944, 2; Sulbout, "Liège," 77–80; SHAEFB, FR No. 9, 5, January 23, 1945, WO 202/689, AA 1230; and Gendarmerie

Theft was even more blatant and widespread where it concerned vital necessities. This was demonstrated most clearly during the winter of 1944–5 when there was not even enough coal for the elderly and sick. The Allied military in Ostend complained that trucks loaded with coal were being stalked by large numbers of civilians – many of them children and old people – and that these carried baskets and sacks hoping for an opportunity to snitch. Also in West Flanders, groups of hard-pressed people in and around Kortrijk repeatedly attacked coal transports. In Kooigem, for example, on the road from Tournai to Kortrijk, 150 civilians stormed a vehicle loaded with 5 tons of coal and made off with it in no time. Local police and English soldiers in nearby Mouscron were guarding the station's coal stocks and at night had to disperse angry mobs eyeing the fuel they so desperately needed. SHAEF in January 1945 acknowledged "that in most cases the pilferers are poor people who are genuinely unable to obtain coal by any other means."[67]

But many Belgians managed to obtain more coal than the ration allowed without getting their hands dirty. Those who had the money turned to the black market just as they had done during the German occupation. And they turned to these irregular lines of supply not just for coal, but for any Allied item imaginable. That large numbers of respectable civilians were stocking up on Allied supplies in the black market became clear during traffic checks just weeks after the liberation. Of the more than 13,000 civilian vehicles pulled over by gendarmes in Brussels in the first half of October 1944, for example, 570 were discovered to have British military petrol in their tanks.

If petrol was scarce, so were blankets, and they too provide an illustration of how pervasive black-market purchases were becoming in Belgian society. In October already, SHAEF noted that, among many other things, there was "an urgent need" for blankets. Once the harsh winter set in, however, Allied blankets became highly coveted not only as bed covers but, since clothing was scarce, as coats too. At the end of February, *Het Belang van Limburg* was commenting that the shortage of coats seemed to have been resolved as many women on Sunday were showing off brand-new outfits. The newspaper hinted at their unusual origin when it noted tongue-in-cheek that some could not help looking like "walking beds." Few of these women would have resorted to theft to obtain blankets. Indeed, many had come by them in what they

Brugge, November 18, 1944, Folder 958, AA 1311.

[67] Gendarmerie Brugge, March 14, 1945, Folder 1017; and February 28, 1945, Folder 1336; and Police Kortrijk, February 7, 1945, Folder 1025, AA 1311. SHAEFB, FR No. 8, 17, January 9, 1945, WO 202/688, AA 1230.

considered a completely legal manner as Allied soldiers quickly learned that, apart from rations and cigarettes, blankets were the perfect gift for families hosting them for dinner. Still, so many Belgians could be seen parading in coats of Allied fabric by the end of winter that it was clear most were buying them in the vibrant black market. "It was found impossible," SHAEF conceded in the summer of 1945, "to reverse public opinion with respect to the use of irregular markets for day to day requirements."[68]

Where it concerned blankets this was borne out when in October 1944, for example, police seized a batch of seventy-five US army blankets from a dealer in Tongeren and in February 1945 discovered another ninety such blankets waiting to be dyed in various colors in a building in Huy. But the illegal trade in army blankets was only the tip of a giant iceberg. There were huge profits to be had from a variety of Allied goods, and those involved in supplying such goods often belonged to organized crime operating on a large scale. SHAEF was well aware that "Sufficient imports and availability of goods are the only means to kill irregular markets." But it would take until the summer of 1945 for those means gradually to materialize. Until that time, even the most enterprising Belgians found themselves barred from legitimate trade in most of the goods the population craved. In May 1945, for example, Allied authorities reported the case of an inhabitant of Liège who was distributing leaflets to GIs encouraging them to ask their families to send over new or used typewriters. The man was willing, he announced, to pay them twice the price in the US. In the leaflet he clearly mentioned his name and address – describing himself as an "Import-Export Manager" – and military prosecutors had to admit that the entrepreneur was not committing any real offense. Nevertheless, in order to discourage more such requests, authorities decided to send the man "a serious warning" for soliciting "unauthorised importation." In such an adverse economic climate, criminal elements doing business in shadowy alternative circuits were bound to thrive.[69]

One of the very first products targeted by those elements was petrol. This was not surprising. At the time of the liberation in September 1944 there were sufficient stocks of petrol in the country to last through

[68] CAC Lt. Jean Crevecoeur, "Controles de la gendarmerie du 2 au 19 octobre 1944," Folder 947, AA 1311; SHAEFB, FR No. 2, 19, October 17, 1944, WO 202/682, AA 1230; Final Report No. 21, 26, July 21, 1945, AA 1798/9; and *HBVL*, February 27, 1945, 2.

[69] *HBVL*, October 25, 1944, 2; CAC Capitaine Perier to Ganshof, February 8, 1945, Folder 1000, AA 1311; and SHAEFB, Final Report No. 21, 26, July 21, 1945, AA 1798/9. On the Liège case, see Major Summers to Colonel Dumon, May 1, 1945 and Ganshof to Major Lerot, May 11, 1945, Folder 894, AA 1311.

that month only. But more petrol imports were not to arrive for Belgian consumption until the national civil import program would take off the following spring. In the meantime, Belgium remained entirely reliant on military stocks for a commodity that British and Americans forces thirsted for more than anything else. This meant that while troops were building giant petrol dumps across the country, civilians were receiving only minimal quantities of rationed fuel. And at least as late as February even the promised trickle of Allied petrol was not being delivered in full.[70]

Against this backdrop of a largely immobilized country, black-market operators were soon being drawn to the sprawling Allied dumps like moths to a flame. This was particularly true when it dawned that there were barely any soldiers guarding these. By November 1944 already, Belgium's military prosecutors were being alerted to the theft of petrol on a large scale. To protect the fuel dump at Kuringen, which stretched along the Albert Canal for 4 kilometers, at least twenty guards were known to be needed at night. Yet the actual British patrol comprised four men and a dog. The result was, one report noted, "massive theft." It was a similar story along the public roads in Leuven, for example, where an entire ship cargo of filled jerrycans was said to have been piled up. Or in Diest, where Belgian authorities feared not only theft, but sabotage too, as not a single guard could be spotted in the vicinity. By mid-November, General Walter Ganshof van der Meersch, Belgium's chief military prosecutor, was urging the Allied command to take action to halt the abuse. With Allied troops needed nearer the front, however, and local police and gendarmerie chronically understaffed, tightening security was not self-evident. As late as May 1945, for example, more than half a year after the first complaints, theft of petrol in the Diest area continued unabated.[71]

Meanwhile, as winter drew closer at the end of 1944, criminal elements turned their attention to yet another form of black gold. Late in December, the Allied military reported that coal worth 350 francs a ton at the pit was being sold for 5,000 francs in Brussels and 6,000 francs in Ghent. The promise of such profits caused coal transports to attract

[70] SHAEFB, Final Report No. 21, 31–2, July 21, 1945, AA 1798/9; and FR No. 10, 20, February 6, 1945, WO 202/690, AA 1230.

[71] For Kuringen, see "Vol et recel d'essence militaire," November 7, 1944, Folder 1336, AA 1311. For Leuven, substitute military prosecutor Peereboom to Ganshof, November 17, 1944, Folder C5-3, AA 1882. For Diest, Commissaris Gerechtelijke Politie Verschaffel to military prosecutor Leuven, November 10, 1944, Folder C5-3; and General Erskine to Ganshof, August 2, 1945, Folder C5-2-5, AA 1882. For the chief military prosecutor's warning, see Ganshof to Colonel Passmore, November 14, 1944, Folder 578, AA 1311.

not just poor people filling sacks and baskets for their personal needs. On its way from the pits in Limburg and the Borinage to the rest of the country, coal dwindled steadily as gangs siphoned off vehicles, barges, and trains whenever these dared halt for too long. It was not unusual, SHAEF mentioned, for a train loaded with 400 tons of coal to have lost 40 tons by the time it arrived in Antwerp or Ostend. Chief military prosecutor Ganshof van der Meersch pointed out that "veritable organizations" had been called into life to facilitate such illegal operations and that in Brussels boys accosted people in the street offering to sell sacks of coal from hidden locations. In January, when the coal shortage reached a crisis point as a result of the German offensive in the Ardennes, Allied authorities admitted to "a very large number of irregularities." Indeed, these were causing the "leakage" of a staggering 12,000 tons of coal a month from wagons in railway yards alone.[72]

But the disappearance of coal was only part of a much larger pattern of theft that in the course of winter began to strain relations between Allied forces and Belgians. As the official food ration remained meager, and at one point even shrank again, lucrative businesses were built with foodstuffs stolen from rich Allied stocks. The gendarmerie's monthly surveys of goods seized from illegal operators read like the inventories of giant supermarkets. In Namur in January, for example: 3 boxes of turkey, 6 boxes of Nescafé, 10 crates of tomatoes, 14 boxes of pork sausage, 36 boxes of condensed milk, 42 boxes of salmon, and 142 boxes of biscuits. Or in Leuven in April: 9 boxes of beans, 17 boxes of jam, 44 boxes of sardines, and 87 boxes of corned beef. Some of the gangs' more spectacular feats were the plunder from American stocks of 16 tons of sugar in Liège in January and 10 tons of chocolate in Limburg in March. Perhaps nothing caused a bigger stir, however, than the theft in the middle of winter of no less than 35 tons of military bacon earmarked for distribution among the inhabitants of Liège. To pilfer abundant Allied stocks was one thing, to steal food from hard-pressed civilians quite another, and public opinion in the Walloon city railed against the unscrupulous villains for almost a week.[73]

And it was not just food that disappeared into the increasingly well-oiled maw of the black market. Nothing that belonged to the Allies

[72] SHAEFB, FR No. 7, 16, December 26, 1944, WO 202/687; and No. 8, 16–17, January 9, 1945, WO 202/688, AA 1230. Ganshof to Procureur Generaal Hof van Beroep Gent, January 15, 1945, Folder 960, AA 1311.

[73] Gendarmerie Namur, MR February 8, 1945, Folder 1075; and Rijkswacht Leuven, MR May 9, 1945, Folder 1063, AA 1311. For Liège, see SHAEFB, FR No. 8, 20, January 9, 1945, WO 202/688, AA 1230; and SE Liège, WR February 3, 1945, Folder 1057, AA 1311. For Limburg, see letter to Lt. Col. Passmore, May 23, 1945, Folder 1335, AA 1311.

could fail to fetch fantastic prices in a society starved of almost any consumer good imaginable. The surveys drawn up by the gendarmerie for Namur and Leuven, for example, also mentioned – among many other non-perishable Allied items seized – cigarettes, cigars, shoes, trousers, gloves, shirts, blankets, tires, and soap. The gendarmerie of Kortrijk in February seized 76 army raincoats as well as 207 kilograms of soap, 751 kilograms of tobacco, tens of thousands of cigarettes, and 4,456 booklets of cigarette paper. There were reports even of radio transmitters changing hands on the black market as well as spare parts for tanks.[74]

At the end of the turbulent winter, someone from within the office of the chief military prosecutor wrote a letter to Baron Holvoet, the Prince Regent's private secretary. In it, he lamented, with a mixture of disbelief and shame: "The theft and dealings in stolen food, goods, and equipment committed to the detriment of the allied armies in Belgium are reaching proportions one does not suspect. The phenomenon at one point developed into something manifestly paralyzing operations. Even at the present time it is one of the factors seriously complicating transport and especially shipping."[75]

Preventive measures

Within weeks of their arrival, the Allied military came to realize the seriousness of the threat that theft was posing. And it prompted them to take increasingly severe countermeasures in concert with Belgian authorities. A first priority was to stop petrol from being plundered. This led local police and gendarmes to engage in regular traffic controls as early as the start of October. They forwarded the detailed results of the surprise checks to General Ganshof van der Meersch. He in turn kept the SHAEF Mission in Belgium informed of how many civilians had been caught using military petrol and to what extent their cases were being brought before the Belgian military tribunals. As the example of the Diest dump has shown, however, shortages of security personnel meant that these efforts had only limited success. Indeed, in the midst of the Ardennes offensive, Ganshof van der Meersch in a circular to the military prosecutors stressed that the theft of fuel was still assuming "considerable proportions," to the extent even that "at certain times motorized columns which had to rush to the theaters of operations were prevented from doing so because of a lack of fuel at the disposal of the armies in Belgium."[76]

[74] Rijkswacht Kortrijk, MR March 8, 1945, Folder 1025, AA 1311.
[75] Letter of March 12, 1945, Folder C5-15-0, AA 1882.
[76] Circular of January 8, 1945, Folder C4-4, AA 1882.

By the time of the German offensive, however, the Allies were even more concerned about the "alarming proportions" of coal being lost to the black market. Coal was fetching "enormous prices" and it was clear that the Belgian authorities were finding it impossible to deal with what were identified as "very big rackets." SHAEF complained that certain elements within mining management and distribution were guilty of corruption. Belgian security forces in turn complained that they did not have enough manpower to prevent the pilfering in stations and along tracks and roads. These circumstances led the Allied command to take "vigorous action" itself and to form the Belgian Coal Distribution Section late in December. This military organization was charged with "the protection of shipments from the mines to the consumer" and it developed a close relationship with Civil Affairs. The organization had its headquarters in Brussels and established a subsection in each of the mining areas. It dispatched a representative to every individual mine "to supervise the labelling and consignment of all trains, barges and lorries." It also lent support to Belgian security forces by posting military guards at railway yards known to be "vulnerable points." On top of that, "flying squads" were organized to be sent to trouble spots across the country. But the military had been sent to fight Nazi Germany, not Belgian corruption, and so they urged local authorities to step up their own fight against the illegal coal trade in tandem with Allied authorities. SHAEF leaned on Ganshof van der Meersch to make the Belgians crack down on pilfering. He in turn put pressure on the military prosecutors, ordering them to mete out harsher punishment and to use their powers to prompt police forces to become more assertive in apprehending offenders.[77]

The Allied authorities also asked the Belgian press and radio to cooperate by reminding people that purchasing coal on the black market was harmful to the military effort and punishable by law. This was just part of a much larger preventive campaign. It had commenced as early as October 1944 when SHAEF asked the government to issue a notice reminding people that it was illegal for civilians to be in possession of Allied equipment or supplies regardless of how they had obtained them. It was clear to most people, of course, that to purchase coal and Allied goods on the black market was illegal. But many found it hard to believe that they were not supposed to accept items from the soldiers themselves, even when offered in return for civilian goods or

[77] SHAEFB, FR No. 7, 16, December 26, 1944, WO 202/687; and No. 8, 16–17, January 9, 1945, WO 202/688, AA 1230. Ganshof to Procureur Generaal Hof van Beroep Gent, January 15, 1945, Folder 960, AA 1311.

services or merely as gifts. Indeed, early in January in Namur even a Belgian military prosecutor turned to the Allied authorities to have this clarified. The response from both the US Civil Affairs and Criminal Investigation detachments confirmed that GIs "under no circumstances" could "legally present" even "minimal quantities" of rations or cigarettes to civilians. Reporting on the Namur case, an SE officer noted that Belgian military tribunals could not be expected to pursue cases as long as Belgians remained confused about what in effect constituted an offense.[78]

That – and the dramatic increase in thefts of all kinds – is why SHAEF's Psychological Warfare branch in the middle of winter decided to launch a long-term "propaganda campaign to re-educate Belgian public opinion on the subject of the black market." The campaign gathered steam in February and its main purpose was to make clear to the population once and for all that there could be no excuse whatsoever for possessing Allied supplies of any kind. Military prosecutors drafted warnings to that extent, emphasizing that to ignore these was to break the law and to harm the nation, and they had mayors across the country post the notices. Ganshof van der Meersch personally intervened to have the same message spread by radio and all of the country's newspapers made sure to lend their cooperation too.[79]

Repressive measures

Meanwhile, however, theft and black-market activities had multiplied to the point where prevention had to be combined with tough repressive action. For this purpose, the Allies sought to join forces with the Belgian gendarmerie and police. They managed to do so in the course of the winter, and not just to combat the loss of petrol and coal. Early in February, for example, a Belgian officer who served as a liaison at the headquarters of the US Ninth Army reported to the head of the Belgian Military Mission that every day Allied goods were being stolen by the truckload in the region. He talked of "an epidemic" of plunder and warned that "an incredible amount" of American food and supplies was being handled by "civilians with few scruples." The Counter-Intelligence Corps and Criminal Investigation Division of the American military were

[78] SHAEFB, FR No. 1, 14, October 3, 1944, WO 202/681, AA 1230. For the correspondence to and from Namur, see Folder C5-0, AA 1882; and Folder 576, AA 1311.

[79] SHAEFB, FR No. 8, 17, January 9, 1945, WO 202/688, AA 1230; and Ganshof to Minister of Justice, February 6, 1945, Folder C5-0, AA 1882. On the press campaign, see Ganshof to Inspecteur Général à la Sûreté de l'État Louwage, February 14, 1945, Folder 576, AA 1311.

doing what they could, he noted, "but they are snowed under." "Can we not," he pleaded, "help them?"[80]

The Allied military certainly thought so. But the Belgian security forces too were eager to link up as they lacked not only the manpower but also the equipment to stem the tide of looting on their own. An SE officer in Liège complained that a crackdown "would have to take place on a vast scale to obtain any significant result" and that the city simply lacked the means for such an operation. The mayor of Antwerp wrote to the Minister of the Interior that police forces in the port were unable to conduct guard duties imposed on them by the Allies because they lacked not only weapons, but also trucks, jeeps, motorcycles, and motorboats. The gendarmes of Namur were even worse off. A report on their activities in January stated that they did not have at their disposal any motorized vehicles to move about the city. Meanwhile, the report continued, Namur's tram lines had not been repaired, the men's bicycles and tires were in bad shape, and making the rounds on foot was no easy task with worn-out shoes.[81]

Cooperation with Allied MPs had already improved early in the year where it concerned illegal trafficking in coal. But in response to the blatant security failures in other areas, Ganshof van der Meersch on February 16 in a secret message urged all military prosecutors to organize weekly meetings to improve the coordination between Belgian security forces and Allied MPs. By March it was clear from many accounts that this was bearing fruit in the form of increased house searches and raids conducted by integrated teams. In the town of Mechelen alone, for example, a report from the gendarmerie for that month mentioned no fewer than 149 operations with the support of British and American MPs.[82]

The cooperation was not without its fair share of problems, however. Military prosecutors in Antwerp province, for example, complained that MPs, with or without Belgian colleagues, were conducting house searches outside the allowed times and without either warrants or prior permission of the inhabitants. Indeed, in some parts of the province those searches were giving rise to serious tension between British MPs and civilians who in some cases insisted on official apologies.[83]

[80] Report from Capitaine-Commandant F. Goffinet, Folder 499, AA 1311.

[81] On Liège, see WR January 20, 1945, Folder 1057, AA 1311. On Antwerp, letter of January 22, 1945, Folder 1493, AA 1311. On Namur, MR February 8, 1945, Folder 1075, AA 1311.

[82] On the improved cooperation on the coal front, see SHAEFB, FR No. 10, 18, February 6, 1945, WO 202/690, AA 1230. For reactions to Ganshof's message, see Folder C5–17–3, AA 1882. On Mechelen, see MR April 1, 1945, Folder 1066, AA 1311.

[83] Krijgsauditoraat Turnhout to Ganshof, April 5, 1945, Folder C5-16–1, AA 1882; and Laureys, "Het bevrijde België," 68.

Allied authorities, on the other hand, found that Belgian security forces were not shying away from theft themselves. Some of the cases were relatively innocent. That which involved the 45th Field Hospital in Malmedy even had a farcical air to it. The gendarmes of Malmedy were housed in the basement of a building that was occupied by the US hospital unit. American supply clerks in various reports at the end of January 1945 testified that in the course of the last ten days "30 bars of soap and an undetermined amount of gasoline" had disappeared from the hospital premises. They did not find it hard to guess who was to blame. Indeed, an American sergeant in one report stated that he had caught "a gendarme trying to extract GI equipment, namely a pair of GI shoes, through a grilled window from supplies stacked outside."[84]

The antics of the gendarmes in Malmedy merely illustrated the extent to which these men shared in the privation of the population at large. But events elsewhere showed that police and gendarmes were also involved in less innocent rackets. In the autumn of 1944, for example, a policeman was charged after a train had been emptied of its load of coal at the station of Braine-l'Alleud, while in March 1945 six policemen were arrested for the theft of military items in Mechelen. The most spectacular case, however, came to light in the mecca of Allied supplies that was the port of Antwerp. In mid-February British MPs raided the homes of fifty policemen who belonged to a special port section in charge of combating theft. In the homes of sixteen of them they found Allied supplies. Half a dozen men were arrested for possessing considerable amounts of stolen food, soap, clothing, and a variety of other articles. One of them was the police inspector who headed the section.[85]

The Allied military authorities were outraged. It was true that the nature and quantities of the supplies found in the homes of the policemen pointed to the fact that they had been stolen for personal use and not to make a profit on the black market. On the other hand, if not even the police could be trusted, there was no hope at all of stemming the tide of theft and corruption in Belgium. Especially troubling in that regard was that the police inspector himself had been charged also with possessing a stolen British Sten gun. Allied authorities therefore insisted

[84] Report Captain Rodney G. Welsh, Detachment D7C1, Company C, 1st ECA Regiment, February 2, 1945, Folder 979, AA 1311.

[85] "Maintien de l'ordre," October 1944, Folder 951; SE Malines, WR March 16, 1945, Folder 1066; and SE report, "Province d'Anvers: Police d'Anvers," February 26, 1945, Folder 944, AA 1311.

Plate 6.2 An American soldier keeps an eye on Belgian workers in the port of Antwerp. (CEGESOMA, Brussels, picture number 29999)

that Belgian military justice should take "adequate measures" in dealing with these perpetrators.[86]

They were sorely disappointed when several weeks later a military tribunal sentenced the head of the port section to no more than five months' imprisonment and then went on to suspend that sentence on the basis of "his previous good character." What upset the Allied military even more was that the mayor of Antwerp in the week following the trial decided to reinstate the police inspector as if nothing had happened. Antwerp's CA headquarters lodged "vigorous protest" with the Belgian authorities, decrying the leniency shown to the inspector. "At a time when the Allied Armies are advancing," they complained in a letter to a provincial SE officer, "a great strain is put on the supply organisation of the army and a leakage on the scale which has now been reached in Antwerp is intolerable." The SE agreed with the Allied military and their combined pressure caused the police

[86] SE report, "Province d'Anvers: Police d'Anvers," February 26, 1945, Folder 944, AA 1311.

inspector to be suspended soon after. Even then, however, the Antwerp interim governor continued to plead the inspector's case. As mitigating circumstances he pointed out to the Minister of the Interior that the Allied goods in the man's possession had been for his own use only and that the events had, after all, taken place "after a long period of great privation."[87]

The role of the Belgian military tribunals

Much of the polemics surrounding the trial of the Antwerp port police reflected the broader debate between Allied and Belgian authorities regarding the role of Belgian military tribunals in the fight against theft and the black market. At first, from at least the end of October 1944, SHAEF was complaining about substantial delays in the prosecution of such offences. It conceded that in part this was almost inevitably the result of the preoccupation of the tribunals with the many collaboration cases. But as the abuses began to take on worrisome forms during winter, SHAEF also bemoaned the lack of a more systematic and severe punishment of these offences against Allied forces. This was causing General Ganshof van der Meersch serious headaches by the end of the year. In a circular to the military prosecutors on December 30 he expressed understanding for the Allied concern. Too much leniency from the Belgian courts, Ganshof van der Meersch said, risked minimizing in the eyes of the public a delinquency "that tends to obstruct and even paralyze the action of the combat forces." But the chief military prosecutor had his own worries too. He reminded the magistrates that the Anglo-American-Belgian convention of May 1944 had given Belgians the right to try offenses against Allied forces so long as they acquitted themselves of this task efficiently. He feared, however, that if the Allied military grew too dissatisfied, they might seize their right under international law to have their own courts take care of matters.[88]

In a letter to his superior, however, such concerns did not prevent Namur's military prosecutor from criticizing what he thought had become too harsh a repression by the end of winter. Indeed, the magistrate's tone at times sounded outright rebellious. If one had to believe the American authorities, he complained, each and every Belgian in

[87] SHAEF Mission (Belgium) to Ganshof, "Sentences by *Conseil de Guerre*," Folder 536; Hq Civil Affairs Antwerp to SE officer Antwerp, "Vols au préjudice des armées alliées," March 16, 1945, Folder 1331; and Governor Clerckx to Minister of the Interior, May 16, 1945, Folder 1331, AA 1311.

[88] SHAEFB, FR No. 3, 17, October 31, 1944, WO 202/683, AA 1230; and Ganshof to military prosecutors, January 8, 1945, Folder C4-4, AA 1882.

possession of even a minimum quantity of rations or cigarettes accepted as a gift from visiting soldiers had to be prosecuted. He was adamant that this was "too strict" a policy by far. "This way," he lamented, "our Allies seem to be taking back with one hand what they give away generously and amicably with the other." And the magistrate insisted that this was not only harmful to public opinion, but that it was ruining individual lives. He noted that some of the recent punishments meted out by military tribunals had been far harsher than they would have been for comparable offenses in peacetime, and that they "were dishonoring perfectly honest people." Given all that, the magistrate announced, the military tribunal of Namur had decided that punishment was "justified" only when military equipment was involved or in cases where it could be shown that Allied foodstuffs had been purchased. And the latter, he warned, was very difficult to do.[89]

The trial of the port police in Antwerp a month later showed that the opinion of Namur's military prosecutor was shared by other Belgian magistrates as well as politicians. And there was support for their view in the press too. The military tribunal of Antwerp at the end of March made sure to forward to the chief military prosecutor a copy of an article in *Le Matin*. The article responded to the recent Allied campaign prohibiting civilian possession of Allied articles no matter what their nature or provenance. *Le Matin*, the article said, had condemned stealing from the Allies on numerous occasions, but this new Allied policy could be described only as "draconian." "Not all Belgians are thieves," the article insisted, "but all – if they are smokers – smoke English or American cigarettes. Not all Belgians work on the docks but all, without a doubt, have consumed chocolate originating from London or Washington." "Moderation and tolerance," the article pleaded, "are the most reliable foundations of an intelligent justice."[90]

At the end of winter the Minister of Justice himself was adding his voice to the debate, though his objections concerned practicality more than the principle of the matter. In a letter to the chief military prosecutor, the minister urged the military tribunals to consider that Belgium's penal institutions were already filled to capacity with collaborators. He therefore instructed them to refrain from "carrying out on a massive scale the sentences of imprisonment for offenses committed against the Allied forces." The scope of the problem becomes clear when considering a survey of close to 1,000 such cases brought before the Belgian military

[89] Letter of February 24, 1945, Folder C5-0, AA 1882.
[90] The newspaper article is attached to a letter dated March 27, 1945, Folder C5-10, AA 1882.

tribunals in the second half of March 1945. The large majority of offenders had been caught with limited Allied supplies. Still, only in a very few cases of possession of no more than a few bars of soap or so did people escape punishment altogether. Though several were given a fine or the choice between a fine and imprisonment, many of the small fry were given no other option than to serve time. Possession of two army blankets, for example, sufficed for one offender to be sentenced to fifteen days behind bars. Nine packs of cigarettes, four bars of soap, eleven bars of chocolate, and more than a kilogram of cheese landed someone else in prison for fifteen days on top of a fine of 700 francs. As long as the quantities were limited, however, offenders did not receive prison sentences beyond two months. Civilians in possession of quantities pointing to black-market trading, however, could count on much harsher punishment. Two months of incarceration, for example, for 60 kilograms of coffee; 3 months for 8 pairs of combat boots; and 18 months for 780 boxes of margarine and 7,536 boxes of corned beef stolen somewhere near Bruges.[91]

As the Minister of Justice noted while these sentences were being passed, the accumulation of such imprisonments threatened to make an already difficult situation inside Belgium's penal system untenable. The problem was increasingly solved, however, by allowing those sentenced to less than two months in prison to lodge a petition for pardon. In the meantime these people would not have to go to prison as otherwise they risked having completed their punishment while awaiting the decision. By mid-May 1945, the military tribunal of Antwerp was reporting that such petitions were being launched "on a systematic scale." As most petitions did result in suspension, they observed, this meant that of fifty prison sentences of less than two months no more than three had actually been carried out. It appears that even SHAEF eventually came to accept this policy, although General Erskine did ask Ganshof van der Meersch to ensure that those sentenced to more than two months would have to go to prison, whether they had a petition for pardon pending or not.[92]

All in all, SHAEF at the end of spring found the situation "far more satisfactory" as a result of this firm but pragmatic approach. Reports in the press of hefty fines and significant prison sentences pronounced by military tribunals warned the population that stealing from the Allied military was no laughing matter. And it pleased Allied authorities that,

[91] The minister's letter is dated March 21, 1945, Folder C5-15-2, AA 1882. For the survey of cases for the period March 16 to 31, 1945, see Folder C5-4, AA 1882.

[92] General Erskine to Ganshof, March 9, 1945, Folder C5-15-1; and Krijgsauditoraat Antwerp to Ganshof, May 15, 1945, Folder C5-15-3, AA 1882.

with sentences now "generally adequate," an end had come to what they had for quite some time been complaining was "undue leniency." Just as importantly, after more than half a year of Allied complaints, the Belgian military tribunals, helped by the arrival of additional legal personnel in some of the cities with the largest backlogs, were at last trying cases "with reasonable promptness."[93]

A survey of the nineteen Belgian military tribunals concluded that between September 1944 and November 1945 they had looked at a total of 51,164 cases involving offenses against Allied forces. These had led to the conviction of 18,508 people. Among the five Belgian cities with the highest numbers of cases were Brussels and Liège, two of the major bases and rest and recreation centers for Allied troops. It was no coincidence that the other three cities – Antwerp, Ghent, and Bruges – happened to be the ports into which had poured all of the Allied abundance so enticing to a people in dire need of almost everything.[94]

The humiliation of abundance

Wounded pride

Allied affluence to many Belgians was as humiliating as it was tempting. "I myself was sixteen," a girl from Antwerp could still recall much later, "I was shabbily dressed and felt ashamed, because I thought these foreign liberators came from rich countries and were rich themselves." It was bad enough to be reminded of the poverty that war had brought. To live in a society where begging had become commonplace was even more painful. Belgians responded with a mixture of gratitude and shame to news that Britain was sending a shipment of used tires in March and that in Antwerp in spring a shipload had arrived from the US with more than 50,000 reconditioned shoes and 2,400 tons of handed-down clothing. People of all ranks were made to feel awkward about such dependence. Within weeks of the liberators' arrival, newspapers across the country were urging parents and teachers to tell children to stop asking troops for candy and cigarettes because it made Belgians look like beggars. "This cannot but leave a poor impression among these soldiers," one Flemish newspaper worried, calling it "a matter of attitude, prestige." Half a century later, a physician from Hasselt still felt piqued by the memory of having to beg the

[93] SHAEFB, FR No. 20, 15, June 26, 1945, WO 202/701, AA 1230; and Final Report No. 21, 28, July 21, 1945, AA 1798/9.

[94] "Justice militaire. 1er mars 1946," 65 and 87, Folder Z34-10-6-0-3, AA 1882.

Americans for penicillin "as if living in the Third World." How much more disgraceful it was then to see one's country descend into thievery. A teenage girl in Seraing remembered bursting into tears when American soldiers, fed up with yet another theft from their convoy, responded by searching every single house in her street. "I was sad," she explained, "that one would do such a thing to our liberators."[95]

The war caused serious injury to Belgian pride. When British troops settled down in Braine-le-Château, they challenged the inhabitants to some football. The Belgian home team lost the first game 7–3. They also lost the next game 3–1. For locals who had experienced nothing but defeat since 1940, the explanation could only be that the soldiers were much faster on their feet because they were better nourished. It was important for Belgians to convince the Allies that it was only because of the war that they and their country were in such bad shape. In Limburg, for example, the regional newspaper as part of its language lessons taught readers how to tell soldiers that it was the occupation that had made them lose weight and how to explain to them that their small country had been a happy one before the war. *Le Matin* in March 1945 railed against the tight restrictions on the possession of Allied items not only because it thought these to be draconian, but also because it considered them deeply insulting. "Honesty," it lectured the Allies, "is not the monopoly of one or a few nations. It is just that man finds it hard to resist the temptation of forbidden fruit when for a long time he has been deprived of fruit altogether."[96]

Belgians clung to anything that served to restore hurt pride. In that regard British General Horrocks showed keen judgment during the liberation in September. As soon as Brussels came into sight, he called forth some of the Belgian troops who had been with them since the Normandy invasion. And he made certain to assign the token forces a prominent place so that they could not be overlooked by the adoring crowds in the capital. Thereafter too, however, it remained important for a downtrodden people to be shown that they were more than wards of the liberating forces. General Eisenhower's much heralded visit to Belgium early in November, for example, gave people across the country an urgently needed boost of confidence. "It has," SHAEF noted, "raised public thought above internal problems and given the Belgians a feeling

[95] Irène Van Cleemput, AB 1591. On the arrival of used clothing from the UK and US, see SHAEFB, FR No. 12, 14, March 6, 1945, WO 202/692; No. 16, 18, May 1, 1945, WO 202/696; and No. 17, May 15, 1945, 14, WO 202/697, AA 1230. Coenegrachts, *Hasselt*, 33. *HBVL*, September 20, 1944, 1. For Seraing, see "Des habitants racontent," 26.

[96] Aelbrecht and Maghe, "Braine," 41; and *HBVL*, September 21, 1944, 1 and October 12, 1944, 2.

of being real Allies." SHAEF's Psychological Warfare branch that same month had the good sense to build on this feeling by designing a poster thanking the Belgians for their assistance in the Allied war effort. It was particularly pleasing then for the population to read in the press at the end of a humiliating winter that as prestigious an American newspaper as the *New York Herald Tribune* had singled out Belgium for its remarkable contribution to the war. Its London correspondent explained to audiences around the world that Belgium, because of the services and materials it and its colony had delivered, was "the first country in the history of mutual aid for this war that gave more to America and England than it received." It goes to show, a Flemish newspaper exclaimed, brimming with pride, that Belgium "in relation to its small and impoverished population carries the heaviest burden of war."[97]

Yet, to be shown this kind of respect by Allied troops became harder as increasing evidence of thieving did much to sour relations on the ground. Early in October 1944 already, annoyed soldiers in the capital scribbled on their trucks "No cigarettes for Papa" and "No chocolate for Mama." It prompted at least one newspaper to warn Belgians against acquiring "the unenviable reputation of being a people of bums." Concerned SE officers during the volatile winter reported that relations were becoming less and less amicable. Civilians who were employed in American depots in Hainaut province, one report stated, vociferously complained about distrustful GIs treating all Belgians as thieves by default. Indeed, the Americans apparently thought it necessary to surround the off-limits sections of the depots with nothing less than mines. Rough body searches made things worse and led to charges of "forced labor" and even of "Gestapo methods." Workers found it particularly upsetting that quite often these searches were conducted "with the help of negro guards," something that triggered a racist reflex among Belgians used to lording it over blacks in the Congo. In mid-January a wildcat strike erupted among dockers in Antwerp. They went back to work only after Allied authorities agreed to provide them with better means of transport. And after the MPs in particular promised that future inspections "would happen in a more civilized way."[98]

[97] Balace, "Bruxelles," 72; SHAEFB, FR No. 4, 1 and 9, November 14, 1944, WO 202/684, AA 1230; and "Wat WIJ doen voor onze Geallieerden," *HBVL*, February 20, 1945, 1.

[98] "Voornaamheid!" *HBVL*, October 10, 1944, 2; SE report on Hainaut, March 22, 1945, Folder 526, AA 1311; and De Vos, "US Forces," 191.

Plate 6.3 American soldiers flaunt their wealth in Liège. (CEGESOMA, Brussels, picture number 30004)

Overabundance and winter rumblings

"The Americans in general regard the Belgians as thieves and freeloaders, and [the Belgians] in general will be happy to see them leave, black as well as white." It was a harsh comment from the pen of a priest in rural Voeren who in November 1944 had still been able to write that his flock "admired the good manners of the Americans and had reciprocated with equal courtesy." But it was April 1945 now and much had transpired during the winter to cool relations significantly in Voeren and elsewhere.[99]

If the liberators during those critical months were put off by the scourge of theft, many Belgians took offense at Allied overabundance. And especially at the humiliating manner with which troops, and above all Americans, flaunted that excessive wealth. Reports from SE officers in Charleroi observed that, since most of the people in this industrial region were laborers and miners who were having a hard time making ends meet, a "chill" had descended on relations with the Americans who were receiving more than they could possibly consume. And that was true not only of meat and fats, but even of luxuries like coffee and

[99] Quoted in Waterval and Lensen, *Basse-Meuse*, 264 and 230.

chocolate. What was making civilians really angry, reports from across the American sector warned, was that GIs thought nothing of wasting food in full view of those going hungry. Convoys of army trucks loaded with food and cigarettes stood parked along the boulevards of Mons without tarpaulins. "The goods," one observer ruefully remarked, "are exposed to the bad weather and are spoiling while the population lacks everything." Elsewhere in Mons, civilians employed by the Americans claimed they saw soldiers throw food in dumpsters day after day. Rather than hand them out to the Belgian employees, GIs in their depots at Cronfestu preferred to burn entire boxes of chocolate bars for no other reason than that they showed slight traces of humidity. People in Arlon were deeply insulted to see Americans plow surplus food into the soil or douse it with petrol to make it unsuited for consumption.[100]

SE officers sounded increasingly alarmed at the effects that this disturbing behavior was having on public opinion. The popularity of the Americans in La Louvière was "crumbling away" because soldiers were squandering food "while the Belgians and especially the children have been deprived of the most elementary things for years." People in Charleroi denounced the "selfishness" of the GIs and it was feared that if this continued "the great majority might turn away from the allied armies." American authorities too came in for severe criticism. Inhabitants of Arlon were retrieving much that was edible from garbage heaps near American camps and could not help wondering why this food was not being distributed in a more "rational" fashion to benefit the local population. And how, people who lived near the large depots at Cronfestu demanded to know, could the waste of such "an extraordinary tonnage" be explained in view of the fact that "one pretends not to be able to send food to Belgium for lack of means of transport?" The population in Liège province, another report noted, is asking out loud why the government is not officially requesting the Allied authorities to intervene on their behalf.[101]

In not a few places Belgians were sounding outright rebellious. The Americans in Liège might be cracking down hard on the black market in military supplies, one SE officer noted, but the population "does not

[100] On Charleroi, see SE reports, February 3 and 24 and March 10, 1945, Folder 1020, AA 1311. On Mons, Dauphin, "La Belgique libérée," 166–9; and SE report, March 8, 1945, Folder 972, AA 1230. On Arlon, SE report, March 31, 1945, Folder 1005, AA 1311.

[101] On La Louvière, see SE report, February 22, 1945, Folder 1054, AA 1311. On Charleroi, SE, WR February 17, 1945 and MR March 8, 1945, Folder 1020, AA 1311. On Arlon, SE, WR March 31, 1945, Folder 1005, AA 1311. On Cronfestu, "Marchandises entreposées par l'Armée des États-Unis," report of March 17, 1945, Folder 527, AA 1311. On Liège, SE report, February 24, 1945, Folder 979, AA 1311.

easily accept measures taken by soldiers who mock misery by throwing away enough food to provision an entire region." "There is talk," an alarmed gendarmerie in Charleroi reported early in February, "of plundering military convoys because people believe that such plunder will not harm the supply of troops who waste without restraint." The military prosecutor in Namur who announced he would not punish civilians for possessing Allied food that they might have accepted as gifts did so not only because he thought this policy too harsh and indiscriminate. He was motivated also, he wrote to his superior, by another consideration: "There is almost no one who does not know from personal experience to what extent our Allies waste their food. People know it and see it. How can one feel guilty when one accepts what one so desperately needs and what may be thrown away when refused?"[102]

Most Belgian observers were convinced that the GIs were "acting without malice" and that they were simply not aware of the humiliation and anger they were causing by their careless display of wealth. In the final analysis, however, the exact reasons for the soldiers' inconsiderate behavior were of little import. "There is in all this," one SE officer suggested, "a lack of psychology that in some way we should delicately signal to our allies." Ganshof van der Meersch wholeheartedly agreed. Indeed, he believed that the situation was grave enough to warrant a more blunt message to the Allied command. "It has been reported to me several times," he wrote to General Erskine in English as early as January, "that the American Armies are destroying or wasting great quantities of army food in front of the local population ... In the very distressing state of the population, this creates, of course, an extremely unfavorable impression and I think that it would be highly advisable to draw the attention of the 12th Army Group to that situation." If this ever happened, the message certainly did not percolate all the way to the troops on the ground. In response to yet another complaint from an SE officer at the end of March, his headquarters in Brussels replied that they were well aware from numerous SE and gendarmerie reports "of the development among the population in certain parts of the country of sentiments regarding authorities and American troops that are not favorable and even hostile." But, the letter stated impotently, all this had already been brought to SHAEF's attention before. "It is important meanwhile," so the advice went, "to undertake whatever is possible

[102] On Liège province, see SE report, March 13, 1945, Folder 526, AA 1311. On Charleroi, gendarmerie report, "Esprit public," February 2, 1945, Folder 972, AA 1311. Military prosecutor Namur to Ganshof, February 24, 1945, Folder C5-0, AA 1882.

to prevent the emergence or development of a state of mind that could become dangerous."[103]

It was the end of winter that caused the crisis mood to recede and with it any danger of public opinion mutinying against liberators who had so much more than the liberated. But dissatisfaction lingered long after the thaw. A month after the war had ended in Europe, a report from Charleroi indicated that people still resented the fact that the Americans were setting up large depots "with products that were useless to the population." That it was not just American troops eliciting such responses was shown a day later. On June 9, 1945, the police in Blankenberge noted that one of the main points of criticism regarding British troops was that they were dumping large amounts of meat and fats onto garbage heaps while all this "could still have served to feed humans."[104]

Economic dependence

It was hardly surprising that people who hailed from countries rich enough to care little about wasted supplies were going to be paid well. That was especially true, one Belgian newspaper pointed out in January 1945, for those who came from "the blessed land of the Dollar." It devoted an entire article to an analysis of what were said to be the spectacular salaries of President Roosevelt and General Eisenhower. But it also highlighted the astonishingly generous pay that even a lowly American private was receiving for service to his country. For Belgians who observed the GIs in shops and cafés all this was hardly news. In December 1944 a disgruntled priest from Voeren noted that even the inflated prices in Visé left Americans unfazed as they stocked up on presents to send home for Christmas. "The Americans buy perfume," he wrote in his journal, "lots of perfume, and they smile at how low the prices are for them."[105]

It harked back to age-old images of America as the country where roads were paved with gold. But it just as easily revived concerns about the rampant economic power of the Anglo-Americans. That power had become particularly threatening by the late nineteenth century. The New Order press during the occupation had shrewdly manipulated

[103] Dauphin, "La Belgique libérée," 166–9; Ganshof to General Erskine, January 1945, Folder 528, AA 1311; and SE to Lieutenant Anspach, March 21, 1945, Folder 526, AA 1311.

[104] Charleroi, MR June 8, 1945, Folder 1020; and Police Blankenberge, WR June 9, 1945, Folder 1014, AA 1311.

[105] "Uit Dollarland," *HBVL*, January 9, 1945, 2. The Voeren priest is quoted in Waterval and Lensen, *Basse-Meuse*, 234.

these fears by calling on Belgians and other Europeans to unite under German leadership against the Anglo-Saxon bloc and its imperialist ambitions. Not that liberated shopkeepers in Visé and elsewhere were unhappy about soaring sales. Or that Belgians were particularly worried in 1944–5 about rapidly diminishing stocks of perfume. But there were fears that so much economic pull might leave Belgium and its more vital resources vulnerable. Those fears took the form of stubborn rumors that, while Belgians were cold and hungry, food and fuel from their own country were being shipped to England as if from a colony. Many Belgians had been craving fats for months, yet stories circulated of rich butter from local dairy factories on sale in shops across the channel. Even more humiliating were whispers in the midst of winter that British ships were being loaded with tons of scarce coal in the ports of Antwerp and Ghent. As the whispers swelled in force, the Allies eventually had no other choice than to refute them most forcefully on the front pages of Belgium's major newspapers.[106]

But unease among Belgians about their country's economic dependence also extended to the question of who would control the domestic market once the war was over. The Allied command sensed early on that this might become a problem. "If the Belgians are prevented from developing their own economy for lack of shipping," General Erskine warned presciently in December 1944, "they are certainly going to accuse the Allies of deliberately stifling the restoration of their industry for selfish reasons." A few months later, at the end of a winter in which many Belgian factories had been idle, SE officers were indeed signaling the emergence of such accusations. In Huy, for example, industrialists who were trying to start up production in February were said to be "encountering numerous difficulties with American authorities." The nature of the problems was not specified. Most probably the Americans refused to release raw materials other than those for priority war production. Or perhaps too many buildings remained requisitioned. But the real reasons for the delays mattered little for local businessmen, who increasingly came away with "the impression that our allies want to allow only their own products on the Belgian market."[107]

That was a threat to industrialists as well as their workforces. And fears were soon being fueled by rumors across the American sector that

[106] On the rumors see, for example, SE Tournai, WR March 10, 1945, Folder 1104; and SE Zotteghem, WR February 2, 1945, Folder 1119, AA 1311; and Janssen *et al.*, "Maasland," 143. On the Nazi press in Belgium and Anglo-American power, see Stirk, "Anti-Americanism," 72–3 and 75.

[107] SHAEFB, FR No. 6, 2, December 12, 1944, WO 202/686, AA 1230; and SE Huy, WR February 17, 1945 and March 8, 1945, Folder 1048, AA 1311.

giant depots were being built up not only for military victory but also with an eye to a postwar economic offensive. Many of the rumors originated with Belgians who worked in the depots. They were astounded not only by the "immense quantities" of supplies, but also by the "extremely diverse" range of American items. Indeed, what raised most suspicion was that many of those items seemed to have nothing to do with the military whatsoever. People in Soignies talked of crates full of combs and lipstick. In Jemappes there were said to be large stocks of feminine beauty products and lingerie. Workers at Cronfestu insisted that the depots held everything from pocket knives to lighters and wallets. One stupefied Belgian employee there insisted he had seen at least 50 cubic meters of crates filled with nothing but playing cards. "An approximate calculation," an equally incredulous SE officer reported, "has enabled me to estimate the packs of cards at one million if the information I was given is correct."[108]

Some of these stories took on lives of their own and became necessarily exaggerated. Most of them were true, however, as they merely inventoried the merchandise that post exchanges on military installations sold to GIs as a matter of routine. But even if people had known this, it would have been impossible for them to believe that soldiers fighting a war were having easier access to consumer articles than civilians who had been deprived of them for so long. Inevitably, therefore, conspiracy theories arose to explain that which did not seem to make any other sense. In Jemappes, for example, an SE officer reported that the population had concluded the Americans could only be building up such stocks "to pave the way for a postwar market that no other industry can compete with." Indeed, the allegations in Jemappes were stirring up sufficient unrest for the SE in mid-March to launch an investigation and to be given access to the depots. The investigating officer afterwards reported that he had found no evidence of supplies for women, although he added that because of the large number of women in the US military such supplies might be present in depots elsewhere. The Jemappes depots did hold large quantities of candy and chocolate, but, the officer pointed out, everyone knew that American troops were "crazy" about sweets and that these were part of their standard ration. In short, he concluded, there was no foundation for "rumors that the American government supposedly engages in commercial activity under the cover of its army."

[108] SE Soignies, WR March 17, 1945, Folder 1098, AA 1311. On Jemappes, see SE report, March 9, 1945, Folder 526, AA 1311. On Cronfestu, see "Marchandises entreposées par l'Armée des États-Unis," report of March 17, 1945, Folder 527, AA 1311.

"What is true," he emphasized, "is that all these rumors seriously sap public opinion's confidence in our allies from the United States."[109]

Such an investigation did little, however, to lay suspicions to rest. A detailed analysis of the state of mind of people in La Louvière, a city not far from Jemappes, still held the following observation at the end of March: "The population, even the working class, is much preoccupied also by certain rumors that claim the Americans in our country are stocking great quantities of diverse merchandise that have nothing to do with troop supply or the pursuit of the war; they fear seeing the Belgian market inundated by foreign products, after the end of hostilities, causing our own work force to become unemployed." This, the report said, continued to cause "unfavorable reactions" among the population. The report's authors were worried enough about these reactions to have copies sent to the Belgian ministers of economic and foreign affairs as well as the Prime Minister himself.[110]

Meanwhile, unrest was growing on yet another part of the economic front. Belgian employers increasingly resented the way in which the Anglo-American militaries were dictating labor conditions. "The agreement under which the Government has undertaken to administer and pay civilian labor used by the Allied forces," SHAEF noted in mid-November 1944, "has worked satisfactorily in most places from the military point of view." But things looked quite different from the civilian perspective. SHAEF in the same November report asserted that civilians working for the Allies were being paid in accordance with the 60 percent increase over the 1940 wages that the Belgian government had decided on after the liberation. Belgian employers insisted, however, that to attract workers rapidly and in sufficient numbers, Allied forces in reality were offering wages that went way beyond the official rates. Indeed, SHAEF at the end of December seemed to agree that all was not as straightforward as it had been letting on when it admitted that there were continuing efforts "to establish more equitable and uniform wage rates." The problems persisted throughout the winter and Belgian accusations became more heated when in spring industrial production accelerated and competition with the Allies for civilian labor grew more intense. Newspapers in April joined forces with local employers, asserting, as SHAEF noted, "that the Allies were spoiling the labor market by high and uncontrolled wage rates." To counter this, SHAEF backed the Ministry of Labor in a press campaign driving home that there was

[109] Reports SE, March 9 and 15, 1945, Folder 526, AA 1311.

[110] Report SE La Louvière, March 28, 1945 and attachment "Extrait d'un rapport en date du 23 mars 1945," Folder 526, AA 1311.

"no justification for the charge" because, after all, Belgian authorities under the Mutual Aid agreements were paying the wages themselves.[111]

This was true, of course. But SHAEF did not mention that in many circumstances Allied forces left the Belgian government no choice but to pay inflated wages. As early as September 1944, Belgian authorities had agreed that the Allies were allowed to engage in "direct employment" of civilians whenever a mayor was unable or failed to supply the required labor. In such cases the Allies could freely negotiate the terms of employment (including wages), while the mayors remained responsible for pay (later to be reimbursed by the government). But even where the mayors maintained active control over the recruitment of workers, Allied forces could exert significant pressure to have municipal authorities agree to wage rates higher than the official ones. One such situation arose, for example, in Liège province when large numbers of mostly American troops were massed together for the spring offensive. A meeting was called on March 22 at the town hall in Verviers to decide on the wage rates for a large number of job categories in the region. These ranged from chauffeurs to masons and electricians, and the Allies urgently needed to fill them all. SHAEF had dispatched a Belgian officer to preside over a meeting that brought together in a single room American officers, local officials, delegates from all of the main unions, and a representative for the employers. The ad hoc commission wasted no time. By the end of the day the group had hammered out an agreement allowing the Americans for most of the jobs on the list to pay on average 25 percent higher wages than the Belgian employers in the region. In a report drawn up after the meeting, an upset employers' representative cried foul. The Allies, he alleged, had seriously twisted his arm to achieve that outcome. He charged that they had "completely modified the atmosphere" by inviting no fewer than seven union delegates as opposed to just one spokesperson for the employers. And he virulently protested "the unexpected meddling" of military personnel who were unfamiliar with the region's economic climate and prior labor agreements. They were, he claimed, too inexperienced to deal with "a question so delicate and complex." Most frustrating of all, he lamented, was that whenever he had launched a "well-argued" attack against their proposals, the American officers had most easily parried it "by appealing to patriotic sentiments."[112]

[111] SHAEFB, FR No. 4, 20, November 14, 1944, WO 202/684; No. 7, 21, December 26, 1944, WO 202/687; No. 14, 1, April 3, 1945, WO 202/694; and No. 15, 10, April 17, 1945, WO 202/695, AA 1230.

[112] SHAEFB, FR No. 1, Appendix C to Section IV, October 3, 1944, WO 202/681, AA 1230; secretary of the Fédération Patronale de l'Industrie Textile to Administrateur-

What annoyed Belgian employers across the country was that such arrangements were causing their workers to become increasingly brazen. The day after the Verviers meeting, for example, leather workers in the area were demanding a pay rise similar to that accorded the employees of the Americans. In Leuven two weeks earlier, personnel of Artois and several other breweries had gone on strike because they claimed that people employed by the Allies on nearby bases were earning 50 percent more. When some months later, perhaps in response to inequitable pay rates in the region, the British military tried to lower the wages of civilian employees at its food depots in Lommel, these too threatened to walk out.[113]

The biggest challenge for Belgian employers, however, was that workers were now using their newfound freedom to vote with their feet. One of the reasons why coal production remained below expectations in the autumn of 1944 was the shortage of miners. An investigation of the labor situation in Hainaut province, for example, found that this was exacerbated by American hiring practices. Miners preferred to work for the US military because of markedly higher wages, but also because of the promise of warm meals rich in calories. There were recruiting problems for similar reasons in other sectors too, even in the midst of winter, when unemployment figures were generally high. When in January 1945 General Erskine expressed concern to the Minister of Defense about the difficulties of attracting more police and gendarmes in Antwerp, the Belgian minister replied that the British military was aggravating the problem by luring people away with higher-than-average wages.[114]

But it was when winter had run its course that a chorus of complaints rose from the ranks of industrialists across the country. Before long, SE officers were bringing a litany of cases to the attention of their headquarters in Brussels. As more and more factories reopened their gates, attracting sufficient numbers of workers proved particularly hard for employers who experienced direct competition from Allied forces offering all kinds of conditions they could not match. Factory owners in Roeselare were astounded to learn that the Allies were not just paying higher standard wages, but that they added significant extra pay for work in the evenings, raised the rate by 50 percent for night shifts, and doubled the remuneration for work on Sundays. "There is not a single private

délégué of the CCI, March 28, 1945, Folder 980; and report SE Verviers, March 29, 1945, Folder 979, AA 1311.

[113] Report Gendarmerie Leuven, March 17, 1945, Folder 1634; and Police Neerpelt, WR June 23, 1945, Folder 1076, AA 1311.

[114] SE memorandum, October 20, 1944, Folder 973 and Minister F. Demets to General Erskine, January 30, 1945, Folder 1493, AA 1311.

business," one report lamented, "that can afford to pay its workers such wages."[115]

In some cases the effects proved crippling. Fifty percent of workers previously employed in a factory in Vorst that produced steel wire and sheeting had failed to return by early April. In large part, it was claimed, because many preferred to work for the Allies. In another business near the capital, a tannery in Zaventem, more than 160 people had been hired by May. But some one hundred positions remained unfilled. And again the irresistible pay and warm meals of the Allies were pointed to as the main cause. Despite efforts since the autumn of 1944 to stem the flow, as late as the end of May 1945 the Prime Minister's office, SE headquarters, and SHAEF were writing back and forth on "the question of the considerable exodus of miners to the American depots." That same month, the gendarmerie reported from Perwez that the question of agricultural labor had become "almost a nightmare" as many fled the fields for the mines or the Allied armies.[116]

Cultural threats

The overwhelming power of the Anglo-Americans caused concern not only about the inroads they were making in the Belgian economy. There were those also who wondered whether the cultural juggernaut the Allies had unleashed could ever be restrained again. Some of the new elements of that surging culture required only minor adjustment. The Belgian foreman at the American rest and recreation center in Eisden at the end of his first day thought nothing of lowering the Stars and Stripes without ritual and climbing down from the roof with a crumpled flag under his arm, until he received some serious scolding from a GI, who told him that this was not how one treated the American flag and that it could carry serious punishment. The thousands of Belgians who listened to a radio speech by the American ambassador on Thursday, November 23, may have wondered why he picked that particular day to address them so formally. But they were soon learning much more about the meaning of that quintessentially American celebration called Thanksgiving. For many, however, the arrival of a competing language was quite another matter. In a cartoon in the *Gazette de Liège* in January 1945 a father and his small son walk past an ice-cream parlor. Signs in

115 "Province de Flandre Occidentale. Objet: Situation à Roulers," January 9, 1945, Folder 1090, AA 1311.

116 SE Bruxelles, WR April 6, 1945, Folder 1018; Gendarmerie Zaventem, MR June 1, 1945, Folder 1118; Ganshof to Capitaine Drapier, May 26, 1945, Folder 893; and Gendarmerie Perwez, MR June 1, 1945, Folder 1084, AA 1311.

the window are screaming for attention in English. A tiny sign timidly announces: "French spoken." The drawing in a joking way betrayed latent anxiety about what the future would hold in store for a people's cultural identity.[117]

Liège was one of Belgium's major American garrisons and the ice-cream parlor's sign might have offered the inhabitants at least some solace that the city was still theirs too. As early as December 1944 an article in another newspaper had described Liège as an American city where people chewed gum, *coiffeurs* had restyled themselves into hairdressers, cinemas showed nothing but Hollywood movies, and libraries could not keep up with the demand for American novels. But such a cultural shift was of particular concern, of course, to those who had made culture their business. Purveyors of the arts – high, low, and middlebrow – scrambled to reposition themselves in a market where Anglo-Americans in the blink of an eye had come to dominate like never before. In terms of its theater programming, for example, the Belgian capital before the war had been regarded as "a province of Paris." Plays of Anglo-American origin had been much less influential. During the German occupation they were banned altogether, although the *Propaganda Abteilung* had made an exception for work by Shakespeare. But war and occupation had caused Brussels' theater world to be cut off from Paris, and in a sense this had provided it with a new élan, allowing a more home-grown art to be given expression. Indeed, some voices in the capital's theater press feared that liberation would mean the return of French domination. Within weeks of the liberation, however, those concerns were drowned by the cultural deluge washing in from the Atlantic. The French come-back stalled amidst the continuing disruption of war. A play with Gaby Morlay in Brussels had to be cancelled, for example, when the French star encountered problems with her passport. Meanwhile, the demand for that which the Germans had prohibited was overwhelming and theaters were quick to put on anything exuding the magic Anglo-Saxon touch. The Belgian capital soon was alive with British plays by Noël Coward and George Bernard Shaw, a slew of American comedies, and countless revues spiced up with contagious jazzy tunes.[118]

Yet, despite this buoyant atmosphere, by the end of 1944 theater revenues were down. People preferred to escape to the more powerful dreamworlds of the cinema. And they snapped up tickets most easily if these promised access to the shiny worlds dreamed up by Hollywood.

[117] Kohlbacher, "Eisden," 34; SHAEFB, FR No. 5, 7, November 28, 1944, WO 202/685, AA 1230; and Sulbout, "Liège," 27.

[118] The article on Liège appeared in *L'Express* on December 22, 1944. See Sulbout, "Liège," 40. Duchenne, "Bruxelles," 12–13, 21–5, and 39–42.

Distributors and cinema operators in Brussels, who before the war had been heavily reliant on French productions, had reasons to be worried about this abrupt change. Not only were they left stunned by the massive shift of demand in favor of films made in the US, they also decried the fact that no new French films were entering the distribution channels. At the same time, rather than see a theater play, many Belgians also preferred to dance away the dark nights to the upbeat rhythms of jazz. But in the Belgian music world too there were voices expressing concern about the Anglo-American powerhouse; voices that sounded small and timid against the confident and swanky blare of the new victors. "As to the question of Belgian pieces," *Sélection Magazine* lamented in January 1945, "they are, for the moment, relegated to second plan … The public from all sides demands English and American pieces." That situation, the Belgian music magazine acknowledged, had already existed before the war, but it now threatened to repeat itself with renewed force. "The jazz music of our own composers," the complaint went, "is going to be pushed out of the market bit by bit … by London and New York. What can we do? We are such a small country!"[119]

The irritations of occupation

Allied relations with women

Rivalries

Nothing caused the male half of the Belgian population to feel more humiliated than the supreme ease with which the liberators established dominion over their women. Tens of thousands of Belgian men in their prime were simply unable to put up resistance because they were far from home as POWs, forced laborers, and deportees. Not quite three weeks had passed since the liberation when *La Wallonie* lambasted women who, it said, by attending Allied dances, were showing disrespect for the men imprisoned in Nazi Germany. The association of deported workers also voiced serious concerns, accusing the Allied soldiers of abusing the situation by shamelessly seducing women who had been alone for too long.[120]

Men in Belgium were scarce. And those who remained were often too young or too old. Or they were wan and thin and poorly dressed.

[119] Marechal, "Cinéma et jazz à Bruxelles," vol. B, 23–4 and 40 and vol. C, 9–10.

[120] The article in *La Wallonie* appeared on September 28, 1944 and is quoted in Sulbout, "Liège," 28. On the deported workers, see Lagrou, "US Politics of Stabilization," 241, note 60.

Plate 6.4 Relations between Allied soldiers and Belgian women would soon give rise to much criticism. (CEGESOMA, Brussels, picture number 29474)

By contrast, the well-fed liberators in their neat uniforms appeared exotic and virile, exuding an almost irresistible sex appeal. Early in November 1944, Limburg's newspaper ruefully observed that the young men of the provincial capital were walking the streets all by themselves, while American soldiers could be counted on to be seen arm in arm with local girls. For the article's title the disapproving journalist changed the expression "New lords, new laws" to "New lords, new love."[121]

Before long, girls dating Allied soldiers were changing tongue-tying first names like Victorine, Lambertine, and Joséphine into the smoother-sounding pet names Vicky, Betty, and Josy. But what women might experience as exciting reinventions, men often regarded as insufferable betrayals. It was the accumulation of indignities like these that increasingly caused local men to be up in arms against their liberators. And it was the dance halls and ball rooms that were shaping up to be the

[121] *HBVL*, November 3, 1944, 2.

main battlegrounds. Allied troops did their best to monopolize these places, eagerly inviting Belgian women to their dances, but quite often bluntly denying access to local men. A nineteen-year-old who had on several occasions received such treatment from the Americans in Dolhain remembered the situation as "somewhat vexing." That was putting it mildly, however, for in many communities it was proving to be a main source of irritation. When the British military in Arendonk announced a ball in the local dance hall, their decision to invite only women triggered such a storm of protest that they were forced to change their mind for the sake of public relations. The British troops in Sint-Niklaas, however, refused to budge on the issue. In response, the town's men retaliated by organizing their own balls without extending invitations to the liberators. "We are afraid," a local SE report noted, "that such trifles might cause feelings harmful to currently much needed good relations."[122]

Not that any alternative circuit of dances attempted by local men ever stood a chance of competing on an equal footing with those organized by Allied troops. Anglo-American charm offensives routinely involved the shameless flaunting of economic and cultural sweeteners to lure women to their parties. Girls in Verviers who on Friday nights agreed to accompany GIs to dances organized by the Victory Club were promised access to the soldiers' movie theater the next day – an especially enticing prospect as it was the only place where the newest Hollywood productions could be viewed. In Liège, a city overrun by American troops, women were encouraged to sign up as members of a semi-official club providing GIs with recreational activities. If they did, they were told, they would receive priority invitations whenever one of the big American stars was scheduled to appear in person. Yet many women were drawn to the Allied dances by the promise of substance as much as glitter. In the summer of 1945 a left-wing resistance paper berated American and British troops for the indecency of bribing girls to their dance clubs with free sandwiches, coffee, and tea.[123]

Such circumstances inevitably caused mounting frustration. One of the much-appreciated English plays in the Belgian capital in October 1944 was *Sérénade à Trois*. A woman who is unable to choose between two lovers avoids the Gordian knot altogether by deciding to keep both. What may have seemed like an elegant solution on stage proved

[122] On the name changes, see Sulbout, "Liège," 118. On Dolhain, see transcript interview Georges Brausch, 4, M348–9, AA 1593. Van Gorp, *Arendonk*, 179–80. SE Sint-Niklaas, WR January 18, 1945, Folder 1094, AA 1311.

[123] Wynants, *Verviers*, 155. For Liège, see Lognard-Poncin and Michel, *Chaudfontaine*, 45. The leftist comment appeared in *Front* on July 15, 1945 and is quoted in Lagrou, "US Politics of Stabilization," 241, note 58.

to be much more problematic in real life. The local press in Limburg responded with alarm to the number of engagements broken off as a result of flings with Allied soldiers. In response to the same problem, a newspaper in Verviers scoffed that soon the town's young men would be uniting in a "club of the abandoned." The divorce rate in Liège in the last year before the war had stood at not quite 13 percent. After the liberation, it jumped from over 9 percent in 1945 to more than 17 percent in 1946 and nearly 22 percent in 1947. Those increases can be adequately explained only by a complex set of factors brought about by the disruption of war. But since 70 to 80 percent of these divorces took place without mutual consent, involving procedures lasting one to two years, clearly many were set in motion in 1944 and 1945, when Allied soldiers were breaking hearts on a massive scale.[124]

The breaking hearts of civilian men can be traced in mournful ditties composed across the country to express ache and despair about loves lost to the liberators. But some of the wronged men were not given to song and refused to accept defeat good-naturedly. Fifty years on, people from Waterloo in interviews about the liberation remembered that the village during the Second World War had refused to submit to a less honorable victory by British forces. On more than one occasion, they recalled, young men had become embroiled in brawls and given their best in fistfights over women. Even a cursory reading of a single regional newspaper reveals that there were quite a few men who carried not just anger in their hearts but murder. In November 1944 a middle-aged man in Genk spotted his eighteen-year-old girlfriend on the street in the company of a soldier, reached for a knife in response, and stabbed her in the abdomen. Several months later, a twenty-four-year-old man in Eisden fired three shots at his fiancée and then killed himself. He did so, *Het Belang van Limburg* explained, because "in his opinion she had too much sympathy for an Allied soldier." A man who returned home from work in the Waterschei mine had no reason to doubt this when he caught his wife in bed with a liberator. The soldier managed to escape. But the miner grabbed the weapon the soldier had left behind and used it against his wife. After he had attempted to kill his children too, the aggrieved husband put the barrel against his head and pulled the trigger one last time.[125]

[124] Duchenne, "Bruxelles," 39; "Een noodkreet over Limburg," *HBVL*, February 8, 1945, 1; Wynants, *Verviers*, 155; and Malevez, "Aspects démographiques," 87–9.

[125] Catoire and de Bellefroid, "Waterloo," vol. II, 2. The stabbing and shootings are described in *HBVL*, November 19, 1944, 2 and March 13, 1945, 1; and in Janssen *et al.*, "Maasland," 138.

Thrill seekers

Some women were driven into the arms of Allied soldiers by feelings of true love that would form the basis of extended relations and even marriage. But in war, much more so than in peace, how much of the attraction was love and how much of it lust? After four hard years of occupation, the liberation released a jumble of pent-up emotions. As the citizens of Paris rose up against the Germans in August 1944, Pablo Picasso caught the ebullient mood in a painting aptly named *The Triumph of Pan*. The work depicts an Arcadian world of joy and dance in which centaurs engage in orgiastic rites with nymphs offering fruit and baring oversized breasts. They all pay homage to Pan in a heavily eroticized scene symbolizing rebirth and regeneration. Into this world of pleasure seeking stepped countless virile-looking soldiers from exotic-sounding places, young men who for years had been denied regular sexual relations.[126]

The consequences were easy to predict but impossible to contain. And they became obvious almost straightaway. "The Germans have barely gone," *De Gazet van Antwerpen* noted disapprovingly, "and droves of women are already homing in on the English Tommies. Acquaintances are being made in no time, dates are arranged, and intimacies are being permitted as if they were old friends." Offended inhabitants of Ghent claimed that just days after the liberation more and more used condoms could be seen littering streets and parks. Newspapers were addressing the licentious behavior of GIs and women in Liège at least as early as November 1944. *La Wallonie* on December 16 printed an open letter to the American authorities in the city, asking them to make clear to the soldiers "that they should calm their conquering instincts." This apparently ruffled feathers in certain quarters because three days later the newspaper printed a rectification, demanding from women too that they showed "more acceptable behavior and the same restraint in their relations with soldiers as in that with civilians."[127]

The exceedingly cold winter, meanwhile, did little to dampen passions. Limburg's newspaper in February urgently addressed the province's girls, saying it understood full well that the sorrows and limitations of war had taken from them five of the best years of their lives, a time that should have been one of pleasure and entertainment. But, the newspaper continued, that could not be an excuse for "the low pleasure and continuous flirting" that were now plaguing the country. The "moral degeneracy"

[126] For the Picasso painting, see Newman, "The Triumph of Pan." On the erotic nature of liberation, see also Brossat, *Libération*, 135–6 and 160–1.

[127] The Antwerp article is reproduced in Van Cauwenbergh, *Antwerpen*, 52. Marchal, *Gent*, 149. *La Wallonie* is quoted in Sulbout, "Liège," 34–5.

was fueled by alcohol and a "dance craze," and not least by the jazz music that made youngsters "jump around for hours." In those circumstances it was hardly surprising that "the inevitable" happened when girls returned home late at night with soldiers they barely knew. On the other side of Belgium's language boundary, Verviers' chief of police readily agreed with this assessment and went on to publish his own stark warning to parents in the local press. Young girls, he claimed, were "in grave danger." Not only because they were "in the grip of a frenzy of pleasure," but also because they tended to be too "impressed by the prestige of the uniform and heroism." That, he wrote, combined with alcohol, dances, and darkness, was a sure recipe for "disaster."[128]

Gold diggers and prostitutes

But the dire warnings of moral decay among Belgian women at the end of a harsh winter also hint at the more mercenary interests underlying the apparent search for thrills. Gaby Bex in Zepperen in 1944 was twenty-six and had two children. Her husband had been a POW in Germany since 1940. She was grateful to have American artillery battalions and quartermaster companies stationed near her village, for they provided her with much-needed work. GIs were happy to bring her their laundry and there were days when she had more than 20 meters of washing hanging out on the lines. But it was grinding work in return for no more than a few bars of soap or chocolate. Inevitably there were women who figured they could extract significantly more material advantage by employing their charms. "And do not," *Het Belang van Limburg* continued its tirade against loose women in February 1945, "tell us it is Patriotism! This behavior is usually driven by selfish motives: it is all about chocolate, soap, and meat." A ditty in the Liège dialect alleged the same, with a refrain mocking GI catcalls: "Mademoiselle listen to me/Zig zig with me/Chocolate for thee."[129]

There is no doubt that the liberators were attracting women from all walks of life. Commenting on the popularity of Allied dances in Heist, a man wrote in his diary in January 1945: "The women who are not involved with the English or Americans are rare, even girls from the better classes." His observation was corroborated by contemporaries across the country. Gold diggers too, of course, could be found in any

[128] "Een noodkreet over Limburg," *HBVL*, February 8, 1945, 1; and "Aan onze Limburgsche Meisjes," *HBVL*, February 11, 1945, 1. The police appeal in the Verviers press was transcribed in a report to the SE of March 22, 1945. See Folder 979, AA 1311.

[129] Celis *et al.*, *Zepperen*, 282 and 290; "Een noodkreet over Limburg," *HBVL*, February 8, 1945, 1; and Lecerf, *Libération*, 363.

class. But it stands to reason that those who had least could see even more incentives to get close to Allied soldiers and their tantalizing supplies. The socialist newspaper *Le Peuple*, for example, claimed that the young women who registered to attend British dances were generally "honorable girls" but "for the most part of modest origins." A careful analysis of the marriage statistics for Liège in 1944–47 suggests that class played a role too in determining who was most likely to marry a GI. More often than not they were girls from modest social milieus whose mothers did not work outside the home even though their fathers held rather poorly paid jobs. All this was not helped by soldiers exaggerating their social status and wooing women with stories that turned grocery shops into supermarkets and dirt farmers into wealthy ranchers. It will remain forever unknown how many women followed their husbands from the Old World to the New impatient to see their vaunted gold mines.[130]

What is certain is that during the winter voices could be heard questioning the sincerity of the feelings women so openly displayed towards the liberators. "Hearts for sale" is how some newspapers summed it up at the start of 1945. Public opinion, and men in particular, thought it disgraceful and demeaning. A doggerel published in one of the Catholic newspapers branded as "sluts" women who feigned affection for soldiers for no other reason than to wheedle cigarettes, chocolate, and cans of corned beef. There was a thin line between this kind of behavior and prostitution. During the liberation, of course, professional prostitutes were involved in very brisk business wherever troops congregated. In Liège at the end of 1944 no fewer than fifty-nine brothels were operating with official authorization. In front of one of nearby Hasselt's brothels, one inhabitant recalled, "The soldiers waited in line, the way we did to buy fish during the war!" A police report in March 1945 claimed that in peacetime there had been no more than ten registered prostitutes in Verviers while now that number had climbed to 150. But the ranks of the professional working girls were swelled by large numbers of amateur prostitutes forced by the exigencies of war to put up for sale much more than their hearts. Flyboys from the American air base at Florennes loved to go to the professional girls in the night clubs of Charleroi. But "public rumor" insisted that each day too "adventuresses" arrived at the Florennes station "and threw themselves into the arms of the Americans in exchange for nylon stockings, cigarettes, alcohol, or dollars." More likely than not this was more than just rumor.

[130] Patteet, *Heist*, 403; "Les Dancings et le péril vénérien," *Le Peuple*, February 1, 1945; and Malevez, "Aspects démographiques," 80–118 and 133. On soldiers exaggerating their social status see, for example, Pauwels, *Canadezen*, 157–8 and 160.

Research into the world of prostitution in Liège during the liberation, for example, points to a large discrepancy between the number of registered prostitutes and the actual number of women selling their bodies to troops for benefits of all kinds.[131]

Reports indicated that by mid-January Belgian public opinion had become gravely concerned about the moral corruption of females of all ages. The SE signaled, for example, that the population of Blankenberge reproached British authorities for having called on women aged eighteen and older to register for the so-called 21 dance club. Since neither men nor parents or guardians were allowed access, the lack of social control during these events was causing much trepidation and scandal. But there was even more outrage regarding the threat to minors. In the autumn of 1944, one of the movies screening in Belgian theaters was *The Whole Town's Talking*. Although the censor had rated the John Ford film of 1935 "morally harmless," children under eighteen were still deemed too impressionable to see it. Yet by the end of winter, early in 1945, the whole country was talking about parents who were allowing minors to experience much worse things in the company of Allied soldiers. This was not unique to Belgium, as similar concerns were raised about intimate relations between very young girls and Canadian troops in Holland and American troops in France. An historian of Paris during the liberation, for example, found it hard to determine "whether this was juvenile prostitution driven by hardship or thrill-seeking by children disturbed by the war." By March 1945, for a number of male students in the university city of Leuven the precise explanation no longer mattered. They had had enough. Hotheads launched a string of attacks on brothels servicing Allied troops. Gendarmes and British MPs had to use force to disperse them. In pamphlets they left behind, the students not only targeted the prostitutes, but railed more generally against "the licentious immorality" of the town's "womenfolk" in their relations with what were described as "brutalized and bestialized soldiers."[132]

Illegitimate children

Even the cooler heads of Belgian criminologists, looking back on the liberation shortly after the mass of Allied troops had left, could not but

[131] The "Hearts for Sale" headlines are mentioned in Patteet, *Heist*, 403, and the Limburg paper is quoted in Celis *et al.*, *Zepperen*, 297–8. On Verviers, see report to SE, March 22, 1945, Folder 979, AA 1311. Sulbout, "Liège," 50, note 107; Coenegrachts, *Hasselt*, 34; Challe, "Florennes," AB 1381; and Sulbout, "Liège," 90.

[132] Police Blankenberge, WR June 9, 1945, Folder 1014, AA 1311. The film rating can be found in *HBVL*, October 21, 1944, 2. Beevor and Cooper, *Paris*, 126. Gendarmerie Leuven, MR April 7, 1945, Folder 1063, AA 1311.

conclude that there had been what they more carefully phrased as "a certain amount of sexual laxity." This conclusion was not based, as had been much of public opinion, on perception. It was derived from statistics revealing the serious consequences of the more liberal sexual behavior of the era. The omnipresence of condoms scandalized many a Belgian during the presence of the Allied troops. And comical stories abound of fidgety parents loath to explain to their children why they should not be playing with such balloons in public. But the problem was that many soldiers preferred to hand out condoms to children as toys rather then use them when spending time with women. On the first consequence of this negligence – illegitimate children – there were, almost inevitably, few reliable figures available. Early in the summer of 1945, when nine months had passed since the arrival in Belgium of the first Allied armies, Belgian papers in both languages claimed that of the 24,000 children born in one month, some 16,000 to 18,000 had been conceived out of wedlock. There was no mention of sources, however, and the numbers appear to be gross exaggerations. The numbers also said nothing, of course, about who in fact had fathered these children. But the timing of the figures' release clearly implied that the press knew who was to blame. Apparently there had also been no doubt about this in the minds of some in Tongeren as early as March 1945. That was when gendarmes on the wall around the town's hospital discovered huge letters splashed in whitewash across a length of nearly 30 meters. "How many girls are expecting?" the graffiti asked. "We point at the men from the USA."[133]

Venereal disease

There was no doubt in anyone's mind about the scale of that other consequence of unsafe sex: venereal disease. VD was a headache for Allied commanders across Europe. The SHAEF mission in Belgium was reporting an increase in VD as early as October 1944. For the Allies the issue was one of manpower and the execution of the war. To prevent VD from causing too many military casualties, SHAEF pressured the Belgian government to take stricter measures in dealing with infected civilians. Early in December 1944, the Minister of Public Health sent a circular to all medical doctors and heads of medical laboratories. In it he reminded them of Belgian legislation dating back to the 1920s and

[133] The criminologists' report is C. Van der Bruggen and Louis C. Picalausa, "Belgian Youth Movements and Problems," in BT, 114–15. For examples of the numbers of illegitimate children, see *HBVL*, July 31, 1945, 2; and *Front* quoted in Lagrou, "US Politics of Stabilization," 241, note 58. Report Gendarmerie Tongeren, March 30, 1945, Folder 526, AA 1311.

1930s, and strengthened during the occupation, that made the reporting to authorities of infections with transmissible disease compulsory. The minister was aware, he said, that physicians had been hesitant to apply these laws to the letter during the German occupation. But he urged them to observe the legislation very strictly now that the liberators had arrived and were expressing "a vital interest" in staying informed to protect their armies. The reminder was not enough for the Allies, however, and SHAEF pushed for even stricter additional legislation. The government eventually obliged by enacting a new regulation at the end of January 1945. This law made it compulsory for any Belgian affected by VD to seek medical treatment and to report the identity of the person thought to be the source of the contagion.[134]

The new law made quite an impression on the population. But for the Allied military it was just the beginning as next they wanted to crack down on the sources of the disease. From their perspective, the problem lay with the women, and especially the prostitutes. In Britain prostitution was unorganized and barely tolerated. For the US War Department the official position was the suppression of prostitution altogether. Not surprisingly then, as early as November 1944, SHAEF had given to understand that it would prefer the Belgian government to enact "laws for the abolition of prostitution." But in Belgium, as in other countries on the Continent, prostitution was more socially acceptable. And it was a legally sanctioned and regulated institution as well, in which brothels were commonplace. By the start of the new year, SHAEF admitted defeat when it announced in a confidential report that the proposed law on banning prostitution had been "indefinitely postponed."[135]

Part of that Allied decision seemed to have been informed also by the realization that authorized brothels offered at least some means of control over the health of working girls. Indeed, the mayor of Leuven in December 1944 had closed down nineteen brothels saying they posed "health dangers." Yet, in February, the British Area Commander himself ordered the mayor to reopen the *maisons tolérées* for his troops. The US military, meanwhile, appeared in two minds about the situation on the ground. Some commanders insisted on a strict enforcement of the official line. The police chief of Verviers, for example, bemoaned the fact

[134] On the pressures exerted by the Allies, see SHAEFB, FR No. 3, 17, October 31, 1944, WO 202/683; and No. 8, 20, January 9, 1945, WO 202/688, AA 1230. For a transcript of the circular, see Ganshof to CAC Lieutenant Van Leckwyck, January 15, 1945, Folder 889, AA 1311. For the VD problem among American troops in Europe, see Schrijvers, *Crash of Ruin*, 179–83.

[135] SHAEFB, FR No. 4, 19, November 14, 1944, WO 202/684; and No. 8, 20, January 9, 1945, WO 202/688, AA 1230.

that American authorities "do not recognize prostitution." They made that clear by posting "off limits" signs for GIs on brothels whose girls were registered with Belgian authorities and forced to undergo regular medical inspections. In Liège, on the other hand, it appears that the American military actively cooperated in the licensing and regulating of scores of authorized brothels in the garrison town.[136]

Verviers' police chief was upset, of course, because soldiers who were denied access to brothels invariably turned to clandestine forms of prostitution, like girls walking the streets. And medical control and inspection of such girls was all but impossible, with sharp rises in VD rates an inevitable consequence. Unregistered prostitutes were thriving enough as it was anyway, even without locally sanctioned brothels being closed to troops. Indeed, these high-risk women were another reason, in addition to the fight against the black market, for Allied and Belgian security services to step up joint efforts early in 1945. They faced an uphill struggle, however. The SE signaled that in rural communities too there was "debauchery" leading to "numerous cases of venereal disease." But, it noted, controlling prostitution in these areas was far more difficult than in big cities, because of a lack of manpower and mayors "afraid of offending voters." Still, the fight against clandestine prostitution in urban areas remained a tall order too. When, in March 1945, news came of a plan to decentralize the police forces of Greater Antwerp, a high-ranking British officer of the city's CA detachment warned the Belgian Military Mission that this was bound to have a dramatic impact. Close cooperation between British MPs and local vice squads, he said, had finally succeeded in reducing the number of VD cases from seventy to ten per week. Decentralization, he predicted, would once again cause the rate to be "out of control."[137]

US authorities in Liège were determined not to let this happen. They used an iron fist in the battle against what one SE report described as "the clandestine prostitution that has made its reappearance in Liège as a result of the presence of large numbers of American soldiers." Frequent raids led to the arrest of so many "suspect women" that a school had to be requisitioned to serve as an extra wing for the hospital normally treating VD patients. In February 1945, however, the authorities took their zeal a step too far in what was described as "a monster raid." American MPs and local vice squads swept down on a particular

[136] Aerts *et al.*, *Leuven*, 49; report on Verviers to SE, March 22, 1945, Folder 979, AA 1311; and Sulbout, "Liège," 49–50 and 87.

[137] On the rural areas, see SE Visé, WR February 24, 1945, Folder 1109, AA 1311. On Antwerp, see Lt.-Col. W. P. S. Curtis to Lt. Van Leckwyck, March 3, 1945, Folder 939, AA 1311.

section of the city, rounded up some 150 women, took them to the police station, and there forced them to undergo medical inspection. The authorities afterwards claimed that some thirty-five women were shown to be infected, five of them with syphilis. But public opinion and the press were scandalized by the random nature of the operation and the fact that it had forced to submit to such humiliation "certain women who were above suspicion and had found themselves on the premises by accident."[138]

Such affronts fed into the growing resentment of a population that wondered why Belgian women were seen as the main cause of the VD problem rather than the soldiers. They were irritated too by the nature of a debate that always revolved around protecting troops. What, people wanted to know, was being done to prevent licentious soldiers from infecting the civilian population? The polemic reached fever pitch in the winter of 1945. And once again the Allied dance halls became a favorite target. Indeed, it appeared that the question of what to do to halt the VD epidemic – shutting down the brothels or closing the dance clubs – was very much a contest about who was to blame for the scourge – Belgian women or Anglo-American troops. In a letter to a fellow officer in the Belgian Military Mission, Ganshof van der Meersch in mid-January 1945 revealed that the government refused to take measures regarding prostitution not only for fear of being "criticized," but also "to put pressure on the Allied military authorities and have them close down all the dance halls they have opened in different centers." When that did not happen, the Minister of Public Health demanded outright that the military halt the organization of such dances. This caused a storm of protest among the Allies. SHAEF said British medical authorities firmly believed these clubs would "decrease the rate of VD rather than increase it." *The Maple Leaf*, the Canadian troops' official newspaper, shot back that the Belgian government would do much better to close down the gory night clubs of Brussels "with their expensive rotgut and loose women." But public opinion remained riveted on the Allied clubs, which never stopped the dances despite the minister's insistence. It was there, *Le Peuple* maintained, that many "honorable young girls" became entangled in "regrettable liaisons." And it was there, many were convinced, that "morality and health often ran the greatest risks."[139]

138 Sulbout, "Liège," 87; and SE report on Liège province, February 24, 1945, Folder 979, AA 1311.

139 Ganshof to CAC Lt. Van Leckwyck, January 15, 1945, Folder 889, AA 1311. SHAEFB, FR No. 10, 6, February 6, 1945, WO 202/690, AA 1230. *The Maple Leaf* is quoted in Pauwels, *Canadezen*, 159. "Les Dancings et le péril vénérien," *Le Peuple*,

Black soldiers as sexual threats

Ironically, there was much unease also about the risks posed by those soldiers who were rarely seen at Allied club dances. There were Belgians who treated the segregated African-American troops in ways often unthinkable in their homeland. They invited them as guests of honor to private family gatherings, for example, from dinners to christenings. And they did not see color as an obstacle even in the more intimate relations between men and women. When a black quartermaster company arrived in rural Zepperen, for example, there soon was much flirting between the soldiers and the local girls, and the GIs left many weeks later amidst "much tears." The same happened more than once in Eisden, where one batch of African-Americans arrived after another at the rest center to get away from the front lines for a couple of days. The goodbyes, a Belgian foreman recalled, were often "touching," not only because friendships were formed, but because many a woman lost her heart to a black GI.[140]

Still, there were many in this small country that ruled a giant African colony who frowned on intimate relations with blacks. Marriages between Belgian women and black soldiers were exceedingly rare. Sufficiently so for *La Wallonie* to spend an entire article on one such union in Liège at the end of 1944, which was cause for much amusement. The same doggerel in Flanders that called gold diggers "sluts" singled out women dating blacks as even more reprehensible. "Whether negroes with skins of bronze, or chimney sweepers, it matters none," one verse ran. "Women do not care as long as they chew gum." For decades, government and church, through publications and exhibitions, had projected a picture of blacks in the Congo as naïve children in need of education. The implication always was, however, that without this *mission civilisatrice* their dark side would take over, unleashing their primitive, predatory, and aggressive nature. That point was driven home most suggestively in the 1930s in colonial publications and documentaries routinely combining the images of pygmies and gorillas. Indeed, some before the war had attacked jazz as a product of this dark side, a style of black music that threatened to barbarize, eroticize, and awaken primitive instincts. Many of these images lingered in a society suddenly confronted for the first time with large numbers of blacks on home soil. As a result, besides doubtless goodwill and

February 1, 1945. The nationwide concern about the role of dance halls is reflected also in Institut d'Éducation et de Documentation Nationales, Chronique, 53.

140 Celis *et al.*, *Zepperen*, 297; and Kohlbacher, "Eisden," 37.

unending fascination, there was much latent fear too. The first time, for example, that a young woman in Bilzen came face to face with an African-American soldier was in her father's café. The one image of the encounter that forever stuck in her mind was that, when paying his bill, the black GI showed her a palm full of coins and condoms.[141]

The association of blacks with unrestrained sexuality was never far from people's minds. And it was given new meaning when reports in the press suggested that it was African-Americans more than any other soldiers who were luring minors to their camps. So many young girls were said to be descending on an army camp of black GIs in Vottem near Liège, for example, that newspapers derisively referred to it as "Harlem's Hotel." A similar problem in Mons took on such proportions that the city's juvenile court appealed to the Belgian Military Mission to intercede with the Allied authorities for the sake of public health and morality. Nowhere, however, was there any reference to the fact that clandestine prostitution thrived near those camps in large part because American authorities declared even authorized brothels off limits to black soldiers. It would have made little difference anyway for a public opinion already alarmed about rising immorality. Insipid allusions in the press and local ditties about black babies played on deep-seated fears of miscegenation. When the police chief in Verviers' local newspaper challenged the town's girls about their relations with Allied soldiers, he did not appeal to their love for the nation, but to "the essential mission that befalls you for the future of our race." More still, he warned against the particular viciousness of VD passed on by soldiers who had arrived in Belgium by way of campaigns in North Africa. In doing so, he harked back to stereotypes of primitive sexuality and debauchery in the dark continent that in 1930 had a Belgian campaign against VD issue a series of postcards tellingly illustrated with drawings of the Congo. By the summer of 1945, Limburg's newspaper was warning girls against relations with "negro soldiers" because so many of them were known to be "morally retarded."[142]

141 For the *Wallonie* article, see Sulbout, "Liège," 67. *HBVL* is quoted in Celis *et al.*, *Zepperen*, 298. On Bilzen, see story related by Elizabeth Rigo, the author's maternal grandmother. On the Belgian images of the Congo, see Vints, *Kongo*, 64, 69–72, and 80–1.

142 On Vottem, see Sulbout, "Liège," 90. On Mons, Cabinet du Juge des Enfants to Commandant Drapier, March 19, 1945, Folder 972, AA 1311. For examples of sneers about children of mixed race, see Lecerf, *Libération*, 363; and Sulbout, "Liège," 98–9. SE Verviers, March 22, 1945, Folder 979, AA 1311. For the 1930 campaign, see Vints, *Kongo*, 78. "Wanneer treedt de overheid op tegen de uitspattingen?" *HBVL*, August 19, 1945, 1.

A losing battle

By then too it was clear that the fight against VD would be a losing battle until the massive presence of Allied troops ebbed away. Despite the circulars, laws, inspections, and raids, the gendarmerie in Namur, for example, reported new increases in VD rates among the female population in January 1945, and again in March and May of that year. By early spring of 1945, the VD rate in Belgium had become so alarming that SHAEF rushed penicillin to civilian hospitals for the treatment of infected prostitutes. The rate of syphilis in Liège perhaps best illustrates the overall trend. It had increased at the start of the war, but reached a plateau by 1943. The liberation, however, caused a huge spike again, bringing the total number of cases in the civilian population to no fewer than 1,671 in 1945. As a result of the withdrawal of most Allied troops by the end of 1945, the rate was more than halved in 1946, and it was back at its prewar level by 1948.[143]

Amidst the alarming statistics, some men, frustrated by the lack of control that their government and society could exert over the mass of foreign troops stationed on Belgian soil, found it much easier to blame women for the debauchery. Several of the newspaper articles on men in Limburg who wounded or killed their partners for having an affair with an Allied soldier called such retribution a "lesson" for women in the province. A revue in Aalst had spiteful men sing that girls "dating a Tommie, a Canadian, or a Sammie" were "as rotten as bad eggs." There were those, however, who, disgusted by the moral decay around them, took the debate beyond the level of the personal to that of the nation. Several reports drafted by SE officers in the American sector, for example, hinted at this betrayal of patriotism most insidiously: they claimed that many of the women who preferred GIs to local men were those who not long ago had gravitated to the Germans.[144]

Allied relations with German prisoners of war

The massive presence of Allied troops in Belgium caused irritations not just where it concerned relations with local women. To empathize

[143] For Namur, see the monthly reports in Folder 1000, AA 1311. On the March 1945 crisis, see Schrijvers, *Crash of Ruin*, 182. Sulbout, "Liège," 89–90.

[144] For the revue, see Neckers, *Bevrijding*, 71. For examples of the SE reports, see Namur, WR January 27, 1945, Folder 1057; and Virton, WR April 14, 1945, Folder 1111, AA 1311. The women's apparent preference for foreign soldiers caused similar feelings of betrayal of "the patriotic sentiment" in France. Torrent, *La France américaine*, 231. By the summer of 1945 in some areas of Holland pamphlets were issued warning women "not to become too friendly with Canadians or they would have their heads shaved." Horn, "More than Cigarettes," 168.

with the Germans was to commit a mortal sin in a country that had experienced the dreadful Nazi yoke for more than four years. Yet, to their consternation, Belgians during the inclement winter of early 1945 suspected that this was exactly what Allied troops were doing. There was a painful irony in the fact that German POWs could count on sharing the rich meals of their captors while Belgian civilians complained they were receiving no more than crumbs from their liberators. "People," an SE officer in Charleroi wrote in February 1945, "envy the German POWs who benefit from the rich provisions of their conquerors." Some Belgians were loath to accept this injustice in silence. Workers, a report on La Louvière noted, "loudly proclaim their indignation" at the fact that German prisoners were receiving "abundant and substantial food" while they were forced to get by on "a subsistence allowance." The SE in Liège observed "rage" among bystanders each time German POWs marched through town merrily "munching oranges." Indeed, to allay suspicions about Allied pampering of German troops, SE agents in Namur province at the end of February paid visits to several POW camps, only to report back to Brussels that they had seen nothing of the excesses played up by the press.[145]

Such confidential reports did little, however, to calm public unrest when that same month a Belgian whispering campaign insisted that American troops in Germany were cozying up to the civilians. Rumors also claimed that Belgian troops on enemy territory had revolted against this behavior and that it had caused friction with GIs. Meanwhile, tension in Belgium over Allied relations with the Germans rose when it became obvious at the end of winter that more and more POWs were being used as workers. In part this was done, despite protests from the International Red Cross, to accommodate the Belgian government, which had asked SHAEF for Germans to work in the coal mines and help clean up explosives in West Flanders province and rebuild the Ardennes. In part it was a solution also to labor shortages in some districts becoming more pronounced as the Allied demand for workers increased with an eye to the spring offensive. But Belgian employees cared little about the economic rationale behind the new policy. They feared losing their coveted jobs to men who had no choice but to work for free. Moreover, they were outraged that the Allies could expect them to work side by side with the former enemy. Workers in Antwerp were so upset by the sight of German POWs on the docks that at one point

[145] Report Gendarmerie Charleroi, [February 2, 1945], Folder 972; SE La Louvière, WR March 30, 1945, Folder 1054; and SE Liège, WR February 10, 1945, Folder 1057, AA 1311. On Namur, see Van Ypersele, "La Belgique libéréé," 30.

they threatened to halt work. The new policy eventually created such a swell of anti-German hysteria that the Belgian Prime Minister had to call on SHAEF to reduce the reliance on prisoner labor and make it less conspicuous.[146]

Allied military successes in the enemy's heartland ensured that anti-German hysteria would stay alive until at least the end of spring. As troops pushed deeper into Nazi Germany, Belgians were left reeling by escalating news of the horrors inside the myriad concentration and extermination camps. Those who refused to accept the printed evidence were quickly convinced by the shocking sight and stories of returning deportees. In Brussels late in April 1945, Buchenwald was "the subject of all conversations," and "a wave of rage and disgust" was said to be building among the capital's "deeply affected public." The same was happening all over the country so that by May renewed indignation with the Nazis and their henchmen gave rise to the so-called second street repression. Collaborators were forced to return home from a collapsing Nazi Germany at the same time that their victims were making the trip back. In some cases enraged crowds were meting out merciless punishment to traitors who were barely given a chance to step down from the train. In Mol, for example, a mob killed a collaborator inside the station and then turned against the family that had been waiting for him, wounding his wife and shaving his daughter's head.[147]

The boiling rage did not remain contained within the stations. Frustrated by the slowness of the justice system and the release of many suspected collaborators for lack of firm evidence, people again demanded a more sweeping cleansing of their communities. In many a village or town anonymous posters warned collaborators to leave in the next twenty-four or forty-eight hours or to risk terrible retribution. Such threats set in motion a stream of refugees. Those who refused to heed the warnings often suffered a much worse fate. In Hainaut province inmates from Buchenwald and Bergen Belsen were placed at the head of processions that snaked to the homes of suspects who had already been released from prison or had never before been charged with treason. Four thousand furious people demonstrated against collaborators

[146] On the rumors regarding GIs in Germany, see SE Visé, WR February 10, 1945, Folder 1109, AA 1311. On the reasons for employing German POWs, see SHAEFB, FR No. 12, 6, March 6, 1945, WO 202/692; and No. 14, 1, April 3, 1945, WO 202/694, AA 1230; and De Vos, "US Forces," 194–5. On unrest in Antwerp and across the country, see Lagrou, "US Politics of Stabilization," 242, note 63.

[147] SE Bruxelles, WR April 27, 1945, Folder 1018, AA 1311; and Laureys, "Het bevrijde België," 69.

in Quaregnon before ransacking their homes. Twelve houses were smashed in Soignies in the wake of a protest march organized by former members of the resistance. Explosives were used in attacks in Flobecq, Ath, and Maffles. Similar scenes unfolded in Flanders. In Antwerp province, for example, the contents from the homes of twenty-six returning collaborators in Geel were burned in the streets and thirty homes in Meerhout fell victim to frenzied looting shortly after an inhabitant returned from the camps. Belgian security forces were especially worried by the reappearance of weapons on the streets, presumably from stocks that the resistance had kept hidden. Gendarmes in Antwerp province appealed to the military for additional vehicles to be able to intervene more rapidly. But British authorities were not particularly forthcoming this time, signaling that they would lend support only when their own lines of communication risked being threatened.[148]

Matters never became that critical. General Erskine kept a cool head. "This is a natural reaction," was his take on events at the end of May, "and does not mean a general outbreak of lawlessness, except on this particular subject." The violence against the collaborators indeed abated by the end of June. However, with the depths of Nazi depravity now starkly etched on their minds, Belgians were bound to look at chummy behavior with German POWs with even more disdain. Relations with the Americans in Namur had turned "cold," one SE report said early in June, because they stood accused of "showering the German prisoners with an almost maternal solicitude and providing them with abundant rations to the detriment of the populations in the occupied countries." In the summer, British troops had many of the 2,300 POWs in the Zandvoorde camp near Ostend perform labor at the nearby Belgian coast. But inhabitants resented the Germans' soft treatment. They could not understand why they had to be trucked to work and why, in rainy weather, the British bothered to provide them with raincoats. The Belgian POWs in Germany, they claimed, had never been given the luxury of such attentive care.[149]

Allied authorities ignored such sensitivities at their own risk. Belgian employees on an American base in Luttre in July 1945 refused to continue work. Representatives from the unions and the OMA rushed to the base to help American authorities defuse the situation. Talks with the

[148] On Hainaut, see Van Ypersele, "La Belgique libéréé," 16; and Dauphin, "La Belgique libéréé," 70–6. On Antwerp, see Laureys, "Het bevrijde België," 69. For the second street repression more generally, see Conway, "Justice," 26–31.

[149] SHAEFB, FR No. 18, 2, May 29, 1945, WO 202/699, AA 1230. Gendarmerie Namur, MR June 9, 1945, Folder 1075; and SE Oostende, WR August 4, 1945, Folder 1082, AA 1311.

employees revealed that American overseers had recently visited the base with German POWs and had appeared to be making jokes at the Belgians' expense. The employees not only felt insulted. They were convinced that the Americans intended to have Germans oversee the Belgians. The Americans were flabbergasted to find that this was the cause of the unrest. They insisted they had never intended to ridicule their employees and strongly denied any plans to bring in German foremen. At the same time, however, they pointed out that they "were bound to respect the German prisoners just like they did the Americans or Belgians."[150]

Problems of discipline

It was irritating to find that troops who were on Belgian soil to keep the Germans at bay appeared to be turning soft on the enemy. That these were mostly rear-area troops who had not seen the enemy at his worst in battle, the population failed to take into account. But Belgians thought it still more disconcerting that Allied troops, whose other *raison d'être* was to ensure law and order, quite often turned out to be part of the problem. Indeed, during the second street repression in the spring of 1945, Allied soldiers, for the most part British, had joined the agitated crowds on numerous occasions. The governor of West Flanders reported that by mixing with demonstrators across the province these soldiers had repeatedly aggravated the situation. "The excellent relations that have formed between Belgians and British," one SE report observed, "seem to have caused the latter to adopt the shortcomings of our fellow-citizens." Whatever the explanation, nothing could justify the behavior of British troops in northern Limburg who actively helped mobs smash homes and even a cinema and hotel said to belong to collaborators.[151]

Allied commanders during the street repression of May and June 1945 hurriedly intervened to call their troops to order. But Belgians had sensed early on that loose discipline was a more systemic feature of the Allied armies. This was certainly true when they compared them with the strict disciplinarians that the Germans had been until shortly before their retreat late in the summer of 1944. Many of the Allied soldiers, of course, were passing through on their way to and from battle, whereas the Belgians had known the Germans almost exclusively as more settled garrison troops. The arrival of front-line troops could be quite unsettling

150 "Procès-verbal de la réunion tenue le 23.7.45 à la Maison Communale de Luttre," Folder III, AA 608/22.

151 "Procès-verbal de la réunion provoquée au ministère de la justice par M. le ministre de la justice en date du vendredi 25 mai [1945] à 10 h 30," 4, Folder 1184, AA 1311; and *HBVL*, May 8, 1945, 1. See also Van Ypersele, "La Belgique libérée," 21.

for civilians. During much of the Ardennes offensive, for example, the town of Tienen hosted large numbers of hardened troops taking a rest from combat. This, an SE officer at the end of December 1944 reported in rather euphemistic terms, gave rise to "an exceptional atmosphere," though he hurried to add that there had been no major disturbances. It was only early in March 1945, when most combat troops had pulled out, that another report could note that the region had at last become "somewhat more tranquil."[152]

Still, the passage of large numbers of combat troops was only part of the story as irreverence for authority seemed to be an endemic streak in Allied troops of all stripes. America's citizen-soldiers almost instantly acquired a reputation for being allergic to rigid discipline. But in the wake of the Germans even the more formal British troops were seen as much less restrained. Nothing illustrates this better than a popular joke making the rounds in Antwerp province. A Tommy walks up to Montgomery, hero of El Alamein, and asks if it is all right for him to go on a short spin in the marshal's jeep. "Ah," an elated Montgomery exclaims, "the discipline of the British soldiers has much improved. Some time ago they would not have bothered asking for permission."[153]

Compared with the enemy martinets, the liberating armies' more relaxed ways generally went a long way in putting civilians at ease. When such habits prevented troops from being reined in, however, they proved to be a very irksome characteristic. As early as the autumn of 1944, for example, Belgian police and gendarmes reported numerous instances of Allied soldiers stealing bicycles and motorcycles, an especially irritating phenomenon given the memory of German behavior in this regard during the retreat. Yet, despite such complaints, as late as June 1945 SHAEF was still urging recalcitrant troops to stop this practice, reminding them in particular that seizing civilian motor transport was a military offense.[154]

Allied troops regularly showed themselves to be a rowdy bunch in other ways too. Hotels requisitioned for American troops at Chaudfontaine between September and December 1944, for example, were treated with total disrespect. The OMA had to cough up a total of more than 370,000 Belgian francs for damages to the forty-two rooms of the Hôtel des Bains alone. Where troops from different Anglo-Saxon nations mixed, things could get even more unruly. Canadian and British soldiers, for example, were quickly known to have difficulties getting along. Brawls between both groups erupted with such regularity in the cafés of Arendonk that

152 SE Tienen, WR December 23, 1944 and March 3, 1945, Folder 1102, AA 1311.
153 The joke can be found in Patteet, *Heist*, 403.
154 SHAEFB, FR No. 19, 12, June 12, 1945, WO 202/700, AA 1230.

local authorities, with the support of the Allied military, decided as early as November 1944 that declaring the places off limits to the Canucks was the only way to calm things down.[155]

There were no easy fixes for many other forms of unruly behavior. These included the recurrent instances of theft and violence to the detriment of civilians. Gendarmerie, police, and the SE diligently catalogued them in countless reports. A survey by the Belgian police alone on interventions regarding Allied personnel in Brussels between September 1944 and March 1945, listed 2 civilians killed, 21 inhabitants wounded, 26 cases of damaged property, and almost 100 cases of theft. The American MPs, if they were not on the spot first, were soon urging Belgian authorities to report such cases "with utmost speed and when possible by telephone." But in the hectic and fluid climate of a war zone these incidents were impossible to prevent and hard to prosecute. The Blankenberge police in a weekly report early in June 1945 listed assault and battery as one of the three main issues of contention between British forces and the population of the coastal town. Most deplorably, one of the victims of British violence that very week had been the president of the local association of Nazi deportees who had tried to prevent his property from being looted.[156]

Sexual harassment and rape

Police in Blankenberge pointed to troops spoiling food as a second issue responsible for discord between the liberators and the liberated. The other concerned the behavior of British troops towards the town's female inhabitants. In Blankenberge, as in British and American zones across the country, this implied more, however, than the annoyance and jealousy caused by consensual relationships. As in any large population of males, and even more so in one deliberately trained in violence, some men of the Allied military took by force what women refused to give of their own accord. That the liberators were not always simply charming but could be quite aggressive in their pursuit of women became clear within weeks of their arrival. As early as October 1944, Limburg's newspaper, always attuned to practical needs in its linguistic column, was also teaching local women phrases like "My sweetheart is a nice Flemish boy," "I am a decent girl," and the more insistent "Leave me alone!" But the problem of sexual harassment was still more pronounced in the larger

[155] Lognard-Poncin and Michel, *Chaudfontaine*, 56; and Van Gorp, *Arendonk*, 179 and 219.

[156] "Interventions police communale de l'agglomération bruxelloise du 3/9/44 au 3/3/45," Folder 528, AA 1311. On the American MP, see Ganshof to provincial governors, March 17, 1945, Folder 574, AA 1311. Police Blankenberge, WR June 9, 1945, Folder 1014, AA 1311.

urban areas that served as logistical hubs and centers for rest and recreation. "In Antwerp," an inhabitant of the nearby town of Heist noted in his journal in February 1945, "people are afraid of going out at night, especially women. They are afraid of being assaulted; it is not nearly that bad in our area." Stories of women who lived in the port city attest to the fact that they thought the Germans much more disciplined and that harassment was much more common after the liberation. People in Brussels in March actually took to the streets to protest the behavior of soldiers toward the female population. They were especially upset with American troops as women were said to have been assaulted on the streets while returning home after dark.[157]

Poignantly, a girl from Antwerp, who was seventeen at the time, claimed that women who showed themselves uncooperative "in the best case could expect a slap in the face." In the worst case, however, soldiers committed the most shameful crime and, in the stilted yet coldly precise words of the American military judiciary, "did, forcibly and feloniously, against her will, have carnal knowledge of a woman." Rape statistics are notoriously hard to come by in any era and even more so during wartime. Criminologists in the 1950s estimated that in Britain during the war no more than 5 percent of rape victims had reported the crime – and this was in a country that did not experience the full chaos of war. Taking into account such underreporting, recent research, grounded in the records of the American Judge Advocate General, suggests that GIs alone probably committed some 2,400 rape crimes in England, more than 3,600 in France, and an estimated 11,000 in Germany.[158]

The same research unfortunately remains silent on the total figures for the much smaller Belgium. Indeed, for reasons that are not quite clear, the files of the American Judge Advocate General mention less than a handful of cases. Newspapers, and even the highly confidential SE reports, generally remain equally silent on the subject, as do the more personal testimonies. The most encouraging explanation – that if it is not in the sources, it must not have happened – is most implausible, of course, given the high number of estimated rape cases in all of the neighboring countries and clear indications of a climate of sexual harassment

[157] For Limburg, see *HBVL*, October 26, 1944, 2. The journal is quoted in Patteet, *Heist*, 403. For the Antwerp women see, for example, G. Van Aerschot and Liliane Wolters, AB 1591. On Brussels, see SE report, Folder 526, AA 1311. Belgium was not exceptional in this regard. Reynolds, for example, notes that the prevalence of sexual harassment in Britain during the war "cannot be doubted." *Rich Relations*, 201.

[158] The seventeen-year-old is G. Van Aerschot, AB 1591. The American military wording of rape is taken from the charges as specified by the JAG/ETO Boards of Review. For the estimates on rapes committed by GIs in Europe, see Lilly, *Taken by Force*, 11–12.

in Belgium. Indeed, Canadian military authorities in Belgium as early as October 1944 were reporting "a small but growing number of rapes and indecent assaults."[159]

Whatever the explanation for the dearth of sources on wartime rape in Belgium, there is fragmentary evidence of sexual crimes. And it speaks volumes on behalf of all of the women who never dared step forward or whose testimonies failed to be recorded. Belgian women accused of collaboration were, of course, the last to consider lodging complaints against their tormentors. Nevertheless, in recent times evidence has emerged of Belgian guards, as well as British and American soldiers, guilty of participating in systematic rape in prisons across the country. Yet rape was never simply a punishment for supposed wartime crimes. It was also a more general manifestation of dark male urges to dominate and humiliate. And as such it chose its victims randomly. Consider the case, for example, of the nineteen-year-old student from Leopoldsburg. On her way back home, late in the evening of October 17, 1944, a British soldier stalked and attacked her in the dark. The girl barely had a chance to resist and was bludgeoned until she lost consciousness. A Belgian who happened to pass by caught the soldier raping the girl and caused him to flee. The girl managed to survive the attack and to summon enough courage to report the crime at the local gendarmerie.[160]

Exactly one week later, on the other side of the language border, a fifty-one-year-old woman in Namur felt safe in the warmth of her home and the presence of her husband. When the bell rang close to midnight, however, and men outside claimed to be the police, the couple made the mistake of opening the door. Two GIs barged in. They had been drinking, were looking for "a whorehouse," and instead had chosen this house simply "because the lights were on." They threatened the couple with a knife, urinated in one of the rooms, then dragged the woman into a bedroom and took turns violating her. It took almost an hour for the ordeal to end and the soldiers to leave. The anxious couple waited another eight hours before reporting what had happened. They had a telephone but did not know the number of the American MP, and the husband was too ashamed to discuss the matter with the Belgian police.

[159] Professor Dr. J. Robert Lilly, author of groundbreaking work on GI rapists in the Second World War, calls the absence of information on this kind of crime in Belgium "one of the curious aspects" of the thirty-four JAG Board of Review volumes that he and a team of volunteer students at Northern Kentucky University were kind enough to trawl for my benefit. Lilly says that he cannot come up with "a good explanation" for the lack of information. E-mail to author, September 26, 2006. On the Canadians, see Pauwels, *Canadezen*, 159.

[160] On the rape of Belgian collaborators, see Balace, "Hoquets," 89–90. Gendarmerie Bourg-Léopold, procès-verbal No. 934, Folder 574, AA 1311.

Only at dawn, when the curfew had lifted, did they venture outside to tell of their frightful night to the American authorities.[161]

Belgian newspapers early in February 1945 in a couple of brief sentences announced that a few days earlier both perpetrators of the Namur rape had, as the sentence had demanded in November, been "hanged by the neck until dead." No such notice has been found in the press on the verdict pronounced in the case of three GIs tried that same February for a rape committed near Mons. Perhaps because the punishment was less sensational. Certainly not because the soldiers' crime was less horrendous. On November 4, 1944, the three privates were on the road in a US army truck. They offered a ride to a woman on a bicycle who was on her way to buy shoes for her young son. She accepted the offer to save time, had her bicycle loaded into the back of the truck, and joined the three soldiers on the cabin seat. The soldiers had been drinking and continued to take swigs from a bottle. When the woman gestured that this was her stop, they ignored her and accelerated. The woman fiercely resisted the GIs' attempts to feel her up and at one point grabbed the steering wheel and put the truck into a ditch. The soldiers managed to get the truck back on the road and next drove it onto a path between fields. There they stopped the vehicle and, in the chilling words of American court documents, "tossed a coin to determine the order in which they would have intercourse." When all three were done in the cab, they dragged the woman into a field, spread a coat out on the ground, and took turns violating her all over again. After more than two hours, the soldiers unloaded the bike and the woman was free to go. Covered with bruises and scratches, patches of hair pulled out with the skin, she staggered to the home of her mother who took her to a doctor and finally to the American authorities.[162]

American military justice had no problem finding the accused from Mons guilty. The difference was in the sentence. The penalty for rape was death or life imprisonment as the court-martial saw fit to direct. The Namur rapists were black and sentenced to death on the gallows in Belgium. The Mons rapists were white and got away with a life of hard labor in a penitentiary in Pennsylvania. A similar pattern emerged across Europe as a racially segregated and discriminatory US military

[161] JAG/ETO, Board of Review No. 1, CM ETO 5561, *United States v. Privates Mervin Holden and Elwood J. Spencer*, vol. 15, 169–83.

[162] For a notice in the press, see *Le Peuple*, February 6, 1945, 2. An SE report mentioned that the execution was widely discussed in French-speaking Belgium and that it prompted people to express the hope that parents would keep a closer eye on minors in particular. SE Mons, WR February 10, 1945, Folder 972, AA 1311. The Mons rape is described in JAG/ETO, Board of Review No. 2, CM ETO 9025, *United States v. Privates Robert A. Clegg, Lyle B. Merritt, and Louis H. Vincent*, vol. 20, 79–91.

punished many more blacks for rape than whites, and punished them much harder.[163]

The black market

There is more than fragmentary evidence to show involvement of Allied soldiers in one of the best organized forms of crime to plague the country. Military authorities had to fight not only the complicity of Belgians in the lucrative black market but that of their own troops too. Late on Monday afternoon, October 2, 1944, Mrs. Verheyden caught sight of two vehicles through a window of her home on the Rue Bordeaux in Brussels. One was an army truck manned by British soldiers. The other was a civilian car. From behind the curtains Mrs. Verheyden spied a civilian carry petrol cans from the truck to his car. He continued to do this until the cans piled up to the level of the windows. When the car finally drove off, it was so packed that one of the passengers had to lean out of the door and hang on to the side. Mrs. Verheyden immediately rushed to the British authorities to inform them of what had transpired in her street. "I reported what I had seen to the Military Police," she later said in a statement to the Special Investigation Section, "as I know it must be wrong."[164]

Wrong it was indeed, and within two days British authorities had arrested a soldier from the 7th Heavy Recovery Section who confessed to having been involved in the shadowy transaction in the Rue Bordeaux with two of his comrades. Such crackdowns did little, however, to stem the tide of fraudulent trade. Much of it was petty. Canadian soldiers, for example, despite repeated warnings from their commanders, continued to sell rations or bars of soap and other small items to make a quick profit on the black market with which to buy a pair of silk stockings or a bottle of perfume as gifts for sweethearts. Much more worrisome, however, were the big rackets run by soldiers who aimed to earn big money and operated like criminal gangs. Canadian soldiers and officers were said to be involved also in the much less innocent sales of everything from petrol to motor parts and diamonds. On Saturday, February 10, 1945, a team of MPs, gendarmes, and SE officers during traffic checks in Bruges pulled aside fifteen civilian cars equipped with tires that belonged to the

[163] On the broader issue of race, sexual crimes, and punishment in the US army during the Second World War, see Lilly's work.

[164] Allied black-market activities constituted similar problems in France and Germany. See Torrent, *La France américaine*, 240–1; and Willoughby, "Sexual Behavior," 156–7. Statements taken by 74 Special Investigation Section, C. M. Police, October 4 and 5, 1944, Folder 1336, AA 1311.

Allied military as well as one unregistered vehicle that the driver insisted had been sold to him by British soldiers.[165]

When the local press that same month cited the *Manchester Guardian* as saying that up to 13,000 American soldiers were AWOL and that half of them were thought to be living off the black market in Paris, people inhabiting the American sector in Belgium had little trouble believing this. Belgians employed in American depots in Hainaut province resented being subjected to ever stricter security measures as if they were all thieves, while the GIs – who they claimed were the worst offenders – were presumed innocent. People in Charleroi took offense, an SE report noted in March 1945, not only at the degree with which the Americans spoiled food, but also at their heavy involvement in the black market. This was barely two weeks after authorities in Verviers had busted a black-market ring specializing in army rations. The seizure of almost 400 kilograms of B rations in one location alone prompted *La Presse Verviétoise* to brand the behavior of both Belgians and Americans involved in the trade as "scandalous."[166]

More scandalous still was that some soldiers thought nothing of considering even weapons acceptable items to trade. In the autumn of 1944, for example, Belgian authorities in Ghent and Roeselare reported that Allied troops were selling both pistols and ammunition. Indeed, British authorities just weeks into the liberation were forced to start an investigation after SHAEF was told by the SE headquarters in Brussels that, according to reliable sources, Canadian soldiers were said to have sold "several hundred revolvers" to civilians in Antwerp province.[167]

One could hardly expect soldiers brazen enough to swindle their own military to be afraid of stealing from civilians, no matter how needy they knew them to be. Inhabitants of Winksele near Leuven were left to wonder why an American soldier staged a holdup to make off with 10 kilograms of butter that were part of the allotment to be purchased with ration cards. Since GIs got more than their fill of butter from their own kitchens, the robber almost certainly headed straight for the black market to unload his catch for a nice profit. GIs who were willing to put their powerful big trucks at the disposal of gangs specialized in hauling coal stood to gain much bigger profits. Even near the end of winter, in

[165] Pauwels, *Canadezen*, 68; and military prosecutor Bruges to Ganshof, February 13, 1945, Folder 960, AA 1311.

[166] *The Guardian* was quoted in, for example, *HBVL*, February 3, 1945, 2. SE report on Hainaut, March 22, 1945, Folder 526; and SE Charleroi, MR March 8, 1945, Folder 1020, AA 1311. On Verviers, see newspaper clipping in Folder 979, AA 1311.

[167] SE Roeselare, WR December 15, 1944, Folder 1090; and Gendarmerie Gent, WR December 23, 1944, Folder 1035, AA 1311. On Tamines, see SE headquarters to Colonel Basseth Wilson, October 16, 1944, Folder 528, AA 1311.

mid-March 1945, the gendarmerie of Baudour near Mons reported the theft of nearly 5,000 kilograms of coke. Witnesses claimed they had seen a US army truck at the time of the crime and two GIs accompanied by some five civilians.[168]

Some soldiers expanded their criminal activities and became involved in the equally lucrative business of importing civilian supplies. By December 1944, for example, SHAEF signaled that Belgian customs were expressing "concern at the amount of champagne and brandy which is being smuggled into Belgium from France in Army lorries." But it was the booty that soldiers brought back to Belgium from Germany that gave authorities the biggest headache. In the enemy's homeland, Allied troops gladly substituted the word "liberating" for what until then had been known as looting, and they were soon showing few qualms claiming the spoils of war. Much of it ended up just across the border, in the provinces of Liège and Limburg. Some of it the troops brought back as presents for Belgians they had befriended and knew to have suffered at the hands of the Germans. GIs from an army engineer unit who had become acquainted with a family in Bilzen one day returned from a foray into Germany to drop off a washing machine "courtesy of Hitler." From the British a family in Peer obtained a magnificent-looking doll as well as a set of glasses in fine crystal, all seized from the enemy. Elsewhere soldiers engaged in a brisk trade of German supplies for their own gain. The SE in Visé in February 1945 reported that the Americans were selling not only German typewriters and sewing machines but even radio transmitters. Just north of Visé, in Limburg, the SE in March was pleading with the Belgian Ministers of Justice, Internal Affairs, and Defense for more vehicles to be able to cast its net wider in the fight against the large-scale trade in goods smuggled in from Nazi Germany.[169]

Allied military authorities did what they could to clamp down on these practices, among others by dishing out harsh punishments to those caught red-handed. In Liège at the end of March, for example, three soldiers were arrested for desertion and involvement in the black market. A court-martial sentenced one of them to thirty years in prison and told the others they would be locked away for life. All in all, however, such examples did little to dissuade the more hardened elements to stay clear of a black market promising huge profits in a country crippled

[168] Gendarmerie Veltem-Beisel, procès-verbal No. 800, Folder 574; and Gendarmerie Baudour, report March 15, 1945, Folder 528, AA 1311.

[169] SHAEFB, FR No. 6, December 12, 1944, WO 202/686, AA 1230. On Bilzen and Peer, see author interview Urbain Schrijvers, December 16, 2005 and story related to author by Elizabeth Rigo. SE Visé, WR February 10, 1945, Folder 1109; and SE headquarters to Belgian ministers, March 15, 1945, Folder 1335, AA 1311.

by want. MPs in Belgium's American sector eventually saw themselves forced to instruct civilians to report any trucks standing idle on the roads on the blanket assumption that they were being used for clandestine trafficking.[170]

Alcohol abuse

Belgian customs authorities on the border with France could attest that alcohol was a major factor in fuelling black-market crime. And American judicial documents demonstrate that rapists often acted under the influence of alcohol. So did murderers. In the trials that the American Judge Advocate General was asked to review, for example, of the eight cases pertaining to the death of GIs at the hand of their own comrades in the Belgian rear, five involved soldiers who had had too much to drink. Reports written by police and gendarmes regularly identified alcohol abuse as a source of much of the soldiers' unruly behavior, from theft and the destruction of property to physical assault against civilians.

Allied troops quickly acquired a reputation among Belgians as hard drinkers. A photo taken in Verviers during the first days of the liberation shows two GIs in a street full of spectators. The exuberant Americans amidst the crowd are acting out a little dance while guzzling beer or wine from a bottle without a hint of inhibition. Civilians blamed many of the glitches in discipline among British and Canadian troops too on alcohol. Late in October 1944, gendarmes in Ghent reported that drunken soldiers could be seen on the streets after dark and that from time to time they frightened the population by firing shots in the air with their pistols. An eight-year-old boy from Bruges, who adored the friendly Canadian soldiers, half a century later could remember only one negative image: the sight of drunken men in uniform slumped in the streets waiting for MPs to pick them up. "That was, of course, understandable," he added, "given that for months on end they had been risking their lives. You are bound to have one too many then. Still, it was something I had never seen among the Germans."[171]

It was not the military, of course, that supplied troops with alcohol. Civilians were all too happy to show their gratitude to the liberators by plying them with wine and beer in copious amounts. Two weeks after the liberation, *Het Belang van Limburg*, in an English-language column on hospitality, was teaching people how to pronounce light and dark

[170] Sulbout, "Liège," 84–5. On the MP pleas for cooperation, see also Lognard-Poncin and Michel, *Chaudfontaine*, 45.

[171] Ruwet, *Verviers*, 106; Gendarmerie Gand, WR November 4, 1944, Folder 1035, AA 1311; and Warnier, *Brugge en september '44*, vol. II, 129.

ale, wine, claret, burgundy, gin, and cordial. Café owners, on the other hand, were quick to spot a golden opportunity in the presence of countless new customers eager to forget the war for a fleeting moment. And they showed few scruples in serving whatever alcohol they could get their hands on in return for hard cash. It became clear to Belgian and Allied authorities within a matter of weeks that the flow of alcohol from civilians to soldiers had to be curbed. By mid-October 1944, MPs were posting notices warning all ranks of all Allied services that it was prohibited to purchase hard liquor from any café, shop, or other civilian source. At the behest of military authorities, mayors across the country declared it illegal for civilians to supply Allied troops with hard liquor against payment, in barter trade, or even as gifts. Also, as early as October, the Allied military were enforcing closing hours on cafés and bars in large cities like Brussels. Smaller places were soon following suit. English authorities in Zottegem in February 1945, for example, told the owners of cafés to close their businesses no later than ten in the evening. American authorities in Spa in March ordered all cafés and hotels to stop serving customers at midnight, one hour before the curfew was scheduled to set in.[172]

The Americans had learned from experience at home in the 1920s that the battle against alcohol was not easily won. As might have been expected, the battle proved even more daunting in theaters of war. Keen to maximize their profits among so many eager customers, owners of bars and cafés after official closing hours gladly transformed their businesses into speakeasies. In Brussels in October 1944 gendarmes and police turned a blind eye because the closing hours had been announced by the garrison commander as a mere "warning" and, as Ganshof van der Meersch had to admit in a letter to SHAEF, this was not sufficient to have the weight of law. Not that those who made a living selling alcohol cared much about legal niceties while surrounded by thirsty soldiers. Even where bars and cafés received clear and unambiguous orders to close their doors at a certain time, trade often remained brisk throughout the night. In Limburg's capital town of Hasselt, American and British troops knew that when certain cafés in the center obediently closed their front doors, they could stealthily slip in via the back doors, causing neighbors to complain of boisterous fun lasting into the small hours of morning.[173]

Much more serious problems resulted from the ban on the sale and distribution of hard liquor. Hard liquor was the preferred drink of soldiers

[172] *HBVL*, September 23, 1944, 2; SE Zottegem, WR February 2, 1945, Folder 1119; and SE Spa, WR March 24, 1945, Folder 1099, AA 1311.

[173] Ganshof to Colonel Bygott, October 27, 1944, Folder 951, AA 1311; and "Het drankmisbruik in Limburg," *HBVL*, December 19, 1944, 1.

keen on washing away war's volatile mix of fear and ennui with the stupor of inebriation. And if the military prevented them from obtaining this cure legally, there were various other ways to get their hands on the miracle medicine in the black market. Already by the middle of October 1944, Namur's military prosecutor was reporting that GIs frequently traded petrol and items of equipment with civilians for alcohol. Shortly before Christmas, a Belgian military court in Liège sentenced a man to three months in prison and a fine. The man ran a business in wines and liquor and had managed to obtain large quantities of US army cigarettes, coffee, chocolate, cans, and fruit bars – all "in exchange for alcohol." Other cases that appeared before the Liège courts revealed that to soldiers a single liter of "cognac" at times could be worth a whole jerrycan of American petrol.[174]

Some GIs might as well have drunk the petrol. When the regular sources of liquor dried up in Belgium, soldiers and civilians cooperated to smuggle brand-name bottles into the country from France and Germany in army trucks. But many more troops began to rely on the cheaper liquor brought to market by a mushrooming number of clandestine distillers. Sugar beets formed the raw material for much of the illegal alcohol, and at one point so many were being used by bootleggers that people claimed this was what was causing the rising price of sugar. Improvised and often run by amateurs, illegal distilleries produced a rotgut that no one who consumed it could predict the effects of. Indeed, gendarmerie reports claimed that some distillers thought nothing of using "the scum of liquid manure" to help bring about fermentation.[175]

One effect of the consumption of clandestine alcohol that was beginning to manifest itself early in 1945 was an increased propensity for violence among troops. More and more reports from the SE, for example, made mention of drunken soldiers in a rage firing their pistols inside cafés and out on the streets and putting up resistance when Belgian or Allied security forces tried to arrest them. But the military was even more troubled to learn that bootleg liquor was causing soldiers to lose their lives. On one of the last days of 1944, a black American soldier was found dead in the cabin of his truck in Gutschoven. A first investigation revealed that he had poisoned himself as a result of "the liberal consumption of bad alcohol." The incident was by no means an isolated one in Limburg province as illegal bootlegging was quickly getting out of hand so close to the front lines. In Tongeren seven GIs had died in similar circumstances by the end of January 1945. At around the same

[174] Military prosecutor Namur to Ganshof, October 16, 1944, Folder C5-0, AA 1882; and military prosecutor Liège to Ganshof, January 4 and 6, 1945, Folder 1172, AA 1311.

[175] On the sugar price, see Patteet, *Heist*, 403. On fermentation practices, see Gendarmerie Tongeren, MR February 8, 1945, Folder 1103, AA 1311.

time, the press claimed that in Neerpelt, the province's north, bootleg had killed four people and rendered seven others blind. It is not clear whether these were soldiers, but British authorities swiftly responded by repeating stark warnings to stay away from hard liquor. Early in March, the SE in Liège, the Walloon province closest to the front, was calling on authorities to pay special attention to "the large-scale sale" of suspicious spirits to troops stationed in the city and passing through.[176]

The Allied military needed little prodding to spring into action against what one gendarmerie report in Tongeren described as "this modern plague." Before long, the US army was posting notices on walls in Tongeren alerting GIs to the serious dangers of illegal alcohol. But with warnings and prohibitions succeeding each other uninterruptedly since at least as early as October 1944, Allied authorities realized that the only successful strategy to eradicate the scourge would be to put pressure on Belgian authorities to crack down on illegal distillers. The Belgians had already claimed some successes. In December they had seized twenty tons of sugar beets earmarked for bootlegging in Bilzen, for example, and a month later exposed a large ring involved in the fraudulent trade in yeast intended for similar purposes.[177]

But the Allied military wanted the Belgians to intervene much more systematically and, as the SE in Liège indicated, "with the utmost severity." The provost marshal of the American Ninth Army, for example, urged the Belgian judicial authorities to take "the most appropriate and the most energetic measures" to put an end to "these crimes against the health of the Allied troops." The press cooperated by reminding people that bootlegging carried hefty fines of up to 70,000 francs and a minimum prison sentence of one year. To dish out sentences, however, Belgian security forces first had to catch the culprits. Gendarmes and police complained that, as in so many other areas of crime fighting, they lacked transportation. But closer coordination between Allied and Belgian authorities did much to make the fight against illegal distillers, among other criminals, gradually more effective. The gendarmerie claimed that in Tongeren alone in the course of January it had closed down fifty-two such rackets. The Ministry of Finance reported to the head of the SE, Ganshof van

[176] On the increase in violence see, for example, SE Spa, WR February 10, 1945, Folder 1099; and SE Namur, WR March 10, 1945, Folder 1057, AA 1311. On Gutschoven and Neerpelt, see *HBVL*, December 31, 1944, 2 and January 22, 1945, 2. On Tongeren and Liège, see Lt. CAC Van Leckwyck to Ganshof, February 7, 1945, Folder 895; and SE Liège, WR March 3, 1945, Folder 1057, AA 1311.

[177] Gendarmerie Tongeren, MR March 8, 1945, Folder 1103, AA 1311; and military prosecutor Tongeren to Ganshof, March 20, 1945, Folder C5-17–3, AA 1882. On the Belgian interventions, see *HBVL*, December 11, 1944, 2; and Institut d'Éducation et de Documentation Nationales, *Chronique*, 51.

der Meersch, that in the first two months of 1945 more than 800 installations had been uncovered and dismantled across the country and that more could be done by disrupting the traffic in combustibles, sugar, molasses, syrup, and yeast. By March 1945, the gendarmerie in Tongeren was happy to report that, to accomplish all this, Belgians and Allies had attained "complete coordination" with weekly meetings that involved the local military prosecutors and police as well as American MPs.[178]

"Reports," the Liège edition of the GI newspaper *Stars and Stripes* said that same month, "of an epidemic of liquor poisoning among American soldiers has brought to light a Belgian bootleg industry run by peasants in the tradition of American prohibition days."[179]

A noisy exit

The sigh of relief the population heaved in March 1945 in response to the successes in the campaign against illegal distillations and the attendant unruly behavior of Allied troops was brief. Ironically, it was the end of the war in Europe early in May that was soon causing large swathes of the Belgian population to feel patently unsafe in the presence of Allied troops. And it was American troops above all others that civilians singled out for their disruptive behavior. This had everything to do with the way in which the US War Department handled the demobilization and redeployment of forces in Europe. The task, to be sure, was a formidable one: even when taking into account the number of US troops required for occupation duties in western Germany, more than two million GIs would have to be shipped out of Europe at short notice.

Most of those were scheduled for redeployment to the Pacific, where the war with the Japanese continued to rage furiously. The others would be going home, but here the War Department complicated matters by devising a point system that would determine who would be so fortunate. The Adjusted Service Rating was fair from the point of view of the individual soldier. But it was not practical in terms of the needs of the military. Points were assigned to soldiers on the basis of time in the service and overseas, battle decorations, and children under eighteen. This meant that the first GIs to be demobilized were the most mature and experienced ones.

[178] On Liège and the Ninth Army, see "Quartier Général de la 9ième armée américaine," March 2, 1945, Folder 536, AA 1311. For warnings in the press see, for example, "Wat staat een alcholstoker te wachten?" *HBVL*, February 1, 1945, 1. On Tongeren, see Gendarmerie Tongeren, MR February 8 and March 8, 1945; and SE Tongeren, WR March 17, 1945, Folder 1103, AA 1311. Ministère des Finances to Ganshof, March 6, 1945, Folder 1635, AA 1311.

[179] "Poison Booze Mart Found," *The Stars and Stripes*, March 12, 1945. Copy of article in Folder C5-17-3, AA 1882.

To keep remaining units at full strength, however, also necessitated the constant reshuffling of personnel. This quickly proved fatal to the unit cohesion that is the basis of any military's discipline. The negative effects on the composure of American troops began to be felt in a matter of weeks. When two atomic bombs in August brought Japan to its knees, redeployment to the Pacific was no longer a priority and the rush to demobilize accelerated. The War Department in September announced the intention of having no fewer than 1.7 million soldiers shipped out of Europe by the end of January 1946. The result was that the pullout took place in such haste and amidst so much noise that even an official US Army study later admitted it resembled an "organized rout" more than anything else.

The collapse of unit cohesion was made worse by the idleness that suddenly followed the hustle and bustle and tension of an active war zone. In the weeks and months that followed Germany's surrender, France and Belgium took on the appearance of huge waiting rooms. The US Supreme Command established four main staging areas for the repatriation of its troops. Three of them were located in France – in Cherbourg, Le Havre, and Marseilles – the other was laid out in Antwerp. Into these flooded hundreds of thousands of men who were as boisterous as they were young: those anticipating more combat in the Pacific, tense and irritable; those selected to go home, elated and impatient. It was a recipe for trouble.[180]

The pressures of withdrawal

How easy it was for relations between troops and the population to turn sour in those conditions became clear in Belgium as early as June 1945. As Allied troops poured in from Germany, renewed pressures on accommodation put "a heavy strain" on the population, SHAEF acknowledged, predicting that "the next few months will be extremely difficult." From Spa to Brussels all available hotels were requisitioned and, before long, much of the country was dotted with Allied clubs, hostels, leave and rest centers, and transit camps. A particularly heavy burden fell on the port city of Antwerp. As one of Europe's major staging areas, the situation in Antwerp, in the words of SHAEF, "necessitated the retention of all the accommodation now requisitioned in that area." But that was not all. On June 1, 1945, US combat engineers on the left bank of the Scheldt, close to the port, began the construction of what would become known as Camp Top Hat. First they, and several thousand German POWs, cleared more than 7,000 mines from an area of some 2 square kilometers. Then the engineers began to erect facilities

[180] De Vos, "US Forces," 157–9 and 192.

for the accommodation and recreation of more than 16,000 soldiers. The end result was a small American town more than a camp. Some 500 wooden constructions and 2,500 tents stretched along smooth, straight lanes named after the famous avenues of New York City. The buildings housed a hospital and dentistry, chapels for three different faiths, a post office, barber shops, movie theaters, and souvenir shops. Kitchens daily served 34 tons of food, 3,000 liters of coffee, 30,000 doughnuts, and mountains of ice cream. Soldiers were even allowed a ration of beer to help them relax. Camp Top Hat had everything. Or so it seemed. For what the camp commander could not and would not provide was that which many soldiers craved more than movies and beer: women and hard liquor. And because both beckoned on the other side of the river, Antwerp became an irresistible magnet for the kind of soldiers who refused to be content with the more wholesome recreation provided by their own military.[181]

"Under these circumstances," one US intelligence officer noted, "a soldier with steam to let off will not stay voluntarily in the best of camps." By September 1945, 90,000 GIs had passed through Top Hat and the port. By mid-April 1946, when the camp ceased its activities, the total number stood at 271,785. Even if the percentage of firebrands among them may have been low, there was sufficient potential for sparks to fly. Indeed, in June already, the SE in Antwerp was making mention of brush fires across the city, involving "trouble and friction between Belgian civilians and members of the Allied armies, mainly Americans." By the end of June, however, things had become particularly tense in what was the city's red-light district, popularly known as "the sailors' quarter." Soldiers flocked to the area, one report noted, because "it truly teems with loose women who officially and non-officially allow themselves to be used sexually for fairly low prices." Drink was an even worse source of trouble. If shadowy cafés illegally measured liquor by the glass, charging steep prices, bootleggers in the district sold cheaper rotgut by the bottle. More often than not, these very bottles were the soldiers' weapons of choice in bar brawls, street fights, and indecent assaults. Soldiers smashed windows, vandalized property, committed theft, and broke into cafés after closing hours. There were countless instances also of soldiers displaying such "a boundless rage" that they were "literally fit to be tied." One report blamed this on the presence of poisonous methanol in much of the bootleg liquor. The inhabitants of this neighborhood,

[181] SHAEFB, Final Report No. 21, 22, July 21, 1945, WO 202/702, AA 1230; SE Spa, WR August 12, 1945, Folder 1099, AA 1311; P. S., "Top Hat: De wachtkamer voor Amerika," *Gazet van Antwerpen*, June 27, 1985; De Vos, "US Forces," 192; and de Pinchart, *Office d'Aide Mutuelle*, 6–7.

however, were a tough lot who had suffered much poverty during the occupation and had become highly disillusioned by the little improvement that the liberation had brought to their lives. They could not be expected, the SE warned, to take these foreign threats lying down. Indeed, shopkeepers were known to keep billy clubs behind counters and, on the last day of June, in response to GIs harassing passersby, a furious crowd attacked the Americans, pelting them with stones in the streets and bombarding them with bottles from upstairs windows. As troops still had to pour into Top Hat in full strength, the SE worried that soon these conditions might lead to full-blown riots with repercussions for relations with the Allies across the country.[182]

The deteriorating discipline among American troops was creating much tension also in the Belgian borderlands with Germany. Between October and Christmas 1945, the largely rural, Dutch-speaking Limburg province was plagued by a series of violent carjackings and armed robberies involving GIs described by the press as "dangerous deserters." Further to the south, however, in the French-speaking city of Liège, things became much worse even than in Antwerp, as large numbers of rowdy demobilized troops were passing through from Germany. The situation was made more volatile by unscrupulous bootleggers who quickly spotted a new market and found it easy to resume activities amidst the mayhem. The gendarmerie in the area reported a new spike in the sale of illegal liquor as well as more deaths caused by the consumption of methanol. As early as June the Liège press was reporting on an impressive number of attacks and aggressions committed by American soldiers. Drunken GIs threw fists in bars and cafés, harassed people in the streets, and smashed shop windows. Soldiers inebriated and sober threatened civilians with guns, forcing them to hand over wallets, watches, and even wedding rings. Jewelry stores were being robbed in quasi-professional fashion and GIs were beaten and stabbed in ugly racial altercations. American banditry in an area of the city known as "Outremeuse" was so rampant that inhabitants were soon referring to it as the "Island of Terror." But even in the most public spaces in the very heart of the city, such as the normally lively Place Saint-Lambert, people stopped feeling safe.

In the summer, the press in Liège, like that in Antwerp, was referring to the American offenders as "gangsters." One newspaper unflinchingly compared Liège with the Chicago of Al Capone fame.

[182] Stéphany, "Belgique," 27; P. S., "Top Hat: De wachtkamer voor Amerika," *Gazet van Antwerpen*, June 27, 1985; Lagrou, "US Politics of Stabilization," 241, note 59; and SE report Cappoen, July 2, 1945, Folder 527, AA 1311.

American authorities were highly embarrassed by the situation and in mid-September organized an emergency meeting with local authorities and newspapermen. Words failed to stem the tide, however, and public relations continued to suffer. As autumn set in and days began to shorten, Liège's inhabitants hunkered down as if under siege, refusing to leave their homes after dark.

The most convenient way for the press in Liège to explain how relations with the Americans could have turned sour so rapidly was to put much of the blame on black soldiers. Based on the accounts in local newspapers, African-Americans appear to have been disproportionately involved in the escalating criminal activity plaguing the city. If that was indeed the case, it may have had to do with the fact that soldiers experiencing unrelenting discrimination were bound to display even lower morale. But, as one local historian has pointed out, it may just as well have been that the press thought it safer to denounce American banditry by singling out the black offenders of a segregated army rather than smearing the entire US military. Whatever the explanation, an article on the lawless "Outremeuse" in October set the tone. "Not a night goes by," *L'Express* railed indignantly, "without an honest citizen falling victim to these savages. The negroes seem to have forgotten the warm reception they received in this country and presently act as if they find themselves on enemy territory." Tellingly, the article no longer bothered to refer to blacks as GIs or soldiers.[183]

Across the country, meanwhile, smuggling and the black market thrived as never before amidst the disruption. In another manifestation of growing racist sentiment, the press enjoyed emphasizing the *black* in black market. And not just the press. Part of a song that people sang in the Liège dialect, for example, sneered: "Since those black soldiers/Have arrived here in our Belgium/They have been selling everything they own." But the truth was that white as well as black soldiers were complicit in illegal business schemes that promised to make them small fortunes before going home. To engage in such business was particularly appealing for members of a military that, now that the war was over, appeared to have more equipment left than it could possibly hope to ship home.[184]

In southern Limburg late in August 1945, and again in Liège early in November, panic erupted when thick clouds drifted in that made

[183] For Limburg see, for example, *HBVL*, October 16 and 17, 1945, and December 14 and 20, 1945. On bootlegging, see Gendarmerie Tongeren, MR August 8, 1945, Folder 1103; and Gendarmerie Verviers, MR September 8, 1945, Folder 1107, AA 1311. Sulbout, "Liège," 120–30.

[184] Sulbout, "Liège," 81–2; and Lecerf, *Libération*, 363.

humans feel nauseous and short of breath and caused cattle to stop grazing and producing milk. Investigations by the gendarmerie eventually revealed that the clouds had been released by American chemical units who had not known better than to clear their camps by setting fire to large amounts of fumigating powders no longer needed. Amidst such abundance there were soldiers who inevitably reasoned that it would make more sense to sell equipment for their own account to those who could use it.[185]

Much money could indeed be made from Allied stocks in a black market where in June 1945 Belgians were willing to pay 4 times the official price of men's shoes, 6 times that of coffee, 15 times that of chocolate, and 20 times that of household soap. In ports across the country, equipment vanished at an alarming rate. In Ghent, for example, the American port security officer in August reported that not only most of the Belgian personnel, but most of the American guards as well – including MPs – were involved in what had become large-scale theft. As American air force personnel prepared to depart from their large base at Florennes, some stashed an entire truck with brand-new boots, drove to the nearby town, and set up shop. When civilians refused to take the bait because they thought the prices outrageously high, the business folded and the GIs returned to base. There they committed the rejected boots to giant bonfires that were already consuming everything from clothing to furniture, musical instruments, and food. Belgians who tried to salvage some of the items from the pyres were turned back because they could not afford the prices the Americans insisted on charging. "The population," an SE officer noted in a damning report, "qualifies these events as the senseless acts of new vandals who remind them of others."[186]

Those "others" were the cause of still more tension in Liège province in September 1945. White and black GIs regularly drove their trucks to Fléron, for example, to unload trash. They used the occasion to sell things like flour, matches, and soap to Belgian men, women, and children who stormed the trucks even before these had come to a halt. What piqued the people of Fléron, however, was not so much the prices the Americans charged, but the fact that they were accompanied by German POWs, whom they allowed to deal with the customers freely. "The respectable part of the population," a gendarme wrote, "stigmatizes

[185] Gendarmerie Tongeren, August 28 and 31, 1945, Folder 1335 and September 7, 1945, Folder 1103, AA 1311; and *HBVL*, September 2, 1945, 1 and November 9, 1945, 1.

[186] SHAEFB, Final Report No. 21, Annexure IX (Part I) to Appendix G, July 21, 1945, WO 202/702, AA 1230. On Ghent, see O. C. port security to Ganshof, August 27, 1945, Folder 1487, AA 1311. On Florennes, see SE report Philippeville, [September 25, 1945], Folder 1085, AA 1311.

the behavior of the Allies which is the cause of this scandalous fraternization between Belgian civilians and German prisoners." As usual, matters became even more tense when women were involved. Belgians had been rattled by whispers of widespread fraternization between GIs and German women in the Nazi homeland. The ultimate insult came, however, when GIs began to be spotted in the company of *Fräuleins* on Belgian soil. The police in Verviers knew that Americans were buying butter from farms in the area that was then smuggled into Germany to be sold at exorbitant prices. With these profits the GIs bought the love of German girlfriends whom they then delighted with shopping sprees in the Belgian town. The police were outraged and thought it "abnormal that a defeated country that was previously an oppressor can take away from Belgians the little that remains in the shops." They tried to intervene but on at least one occasion were cursed and manhandled by American officers. The final straw came when the Americans in Verviers organized a Victory Ball a year after the liberation. To their astonishment, the Belgians at the ball learned that four GIs had brought German dates – *Bochesses* as the police report called them less respectfully. This immediately caused "the Belgians to refuse to dance with the Americans to protest the presence of German women who appeared to be making fun of them." The GIs and their dates eventually had no choice but to flee before "the general outcry." This outcry resonated as far as Brussels when the National Federation of Political Prisoners sent a letter to the Prime Minister expressing strong dissatisfaction with the behavior of American troops in Verviers.[187]

A loosening grip

What made the lawlessness among Allied and especially American troops so difficult to contain was that the rapid withdrawal did much to loosen the military's grip. At the top of the command structure, the combined SHAEF Mission to Belgium under the firm leadership of British General Erskine was dissolved on July 14, 1945, to make room for a separate American and British Mission. This, of course, made Allied coordination more difficult. But it also required redefining the responsibilities and communications between the now more fragmented Allied command and the Belgian government. In one of its last reports

[187] Gendarmerie Fléron to Brussels headquarters, September 21, 1945, Folder 979, AA 1311. On GI fraternization in Germany, see SE Visé, WR September 1, 1945, Folder 526, AA 1311. On Verviers, see police reports Nicolas Viellevoye, August 20 and 21, 1945, Folder 979; Gendarmerie Verviers, MR September 8, 1945, Folder 1107, AA 1311; and *Le Peuple*, August 30, 1945, 2.

in June, SHAEF expressed awareness that, even during redeployment and demobilization, "internal disorder may arise from time to time in Belgium." To deal with those exigencies, SHAEF made clear that it was the Belgian government that carried primary responsibility, not only for the internal order of the country, but also for the security of the Allied lines of communication. The principle was established that Allied commanders would intervene only "when Allied interests were directly threatened."[188]

In other words, as long as rowdy troops threatened only Belgian interests it was a problem for Belgian authorities that could no longer count on strong Allied support. This problem was compounded by the fact that, on the ground, the ranks of the MPs became precariously thin in the course of the pullout. The SE in Antwerp, for example, pointed out that there were no American MPs present in the troublesome red-light district and that, when called in to quell disturbances, they often arrived too late. The gendarmerie in Vilvoorde in August expressed extreme concern at "the misconduct of American soldiers" who were said to be committing almost daily "assaults on persons or property." They had been trying, they noted, to get a permanent MP post established in Vilvoorde, but all to no avail. MPs did intervene in Verviers during the row over the presence of German women at the Victory Ball. But they were blatantly unsuccessful and this may well have had to do with the fact that more and more MPs were being drawn from the very units that they were supposed to control. This was a practice American commanders increasingly resorted to in regions where not enough MPs were available, knowing full well that comrades would not make good policemen.[189]

All this served to weaken the authority of the MPs in the face of ever-mounting challenges to military discipline. Following the emergency talks in September, American authorities in Liège decided to attach as many MPs as they could spare to local police stations. They also had them patrol the streets after dusk in tandem with Belgian security forces. But their failure to make much of an impact is perhaps best illustrated by the fact that in November a gang of black GIs in "Outremeuse" chased four MPs in an attempt to avenge the arrest of one of their comrades. Crime

[188] SHAEFB, FR No. 20, 1 and Annexure II to Appendix E, June 26, 1945, WO 202/701, AA 1230.

[189] On Antwerp, see SE report Cappoen, July 2, 1945, Folder 527, AA 1311. On Vilvoorde and Verviers, see Gendarmerie Leuven, MR August 8, 1945, Folder 1063; and police report Nicolas Viellevoye, August 20, 1945, Folder 979, AA 1311. On MP policy, see Chief of Military Police for the Provost Marshal to Ganshof, December 8, 1945, Folder C5-17-6, AA 1882.

was rampant even in the very street where the Counter-Intelligence Division had its headquarters. In December nervous Liège policemen and American MPs fell victim to friendly fire as they mistook each other for troublemakers.[190]

A factor further complicating the situation was that in redefining the responsibilities of government and military, the Belgian security forces were left in the dark about their role in response to Allied misconduct. Ganshof van der Meersch at the end of November 1945 wrote to the Head of the American Military Mission to Belgium that he had made it very clear to the police and the gendarmerie that they were not allowed to intervene in cases of Allied soldiers disturbing public order. But the American chief of Military Police was quick to correct Belgium's chief military prosecutor. He pointed out that Belgian authorities *did* have the right to arrest Allied soldiers who had broken the law – even when this did not involve civilians or civilian property – and to detain them until they could be handed over to Allied authorities. "With particular reference to this time," the American was keen to emphasize, "when the ranks of the Military Police are so depleted by redeployment, such 'interference' is doubly welcomed – more and more emphasis will have to be placed on assistance and cooperation from the Belgian police in bringing American offenders to order."[191]

This was easier said than done, however. The recently purged and tentatively rearmed Belgian forces remained relatively weak in the second half of 1945. Moreover, relations between Belgian police forces and American MPs were often strained. During the summer, for example, there were clashes in Mechelen, while in Ghent there was a serious incident when MPs humiliated gendarmes by disarming them at gunpoint in full view of Belgians at work on the docks. Still more friction arose over the issue of house searches. There was much anger in the region of Mons, for example, when on several occasions American MPs proceeded, sometimes at night, to search private homes for stolen goods without the assistance of Belgian police forces. Again the potential for friction was heightened by misunderstandings about Allied competences now that the war in Europe was officially over. By mid-October both the Head of the British Military Mission to Belgium and the Head of the American Mission had confirmed in writing that, since the cessation of hostilities, the right to house searches belonged to the competent Belgian authorities only. Yet, strangely, in early November Ganshof van der Meersch in

[190] Sulbout, "Liège," 125–6.
[191] Ganshof to Chief of the American Mission to Belgium, November 20, 1945 and Chief of Military Police for the Provost Marshal to Ganshof, December 8, 1945, Folder C5-17-6, AA 1882.

a circular was still informing Belgian military prosecutors that Allied MPs also had that right.[192]

What the lack in police strength and coordination meant for ordinary citizens during the helter-skelter withdrawal became most obvious in Namur. The SE in mid-August described relations between GIs and civilians there as "frankly bad." That month alone, their report showed, GIs had been involved in disturbances and assaults almost every day, including a failed attempt by an American to strangle a woman with a rope after she rejected his advances. Incidents mushroomed rapidly later that month, especially in and around bars and dance halls. After closing hours late at night, drunken soldiers harassed frightened inhabitants, ringing door bells while whining in clumsy French they wanted to sleep "avec Mademoiselle." People demanded that one of the city's main parks be closed at night because it had become "a place of orgies."

Belgian policemen in Namur did what they could. But, as was the case elsewhere, GIs often refused to submit to their authority. When not in the company of MPs, Belgians who tried to stop American jeeps and trucks ran the risk of insults and obscene gestures and, worse, of being run over. Indeed, two policemen who intervened on their own in a bar brawl between GIs were reported to "have been beaten savagely." Meanwhile, the number of MPs in Namur seemed totally inadequate. Owners of dance halls, bars, and hotels repeatedly asked for MPs to be stationed nearby. When that did not happen, they were forced to take emergency measures and unilaterally announced that their businesses would close as early as six in the evening. Their concerns were shared, however, by broader segments of the population. "The question of 'morals' is the topic of all conversation," someone from the Belgian Ministry of Defense remarked on the disturbances in Namur. "The Americans form the main subject: theft, assaults, rapes, etc. ... The opinion is that the MP seems to be completely uninterested in the conduct of the Americans and people ask themselves why the government *does not want* to take measures to protect the Belgians." "People," the officer wrote in a report three days later, "talk of defending themselves and riots are to be feared," his words echoing warnings the SE had raised in Antwerp two months earlier. Some in Leuven at the end of 1945 traded words for sticks and clubs. "It has occurred many times," an unhappy company

[192] On Mechelen, see Laureys, "Het bevrijde België," 68. On Ghent, Ganshof to Chief of SHAEF Mission to Belgium Major-General Erskine, July 14, 1945, Folder C5-17-5, AA 1882. On Mons and the issue of house searches, Chief of American Military Mission to SE, September 15, 1945, Folder C5-16–3; Chief of British Military Mission to SE, October 11, 1945, Folder C5-16-5-1; and Ganshof to military prosecutors, November 9, 1945, Folder C5-16-5-2, AA 1882.

commander complained to the mayor in December, "that isolated American soldiers in the darkness have suffered cowardly attacks at the hands of so-called students."[193]

Liberation as occupation

It was by no means only the Americans who caused disturbances in Europe following the surrender of Nazi Germany. Canadian troops, for example, on July 4 and 5, 1945, caused riots with much looting and damage in the English town of Aldershot. Yet even the American press was making much of the widespread arrogance and misbehavior that appeared to be characterizing US troops in particular. The respected magazine *Time*, for example, in November 1945 admitted that across Europe this had often caused relations with civilians to become "strained to the utmost."[194]

Relations certainly became strained with the Belgian press. This might have been expected where it concerned communist newspapers, which had always relished singing the praises of the Soviet troops above all others. But the US embassy in Belgium, increasingly worried about anti-American sentiment, observed that the powerful Catholic press too was becoming much less accepting of the American presence. This had to do with the complex question of the future of the Belgian king and the opinion among Catholics that American authorities were at odds with their position. But the political issue easily tied in with their much broader concern about the American impact on Belgian moral standards.[195]

Ironically, the erosion of Belgian moral standards by all accounts appeared to be accelerating exactly at a time when troops were pulling out. Amidst the faltering control, civilians in their relations with the Allies became increasingly reckless. To get at petrol, thieves in and around Hasselt on several occasions undertook the sabotage of British pipelines, causing thousands of liters to spill into the soil. Theft from the army depots in and around Liège became so flagrant that American guards received orders to shoot at suspects. Groups of young boys

[193] "Rapport de Namur du 18 août 1945" and Lt. Col. Mampuys to SE, August 25, 1945, Folder 527; and report Gendarmerie Namur, August 21, 1945 and Lt. Col. Mampuys to Ministre de la Défense, August 28, 1945, Folder 1000, AA 1311. Aerts *et al.*, *Leuven*, 49–50.

[194] On Aldershot, see *Le Peuple*, July 7, 1945, 1; and Stacey and Wilson, *The Half-Million*, 170–1. On the American press, see Lilly, *Taken by Force*, 94; and Willoughby, *Conquering Heroes*, 149.

[195] Lagrou, "Een oorlog achter de rug," 130; and "US Politics of Stabilization," 225–6.

pilfered trucks with such distressing regularity and bravado that the press in Limburg described their antics as "gangster behavior," while judges in Brussels appealed to Ganshof van der Meersch for more advice on the means at their disposal to punish them hard. Simultaneously, the plague of VD spread ever more insidiously. In the summer of 1944 a single doctor in the small town of Athus had been seeing four or five inhabitants infected with syphilis; a year later he was caring for eighteen such patients and claimed to know of another seven who were refusing treatment.[196]

On July 20, 1945, the SE reported from the industrial city of La Louvière: "The population [in the region] has grown tired of the Allied troops. That attitude is due to the fact that we have emerged from a long enemy occupation only to find it replaced with another foreign occupation." By the time the last of the liberators withdrew from Belgian territory, the OMA had put together more than 60,000 files involving some 200,000 Belgian individuals or parties who had suffered material or physical damages as a result of "abusive, wrongful or criminal acts committed by members of the Allied armies." No wonder then that the attitude of the people in La Louvière was shared even by people in the normally quieter countryside. "They have brought to us," a report on the Americans in Visé summed up on the first day of September 1945, "habits that the population was not accustomed to: gangster exploits across Belgium, the propagation of venereal diseases, massive requisitions of buildings, and the exploitation of interests vital to our national economy. That atmosphere has made even a region as hospitable as ours embrace the current saying: 'from our liberators, oh Lord, liberate us.'"[197]

[196] On Hasselt, see several cases in Folder 1044 as well as SE Sint-Truiden, WR June 2, 1945, Folder 1095, AA 1311; and de Pinchart, *Office d'Aide Mutuelle*, 6. Sulbout, "Liège," 83–5. On juvenile crime in Limburg and Brussels, see *HBVL*, June 22, 1945, 2; and Parquet de la Cour d'Appel de Bruxelles to Ganshof, August 8, 1945, Folder C5-21, AA 1882. SE Athus, WR August 4, 1945, Folder 1006, AA 1311.

[197] SE La Louvière, WR July 20, 1945, Folder 1054, AA 1311; *La Réparation par l'Office d'Aide Mutuelle*, 182–3; and SE Visé, WR September 1, 1945, Folder 526, AA 1311.

Epilogue: A tide of change

Cries for normalcy

Parading the end of war

May 1945 in many ways was September 1944 all over again. They were days of hatred when Belgians in a new spasm of exorcism turned against anyone in their midst suspected of patriotic treason. But they were, above all, days of victory when the spectacular news of Hitler's death and Germany's surrender brought civilians to the streets united in feelings of boundless joy and relief. "The victory of the Allies in Europe and the total capitulation of Germany," the gendarmerie in Dendermonde wrote, "has caused an enthusiasm among the population that cannot be described." "Victory!" a girl in the capital scribbled in her diary on May 8. "Once again Brussels is a human tide exploding with happiness. There does not seem to be a single bottle of wine left in the shops." Some 500 couples danced the night away on Roeselare's market square while another 5,000 elated spectators sang along to the merry tunes. A week later, thousands in Sint-Truiden flocked to see a hastily arranged parade to mark the end of the war. The British contingent received a deafening applause and airplanes from the nearby American base joined in with a show of fireworks "that made the elation and joy climax."[1]

But even the dancing and singing and pyrotechnics failed to match what people truly felt inside during those heady days in May. It was, a Walloon school principal from the village of Felenne explained in his journal, more like "an internal frenzy," a jumble of emotions that "could not express itself noisily." Among them was a tremendous feeling of expectation. After years of upheaval and fear, people longed to return to their old lives of normal times. For that to happen, however, the first wish of many Belgians was to be reunited at last with those swept away by the tides of war. Most had ended up on enemy territory

[1] Rijkswacht Termonde, MR June 6, 1945, Folder 1100, AA 1311; Stéphany, "Belgique," 27; *Roeselare Bevrijd*, 142; and *HBVL*, May 16, 1945, 1.

in a variety of circumstances and conditions. At the time of Belgium's liberation, an estimated 200,000 citizens were at work in Germany. Some were volunteers, others had been deported as forced labor. More than 64,000 Belgians remained in Germany as POWs. Most of them were Walloons as Hitler, in a deliberate policy of divide and rule, had liberated all Flemish POWs except career soldiers as early as June 1940. Finally, some 43,000 Belgians had been deported as political prisoners. News of punishing Allied bombing and the shocking descriptions of conditions in Nazi concentration camps that surfaced in April 1945 had heightened the anxiety of anyone with relatives or friends in Germany.[2]

Some of the first Belgians began to be repatriated when the Allied troops pushed deep into the lion's den during the spring offensive. The first Walloon POWs, for example, arrived back in Belgium in March 1945. With the unconditional surrender of Germany early in May, however, the process was accelerated for all Belgians who wished to return home. By June an average of between 4,000 and 5,000 repatriates were arriving in Belgium every day. The final statistics of SHAEF and the United Nations Relief and Rehabilitation Administration (UNRRA) show that a total of 300,000 Belgians had returned from Germany and that, with the exception of a small minority, all had done so before August 1945.[3]

The rapid repatriation turned the summer of 1945 into a season of celebration. In many a village the return of the last prisoner was a cause for impromptu festivities. By the time the party ended in Bruyères, for example, the hamlet's inhabitants had downed an impressive fifty-two liters of *peket*, the strong local gin. Across the country, however, there soon was a proliferation of much more formal and better-organized celebrations in the shape of so-called peace parades. Parades had been an important feature of social life in a prewar Belgium that had used them for anything from the installation of a mayor to the veneration of a saint. During the German occupation, however, few parades had been permitted. Now that the final surrender of the oppressive regime had been secured and the surviving victims had returned, people reinstated the culture of parades with a vengeance. Between June and September 1945 there was barely a village, town, or city in Belgium that did not have its own peace parade to celebrate the victory over Nazi Germany.[4]

They were elaborate events that involved most of the local organizations as well as entire neighborhoods. People marched in bands, rode by

[2] Georges Dejardin, "Journal," AB 89. For the "wave of anxiety," see SHAEFB, FR No. 16, 1, May 1, 1945, WO 202/696, AA 1230.

[3] Lagrou, *Legacy*, 82–3, 87, and 94; De Vos, *Bevrijding*, 111; and Stéphany, "Belgique," 30.

[4] For Bruyères, see Dechaineux, "Herve," 156.

on festooned bicycles or horses, or formed part of groups enacting key scenes of the war on floats. The parade in the village of Vlamertinge, for example, consisted of no fewer than forty-six bands, troupes, and floats, while that in the town of Londerzeel counted almost 100 troupes on floats alone. At times there seemed to be more participants than spectators. The gendarmerie in Brabant province reported that in the small village of Waanrode an impressive 500 people had participated in the peace parade and that an astonishing 6,000 people had done the same in Schoonderbuken, a borough of the town of Scherpenheuvel. Most of the liberating armies sent delegations to the giant victory parade in Brussels on September 3. Provincials who had never before set foot in the capital now traveled to Brussels just to see this magnificent parade. People climbed into trees to make sure they did not miss a beat and even seasoned journalists later admitted they had never before seen anything like this celebration, which kept the capital awake for forty-eight hours.[5]

Many of the parades were conceived in gaiety and humor. Floats were flanked by young girls selling sweets and participants frequently wore the funny noses and masks of the carnival season. The Germans were ridiculed, their swastikas smeared with cow dung, their rifles replaced by brooms – all to the sound of cathartic laughter. But many of the troupes also enacted scenes of terrible suffering that through the often chronologically arranged parades were woven into meaningful narratives of the community's history and sense of identity. This communal acting out not only helped to assuage traumatic experiences, it also served as a means of closure to a period of war that had lasted painfully long.[6]

Saying farewell to the Allies

There was a much longer period of closure relating to the Allied troops. Communities across Belgium were bidding formal and often emotional final farewells to their liberators long before the problematic withdrawal of the summer was set in motion. Commenting on the wild enthusiasm with which the Allies had been received in Flanders and the Walloons, *Le Soir* in a major article on the front page in September 1944 had expressed the hope that the Belgians would hang on to this "instinctive impulse." "May they never," the newspaper had pleaded, "allow any person, under

[5] For Vlamertinge, see Quaghebeur and Verbeke, *Ieper*, 182. Vermaesen, *Londerzeel*, 99–100. The gendarmerie reports on the July parades in Brabant are in Folder 951, AA 1311. For Brussels, see Stéphany, "Belgique," 31.

[6] For insights into the function of parades, I thank anthropologist Amanda Wise for presenting the paper "Traumatic Memory and the Embodiment of Political Identities among East Timorese Refugees" in the "War and Memory" forum at the Centre for Peace and Conflict Studies, University of Sydney, August 4, 2006.

whatever pretext, to abandon either that enthusiasm or that gratitude!" Certainly, by the spring of 1945, despite serious currents of discontent, the "instinctive impulse" towards the Allies on the whole remained a very positive one. Myriad Belgian cities and towns invited their liberators back, determined to pay homage more properly than had been possible in the chaos of the previous fall. When, at the end of April, elements of the 2nd US Armored Division passed through Belgium on the long way home, Hasselt hailed its liberators with an impressive ceremony that packed the market square with spectators. An overwhelmed American general and his staff were dragged off to the town hall for speeches, flowers, toasts, and the signing of a special guest book. The town of Wervik had the commanding officer of the 1st Highland Light Infantry come over all the way from Germany for its commemoration. When he arrived, young girls in fancy white dresses normally worn for first Communion welcomed him with flowers. The population went on to honor him and his men with a ceremony at the monument of the dead, a religious service involving three choirs, and a magnificent procession. Meanwhile, General Eisenhower and several other high-ranking American and British officers visited the giant military cemetery at Henri-Chapelle for Memorial Day. They were joined by the governor of Liège as well as thousands of ordinary civilians who silently and respectfully took their places amidst a sea of crosses and stars.[7]

Such ceremonies of heartfelt thanks continued unabatedly even as the summer's chaotic withdrawal was taxing the civilians' patience like never before. The people of Bruges on July 21, 1945, Belgium's national holiday, invited Lieutenant Roy Firth, the first officer to enter the city during the liberation, to be their guest of honor. On the same day, they gave a rapturous welcome to Major General W. H. Foster, commanding officer of the liberating Canadians, who was made an Honorary Citizen. In September, six British soldiers who had been killed during the liberation of Hasselt a year earlier were transferred from their temporary graves to a final resting place in the city's cemetery. The coffins were greeted by the governor of Limburg, the city council, magistrates, the fire brigade, the police corps, the Red Cross, youth movements, a detachment of the Belgian army, organizations of war veterans, resistance fighters and

[7] "Enthousiasme et gratitude," *Le Soir*, September 24–5, 1944, 1; Vanstreels, *Hasselt*, 104, 107, 110, 117, and 119; Decuypere, "Comines-Warneton," 536; and Sulbout, "Liège," 101–8. Even in France, where the winter had brought problems similar to those in Belgium and suspicion towards the Americans ran deeper, the "instinctive impulse" remained a positive one. An opinion poll in January 1945, for example, showed that 62 percent of the French thought the GIs "were behaving correctly." Admittedly, this was before the American withdrawal, when troops turned particularly rowdy. Torrent, "L'Image du soldat américain," 240.

political prisoners, children from all of the city's schools, and countless other inhabitants from all walks of life. More emotional still that same month was the solemn pilgrimage that French-speaking civilians undertook to Neuville-en-Condroz, a second massive American cemetery in Belgium, where many GIs were buried who had been killed during the Battle of the Bulge.[8]

As the ceremonies, honorary citizenships, and pilgrimages demonstrate, none of the gripes, complaints, and exasperation ever convinced the population at large – not even during the difficult closing months of 1945 – that it had not been worth having Allied troops on home soil. "Generally speaking," the SE commented in their report on the tension between civilians and GIs in Antwerp in June, "these conflicts do not leave behind deep traces of resentment." This was the case, the report noted, "because thanks to the psychology of the times people are able to forgive the liberating soldiers much." The SE pointed out also, however, that the generous financial compensations provided by the various Allied Claims Services in cases of damage and injury went a long way to defuse much ill-feeling. Still, it was never just cold calculation that kept the special relationship with the Allies alive. The bond between liberators and liberated ran much deeper and was exemplified by many a gratuitous act of solidarity and affection long after the liberation. Much of the wanton destruction of superfluous equipment by GIs on the Florennes air base in September 1945, for example, could be forgiven by inhabitants in the knowledge that, a week earlier, the 344th Bomb Group, before pulling out, had adopted a Belgian orphan, organized her visit to the airbase as well as a party, and collected a large sum of money to support her. The Sisters of Vorselaar in their journal referred to the presence of foreign troops in their convent in Olmen as five separate "occupations" – three of them German, two English. But in doing so, they in no way intended to suggest that having the British over was something onerous. Not only did the Sisters receive financial compensation for both stays. "The English," the journal also mentions, "were very favorably disposed towards us and had us share in their abundance." When they left, the equally grateful Tommies were happy to present the Sisters with a fine statue of the Sacred Heart almost a meter in height.[9]

While the Allied soldiers prepared to leave, Belgian civilians were becoming impatient to get their lives back to normal as soon as possible. Daily concerns about coal and butter began to overtake the larger issues

[8] Warnier, *Brugge bevrijd*, 60–2; *HBVL*, October 30, 1945, 1; and Sulbout, "Liège," 101–8.

[9] SE report Cappoen, July 2, 1945, Folder 527, AA 1311; Challe, "Florennes," 34, AB 1381; and Zusters van Vorselaar, "Dagboek," 3, AB 711.

of war and peace as soon as Nazi Germany surrendered. SHAEF early in May expressed the desire that the period of military responsibility for Belgium in terms of supplies should end with the July deliveries, petrol and coal being the only exceptions. The Belgian government later that month announced that it would assume responsibility for essential civilian needs at the start of September. The police in a report on the mood of the population in Bruges early in June noted that the three main topics of conversation were repatriation, purges, and the coal stocks for the coming winter. A high rate of absenteeism among mine workers combined with a large number of stoppages and strikes to make coal a nagging concern for people who all too vividly remembered the fight against the cold during the last winter. By the end of June, SHAEF admitted that coal production was causing "more headaches than anything else," both in terms of heating Belgium's homes and powering its industry. Other than that, however, things were looking up for the Belgians. As far as fuel and raw materials permitted, industry was working at full capacity by July. And, SHAEF noted that summer, "While there are no large reserves, the day has been passed when the chain of supply was direct from ship to stomach." The heads of cattle were increasing and the prospects for their winter feed looked good. Indeed, reports on the coming harvest sounded promising altogether. Reasons enough for SHAEF to sound upbeat in one of its final reports on Belgium: "This winter will be hard for many people in Europe. There will be millions without houses, with inadequate clothing, with little food and no coal. These conditions need not exist in Belgium if the Belgian people really take their coats off and work hard during the next 4 or 5 months."[10]

Whispers of change

The school principal from Felenne who on May 7 expressed doubt in his journal that the utter joy of liberation could ever be properly expressed, a day later nevertheless confided to paper his wish for the future: "That upon the return of justice, the poet can think of his verses again, the violinist of Bach, the laborer of cultivating his field, the simple mortal of a stroll, of a voyage, free, free!"[11]

The end of the war would allow Belgians to enjoy all and more of these simple pleasures soon enough. Yet, no matter how hard they

[10] Commissariaat Brugge, WR No. 37, June 2, 1945, Folder 958, AA 1311. The SHAEFB reports are FR No. 17, 20, May 15, 1945; No. 18, 19, May 29, 1945; No. 20, 1–2 and 13, June 26, 1945, AA 1230; and Final Report No. 21, 23 and 26, July 21, 1945, AA 1798/9.

[11] Georges Dejardin, "Journal," May 8 and 9, 1945, AB 89.

Plate 7.1 Belgian, British, and American flags in Liège hail the arrival of a new era. (CEGESOMA, Brussels, picture number 29585)

would work with their coats off in the coming months, they would never again manage to reclaim life as they had known it before the war. The trauma of war, the humiliation of German occupation, and the exhilaration of liberation had seeped too deep into the foundations of society for that. Their combined impact made five years feel like an eternity. In September 1944 the Pierlot government returned from exile in London for only a short stint, estranged from a people that never again fully accepted it for not having shared their hardship. The prewar parliament, minus the representatives of the collapsed New Order, was restored and would remain in place for another year and a half until the first postwar elections were held in February 1946. All that time, however, its members limped along, realizing full well that they too were no longer the true representatives of the people. "This parliament," an astute correspondent from France noted, "dates back to 1939, in other words to a century ago." The feeling was similar at the local level. On September 14, 1944, the liberation in Verviers was celebrated with a band, veterans holding flags, and men and women of the resistance marching proudly in their uniforms. Behind them in the parade followed the mayor, two aldermen, and a judge. Not on foot like the others, but in a stately horse-drawn carriage. Such a scene, juxtaposed with the memory of German *Panzers* and the omnipresence of American jeeps, appeared archaic and suddenly strangely out of place.[12]

Not that the Belgian political establishment in the aftermath of the war experienced anything like a tabula rasa. Historians have shown how pillars like the judiciary and police were firmly restored to their former selves as quickly as possible. And they have described in great detail how parties and unions emerged from illegality to be at the heart of politics again in almost no time. During the war, some in the resistance, especially on the far left, had dreamed of radical change and their involvement in the construction of yet another new order. But the political elite quickly reclaimed power during the early stages of the liberation, never to let go of it again. They hastened to rebuild, stabilize, and strengthen the prewar political system. This, of course, involved dismantling the far right that had fundamentally challenged the system before and during the war. But it also, almost immediately after the liberation, entailed the containment of communism, first and foremost in the form of the armed resistance. When a new parliament was at last elected early in 1946, many new and younger faces replaced the old guard. Other than that, however, nothing much changed in terms of the strength of the traditional parties and their power relations. King Leopold III, of course, would fail to return to his prewar role because of the controversy surrounding his behavior during the German occupation. But even though the monarch fell victim to the war, the Belgian monarchy as an institution managed to survive when Leopold's brother, Charles, in the interim position of Prince Regent, gained sufficient time for Leopold's son, Baudouin, to come of age and take over.[13]

With their focus on the political restoration, many Belgian historians as late as the 1980s emphasized that it was wrong to consider the Second World War as a major fault line and that the real sea change could be found in the 1960s rather than the 1940s. Then, at the fiftieth anniversary of the liberation, an important collection of essays went a long way

[12] The correspondent worked for *Parisien Libéré* and is quoted in Gotovitch, "Communistes et résistants," 63. Ruwet, *Verviers*, 98–9.

[13] Huyse and Hoflack, *De democratie heruitgevonden*; Lagrou, "Résistance"; Gotovitch, "Communistes"; and Witte *et al.*, *Politieke geschiedenis*, 231–42.

towards qualifying this interpretation, demonstrating that rather than bringing firm restoration, the end of the war had landed Belgium somewhere "between continuity and change." That was true politically, not in the least through the "reinvention" of a democracy that many even in the political establishment had turned their backs on in the 1930s. Others posited that an examination of culture and mentality instead of structure and organization was bound to reveal "an undertow carrying the germs of a fundamental renewal." Most prominently among them was Rudi van Doorslaer, who was struck by the extent to which individuals continued to identify the war as a turning point in their lives. My book argues that the latter thesis gains force when the war is looked at from the perspective of the Anglo-American liberation and its impact. It was the hard power of the Allies, of course, that allowed the Belgian political elite to reestablish itself in September 1944 and to withstand pressures for more radical change in November. Simultaneously, however, it was the extraordinary soft power of the Anglo-Americans – their now unparalleled ability to lead by example – that made them into a catalyst of change in a variety of spheres.[14]

The cult of abundance

Security cravings

If any one emotion stood out amidst the turbulent reactions of liberated Belgians, it was that of a deep longing for improvement. For a people that had known years of shortages under the Germans and was experiencing the humiliation of having to beg and steal from the Anglo-Americans, the longing for a better life involved above all an obsession with material progress. At the end of September 1944, one Flemish newspaper was confident that peace would usher in a democratic renaissance. Tellingly, however, the newspaper was not in the first place referring to political democracy, but "democracy in this sense: that the standard of living will be much higher than before the war." That the social and economic expectations now went beyond what had been known even before the war by no means surprised Guillaume Jacquemyns, a Belgian sociologist who had conducted research among industrial workers during the German occupation. What people would want after the war, he had been predicting, was not only improved well-being and renewed dignity,

[14] The collection of essays is Huyse and Hoflack, *De democratie heruitgevonden*. Van Doorslaer's essay is "De oorlog tussen continuïteit en verandering: Vragen en problemen," 17–26.

but also – and especially – more security. "People," he strongly sensed, "desire being surrounded by sympathy."[15]

Belgians during the occupation had suffered together and they now insisted on enjoying the fruits of peace together. That was the essence of the new social solidarity that was born from the war and stood to replace the paternalistic principle of social assistance. The resounding message was heard loud and clear not only by researchers like Jacquemyns. As early as October 1941, Christian and socialist leaders of the labor movement as well as representatives for the employers had been meeting clandestinely to prepare for the new socioeconomic climate of the postwar. Five months before the liberation, they had hammered out a so-called Social Pact of which the idea of social security was a key component. In London, meanwhile, the Belgian Commission for the Study of Post-War Problems (CEPAG) had been thinking along similar lines. CEPAG served as the think tank of the Belgian government in exile from early 1941 until the liberation, and stood under the direct authority of Prime Minister Pierlot. Despite the different philosophical and political backgrounds of the commission's members, they all agreed that the inter-war system had failed and was in need of a thorough overhaul. They also agreed that the individual's dignity and needs should be central in devising new socioeconomic structures. The interests of labor and capital in future were to serve "a regime in which *all* enjoyed security and could satisfy their legitimate needs." In doing so, a careful balance would have to be struck whereby "the social wishes" of the people would be met while at the same time allowing "as much individual freedom as possible."

The key legislation that introduced social security for the mass of wage earners in December 1944 came as close as possible to establishing such a balance. Employees, employers, and the state would henceforth contribute to a system of compulsory social insurance that, as CEPAG had suggested, covered "all aspects of a person's life that escaped the individual's control, plus some additional benefits." The new system aimed at softening the trauma and pain of war while at the same time paving the road for a more civilized country characterized by social peace.[16]

The Belgian welfare state that was established in 1944–5 might not have been conceived had it not been for the hardships of the Nazi occupation and a culture of social experimentation preceding the war.

[15] "Handen te kort!" *HBVL*, September 24–5, 1944, 1 and Jacquemyns, "La Société belge," 384–9.

[16] Veraghtert, "Naoorlogse economie," 70; and Henau, "Shaping a New Belgium," 112 and 116–19. See also Witte *et al.*, *Politieke geschiedenis*, 254–5 and 258–9.

But the concept of the welfare state during the war also received strong impulses from the Anglo-Americans and especially Britain. Fascism formed an ideological as much as a strategic threat for much of the world. That is why, in a meeting in August 1941, Roosevelt and Churchill insisted on issuing a statement of common purpose in the war against the Axis powers. Of the eight propositions outlining their ideology, point five of the so-called Atlantic Charter addressed the socioeconomic component. In it the leaders very clearly expressed a desire to see "improved labor standards, economic advancement and social security." Roosevelt, of course, had forced the federal government to demonstrate, in the form of the New Deal during the Great Depression, at least a basic form of social responsibility in a country traditionally enamored with economic liberalism. Indeed, Nazi propaganda in Belgium seized on this opportunity to gloat that even the liberal economic order's biggest champion had broken ranks and that the US "merely promised what the New Order was already achieving." War and a booming economy, however, soon gave rise to a tide of American conservatism threatening to roll back Roosevelt's social accomplishments. This left Britain, another paragon of laissez-faire economics, to position itself within the Allied coalition as the leading advocate of a new and more humane liberalism. Eager to rally public support in the midst of the German air war against British cities, Churchill ordered a report on the country's social ills and on how to address these head-on after the war. Sir William Beveridge presented an elaborate blueprint for a welfare state as early as December 1942. There was support both within the ranks of conservatives and socialists for Beveridge's ambitious plan blending private enterprise with state socialism. The stratagem aimed at neutralizing both fascist and communist appeal and, as historian Randall Woods has pointed out, "seemed tailor-made for the war-damaged, postindustrial societies of Western Europe because it promised social security without undermining democracy or diminishing individual liberty."[17]

Indeed, as the BBC and the resistance press spread news of the benefits that such a plan might bring to the rest of Europe in case of an Allied victory, Nazi propaganda thought it necessary to denounce it as a false promise that would not survive the war. Given this background, it was not surprising in the first months after the liberation to find in the Belgian press, which to a large extent was fed from British sources, rave reviews of Britain's innovative and wide-ranging charter of social security. Newspapers pored over the details of the model Beveridge

[17] Woods, *A Changing of the Guard*, 397; de Grazia, *Irresistible Empire*, 338–40; and Stirk, "Anti-Americanism," 77.

plan with great interest, informing their readers of a national health plan, universal secondary education, and subsidized housing as well as generous schemes for the unemployed, sick, aged, and families. The wonder lasted until Belgian political leaders in December 1944 at last made good on their own wartime plans for a beneficent system of social security. This system, one of Belgium's social architects emphasized, was "henceforth recognized as irrevocable" and "in direct contrast to the frightful insecurity to which the enemy reduced us."[18]

Material desires

The newly liberated Belgians in the economic sphere longed for more, however, than just security. Years of rationing and deprivation had made sobriety and frugality ugly words tainted by the painful memory of an endless war. They might not have been so audacious as to wish for abundance so soon after the conflict, had it not been for the presence of Allied and especially American troops acting as living billboards for a society of plenty, which is perhaps why, as Alain Brossat notes in his work on France in 1944–5, so many of the liberated have found their memory of "the American moment" so irrevocably condensed into a number of "fetish objects" like chewing gum, cigarettes, instant coffee, the jerrycan, and the jeep.[19]

As millions of American soldiers and their impressive equipment were shipped overseas, they exposed large parts of the globe to the standards of what was the most advanced consumer society. Melanesians in the Pacific, for example, were so impressed by the machinery and supplies of the GIs, next to which even the material goods of the Europeans and Japanese paled, that they considered these irrefutable proof of their divine origin. After the war, several of the island peoples adapted their most ancient oral traditions to incorporate a mythical land by the name of America. Many others adopted "cargo cults" in the belief that material wealth could be obtained from that distant source through ritual worship.[20]

Belgians were not Melanesians. They stopped short of attributing to the Americans divine powers and were under no illusion that material progress could be accomplished through rituals and incantations. They, like many other Europeans, had been introduced to American consumer

[18] De Grazia, *Irresistible Empire*, 339–40. The comment was made by Henri Fuss in his 1945 article "Social Security in Belgium," in BT, 117. Belgium's social renewal was, of course, only part of a much broader consensus in the West regarding the new role of the state. See, for example, Duignan and Gann, *Rebirth*, 178 and 574–7.

[19] Brossat, *Libération*, 163–4.

[20] Schrijvers, *Japan*, 238.

practices and ideas as early as the turn of the century. The waves of this consumer culture had surged in the wake of the First World War, only to recede during the Great Depression of the 1930s. Now, however, the tide turned again with a vengeance as GIs, backed up by a humming economy, flooded into an Old World ruined and impoverished by yet another conflagration. In these exceptional circumstances they could hardly fail to sweep people off their feet and impress them with the American model of how the future might look.[21]

For Belgians who during years of austerity and deprivation had developed an insatiable appetite for material goods, American scenes of surplus at the end of the war beggared belief. The British military left few stocks behind as they shipped most equipment home and transported some of it to their German zone of occupation. Aware that their economy was producing more equipment than they themselves could possibly use, the US military reasoned that shipping their considerable European stocks home or to the Pacific would be more costly than simply leaving them behind. As chemical units in southern Limburg set fire to their stocks of fumigating powders in the summer of 1945, gendarmes had to stop civilians from venturing into the acrid smoke to carry off empty wooden crates and other items in everything from trucks to wheelbarrows. Entire barracks and airfields were left behind without American troops bothering to dismantle them. In September, for example, people in Florennes flocked to the abandoned American airbase and stripped it of bricks, steel, and coal long before Belgian authorities could restore a measure of control.

But the Americans left behind much more than weaponry and basic building materials. To ensure a more efficient and orderly liquidation of the massive stocks in Belgium, an agreement was eventually signed between both governments in September 1946, which gave OMA the task of inventorying, storing, and selling them. It was agreed that half of the money from the sales would go to the US. The Belgian agency found the supplies to be so "extremely abundant and varied" that it earmarked huge depots in twenty-four places across the country for stockpiling purposes and took almost seven years to dispense all of the goods made in the USA during the Second World War. The abandoned stocks included civil engineering and telecommunications equipment, petrol products, trucks and cars, tents and textiles, machinery and tools, electrical materials, chemical substances, and supplies for doctors, dentists, and

[21] On the mechanisms and impact of America's globally expanding consumer-oriented capitalism see, for example, Rosenberg's *Spreading the American Dream* and de Grazia's *Irresistible Empire*.

hospitals. During the first year of liquidation, OMA employed 2,380 laborers, 880 guards, and 370 clerks in the scattered depots and another 500 people in its Brussels headquarters. By the end of 1947, the total value of the massive clearance sale was estimated at 1.2 billion Belgian francs. OMA reported that more than a quarter of this revenue came from the export of supplies that "were too large in quantity for Belgian consumption or too rare or unknown in Belgium."[22]

If some of this was hard to believe, much of it proved effortlessly seductive. Belgians did not develop the equivalent of a Pacific cargo cult, but they certainly bought into the American cult of abundance with barely disguised eagerness. Historian Mark Mazower is right in pointing out that in the postwar period, because of an initial lack of money to spend, the "production of desires" manifested itself quite some time before the actual "purchase of goods." But rather than the advertising agencies and retailers of the 1950s that Mazower identifies, it was the Allied and especially the American publicity convoys of 1944–5 that set this production of desires in motion. Belgian soil certainly was fertile enough to allow such a consumer culture to catch on straightaway. "Left to his own devices," Guillaume Jacquemyns observed during the occupation, "the worker has come up with his ideal outside of the influence of propaganda." That model for the future, he explained, no longer revolved around the old slogans of "work and bread" or "bread and games." And it also went beyond the simple demands for security and dignity. There was now a strong longing, he sensed, for a "well-being" that superceded the issue of daily bread and instead encompassed "everything that had to do with one's existence." Belgian policymakers in exile and underground drew similar conclusions during the war. They realized that a future economy would have to be designed for the function of serving human needs. But they were also aware that those needs now had to be defined in terms of giving all members of society a chance not just of security but also – as the American constitution had boldly put it as early as the eighteenth century – of happiness.[23]

Since Jacquemyns sufficiently elaborated on this wartime mentality to make clear that the aspirations were material rather than spiritual, he was essentially saying that his society had become one not only of urgent

[22] On Limburg, see Gendarmerie Tongeren, August 28 and 31, 1945, Folder 1335, AA 1311. Challe, "Florennes," 34, AB 1381. De Pinchart, *Office d'Aide Mutuelle*, 8–11; and De Vos, "US Forces," 191.

[23] Mazower, *Dark Continent*, 307; Jacquemyns, "La Société belge," 384; and Henau, "Shaping a New Belgium," 118. David Reynolds contends that GIs played a part in the promotion in Great Britain of what would eventually become known as consumerism: *Rich Relations*, 437.

needs but also of smoldering wants. Belgians could and would no longer be satisfied with a life of subsistence. And American troops liberated their minds into believing not only that a life of affluence was perfectly feasible, but that it lay waiting just around the corner, to the point even where some in Belgium were having trouble hiding their impatience within mere weeks of regaining their freedom. "Relations between the population and the American army are most cordial," the SE reported from Arlon on October 7, 1944, "but there is nevertheless a slight disappointment because the promised abundance is not arriving immediately." For people exhausted by war and propaganda, nothing proved more soothing and appealing than the thought of retreating into a secure shell of material comfort. In contrast to the exuberance of May 1945, the SE wrote from Ostend in August, the surrender of Japan had "not given rise to a special expression of feelings of happiness." "Japan is, of course, so far away," the report explained, "and the population does not sense a direct connection between the Pacific war theater and their interests here." "What the public does understand," the SE emphasized, "is that shipping cargo will become available for the transport of products from overseas that we cannot do without."[24]

Later that same year, the largest shops of Liège collectively bought advertising space in the newspaper press. The slogan "Long live peace!" featured side by side with "The end of bad days!" *Grand Bazar*, *Innovation*, and *Bon Marché* confidently announced for the near future "a varied selection of products of good quality at normal prices." That they would soon be able to offer such prices, they proudly explained, was thanks to "their rational organization" as well as "their close relations with the exporting countries." Substantial pay increases in 1944 and 1945 and a rapid industrial resurgence fueling employment had foreign observers talk about "the Belgian miracle" before there was any mention even of a Marshall Plan. This miracle was translated almost immediately into a rising demand for consumer items, a trend further strengthened by a redistribution set in motion by the newly introduced social security system. In fits and starts, Europe's old bourgeois regime of consumption in the postwar years would be transformed inexorably into one of mass consumerism. Belgium was among the spearheads of that transformation and, in order to keep the momentum going and its population happy as well as productive, gladly integrated itself into what historian Victoria de Grazia has called America's Market Empire.

[24] SE Arlon, WR October 7, 1944, Folder 993; and SE Oostende, August 18, 1945, Folder 1082, AA 1311. There was a similar eagerness in France to see abundance arrive with the liberating troops. See Torrent, *La France américaine*, 16.

It took the Belgian retail trade slightly more than two years after the war to exceed its prewar volume. Visiting Belgium for the American State Department in mid-1946, economist Charles Kindleberger in a letter to his wife expressed surprise at the quantities of luxury items that were being imported from the US. These included cars, spirits, soft drinks and, above all, expensive nylons, of which in 1947 alone Belgians purchased some ten million pairs. Indeed, there were voices in Europe that criticized Belgium's politics of abundance so soon after the war. And there were those in Belgium who felt no less concerned about the narrow focus on material gratification with which many emerged from the conflict. Catholic philosopher Marcel De Corte, for example, as early as April 1945 wrote a book in which he called on people not to loose sight of balancing "the superficial and the profound, the quantitative and the qualitative."[25]

Technological promises

Ironically, what boosted the material expectations when the war ended were the tremendous technological and scientific advances spurred on by militaries geared towards destruction. It was the task of the postwar generation, Catholic politician Pierre Wigny wrote at the end of 1945, "to build a new society in accordance with the great fact of our day that man, as the master of technology, has a formidable economic power which should make him free and not enslave him."[26]

That Wigny could sound so optimistic in a world largely in ruins as a result of escalating technology had everything to do with the fact that it was *Anglo-American* man who now was the undisputed master of technology and that Belgium had the good fortune of squarely belonging to his camp. It was not a coincidence, for that matter, that Wigny was writing for an American journal that was putting together a special issue called *Belgium in Transition*. This transition, among many other things, compelled Belgium, after four years of German exploitation, to catch up with technological progress by relying on the US and Britain for the replacement of worn-out equipment and outdated methods.[27]

"Modernity," Michael Saler has pointed out, "is one of the most ambiguous words in the historian's lexicon." Still, when understood as

[25] The advertisement is published in Gaier, "Réflexions," 22. On the Belgian economy in the immediate postwar years, see Veraghtert, "Naoorlogse economie," 70–1. Both "Market Empire" and "bourgeois regime of consumption" are concepts taken from de Grazia's *Irresistible Empire*. De Corte, *Du fond de l'abîme*, 114–15.

[26] Wigny, "Belgium Today and Tomorrow," in BT, 179.

[27] Ibid., 183. The journal is *The Annals of the American Academy of Political and Social Science*.

machine or techno civilization, there existed no doubt, even in the minds of the British, that it was the US that had commenced its ascendancy to the acme of modernity as early as the turn of the century. American economic growth in the 1920s caused European entrepreneurs from Britain to Russia to study the methods of Fordism and Taylorism. Others in the Old World saw a threat more than an opportunity as they, like Kafka in his *Amerika*, emphasized the mindless standardization and anonymous mass production that they feared would destroy culture. Meanwhile, however, the Old World, and its German-speaking parts in particular, managed to hang on to its reputation as a scientific stronghold even through the shockwaves of the First World War. Indeed, as Hitler forcefully beat back the Great Depression, and as his troops conquered much of Europe with awe-inspiring discipline and technology, it appeared to many that Nazi Germany had eclipsed America as a robot nation. But, of course, nothing much remained of the image of the clanking robot that a Dutch cartoonist had drawn in May 1940 when, in the autumn of 1944, mauled German troops withdrew on bicycles and horses. Even then, however, Nazi Germany managed a last spasm of futuristic terror by launching a mass of V weapons in the winter of 1944–5. Belgians were soon referring to the unmanned flying objects as "robots" and in popular parlance the homes they destroyed were often said to have been "robotized."[28]

Fearsome and memorable as it may have been, however, the *Vergeltungswaffe* offensive inevitably fizzled in a matter of months as Allied troops pushed deeper into enemy territory. Meanwhile, Anglo-Americans quickly smothered the memory of German technological prowess with a vast array of quality products and novelty items fabricated on a massive scale. This was perhaps nowhere better illustrated than in Zepperen's peace parade in July 1945. As was the case in many such parades, the terror of the *Vergeltungswaffe* was prominently displayed in the form of a self-made copy of the V1. To make Zepperen's replica look more realistic, however, the German robot bomb had been made to emit smoke. Closer inspection revealed to onlookers that the malignant-looking fumes were being pumped into the harmless V1 by way of the exhaust pipe of a massive American truck. The powerful Dodge steadily rumbled along amidst the parade's bicycles and horse-drawn wagons.[29]

Indeed, for a country with a hopelessly outdated and dilapidated car pool, motorization at the end of the war continued to be what made the

[28] Saler, "Modernity and Enchantment," 694. On the European response to American modernization, see Wagnleitner, *Coca-Colonization*, 20–4.
[29] Celis *et al.*, *Zepperen*, 299.

Anglo-American armies look most impressive in the streets. British soldiers could grant children no greater pleasure than to lend them a ride on their motorcycles. Women and girls had a distinct preference for a photo with a GI beau in front of or seated in a jeep. Many a Belgian entrepreneur resumed business in the cabin of a Chevrolet or an olive-drab truck adorned with the Maple Leaf, all from Allied war stocks. Anything Anglo-American with a motor, it seemed, became invested with the magic power of a status symbol. Apart from foodstuffs, raw materials, and clothing, the main Belgian imports from the US by the end of 1945 were industrial equipment and trucks. Gone were the prewar, Kafkaesque fears of the coldness of America's techno civilization now that its very machines had quashed the terror of the Nazi regime. America, a leftist youth paper wrote admiringly, was the land of mechanics, haste, and speed.[30]

With much of the continent dead in its tracks, this meant that the future inevitably belonged to the Anglo-Americans. SHAEF was keen to exploit that image and did so successfully through its hugely popular exhibitions on the war effort, which put great emphasis on aviation in particular. For one of the exhibitions in July 1945, for example, SHAEF specifically ordered the RAF to provide a Mosquito, Auster, Typhoon, and Spitfire and the USAAF to deliver a Piper Cub, Marauder, Mustang, Lightning, and Thunderbolt. Such efforts undoubtedly went a long way towards strengthening perceptions of the Anglo-Americans as technologically superior. Gone were the days of awe for the Stuka and Messerschmidt. If, at the end of 1944, 60 percent of people in neighboring France, for example, were convinced that the Soviets had the strongest land army, 52 percent of the French believed that Britain possessed the most powerful navy, and 72 percent that the US had no equal in the world in terms of air power. Once the reports from Hiroshima and Nagasaki began seeping through, no one could have doubted that the latter was true. Even then, however, the Belgian press emphasized that due should be given to the British too in terms of the development of aviation technology. Newspaper *Het Volk*, for example, at the end of August 1945 wrote: "More and more it appears that this war in the first place has been a victory of Anglo-Saxon science and technology. The atomic bomb is convincing proof of this, but a no less ingenious tool of victory has been what the English call Radar."[31]

30 For the Belgian imports, see Koulischer, "Belgian-American Relations, 1944–45," in BT, 176. The paper, *Bevrijding! Het blad van de arbeidersjeugd*, is quoted in Janssen *et al.*, "Maasland," 126.

31 SHAEFB, FR No. 20, 5, June 26, 1945, WO 202/701, AA 1230; Torrent, *La France américaine*, 277; and *Het Volk*, August 21, 1945, 1.

The article appeared under the dramatic headline "Radar saved civilization!" But the combined technological and scientific superiority of Britain and the US did more than enable these nations to defend their allies across the globe. It also provided them with the power to make that world a better place. The war had done much to put at the disposal of the US, and to a lesser degree Britain, new and improved technologies with social as well as military applications. Nazi intolerance had significantly contributed to this process by forcing countless scientists, many of them Jews, to seek a haven in Anglo-Saxon countries. The effects of the brain drain on Germany were devastating, especially in the fields of chemistry, physics, and medicine. Many articles in the Belgian press raved about the potential of British radar and American nuclear energy for peaceful purposes. But a people whose health had suffered gravely during the past four years understandably fixed their gaze first and foremost on the medical advances that the Allies were introducing.[32]

The war had caused the research departments of Belgium's medical schools to fall significantly behind in terms of instruments and equipment. They were looking forward with impatience to the day when imports from Britain and the US could get underway. Meanwhile, Allied medical personnel did what they could to lend a hand. American hospitals in Liège in 1944 organized a series of conferences aimed at transferring newly acquired knowledge to the city's physicians. In 1945, in the wake of the Ardennes offensive, American physicians were flown in to assist Belgian authorities in the fight against "epidemics of infantile paralysis." The liberators assisted Belgian authorities also with the repatriation of its citizens. They provided air transport and helped with disease prevention in the form of DDT, first used on a large scale by the Allies during the typhus epidemic in Naples in 1943. Still, as a cure for countless bacterial infections it was penicillin, above all others, that continued to be hailed as the new miracle drug. Though it was the Americans who had managed to mass produce it beginning in 1943, the discovery had been made in Britain as early as 1928. On November 30, 1945, shortly after he had been awarded the Nobel Prize for medicine, Alexander Fleming was made a *doctor honoris causa* by the Catholic University of Leuven. The British scientist received the honor amidst acclamations from an admiring and grateful Belgian audience.[33]

[32] For the impact of the émigré scientists on the US and Britain, see Duignan and Gann, *Rebirth*, 615–16.

[33] Jean La Barre and Paul Bastenie, "Medicine and Medical Research," in BT, 102; Sulbout, "Liège," 52; Koulischer, "Belgian-American Relations, 1944–45," in BT, 178; Lagrou, *Legacy*, 91; and Stéphany, *1945*, 269.

It was an optimistic audience too. Medical discoveries like Fleming's were bound to increase life expectancy. In addition, Allied military technologies – from long-distance aircraft to nuclear power – promised to save people much time. More leisure in turn would help spawn a mass consumer culture that would act as a balm for the bad memories of war. Indeed, some industries made the transition from an economy of war to one of peace with seamless ease. "There they are!" a 1946 publicity slogan cried out over a drawing of the British Channel and in a reference to the D-Day invasion. But, instead of warships, what was heading for the Continent in the drawing was a convoy of boat-sized radios. "Everyone knows," the advertisement for British radio brand Ultra told Belgian consumers, "that the British radiophonic industry throughout the war has been a leading pioneer." And it asked potential buyers to consider the high quality of this new radio model given that not a single RAF aircraft had taken off during the war without at least one Ultra component. Even then, however, British radios were no match for American movies. The Belgian press not only raved about Hollywood's stars of flesh and blood, they were enthused also by technological novelties like Technicolor and 3D, all of which possessed the tantalizing potential of making dreams on the silver screen seem real. "Even before the war," one Belgian newspaper wrote on the movie industry in 1944, "it was customary to expect the surprises to come from America. Now we have been cut off from this wonderland for four years. And if we hear about the developments just in this one field, we can rest assured: we are going to be astonished!"[34]

Pierre Wigny foresaw that what was in the making would alter society dramatically. "Humanity," he told his American audience in 1945, "which for thousands of years had to fight poverty, is now faced with the task of organizing the abundance which can be provided by those innumerable and indefatigable robots of iron, the machines. Our social institutions are not yet adapted to this new world." Not that this prevented his countrymen from embracing this brave new world, and especially the continent on the other side of the Atlantic, head over heels. The Second World War had barely ended when an important mission representing Belgian scientific institutions was on its way to visit American universities and laboratories. "People who before the war knew nothing or very little about American ways of life," the foreign editor of socialist newspaper *Le Peuple* observed, "now take a keen interest in American

[34] The advertisement is published in Stéphany, "Belgique," 37. On Hollywood movie technology, see *HBVL*, September 16, 1944, 2.

technical achievements and in the intellectual and scientific activity of the United States."[35]

The erosion of authority

The sympathy that people craved at the end of the war extended far beyond the purely material desires that would help shape the welfare state and consumer society. Total war had demanded sacrifices of everyone and had caused all to suffer. Historian Arthur Marwick has argued that modern war in that regard has tended to increase the sense of status, or at least the self-consciousness, of classes and communities formerly ignored or taken less seriously. Among ordinary Belgian workers sociologist Guillaume Jacquemyns certainly detected a fundamental change of mind heralding a challenge to the dominance of the bourgeoisie. "What can upset the laborer or employee just as much as the fear of insecurity," he noted, "is the sense of injustice, of privilege, of favors." "People," he went on, "want to see certain distances disappear. They object to those who put themselves apart, who consider themselves to be essentially different from the human community and who show it, and make one feel it."[36]

The rigid social order was shaken, Jacquemyns noted, not only because war had destroyed and disrupted much of society, but also because in some unexpected ways it had opened up new vistas that promised to erode provincialism. "Workers whose lives were particularly narrow and whose possibilities for advancement were excessively limited," the sociologist wrote, "have traveled, worked with people greatly different from themselves, established relationships with people of all nationalities, learned new customs, and gained realization of things they had not dreamed of (social and otherwise)." Jacquemyns specifically mentioned the experience of the 200,000 Belgians who had volunteered or been forced to work in Nazi Germany. But since he was writing in an American journal at the end of 1945, he might just as well have been alluding to the hundreds of thousands of Belgians who had worked for, or had otherwise become closely acquainted with, the Anglo-Americans at home. Indeed, conservative elements in Belgium and across Europe, from Britain to Germany, were particularly anxious about the mass presence of Americans that the war had suddenly made possible. This anxiety harked back all the way

[35] Wigny, "Belgium Today and Tomorrow," 179; and Koulischer, "Belgian-American Relations, 1944–45," 177–8, both in BT.

[36] Marwick, *War and Social Change*, 11–14; and Jacquemyns, "La Société belge," 386–7. For the broader European context of what Mazower does not hesitate to call "a social revolution," see the section "Reviving Democracy" in his book *Dark Continent*, 186–94.

to the nineteenth century, when America's rising mass democracy had aroused much distaste for that society among European elites at different ends of the political spectrum. If those elites had not been able to hide a measure of admiration for America's technology, management skills, and efficiency, they showed much trepidation in the face of an egalitarianism that was the other side of what Dutch historian Rob Kroes has called its "unfettered modernity." It was the blatant egalitarianism more than anything else that made America a potentially subversive force in the eyes of anyone keen on preserving and cultivating the advantages of status, whether economic, political, or cultural. And it was those most threatened who traditionally had been keenest to associate America with decadence, degeneracy, and *Unkultur*.[37]

Historian Golo Mann observed that Germans as a result of the Nazi cataclysm "had lost their respect for authority, both public and private." To a degree this is what the forces of war, occupation, and liberation also brought about among Belgians. Public authority had suffered the most serious and visible erosion. People had lost faith in the country's key institutions, all of which had been obliged to seek an accommodation with the Nazi occupier. Most Belgians regarded the government that returned from exile in London as weak, ineffective, and outdated. Because of his authoritarian tendencies and flirtation with Nazi Germany, many Belgians thought even the king unfit to return to the throne. People felt deeply disappointed and betrayed. That is why they vociferously demanded a thorough investigation of anyone suspected of misbehaving during the war. Whether on a national or local level, those in positions of responsibility would have to be held accountable for their actions. Historian Martin Conway sees in this "reflected the wider change which had taken place in popular attitudes." "The events of the war years," he observes, "had cracked open the pervasive culture of deference within Belgian society and had created expectations of a new relationship between governors and governed."[38]

Youth

But the war had done much to weaken private authority too. Parents had been so busy making ends meet during the occupation that they had allowed their children a freer rein perforce. Indeed, many fathers had been completely absent for several years and, as Jacquemyns observed

[37] Jacquemyns, "Readjustment Problems of the Repatriates," in BT, 86; and Kroes, "European Anti-Americanism," 428. For the British and German view of America as a subversive force see, for example, Reynolds, *Rich Relations*, 35 and 38–9; and Poiger, *Jazz, Rock, and Rebels*, 13–17.

[38] Mann is quoted in Marwick, *War and Social Change*, 145. Hardenne, "Entre les Belges et leurs libérateurs," 286; and Conway, "Justice," 32–4.

in 1945, "Often the repatriated is amazed at the great independence of his children." It was equally common for children born at the start of the war not to respond to their returning fathers at all. Parents would find it as difficult as schools, a high-ranking education official warned, to reassert their authority over young people who had lived through exceptional times: "The difficulties of getting all sorts of commodities, in particular food, compelled a great many people to live on and from the black market. Mendacity and robbery thus developed very often with the efficient aid of young people. Resistance to the enemy encouraged recourse to tricks; and children were taught to lie in order to save their parents, friends, and even themselves from deportation." Seventeen-year-old Jacques Dieu certainly fitted that profile when late in September 1944 he had to return to school. "Since May 1944," he recounted, "we had lived without discipline apart from that freely consented. We had not had classes and passed final exams that did not amount to much." His father was a doctor and during the liberation Jacques had lent him a hand at the local hospital in Frameries near Mons, where he had seen things he would never forget. "And then there was the start of school," he grimly recalled. "We fell into the hands of a principal who wanted to subject us to the strict discipline of the Jesuits. It was the beginning of a nine-month battle."[39]

After more than four years of occupation, rationing, uniforms, commands, and threats, teenagers were sick and tired of discipline. And they found an army of allies in the liberators pouring in from the Anglo-American world. Compared with the Germans, their more relaxed manner, material abundance, fun movies, and swing music could not fail to make the impression on young people of a counterculture. Official reports were aghast, for example, at the number of mid-teenage girls who flocked to the camps of these soldiers and managed to get access to their dances. Jan Poupaert was only eleven at the time of the liberation. But the sight of Canadian soldiers in Ghent, who did not seem to take authority too seriously and could regularly be seen drunk in the streets, made a permanent impression. "Perhaps," he mused more than half a century later, "it is because of that freedom of thought and lack of discipline that I still feel so intimately connected with the Canadians of my youth?"[40]

[39] Jacquemyns, "Readjustment Problems of the Repatriates," in BT, 79. On the erosion of parental authority, see also Stéphany, "Belgique," 30. The education official is J. J. N. Kuypers, "The Educational Problem," in BT, 107. Dieu is quoted in "La Libération vue de la clinique Notre Dame à Frameries," *La Province*, September 9, 1994.

[40] Poupaert is quoted in Warnier, *Brugge en september '44*, vol. II, 130.

"Youthfulness" was what a Mass Observation report in Britain during the war said remained the focus of the stereotype of the US. American cultural expressions of that juvenescent energy – jazz, the Charleston, and Hollywood movies – had been appealing to adolescents in Europe from as early as the 1920s. As the depression paralyzed the Old World as well as the New, however, and Hitler seized power in Germany, for a while the fit bodies of Nazi youth in crisp uniforms and dense formations appeared to be the new wave of the future. But as the war sapped the Reich's energy and decimated its young, Nazi officials worried about the increasing appeal that *Amerikanismus* was again exerting on Europe's youth. *Amerikanismus* was understood to represent a relaxed and fun-loving style that emphasized the individual and hence was inherently anti-authoritarian. It also unabashedly praised material possessions and consumerism and thus was inevitably at odds with a heavily regimented society geared towards war. To embrace American symbols then was to challenge the totalitarian regime of the Nazis. Which is exactly why the clubs and gangs of the Zazous in France, the Schlurfs in Austria, and the Swing Jugend in Germany insisted on listening to American records and proudly wore names like Ohio Club, Navajo Pirates, and Harlem Club. "Their ideal," one disapproving Nazi report said of the German Swing Jugend, "is democratic freedom and American casualness."[41]

These groups remained a relatively limited and mostly, though not exclusively, middle-class phenomenon. Nevertheless, they and the much larger segments of youngsters who listened to BBC broadcasts of American jazz and swing, were a source of concern for Nazis who, in the words of historian Peter Stirk, saw themselves "as a party of youth in a literal sense as well as a metaphorical one." That explains why the Nazis in the *Brüsseler Zeitung*, for example, tried to counter this trend by portraying American youth as the victim of a plutocratic system that accepted high rates of child mortality as well as child labor. By the fall of 1944, however, the Nazis in Belgium had lost both the literal and the metaphorical battle. By then, as Duignan and Gann have noted, fascism "no longer appeared – as it had during the 1930s – the cause of youth, and of a banner-waving future. Instead, the US and Britain had out-produced, out-organized, out-thought, and out-fought the Axis powers." Angèle Eeckhaut as a young girl in Ghent during the German occupation had known only austerity and restrictions. But then, when the Allies arrived in September, it felt, she remembered, as if suddenly

[41] Reynolds, *Rich Relations*, 435; Beck, "Anti-Nazi 'Swing Youth,'" 47 and 50; Poiger, *Jazz, Rock, and Rebels*, 26–7; and Willett, *Americanization*, 89.

"everything was possible." She ended up marrying a GI and eventually traded the Old World for America.[42]

Historian Fabrice Maerten, in research on the French-speaking part of Belgium, has made the point that the mentality of young people had begun to undergo fundamental transformations as early as the end of the First World War. This is when the emergence of a consumer society, spurred on in part by the American model, gradually made them embrace individualism and become politically disengaged. The shift was reflected, for example, in the decline of membership in both Christian and socialist youth movements. Maerten argues that the depression of the 1930s and the Nazi occupation, with "their collective constraints and impetus of solidarity," had merely "slowed down and/or masked an evolution that would become glaringly obvious again with the arrival of the Allies."[43]

But, although Maerten is keen to emphasize that the profound change in mentality did not originate in 1944, he does not deny that the huge presence of Anglo-Americans did much to accelerate the reemerging trend. This probably helps to explain why the change appeared to be so abrupt to many in Belgium and why adults and authorities worried about youth as a force of destabilization. On the one hand, society was pinning all its hopes for a better future on young people more than anyone else. "We wish to eliminate," socialist newspaper *Vooruit* announced in April 1945, "all moral shortcomings that found such fertile soil during the occupation." An ambitious task for sure, but *Vooruit* was convinced that, if the educational system became better organized and teachers were more generously rewarded, a new generation would arise that – in contrast with the old and discredited one – was guaranteed to adhere to values such as honesty, justice, and tolerance.[44]

However, the socialist newspaper, in its list of values for young people to aspire to, in the same breath mentioned "respect for authority," and it was in this sphere that many feared the lofty project for the future was being derailed. The Catholic press in particular ranted against children who were allowed to run wild. "Not just in the cities and the workers' quarters," one newspaper lamented a year after the liberation, "but even in our good old villages things are going downhill. Modern youth has no more guidance in life, has lost its bearings and just lets things roll … These days children no older than 14–15 go where they want,

[42] Stirk, "Anti-Americanism," 71 and 79; Duignan and Gann, *Rebirth*, 705–6; and Eeckhaut, interview No. 517, AA 1450.

[43] Maerten, "Jeunesse et résistance," 304–5.

[44] "De noodzakelijke herklasseering van de onderwijzers," *Vooruit*, April 21, 1945, 1.

to cafés, cinemas, and dance halls. And since the liberation our boys and girls have seen and learned things that have had a perverse impact on their young natures." Boys and girls alike, it was said, were enjoying "strong cognac and exotic cigarettes as if there were no tomorrow." Allied uniforms appeared to have the effect of magnets on girls. Teenage girls hung around trucks and dance halls hoping to be picked up and not caring if the GIs were black or white. On train and tram girls and soldiers were "in each others' arms, in poses that are far from edifying." It is not difficult to recognize behind such concerns about moral corruption, older European images of American habits as culturally shallow, vulgarly materialistic and, ultimately, insidiously subversive. In that context, arguments between adolescents and adults over American influences can be understood, in the words of historian Uta Poiger, as "contests over moral, cultural, and political authority."[45]

Order could only be restored and control regained, the Catholic press argued, if mayors and police cracked down hard on such excesses and if schools were finally allowed to hold regular classes again. The latter was "as urgent and important as battling the alcohol plague and the dance craze." But as long as Allied troops remained in Belgium in large numbers, many schools were to serve military purposes. That is why the Catholic press increasingly called upon parents "to think and act! Because, ultimately, they are to accept most of the blame." The police chief of Verviers certainly could not have agreed more with that assessment when he appealed to the population to be aware of the many dangers girls were running in the presence of American soldiers at dances and in the dark. "Parents," he concluded his exhortation in the local press, "nation and nature make you responsible for your children. It is your duty to enlighten them – better too soon than too late – and to exercise over them an authority that is intelligent, but above all firm."[46]

Some of the nation's politicians and educators, however, understood that the youth they were dealing with at war's end was exceptional in its experience while at the same time crucially important for the country's regeneration. "As a result of this war," a Belgian education official recognized, "many children of 14 have had more experience of life than any children of their age had had previously. They have shared their

[45] "Ouders luistert eens!" *HBVL*, September 22, 1945, 1 and "Wanneer treedt de overheid op tegen de uitspattingen?" *HBVL*, August 19, 1945, 1. Poiger, *Jazz, Rock, and Rebels*, 2.

[46] "Is de wet op den leerplicht afgeschaft?" *HBVL*, March 22, 1945, 1 and "Een noodkreet over Limburg," *HBVL*, February 8, 1945, 1. The police appeal in the Verviers press was transcribed in a report to the SE of March 22, 1945. See Folder 979, AA 1311.

parents' concern, they have shared the resistance movements, they have shared the anxieties of the country about the war, and they feel that they belong to a community that is their own." This prompted policymakers to use more conciliatory language. Rather than run the risk of further alienating young people, they promised to coopt as many of them as possible by accepting their unique identity and responding to their strong wish to be heard. In an article written in 1945 for a prestigious American journal, August De Schryver, a Catholic minister who had been in exile in London, readily acknowledged the sacrifices that young people had made during the war. "These efforts," he said in describing how his party was reinventing itself as a more broadly based people's party, "naturally gave them considerable standing in the eyes of the public, and it is from their ranks that we have drawn a new and active leadership." A representative of Belgium's Liberal Party in the same journal emphasized that they too, in a congress at the end of 1945, had made certain to take up "the wishes of young people – their political, economic, and social aspirations." Still in that same American forum, an education official foresaw a near future where "More time will be given to games and physical culture. Closer cooperation between teachers and parents will be cultivated, and meetings will be encouraged where views will be exchanged on the new methods of education." The creation of a more responsive and inclusive educational climate promised, he believed, to "make of our children better citizens, better Belgians, and better democrats, ready to cooperate with all those in the world who share the same ideals."[47]

Women

But how could schools promise to make better democrats of girls when the political system still did not allow their mothers to vote in parliamentary elections? Belgian women had shared with men the hardships of total war, from food shortages to the Allied air raids and German V weapons. And they had been forced during the conflict to take on a variety of new responsibilities and challenges. "It is not exceptional," sociologist Jacquemyns observed during the occupation, "to encounter in the most humble households examples of courage in the face of adversity, courage bordering on heroism. Women in particular stoically battle the difficulties of every day, without ever allowing themselves to be defeated." That was especially true of the French-speaking part of the country where many husbands remained POWs until the spring of 1945 and women, in addition

[47] J. J. N. Kuypers, "The Educational Problem," 109–10; De Schryver, "The Christian Social Party," 7; and René Drèze, "The Liberal Party," 22–3, all in BT.

to protecting and caring for children, had to take on jobs, care for farms, or manage shops. "Some," Jacquemyns noted at the end of 1945, "have not been able to renounce this authority overnight. This change of relationship is especially marked in cases where the wives formerly played a submissive role without responsibilities except those of the homemaker."[48]

Was it at all fair and justified, after five disruptive years that had shaken the existing social order, to ask women to reassume their traditional identities in the private home and accept secondary roles in a male-dominated society? Belgian men, after all, had failed in their traditional roles of protectors of the public nation. Hence the humiliation of arrogant Germans parading in the streets and the embarrassment of swooning women storming cocky Allied liberators. Hence also, during the parades in 1944 and 1945, the sight of Belgian women of the resistance walking side by side with wan male comrades in ragtag outfits. Anglo-American troops, meanwhile, were offering the Belgian population glimpses of a still more assertive female future. In convoys across Flanders many a British woman could be seen casually handling the steering wheel, for example, while in peace parades from Arlon to Charleroi sizeable delegations of American females proudly showed off their uniforms and shining insignia. The Belgian press had been intrigued by this phenomenon from day one. Noting the presence of uniformed British women in the streets of Brussels, *Le Soir* explained to its readers on September 15, 1944: "Besides the millions of women who, in all parts of the Empire, work night and day in the war factories, some 800,000 women have enrolled in the three armies of land, sea, and air." They did not take part in combat, the newspaper was quick to point out, but that did not stop them from "taking care of even the roughest jobs." A month later, *Le Soir* was clarifying the meaning of the alphabet soup of WAF, WAAC, WRNS, WAVES, and so many other acronyms representing the hundreds of thousands of women in the military forces of Great Britain, Canada, and the US. On October 27, 1944, the same newspaper splashed a large photo of female soldiers on its front page, exactly one week after it had done the same with a photo of black GIs.[49]

That there was a huge interest in the new reality of women in uniform was shown not only by its coverage in the Belgian press. The

[48] Jacquemyns, "La Société belge," 370, and "Readjustment Problems of the Repatriates," in BT, 79.

[49] For photos of female GIs in the parades, see Triffaux, *Arlon*, 86; and Neufort, *Charleroi*, 271. "Les Femmes dans l'armée britannique," *Le Soir*, September 15, 1944, 2; and "Femmes soldats," *Le Soir*, October 12, 1944, 1. *Le Soir* exaggerated the number of women in the British military, which was closer to 450,000. 350,000 women served in the US military and 40,000 in the Canadian services. Thébaud, "Deuxième guerre," 238.

Plate 7.2 American female soldiers participate in a parade. Charleroi, June 1945. (Photo Neufort, CEGESOMA, Brussels, picture number 92969)

most popular publication put out by SHAEF's Psychological Warfare Division in Belgium, for example, was a booklet called *Eve en salopette* or, in other words, *Eve in Overalls*. It topped other popular booklets on insignia, the cinema, and America. Such background information was needed to help people come to terms with what was considered to be quite a watershed in the blurring of gender boundaries. It took time for the headmaster of a school in Genval, for example, to get used to the sight of no fewer than eighty young British women in uniform settling down in the area in February 1945. "They are dressed like the men, in dark blue-gray," he noted in his journal with a hint of unease, "and take care of radiography. We see many of them pass by and the only thing that allows us to distinguish them from the men is their hair."[50]

Belgians may have found such occurrences less startling in the American military. Influenced by the Calamity Janes of the frontier and the flappers of the Roaring Twenties as portrayed in movies and the sensationalist press, Europeans had come to regard American women as strong, emancipated, domineering and, if not masculine, gender neutral. During the liberation, reports on American women like iconic Rosie the Riveter making up the largest female labor force in the Western world did much to strengthen this image. *Het Belang van Limburg*, in an article with the English title "Modern Times," reported that GIs had experienced a tremendous culture shock in North Africa, not the least because of the hard lives of the Muslim women. This was to be expected, the newspaper explained, for if in Europe women were treated with "the necessary respect," the GIs came from a country where females enjoyed "unlimited freedom." What this meant in practice a representative of the American National Federation of Business and Professional Women was keen to clarify in rather glossy terms during a visit to Belgium in September 1945. She emphasized that her country had just celebrated twenty-five years of women's suffrage and had been sending female representatives to all major international conferences from Bretton Woods to San Francisco. And *Het Volk* also quoted her as saying that an American woman "could be called upon to play just as important a role as a man: she could even become president of the United States." At the same time, however, she hurried to dismiss as false the Hollywood image of the US as a country of "divorced women in search of something sensational."[51]

Yet the mere sight of Allied women in uniform was causing sensation enough among Belgian men and women alike. The Allied airfield at Cerfontaine was surrounded with hospital tents from which C-47 Dakotas collected the badly wounded. One photo of the area shows a female American officer with two male colleagues. The woman is surrounded by some ten excited local girls while an older Belgian woman

[50] SHAEFB, Annexure I to Appendix D, January 23, 1945, WO 202/689, AA 1230; and Boulet, "Journal," February 5, 1945, AB 1298.

[51] *HBVL*, September 20, 1944, 2; and "De emancipatie van de Amerikaansche vrouwen," *Het Volk*, September 7, 1945. On the European image of women in the US, see Wagnleitner, *Coca-Colonization*, 26; and Poiger, *Jazz, Rock, and Rebels*, 14–15.

admiringly has her arm around the unusual GI. Lydie Degueldre was twenty when she became acquainted with British female soldiers in Kapellenbos near Antwerp. She ended up befriending several of these remarkable young women and half a century later was still writing letters and paying them visits. Surely, Belgian women who had experienced such eye-opening encounters, and many others like them who in a matter of years had witnessed dramatic changes in society, would not accept, as the war ebbed away, meek submission to the male authority of old?[52]

In part they did not have to, of course, because some things never went back to being the same again. On the political front it would take until 1948 for women in Belgium to obtain the right to participate in parliamentary elections. But the battle was raging in the open at least as early as 1945. The Catholic press in the fall of that year was blasting the socialists for their delaying maneuvers, accusing them of fearing too much of an increase in Catholic voting power. But women's organizations were even more vitriolic in their condemnations – and more concerned about the ethical issue than the political gamesmanship. In response to the foot-dragging, the National Federation of Liberal Women expressed "deep regret" in a letter to the Prime Minister, labeling the strategy as "anti-democratic" and "an injustice." The National Federation of Christian Labor Women on the Prime Minister's doorstep dumped a petition signed by women from 1,200 municipalities. In it they virulently denounced decades of "vain promises made by men and parties." "Women and mothers," they rebuked the male political establishment, "for four years have saved the population from famine, slow wasting away, the lack of clothing, moral decline, and treason. They therefore do not deserve to be regarded as inferiors by the government."[53]

The polemics over the issue of the vote were accompanied by signs of a much broader change in mood. While the youth faction of the Liberal Party during a congress in 1945 discussed what one of its male leaders called "the problem of women," the National Federation of Liberal Women during a congress of their own adopted a more constructive tone, approving a program that was not just political, but also economic and social. In April 1945 an organization called the Union des Femmes held a meeting in the cinema Carrefour in Liège. Fifty women and four men attended. So did a member of the local gendarmerie. The meeting, he dutifully reported to the SE in Brussels, had discussed the issue

[52] For the photo of Cerfontaine, see Roba and Leotard, *Walcourt-Beaumont*, 223. Lydie Degueldre, AB 1591.

[53] On the socialists see, for example, "Angst voor de … vrouwen," *HBVL*, October 26, 1945, 1. For the women's protests, see "Krachtig en waardig protest van de arbeiders-vrouwen," *Het Volk*, October 29, 1945, 1.

of increased family allowances and improved hygiene in maternity hospitals and nurseries. If this had sounded harmless enough, however, the woman who presided over the meeting, a school headmistress, had also demanded equal pay for equal work and a "fight against the prejudices and obstacles preventing the female elite from obtaining access to the highest posts in the domain of politics, pedagogy, science, industry, and commerce." Those present had applauded these suggestions and agreed that what was needed to accomplish all this was "an equality before the law similar to that of men." There had been, the gendarme signed off, no incidents.[54]

That same spring there was an incident, however, at the Brepols company in Turnhout. When the employer announced that women would no longer be allowed onto the work floor without stockings, the following day all of the girls in a show of solidarity and defiance showed up barelegged. It was a clear signal that they were no longer willing to accept interference in their personal lives. And it was just one signal among many. A popular Belgian riddle in 1945 asked what the difference was between the occupation and the liberation. Answer: during the former, women had to hide their men; during the latter, men their women. The joke betrayed the impotence of Belgian men during the war. But it also hinted that the liberation's licentiousness could not have arisen if Allied troops had been oversexed but Belgian women completely unwilling. The loosening of social controls, the presence of large numbers of young and exotic liberators and, not unimportant in a predominantly Catholic country, the sudden mass availability of contraceptives in the form of condoms, allowed many women actively to pursue sexual pleasure during the liberation. Historian Marilyn Lake has made the case that this "wartime stimulation of female desire" was carried over into marriages old and new in the form of "high expectations of personal pleasure." Indeed, there were more drastic ways for women to challenge male authority than baring their legs as in Turnhout. With sexual as well as household roles shaken up, some women may have renegotiated their marriages. Others, however, decided to take full control of their personal lives by filing for divorce. A majority of the high percentage of women in Liège who became divorced in 1947, for example, had been married between five and fifteen years. The average age of the divorcées was between thirty and forty and most of them went ahead with the decision without holding a job outside the home. One of them was Elizabeth Rigo. She would eventually take on a job as a saleswoman in Hasselt to

[54] René Drèze, "The Liberal Party," in BT, 22–3; and Gendarmerie Liège, report April 23, 1945, Folder 1458, AA 1311.

provide for her daughter from an unhappy marriage. But before that, she moved from Liège to her father's home in Bilzen. When the powerful village priest paid a visit to try and save her marriage, the woman was undaunted. Emboldened by five years of independent decision-making in the absence of her POW husband, she pointed to the door and told the prying priest that her personal life was none of his business.[55]

Numerous and brave as women like Elizabeth Rigo may have been, however, males generally managed to contain and roll back much of the autonomy that women had obtained as soon as the war neared its end. Indeed, some historians have asserted that the widespread shearings of women in 1944 should be understood not just as political reprisals against collaborators, but also as "gender-based violence." Corran Laurens's argument is that such acts of supreme humiliation – which Alain Brossat poignantly calls the "uncrowning" of women – "represent both an attempted symbolical reversal of women's emergent power, and an exorcism of the image of threatened masculinity from public memory." As such, Laurens maintains, they "act as a warning to women to revert to their expected socio-cultural peacetime role."[56]

But the victims of shearings formed only a tiny minority of women. Mark Mazower argues that the large mass of women in Europe accepted a return to the cult of domesticity as a result of much larger pressures that were no less compelling for being less violent. One was the long-standing fear of a demographic decline that was given added impetus by the war's massive loss of life. A 1945 analysis of Belgium's economic future was typical, for example, when it predicted that difficulties would "arise from the shrinking number of young workers because of the decline in the population." This, however, was a concern for the more distant future. The immediate worry was that the end of the war might herald a return of the Great Depression. Which in turn meant that the number one priority was to make sure that men, the breadwinners of old, would find as many jobs as possible. In this regard even the Allied authorities showed old-fashioned reflexes that belied their supposed progressiveness as extolled in the Belgian press. It was specifically agreed in writing between the Allies and OMA, for example, that the salary of women employed in equal functions and capacities would be

[55] On Brepols, see Van Gorp, *Arendonk*, 220. The riddle is mentioned in "Gaan wij den berg af?" *HBVL*, September 9, 1945, 1. Lake, "Female Desires," 275 and 282–4. Lake has come to these conclusions on the basis of research on the presence of GIs in Australia. On Liège, see Malevez, "Aspects démographiques," 87–9.

[56] Laurens, "La Femme au Turban," 155 and 176–7; and Brossat, *Libération*, 148. See also Kelly, "Reconstruction of Masculinity," 117 and 119–20; and Virgili's excellent *France*.

only 80 percent of that of men. SHAEF was just as satisfied to report at the end of June 1945 that, despite the mass arrival of male repatriates, the unemployment figure had slightly decreased, "largely because many women left the labour market at the return of their husbands."[57]

But did they do so solely to comply with the pro-natal appeals of government and Church? An article in the local press at the start of spring announced that girls in Sint-Truiden could soon attend forums "on marriage and family affairs." Turnout was expected to be so large that the meeting hall *Patria* had been reserved for nine successive Thursday evenings. Mazower indicates that such meetings were popular across Europe not just in response to the call of the nation, but also because "the desire to retreat from the world of ideological strife contributed to an idealization of domesticity." A Mass Observation report in Britain concluded: "the larger number of opinionated women *want* to return to, or start on, domestic life when the war is over."[58]

What the British opinion poll predicted was borne out by the massive baby boom that mushroomed in 1945 and would not abate in Western industrialized countries until the early 1960s. Demographic statistics for Liège show that in 1947 and 1948, the same years that witnessed a significant spike in divorces, births climbed from 12.5 per 1,000 inhabitants on the eve of the war to 17.4 and 18.5 respectively. Still, in 1945 there remained much uncertainty and confusion about what the future would bring for the family and the role of women. This can be gleaned from the contrasting roles that women played in the peace parades during the summer. A float in Sint-Katelijne-Waver named "Women Who Represent the Future" carried along more than a dozen young girls in neat white dresses symbolizing innocence and virgin-like purity. In a similar vein, the young women in Charleroi and Nonceveux who were given the honor of personifying America's Statue of Liberty were representing a moral uprightness considered typical for their gender in the nineteenth century. Likewise, a group of very small children in Chevron were dressed up in compliance with the most traditional of gender codes: the boys as farmers, soldiers, and professionals in tie and suit; the girls as nurses in immaculate white. On the other hand, however, there was much more assertive cross-dressing in Oostvleteren, where women on a float in front of the Allied flags played the role not only of nursing personnel, but of wounded soldiers in uniform as well. A group in Eeklo, enacting a scene from the Belgian revolt against the Dutch in 1830, struck

[57] Mazower, *Dark Continent*, 212. Jean-Charles Snoy et d'Oppuers, "Economic Problems in the Long Pull Ahead," in BT, 159. OMA, Emp-2500, 4, AA 1341. SHAEFB, FR No. 20, 17–18, June 26, 1945, WO 202/701, AA 1230.

[58] *HBVL*, March 28, 1945, 2. Mazower, *Dark Continent*, 212–13.

even more assured a pose as it was composed solely of women armed with swords and spears. Men heard the rumble of revolution on the other side of the language border too. In the small village of Oneux near Comblain, a large placard with the slogan "Men of Tomorrow" served as the separation between two rooms of an imaginary home on a float. In the back, women sat at a table doing nothing: they were dressed up and confidently relaxed. In the front room stood the new-age men: one had his shirt off, the other had his sleeves rolled up, still another was ostentatiously feeding a baby a bottle of milk.[59]

Church

If the men in Oneux responded to the perceived erosion of traditional authority with humor, the powerful Catholic Church in Belgium saw little reason to be amused. This was ironic because on the surface it did not seem to have much reason to be perturbed. The occupation had strengthened the moral prestige of clergymen who, through word and deed, had often caused the wrath of the collaborationist press and reprisals from German authorities. This, public opinion observer Paul Struye asserted, had found an "echo in all classes, among non-believers and believers." Fear and worries had caused people to flock to the churches during the war, and in the wake of the liberation thousands upon thousands in Flanders and the Walloons participated in huge processions to honor the Virgin Mary as their protectress. Similar gratitude was expressed in open-air masses that were celebrated in market squares across the country in September 1944. In that which was held in the capital's Grand Place soon after the Allies' arrival, dozens of priests took part, while countless inhabitants kneeled on the rough cobblestones in sincere devotion.[60]

Yet, while the pool of candidates for priesthood and religious orders expanded significantly immediately after the war, the number of people attending church tapered off as soon as the liberation was a fact. One of Roeselare's priests bemoaned that even the *Te Deum* of the liberation had drawn only half the flock he had grown used to, and he was quick to blame the setback on those he scathingly dubbed "war Christians." But there were other challenges too. The far right's cataclysm had unleashed the forces of the left across Europe. In response to Radio

[59] For Liège, see Malevez, "Aspects démographiques," 64. The photo of Sint-Katelijne-Waver is reproduced in De Roey and Van Hee, *Bevrijding*, 22; that of Charleroi in Neufort, *Charleroi*, 291; and that of Nonceveux in Henry, *Aywaille*, 121. The other photographs are part of the CEGESOMA collection, respectively Nos. 104402, 92673, 92689, and 104375.

[60] Aelbrecht, "Églises," 38, 72–3, and 115; Struye, "Sentiment public," 182 and 226; and Gérard, *Libération*, 128.

Moscow's complaints about the Vatican's anti-Soviet rhetoric, Catholic newspaper *Het Volk* in June 1945 defiantly shot back, "What do they want? For the Pope to protest the persecution and murder of priests at the hand of the Germans, but to remain silent when the same happens in Poland, Croatia, or Hungary?" But the horror and hardship of war had caused Belgium's own society to experience a significant turn to the left. This had also strengthened the Catholic Party's labor wing, forcing it to become more centrist and less confessional as it tellingly renamed itself the Christian People's Party in August 1945, a move the episcopate regretted and resented.[61]

There was, however, also a certain sense of unease about the mass presence and growing influence of Anglo-American forces. In a 1944 speech before parliament in which he expressed his country's gratitude to the US, the Belgian Minister of Foreign Affairs, Paul-Henri Spaak, made much of the "democratic ideals and Christian civilization, to both of which they are attached by unshakable faith." But this statement conveniently glossed over the fact that America, like Britain and Canada, was a Protestant country at heart whereas Belgium was a deeply Catholic nation. Even in contacts between ordinary soldiers and civilians some of the long history of religious suspicion shone through. To many a Canadian soldier in West Flanders, for example, the numerous crucifixes and depictions of angels and saints were reminders of "a strange world, full of taboos and symbols" – a world that made "shivers run over a Protestant back." A village priest in Voeren estimated that of the 250 British soldiers who settled down in the convent of the Ursulines in December 1944, no more than twenty or thirty were Catholics. And he maintained that, although their officers were kind to the women from the outset, it was only the "good mood and geniality" of the nuns that finally made "the protestant prejudices fall away."[62]

Clearly, prejudices were stubborn on the Catholic side too. In an article on religion in Britain, *Het Belang van Limburg* in October 1944 reminded its readers that Catholics there had suffered persecution from the fifteenth to the nineteenth century, had waited until 1926 to obtain equal access to government jobs, and were still not allowed to sit on the throne. Pointing to the differences with England's Low Church in particular, the article magnanimously asserted that, despite the fact that few ever visited a church, many among them were "well-meaning people." The article was nevertheless keen to point out that the number

[61] Aelbrecht, "Églises," 110; *Roeselare Bevrijd*, 130–1; "Sovjet-propaganda tegen den Paus," *Het Volk*, June 1945; and Witte *et al.*, *Politieke geschiedenis*, 252–3.

[62] Spaak is quoted in Grégoire Koulischer, "Belgian-American Relations, 1944–45," in BT, 172. Pauwels, *Canadezen*, 75. Waterval and Lensen, *Basse-Meuse*, 234–5.

of Catholics in England was large and growing and that conversions, even of high-ranking figures, were increasingly common. That autumn the same Catholic newspaper put the best possible spin also on the religious situation in the US. Blatantly skirting the fact that this huge and powerful nation in history and tradition was solidly Protestant, one article manipulated the statistics to such an extent that an uninformed reader inevitably came away thinking that the total number of American Catholics exceeded that of Jews and members of the Protestant denominations combined. In a more stridently assertive tone, yet another article in the regional newspaper, taking much reassurance from the sight of GIs wearing rosaries, was keen to conclude: "This religion that has spread among all nations, races, and languages – its people as brothers among each other and as children of one Mother Church – has to be the only true religion."[63]

Het Belang van Limburg even helped pave the way for proselytism among American and British troops in the province by printing a language column on religion that included the phrases: In our town/village all churches are Catholic. The Catholic church is in the first street on the left/right. Are you a Roman Catholic? I am a Catholic, I am glad that you are too. There were quite a few occasions where those who could not respond to the latter question in the affirmative encountered a rather more tempered enthusiasm. Of the three British soldiers assigned to the Vangeloven farm in Opitter, two were Protestants and one was a Catholic. But although the children preferred to be around Ron, one of the Protestant soldiers who was married and had children of his own, their father would not let them. "He does not go to mass," was how their father put it, afraid that the heretic might prove to be a bad influence.[64]

This was even more of a worry where it concerned daughters. Limburg's newspaper again demonstrated that it was well aware of what was on parents' minds when, in yet another language column, this one on "personal matters," it printed side by side the questions: "Are you married?" and "What is your religion?" Many a parent in Belgium suffered sleepless nights knowing that their daughter was adamant about marrying an Allied soldier of whom they knew nothing for certain, either in terms of religious affiliation or social background. Priests were most eager to help secure guarantees for the religious orientation of local girls and their future offspring. A Canadian soldier in Bruges had claimed

[63] "Kijkjes op Engeland: De godsdienst," *HBVL*, October 10, 1944, 1; "De Vereenigde Staten," *HBVL*, September 13, 1944, 1; and "Zij zijn niet verlegen," *HBVL*, October 22, 1944, 1.

[64] "Spreekt Engelsch," *HBVL*, October 11, 1944, 1, and interview Jan Vangeloven by author, December 9, 2005.

time and again that he was as Catholic as the eighteen-year-old Huguette Van Iseghem whom he firmly intended to marry. But that did not stop the girl's parents from enlisting the aid of the local shepherd. The priest not only called on the unit's chaplain to have the man's Catholic credentials verified, he even wrote a letter to the Montreal parish where the soldier had grown up. For soldiers who made no secret of the fact that they were Protestants, the easiest way out of the conundrum was to satisfy the local community by embracing their sweethearts' religion and seeking conversion.[65]

Given the population's innate suspicion of any faith other than Catholicism, the Belgian episcopate did not indicate much fear of Anglo-Saxon Protestantism as such. They did express serious concern, however, about the more indirect challenge to their authority posed by the materialism and consumerism of the US in particular. This was no surprise as popes in encyclicals dating as far back as 1891 had condemned not only godless communism, but also the excesses of liberal capitalism. As the Belgian Church watched "the fetishism of goods" spread among its flock during the liberation, it feared more than anything else that the family would suffer as a result. After all, even before the war the perception in Europe had been that America, the mecca of materialism, had become a nation of spoiled children, pleasure-seeking women, and high rates of divorce.[66]

If Belgium were to emulate the American model, it would weaken the traditional family and thus the cornerstone of Catholic society and Church power. Rather than let that happen, the episcopate went on the offensive. Sociologist Jacquemyns indicated that in some instances the prolonged absence of the father had already started "a process of family disintegration." He also claimed that where children had become too independent for the father's liking, he often "blames the mother for the changes which have occurred." The Church was quick to add its voice to that of concerned fathers. The diocese of Namur prepared a letter for parish priests that dealt with the issue of returning POWs. In it, women were asked to make great efforts to pamper their husbands, and to refrain from bothering them with too many questions, while making sure to show an interest in the stories they chose to tell. At the same time, the bishop of Bruges sternly reminded parents of their legitimate authority and the urgent need

[65] "Spreekt Engelsch," *HBVL*, September 16, 1944, 2, and Warnier, *Brugge bevrijd*, 81. For examples of Allied conversions, see Roden, *Tessenderlo*, 263–4; and "Amerikaansch Sergeant bekeerde zich te Sint-Truiden," *HBVL*, March 20, 1945, 1.

[66] Domenico, "For the Cause of Christ," 625 and 629; Poiger, *Jazz, Rock, and Rebels*, 20; Wagnleitner, *Coca-Colonization*, 26; and Duignan and Gann, *Rebirth*, 560. The quote is from Mazower, *Dark Continent*, 310–11.

to eliminate among children "that spirit of independence and revolt, that spirit of narrow-minded and mean criticism that demolishes all."[67]

By restoring the traditional family, Church authorities also hoped to put an end to what they saw as a breakdown in public as well as private sexual behavior. The purpose of marriage, the bishop of Bruges reminded, had always been and remained procreation. To reject children, he threatened, was to reject God. Empty cribs resulted from people's "wickedness" and constituted "a curse on nations and families." There was, however, plenty of evidence that for many during the euphoria of newfound freedom, sex had taken on purely recreational purposes. The rampant teenage flirting and numerous illegitimate children attested to this. So did the plague of venereal diseases, the crimes of passion, and the rising rates of divorce. "In legalized divorce," *Het Volk* maintained in January 1945, "lies one of the deepest causes of current world chaos." But Belgian clergy were more immediately concerned with the moral chaos playing out on their very doorstep. The day after the big liberation dance in Zulte, a small community in East Flanders province, used condoms could be traced from the surrounding fields all the way to the parish hall and its basement.[68]

British troops had organized the dance in Zulte and it was the Allied dances that were soon drawing most of the Belgian clergy's ire. Indeed, their response to the sudden change in sexual mores, seemingly brought on by the mass presence of Anglo-American troops, almost resembled moral panic. The Church hierarchy weighed in from the lowest level to the very top. On Saturday, December 16, 1944, the Germans launched their massive counteroffensive in the Ardennes. That, however, did not stop one of Bastogne's Franciscan fathers during mass the following morning from lambasting parents for the indecencies he believed to have taken place at a ball organized by the Americans. From his pulpit he warned the adults to watch over their children and daughters more closely. He also reminded them of what the Romans had done to Hannibal's troops in Italy after their strength had been sapped by a winter of decadent pleasure at Capua. History tended to repeat itself, he thundered, the sounds of war audible in the distance, and American troops, like the Carthaginians, might be asked to pay for their sins.[69]

The head of the diocese of Bruges in a letter to his flock early in February 1945 was more careful not to offend the Allies. He thanked

[67] Guillaume Jacquemyns, "Readjustment Problems of the Repatriates," in BT, 79; and Aelbrecht, "Églises," 62 and 79.

[68] Aelbrecht, "Églises," 62; "Pleidooi voor het Christelijk gezin," *Het Volk*, January 7, 1945, 2; and *Bijdragen Zulte*, 87–8.

[69] Schrijvers, *Unknown Dead*, 112.

the liberators for their sacrifices and instead preferred to put the onus on "certain girls and women" whose "thoughtless and foolish behavior" he condemned, warning that, "One should not confound liberty with licentiousness." That same winter, Cardinal Van Roey, Belgium's most powerful prelate, in a letter read aloud in all parishes and widely quoted by the Catholic press, sketched a dire picture of the indecency and immorality fueled by such "worldly pleasures" as "public dances." He was especially alarmed, he noted, to have learned that even those from "honorable social milieus" were setting a poor example in this regard. "Those who shamelessly violate the laws of chastity," he rebuked his audiences, "whether in the matrimonial state or outside of marriage, those who scandalize and engage in evil, not only by their deeds, but by their attitudes and the way they dress, do they not fear that, rather than seeing an end to the calamities, they are provoking curses from Above over the corrupted world?"[70]

A new world order

Anglo-Saxon power: hard and soft

In Mopertingen, a tiny village in Limburg province, the parish priest during morning mass on Sunday, April 1, 1945 did not hold back either from attacking the corruption of society. Not only did he resolutely blame the English and Americans for the erosion of morals in Belgium. He also decried the imprisonment of the village's collaborators, many of whom the priest thought innocent and subject to ill treatment. The churchgoers barely allowed him to finish his tirade, his words drowning in loud booing and the angry banging of chairs. The priest, an SE officer claimed in a report on the incident, was known to have had sympathies for the VNV, a Flemish collaborationist organization.[71]

To point to the imperfections of the Anglo-Saxons in 1945 was one thing. To try and brush over the horrific crimes of Germany's New Order, however, was indefensible and unacceptable. Many in Europe during the hard times of the 1930s had turned away from the liberal, democratic order and towards a more authoritarian future. Public opinion in Belgium in the summer of 1940 had been, as Mazower observes, in the grip of "anti-parliamentary rage," greeting the news of German victory with "palpable relief." Hendrik de Man, president of the Belgian Workers' Party and a close adviser of King Leopold III, in his famous manifesto had declared: "This collapse of a decrepit world, far from

[70] Aelbrecht, "Églises," 61 and 37–9.
[71] SE Tongeren, report April 16, 1945, Folder 889, AA 1311.

being a disaster, is a deliverance." After four years of Nazi occupation, however, that summer now appeared to have unfolded in a distant age. "The German occupation," the reinstated mayor of Arlon noted in a proclamation on the day of liberation, "bearable in the beginning, did not take long to degenerate, in all of the occupied territories, into a regime of oppression and terror without precedent in history." In a book he started writing on the war some weeks later, Catholic philosopher Marcel De Corte faulted the Nazis for their "pretentious geopolitics," "brutal instincts," and "racist mythology." "The national-socialist revolution," he indicted, "is the supreme nihilistic revolution, that says *no* to all concrete values, to the human being, to the family, to the profession, to the fatherland, and to God: it is essentially the Revolution of Death."[72]

If the Second World War had been a clash of ideologies as much as a grab for territory, Nazism had squandered any chance of winning the hearts and minds of Europe. "National Socialist rule," historian Nico Wouters has noted, "had tried to wipe out liberal democracy between 1940 and 1944 in Belgium, but ultimately had only succeeded in turning the previously contested liberal democracy into the dominant and unquestioned form of legitimate government after 1944." There was no question either about who would be the leaders of the new democratic camp to which Belgium now professed to belong wholeheartedly. Many certainly believed that Germany had forever forfeited its claim to authority. "She will no longer count," *Pourquoi Pas?* announced in its special liberation issue on September 8, 1944, "and it is no longer necessary for her to count in the political game of Europe and the world." If Belgium after the First World War had looked to France for leadership, there was no hope of this repeating itself after the Second World War. The insults at the address of the defeated Belgians and their king in May 1940, the humiliating collapse of the French army in June, the politics of the Vichy regime – all had made an indelible mark on the small neighbor. "The loss of affection among the Belgians for France is one of the most striking phenomena of these past months," Paul Struye observed after one year of occupation. "It is obvious everywhere, in all layers of the population."[73]

[72] Mazower, *Dark Continent*, 142–4; Triffaux, *Arlon*, 48; and De Corte, *Du fond de l'abîme*, 32.

[73] Wouters, "Municipal Administration," 407. On the Belgian rediscovery and "reinvention" of liberal democracy, see also van Doorslaer, "Oorlog," 17 and 21–2. On the European phenomenon, see Mazower, *Dark Continent*, 187–9 and 196. Reprint of special liberation issue in *Pourquoi Pas?* September 5, 1984, 7. Struye, "Sentiment public," 86.

It is true that General de Gaulle paid a visit to an elated Brussels in October 1945. He came by train and was cheered by people in every station on the way to the Belgian capital. But, as one welcome poster put it, Belgians saw de Gaulle as "the soul of the French resistance." The resistance, however, could not be equated with all of France. In its front-page coverage of the visit, *Het Volk* hailed the tall and erect Frenchman not as one of the liberators, but as the head of "an ally just as unfortunate as ourselves." That France earlier in the year had not even been invited to Yalta, where the big powers had decided much of Europe's and the world's future, had left the Belgian press gasping. Newspapers regretted to report that even France's famous soft power – its radiant cultural appeal – had lost much of its former glow. Parisian women were still charming, noted one Belgian paper, but they rarely wore hats any more and thought perfume too expensive. The lights that had once given the city such fame now went out early in the evening. The boulevards belonged to American jeeps and trucks. "Paris," the article headlined sadly, "is Paris no longer."[74]

In Europe's gaping power vacuum it was the Anglo-Americans who had found the Belgian hearts and minds ripe for the picking. Even before the liberators arrived in Brussels early in September 1944, chalked slogans on walls read "England and America forever." Prime Minister Pierlot, back from a long exile in London with his government, in a speech before parliament that same month dwelt long on the special relationship with Britain and, when mentioning the invaluable contribution of the US, brought both chambers to their feet for an emotional applause. The Anglo-Americans were the new and undisputed fount of power. King Leopold III, in something akin to a political testament at the end of the war, defended his authoritarian stance and warned against the Allies as potential new occupiers. If that did much to help diminish his chances of a return to the throne, his brother Charles as Prince Regent restored confidence in the monarchy by following the constitution to the letter as well as steering a course "unequivocally in favor of the Allies" (already during the occupation a German diplomat had described Charles as a "well-known anglophile"). Meanwhile, successive Belgian governments also learned to rely on the powerful Allies to strengthen their position, first by magnifying the threat of the leftist resistance in 1944, then by exaggerating the possibility of a right-wing coup in 1945 by supporters of King Leopold. "We find," the American

[74] The poster is quoted in Caudron, *Nord Pas-de-Calais*, 171–5. "België groet Generaal de Gaulle," *Het Volk*, October 10, 1945, 1; and "Parijs is Parijs niet meer," *Het Volk*, October 4, 1945, 1.

ambassador to Belgium complained in a report to Washington, "that the Belgians are very glad, even too glad, to lean on us."[75]

No wonder then that the Belgian political establishment tried hard to convince the Allies that they were worthy of their support. And they were well aware that nothing would create more goodwill than to emphasize adherence to the democratic principles of the new club. In an article drafted in 1945 for American political scientists, Pierre Wigny explained that, although Belgium was a monarchy, the king was merely "a factor of unity" whose authority was "purely moral." "Nobody," he hastened to say, "wants a personal line of policy from the king." Moreover, "Being a constitutional monarchy, Belgium first of all wants to be a democracy," Wigny made sure to emphasize. "Democracy is a tradition in this old region where the municipal liberties reach as far back into the Middle Ages as the Great Charter in England." Sensing the main weakness of his pitch, Wigny also pledged that full voting rights would soon be extended to women.[76]

The economic pull of the Allies proved as seductive and addictive as their political power. "Today," SHAEF reported as late as June 1945, "Belgium is in an extremely healthy position but still absolutely dependant on continued assistance from the Allies." Belgium was one of the few countries that had engaged in reverse lend-lease aid the total value of which exceeded that of American lend-lease assistance. But the sheet was more than balanced when this was followed by $90 million in aid and continuing American assistance in the framework of the UNRRA. Meanwhile, 130,000 Belgians remained employed directly by the Allied armies in various services in the summer of 1945, and 35,000 as late as March 1946. As soon as Germany had been defeated, observers from many parts of the country had begun expressing concern about what might happen when these mighty employers would eventually pull out completely. Exports were the key for Belgium to guarantee full employment in the long term and to pay for the import of raw materials. With more than 40 percent of Belgian products exported to countries outside Europe before the war and the economies of continental neighbors now largely paralyzed, Anglo-American countries held an important key to future prosperity. In yet another article compiled for an American audience in 1945, a high-ranking official of the Ministry of Foreign Affairs made a point of selling Belgium, with its North Sea and Congolese

[75] For the slogans, see de Sany-Norro, *Forest-Vorst*, 27. "Discours de M. Pierlot," *Le Soir*, September 21, 1944, 2. On the king and his brother, see Witte *et al.*, *Politieke geschiedenis*, 240–2; and van Goethem, "Le Prince Charles," 330 and 360. On the manipulation of the Allies, see Lagrou, "Résistance," 130.

[76] Wigny, "Belgium Today and Tomorrow," in BT, 180.

outlets to the vital ocean, as an unmistakable member of "the Atlantic family."[77]

The soft power of the Allies, meanwhile, perfectly dovetailed with their hard power. While the war caused Paris to lose much of its cultural luster, it put Britain and America in an excellent position to leverage their moral leadership through cultural diplomacy. With the help of Books and Periodicals Commissions in Britain and the US, the Rockefeller Foundation, and the Civil Affairs division of the US Army, Belgian universities and institutions in 1945 received thousands of scientific books and hundreds of journal issues of Anglo-Saxon origin. Much more attention, however, was paid to the return of one of Belgium's quintessential historic paintings. In the spring of 1945, American troops recovered Van Eyck's *Adoration of the Mystic Lamb*, the world-famous altarpiece, from a salt mine in Austria. The Nazis had taken it away as part of their large-scale scheme to rob Europe of its art. The Allies realized full well the public relations value of handing back such potent national symbols and the advantages of being seen as protectors of the Old World's cultural heritage. Belgian authorities on their part insisted on expressing their gratitude by arranging that representatives of the US military would hand over Van Eyck's medieval masterpiece on September 3, exactly one year after the capital's liberation. The ceremony was attended by the Prince Regent, politicians, clergymen, academics, and various cultural figures, and the Belgian press made sure to cover the event extensively.[78]

A month later, Cardinal Van Roey and many other officials were present in Antwerp for an even more symbolic transfer that would soon be reverberating in towns and villages across the country. The Allies in Germany had been recovering many of the giant church bells that the occupier had taken down and shipped home to be smelted into arms. In a deeply Catholic country where church bells determined much of the rhythm of each day, the German move had been seen as the ultimate insult and one of the most hated moments of the occupation. As the ship with its cargo of 835 bells pulled into port in October 1945, Cardinal Van Roey condemned the assault on Belgium's religious and cultural heritage and called those who thought nothing of forging holy objects into deadly weapons "vandals and barbarians." How easy it was for the Allies to win the hearts and minds of the Belgians by mobilizing trucks and

[77] SHAEFB, FR No. 20, 1, June 26, 1945, WO 202/701, AA 1230; De Vos, "US Forces," 191; Léon-H. Dupriez, "Belgium's Unemployment Problem," in BT, 151; and Fernand Van Langenhove, "Belgium's Role in Europe," in BT, 161.

[78] Beyen, *Oorlog en verleden*, 259–61 and 254–5.

Plate 7.3 Belgian church bells return from Germany. Antwerp, October 1945. (CEGESOMA, Brussels, picture number 92634)

cranes and helping to restore the beloved bells, bedecked with flowers, to their rightful place even in the smallest of villages.[79]

The tectonic shift of power in 1944–5 was perhaps best reflected in the sudden emergence of English as the favorite foreign language by far for Walloons and Flemish alike. "Since French was of much greater international importance than the Flemish language," Professor Georges Smets explained to an American audience in 1945, "it conferred upon the Walloons a feeling of superiority." But if French had always been the language of power in Belgium and German that of the past four years, people had awoken to English as the new medium of influence even before the end of the occupation. "Many Belgians," Paul Struye noted as early as the start of 1944, "are learning or relearning English." The wife of a businessman in Londerzeel during the liberation wished she had. Her husband, she claimed in a desperate letter to General Erskine, had wrongfully been detained as a collaborator. She, like many others in her situation, implored the British general to use his power to help her.

[79] "835 klokken te Antwerpen toegekomen," *HBVL*, October 10, 1945, 1. For photos of the Allies returning bells to the small village of Sint-Pieters-Voeren, see Vierstraete *et al.*, *Fourons libérés*, 14.

Her husband, she wrote, had merely stood up for his Flemish identity. His credo during the war had always simply been: "Neither frenchified nor germanized." But now the woman was struggling to explain all this in two pages of yet another foreign language. "I must ask the help of a friend to send this writing in English," she apologized clumsily. "I hope that after Your benevolent intervention my children will be able to thank you in the English language." If the businessman's wife realized that in the future nothing but benefits would accrue from identifying with English, so did Flemish university students in Ghent. On the evening of March 30, 1945, several hundred of them were eagerly awaiting an evening's entertainment in the Ancienne Belgique. When the program started, they did not mind that the announcements were translated into English for the benefit of Allied soldiers in the audience. On the contrary, they cheered each time this happened and sang heartily along with the English songs in the repertoire. They were outraged, however, to hear that the announcements were being made in French first and only then in their own language. The angry catcalls grew louder as the evening progressed, until finally a smoke bomb ended the performance in chaos.[80]

American superpower

Nothing changed more drastically as a result of the war than Belgium's international orientation. Winston Churchill, once a leading figure in the Boer War, which had caused so much suspicion of the British in Belgium, now personified a Britain that Belgians loved and admired and looked to for leadership in Europe. "We continue to trust him for the future of our country," Limburg's newspaper pledged in September 1944, "just as we trusted him in the past and remain grateful to him, him and his courageous people!" The BBC had given Belgians as much hope as news, London had provided refuge for the Belgian government in exile, and a British general was running much of the country as head of the SHAEF Mission. No wonder then that in peace parades across the country in the summer of 1945 gratitude was expressed to the British liberators, the legendary British navy, and the indomitable British people. But it was the voice of Churchill that Belgians had listened to on the radio for the announcement of Germany's capitulation on a splendid, sun-drenched May 8. And it was Churchill who figured in the parades as the most admired Brit by far. Two men in the village

[80] Georges Smets, "The Flemings and the Walloons: Conclusions," in BT, 132; Struye, "Sentiment public," 252; undated letter from Delphine De Meersman to General-Major Erskine, Folder 1194, AA 1311; and SE Gent to Ganshof, March 28, 1945, Folder 1470, AA 1311.

parade of Beselare near Ieper proudly displayed a giant "V." Alongside the famous victory sign, they carried a large painting made by the local priest. In it the British leader could be seen crushing the heads of Hitler and Mussolini with his feet. When, in November 1945, Churchill finally visited Belgium in person, he received rapturous welcomes from adoring crowds in city after city. Paul-Henri Spaak's eulogy to the British Prime Minister in parliament was more subdued but no less powerful. The Belgian foreign minister could hardly keep his emotions in check when he concluded his speech with the soft and humble words, "Thank you, Sir."[81]

Such scenes were reminiscent of Europe's euphoric reception of American President Woodrow Wilson when he arrived for the Paris Peace Conference at the end of the First World War. But then the US had refused to join the League of Nations, had isolated itself from much of the world's affairs, and had vanished into a deep economic crisis. Now, however, after barely four years of involvement in the Second World War, the US loomed larger than ever before. And the man personifying the new Anglo-Saxon superpower had succeeded in making Wilson's failures a distant memory. Indeed, at the end of the war many in Belgium had no doubt that President Roosevelt was more important than Wilson and more powerful than Churchill. This explains the scenes of tremendous shock and emotion when it was suddenly announced that on April 12, 1945, just when it seemed that Germany was about to collapse, Roosevelt had died. "The death of the President of the United States," SHAEF noted, "has come as a severe blow to Belgium where he was immensely popular and respected." "The entire country," *Vooruit* headlined, "is in mourning." *Le Soir* described the feeling among the population as one of "consternation." Some of those guarding suspected collaborators in a Charleroi prison even vented their frustration and anger on the inmates.[82]

The death of the American president, an SE officer in Mechelen reported, was the main topic of conversation among people from all walks of life. Radio broadcasts talked about nothing else and when René Boulet, headmaster of a school in Genval, went to the local mill for flour, even there worried people gathered round a radio. Meanwhile, in the Belgian capital, the Prime Minister as well as the presidents of both houses of parliament made emotional speeches honoring the deceased American leader. Provincial governors ordered municipalities to have flags fly

81 "Winston Churchill," *HBVL*, September 20, 1944, 1; Quaghebeur and Verbeke, *Ieper*, 194; and Stéphany, "Belgique," 32–3.

82 SHAEFB, FR No. 15, 2, April 17, 1945, WO 202/695, AA 1230; *Vooruit*, April 14, 1945, 1; *Le Soir*, April 14, 1945, 2; and Van Ypersele, "La Belgique libérée," 16.

half-mast. Verviers was one of many cities to organize an impressive official tribute to the president. A life-size portrait of Roosevelt was placed at the Monument de la Victoire amidst flowers and wreaths. Policemen, gendarmes, and veterans with their flags came together to form a guard of honor. Men, women, and children crowded the square, their heads bare and bowed. Within a matter of weeks, the universities of Leuven and Liège were honoring Roosevelt with posthumous honorary doctorates while even the smallest of villages were renaming streets after him. And still the Liège-based newspaper *La Meuse* complained that Belgium had not done enough and should have organized some kind of national demonstration of respect for the unequalled American president.[83]

Newspapers readily agreed that Roosevelt had been of incomparable importance in recent world history. "His people," *Le Soir* printed in bold, "owe to him both an increase in power and a new moral appeal. But it is all of humanity that is in his debt, and the homage due to him is without limits." Roosevelt was, *Het Volk* asserted, "The most powerful man of his time." *Vooruit* headlined that the admired American had entered history, "As one of the biggest statesmen of all times and as the passionate champion of world peace." Roosevelt, the mainstream Belgian press agreed, had reached this status by mustering the courage to confront America's deep-rooted isolationism. Already during the American elections in the autumn of 1944, Belgian newspapers had made it very clear that they preferred Roosevelt to remain president of the US. *Le Soir* had endorsed Roosevelt's program and quoted an English journalist as saying that "rarely the destiny of the world had depended to such a degree on the domestic politics of a great democracy." In relieved response to his reelection, *Le Peuple* on November 10 had cheered that "the Americans have broken once and for all with traditional isolationism." Political opponent Thomas Dewey might well have embraced Roosevelt's international orientation, the socialist newspaper had noted, but that did still not cause Belgians to trust a Republican Party which in its ranks counted many traditional isolationists. And now, suddenly, in the spring of 1945, when things had finally begun to look up again, hopes for a better world were cruelly called into question. Limburg's Catholic newspaper asked its readers to remember that until only a few years ago the attitude had been: "America stands all by itself! It pays no attention to what happens elsewhere in the world! A dangerous mentality that Roosevelt gradually had to eradicate, a task in which he admirably succeeded." Belgians needed little reminding of the dangers that a return of such a mentality

83 SE Malines, WR April 13, 1945, Folder 1066, AA 1311; Boulet, "Journal," April 13, 1945, AB 1298; Ruwet, *Verviers*, 123–8; and Sulbout, "Liège," 101–8.

Plate 7.4 The *Stars and Stripes* are prominently displayed in a peace parade. Koersel, June 1945. (CEGESOMA, Brussels, picture number 7073)

would pose. "The announcement of the unexpected death of President Roosevelt," the SE reported from La Louvière, "has caused a profound sensation in public opinion; in a first reaction, opinion is alarmed at the possible consequences for the policy of the United States after the war. People fear a return to the isolationism that has led to the rearmament of Germany."[84]

It took Belgians some effort to get used to Roosevelt's successor. "Who is Senator Truman?" one newspaper asked itself; another badly misspelled his name as "Trewman." But Belgians soon grew as familiar with Truman as they would with every new American president of the twentieth century. They quickly realized that for them too the American Century had arrived. "In absolute as well as in relative terms," Norwegian historian Geir Lundestad has noted, "America's position after the Second World War was much stronger than Britain's had been at the height of *Pax Britannica*." As Truman increasingly signaled that this time his country could not and would not refuse the political and moral leadership that came with global power, America cemented its position as the epicenter of modernity. "Since that war," Dutch historian Rob Kroes has written, "America has appeared in a radically different guise, as much more of a potent force in everyday life in Europe and the larger world than ever before." It was no different in Belgium. The older image of America – that of the land of the Wild West – continued to coexist with the new as it had done before the war. Indeed, it was to avoid confusion with present-day America that the OWI during the war had insisted on having Western movies clearly dated in a foreword. Not that such interventions did much to stop the peace parade in Londerzeel from depicting the American people as cowboys on horseback or a theater troupe in Andenne from impersonating them dressed up in hats, bandanas, and cowhide pants. But a standard float in peace parades in the summer of 1945 would also often represent the US by means of an elaborate copy of New York's Statue of Liberty. And a wood-and-canvas replica of a Sherman tank in a parade organized by the inhabitants of Barbençon was adorned not just with flowers in the form of a "V," but also with the name "New York" painted on it in big white letters. It was New York – not Paris or London, where the lights had gone out – that had come to represent the unassailable future.[85]

The future of American preponderance had many faces. *Vooruit* noted that the US would now be financing much of Europe's economic recovery.

[84] *Le Soir*, April 14, 1945, 1, and "Roosevelt ou Dewey?" November 7, 1944, 1; *Het Volk*, May 8–9, 1945, 4; *Vooruit*, April 14, 1945, 1; *Le Peuple*, November 10, 1944, 1; *HBVL*, April 14, 1945, 1; and SE La Louvière, WR April 13, 1945, Folder 1054, AA 1311.

[85] *Het Volk*, April 14, 1945, 1, and *HBVL*, April 14, 1945, 1. Lundestad, *United States and Western Europe*, 27. Kroes, "European Anti-Americanism," 427. On the OWI, see Reynolds, *Rich Relations*, 180. Vermaesen, *Londerzeel*, 99 and 111; Vandenbroucke, *Andenne*, 144; and Roba and Leotard, *Walcourt-Beaumont*, 216.

The US had already been transformed from a debtor into a creditor nation during the First World War. Lend-Lease, and even more so the creation of the International Monetary Fund and World Bank as agreed at Bretton Woods in 1944, stood to strengthen that position. Two wars in twenty-five years, *Vooruit* concluded, have caused New York to replace London as the world's "financial heart." The socialist newspaper made no bones about this. "Without a doubt," it editorialized, "the Americans, with all this, have the best intentions." Economic recovery would eradicate unemployment, while at the same time preventing autarkic and isolationist tendencies and safeguarding world peace. If this would lead to the kind of economic activity that selected Belgian journalists were witnessing firsthand in the US in the summer of 1945, the potential for the future seemed limitless. That future could be glimpsed not just in New York, but in almost every American metropolis. "The overwhelming facts stand in sharp contrast with the limitations of words," wrote a reporter who had just visited some industries near Chicago. "How to describe the biggest steel factory in the world with the standard vocabulary?"[86]

How, for that matter, to describe American technology with commonplace words? The same journalist who toured Chicago some weeks later filed a story on the newly built Pentagon in Washington. The article appeared on *Le Soir*'s front page on August 8, 1945, and described the impressive construction as "a labyrinth" where no fewer than 33,000 personnel were hard at work making plans for the military. On page two of the same issue, a small headline announced, "The most powerful bomb in the world has been dropped on Hiroshima." News of the most devastating weapon to have emerged from America's military establishment was rather subdued during the first days because few were immediately aware of the watershed it represented. The Belgian press initially talked about the new device as if it were merely a more lethal conventional weapon, 2,000 times more powerful, for example, than the so-called British blockbuster bomb. It took some time for the exceptional nature of the weapon to make the front pages and for words like atomic, uranium, and radiation to enter the discourse. Some expressed fear for the future and a French physicist was quoted as saying that soon these weapons would be capable of wiping out all life on earth. But it was not in a French laboratory that nuclear fission had been developed, and the Belgian press preferred to focus on the advantages that Anglo-Saxon sources claimed this spectacular new energy source held in store: the BBC, for example, which reported that soon a mere teacup of uranium fuel would suffice to power the luxury liner *Queen Mary* across the

[86] *Vooruit*, December 13, 1945, 1; and *Le Soir*, July 14, 1945, 1.

Atlantic or a physicist from the University of Southern California who predicted that even travel to the moon now belonged to the realm of possibilities.[87]

In a country whose colony would be the main producer of uranium for years to come, such musings sparked a fascination with the atom that would make it the shining symbol of the World Exposition in Brussels in 1958. But Belgians in 1945 did not have to look into the future to be amazed by American technological advances. Jules Verne's characters might have needed eighty days to circle the globe in a hot-air balloon, *Het Volk* reported, but *Pan American Airways* had just announced that it would have one of its passenger planes fly around the world in just eighty-eight hours. An American transport plane, meanwhile, was making the shorter trip across the Atlantic to land on Melsbroek air base with a very special cargo. Just days after the destruction of Hiroshima and Nagasaki, it was unloaded amidst reporters and Americans in uniform. Photographs in newspapers showed what was called the first of several "steel lungs." These were special machines, *Le Soir* revealed, to use in "the fight against infantile paralysis." It was just the beginning of an avalanche of new life-saving devices and knowledge pouring in from America. A key role in the transfer of recent advances in medicine and surgery was played by the Belgian American Educational Foundation. This organization, like so many others at the end of the Second World War, had its seat in New York. But its origins went as far back as the aftermath of the Great War, when it had been created with American financial support under the aegis of Herbert Hoover.[88]

"The Belgian people," socialist newspaper *Le Peuple* asserted in a major article on the front page early in July 1945, "know how much they owe to the great American democracy, and it is from the bottom of their hearts that they share the joy of Americans in the celebration of Independence Day." Its Flemish counterpart, *Vooruit*, some weeks earlier had already used a tribute to the American dead of the First World War in the Flanders Field Cemetery at Waregem as an occasion to plead for a more intimate Belgo-American friendship: "Flanders Field serves as eternal testimony to the ties of friendship that bind our two peoples. The heroes ... rest in Flemish soil that is the earth from which must grow ever more affection and goodwill."[89]

[87] "Overgave of vernietiging," *Het Volk*, August 8, 1945, 1; and "De atoomenergie gaat de aarde van uitzicht doen veranderen," *Het Volk*, August 10, 1945, 1.

[88] "Een reis om de wereld in 88 uur," *Het Volk*, July 11, 1945, 1; *Le Soir*, August 14, 1945, 1; and Jean La Barre and Paul Bastenie, "Medicine and Medical Research," in BT, 101.

[89] *Le Peuple*, July 5, 1945; and *Vooruit*, May 31, 1945, 1.

Red fascism

There were, however, also concerns about what the unprecedented power of the Anglo-Americans might mean for the future. Economic concerns had already been aired in the winter of 1944–5 and they refused to go away as the year drew to a close. "More and more, word has it among people from all social milieus," the gendarmes reported from Liège, "that the allies, and the English in particular, are taking away the best of Belgium, coal – panes of window glass – sugar – etc." People in Izegem feared for the future of their shoe industry and for their livelihoods when news reached them that from the giant American factories 300,000 pairs of shoes were on their way to Belgium. Such fears increased when rumors began circulating that the Allies did not intend to abandon Belgium's key infrastructure at the end of the war. Despite firm denials in the press, word continued to spread that the British and American governments would be leasing major airbases and even the port of Antwerp. The American embassy in Brussels on October 8, 1945 reported to Washington that the communist press in particular was accusing the US of delaying the recovery of devastated countries so that their weak economies would allow American businesses to implant themselves.[90]

If people in the street expressed anxiety about the hijacking of their economy, some in the mainstream press raised more concern about the future of Belgian sovereignty. Such unease was being vented fairly shortly after the liberation and was a response to plans unveiled at Dumbarton Oaks in the US for a new international organization to replace the League of Nations. It did not sit well with those who had the opportunity and time to examine the specifics of the proposed United Nations that a handful of large nations in the powerful Security Council would be determining the fate of the world. Socialist politician Louis de Brouckère, for example, did not believe that China would play "a fundamental role" in the Security Council. That meant, he calculated, that "one seventh of the world's inhabitants would decide over the peace or the war that will involve all others." "That is not," he emphasized, "as far as I am concerned, how I understand democracy." Lucien Fuss in *Le Soir* concurred when in January 1945 he said he was in favor of the creation of an Atlantic community only if smaller nations would be treated as the equals of larger ones. "Is this impossible?" he demanded to know. "Is this wish the expression of unforgivable

[90] Gendarmerie Liège, MR August 4, 1945, Folder 1057, AA 1311; SE Roeselare, WR September 22, 1945, Folder 1090, AA 1311; Institut d'Éducation et de Documentation Nationales, *Chronique*, 133, 134, and 168; and Sulbout, "Liège," 76, note 19.

naïveté? ... Belgium admires the United States, Canada, Great Britain, France, and it has reasons to love them profoundly. But it must be able to love them with confidence ... We want to be little loyal allies, but with respect for our individuality, our total independence."[91]

But the procedural intricacies of the UN did not seem to resonate with the larger public as much as the blunt wish for peace. The special liberation issue of *Pourquoi Pas?* on September 8, 1944, had expressed that wish most forcefully: "Let them create a United Nations of Europe or a United Nations of the World, so be it! Let them do what they want, as long as they establish before all else a solid peace, in the shadow of the whims that may sprout from the brain of the Germans, a gendarme's peace, with a number of cannon, aircraft, and bombs capable of enforcing it." Now, a year later, despite reservations expressed by insiders in the press, the SE did not appear to be picking up rumors accusing the Anglo-Americans of employing the UN to further their own ambitions. Indeed, in peace parades across the country during the summer of 1945, the UN, and the Conference of San Francisco that established it, formed recurrent themes of hope. And bystanders much enjoyed the spectacle of Belgians walking side by side with the flags of the world in their hands. Regardless of how strongly Belgian representatives in San Francisco had objected to the idea of the right of veto in the Security Council, their parliament in the autumn did decide to ratify the charter. *Het Volk* accepted that this was best for the nation "because we had to choose the lesser of two evils and because it is better to have a charter than none."[92]

Indeed, by the autumn of 1945 many Belgians were eager to have in place at least some kind of world organization for peace because they were more afraid of the Russians than the Germans. The perception of the Soviets underwent a significant shift in less than a year after the liberation. Prior to the invasion of Normandy, nothing had lifted spirits more than news of the crushing defeat inflicted on the Germans at Stalingrad. In September 1944, Prime Minister Pierlot's mention of the Soviet Union in his speech before parliament had incited applause that was long and loud. Even the department stores Grand Bazar and Innovation, temples of capitalism, had thought nothing of displaying the portrait of Stalin next to that of Roosevelt, Churchill, and de Gaulle. In February 1945, just weeks after the Anglo-Americans had pushed the Germans out of the Ardennes with much difficulty, SHAEF assessed the country's opinion about the ally in the east as follows:

91 "Les Nations Unies," *Le Peuple*, October 23–4, 1944, 1 and 2; and "D'une semaine à l'autre," *Le Soir*, January 30, 1945, 1.

92 Reprint of special liberation issue in *Pourquoi Pas?* September 5, 1984, 6–7; and "Over den moeilijken vrede van morgen," *Het Volk*, November 5, 1945, 1.

There are also many Belgians, particularly amongst the working classes, who consider that Russia is winning the war and would still do so whatever the British and Americans might do. There are other Belgians who dislike intensely the idea that Russia will overthrow Germany as it brings to the surface their worst fears (stimulated by German propaganda) that the whole of Europe is in for a Communist bath. Between these two extreme views of adoration and fear of the Kremlin there is a very large and solid block of Belgian opinion which just wants to live, work and reconstitute Belgium.[93]

But the solid block of Belgians who did not worry much about communism steadily crumbled that year as more and more news of Soviet intransigence and outright hostile behavior surfaced. The press at the start of 1945 had quoted Roosevelt as saying that, although differences of opinion with the Soviet Union were inevitable, rumors of discord were false and the result of German propaganda. When spring came, however, the trusted American president was no longer there to calm such concerns, and reports to the headquarters of the SE indicated that rumors were mushrooming into fear. There was talk of multiplying disagreements and of the Soviets obstructing progress at the San Francisco talks. By the end of May there was talk even of the possibility of war between America and Russia and of the dire consequences of this for Belgium. Socialist newspaper *Vooruit* on May 30 squarely addressed the question of war weighing so heavily on the mind of "the man in the street." In an editorial it concluded that war could be avoided only if the West would abandon its obsession with a communist grab for power across Europe and the Soviets their fixation with the existence of a Western reactionary alliance aimed against them.[94]

Such balanced assessments were harder to come by, however, when, in the wake of Germany's defeat, more and more political prisoners, forced laborers, and POWs returned to Belgium with stories of misconduct and harassment perpetrated by the Soviet liberators. By June people in Flanders as well as the Walloons were repeating allegations of unruly Soviet troops robbing, beating, and even murdering Belgians. It was also being whispered that the threat of rape was so common that some frightened women had arrived in the Anglo-American sector dressed as men. Such stories, the SE reported from Bruges, elicited plenty of comments about Soviet "mentality and conduct." And

93 For Stalingrad, see Struye, "Sentiment public," 218. "Discours de M. Pierlot," *Le Soir*, September 21, 1944, 2; and SHAEFB, FR No. 11, 1, February 20, 1945, WO 202/691, AA 1230.

94 "Een rede van President Roosevelt," *HBVL*, January 9, 1945, 1. On fear of war with the Soviets see, for example, SE La Louvière, WR April 13, 1945, Folder 1054; SE Ronse, WR May 25, 1945, Folder 1088; and SE Roeselare, WR June 2, 1945, Folder 1090, AA 1311. "Wrijvingen met Sovjet-Rusland?" *Vooruit*, May 30, 1945, 1.

they only served to fuel the already existing unrest about war that the Soviets had given rise to through their obstinacy in San Francisco, their territorial ambitions in Europe, and "their feeling of superiority" towards the Western allies.[95]

If Catholics were irritated by the lack of enthusiasm among the Anglo-Americans for their wish to see King Leopold III return to the throne, by the summer of 1945 they were making no secret of who they thought constituted the real enemy. In towns across Flanders chalked slogans could be seen on walls and streets exclaiming not only "Long live the king," but also "Down with communism" and "Hammer and sickle = Swastika." The Catholic press, meanwhile, had a field day highlighting Soviet ambitions in Eastern Europe, Northern Africa, and the Middle East. Both *Het Volk* and *La Libre Belgique* lavished much attention on bizarre incidents in Brussels that saw Soviet soldiers seize a person from a center for repatriates and kidnap another and whisk her off to their embassy. But socialists too by the summer of 1945 were questioning what kind of future there would be if the Soviet Union did not manage to restrain its more aggressive impulses. In an article intended for an American audience, Victor Larock, the political director of *Le Peuple*, had no qualms about repeating that capitalism "involves forms of exploitation of workers." But he also insisted that what socialism wanted was "a free democracy" in which no citizens would be "subject to the material or moral tutelage of any foreign agency." If Larock left the identity of that agency vague, Louis de Brouckère, in the wake of the detonation of two atomic bombs, expressed himself more clearly. Acknowledging the military and industrial advantages of atomic energy, he nevertheless thought it absolutely vital "to prevent any dictatorship from coming into its possession." With such warnings in mind, few Belgians could have felt at ease watching the huge Allied parade go by in Brussels on the first anniversary of the liberation. All of the Allied nations, great and small, were proudly represented. The Soviets, however, after a long silence, had declined to take part.[96]

[95] For the Soviet stories see, for example, Rijkswacht Gent, WR May 27, 1945, Folder 1035; SE La Louvière, WR June 1, 1945, Folder 1054; and SE Roeselare, WR June 30, 1945, Folder 1090, AA 1311. Bruges report Albert Van Kerckvoorde, no date, Folder 1017, AA 1311.

[96] For the slogans see, for example, SE Louvain, WR July 15, 1945, Folder 1063; and Rijkswacht Hasselt, MR August 6, 1945, Folder 1044, AA 1311. On Soviet territorial ambitions see, for example, *Het Volk*, September 4 and 20, 1945. On the Brussels incidents, see *Het Volk*, September 21, 1945, 1. Larock, "The Socialist Party," in BT, 15. De Brouckère, "Encore la bombe atomique," *Le Peuple*, August 14, 1945, 1. For the parade, see Stéphany, "Belgique," 31.

American hegemony: tolerant and tolerable

In such a deteriorating international climate, objections to the way the Anglo-Americans were wielding power appeared increasingly petty if not counterproductive. In 1943, Paul Struye had written: "People are convinced that Great Britain is fighting for its hegemony but are no less convinced that its interests coincide with ours and that its hegemony, even if it becomes more pronounced, will be tolerant and tolerable, whereas that of the Germans will be neither one nor the other." In 1945, Struye could have made an identical observation, but with the Soviets in the role of the Germans. Simultaneously, however, there was also a growing realization among Belgians that the US was destined to be the new Britain. The war had convinced policymakers that a return to Belgium's traditional position of neutrality was no longer a viable option. It had at first appeared most logical to the exiled government in London to look to Britain for leadership on the European continent after the war. "The United States seem to me too distant," Paul-Henri Spaak had explained in April 1942, "Russia too different, from too many points of view, France has become too weak and Germany too hated." As a result of the new course, the Belgian military was rebuilt with everything from Sten guns to Spitfires and Britain was to remain influential in Belgium from the liberation to as late as 1947. A prominent Belgian archivist in 1945 hurried to put together a book tracing the diversity and quality of relations between the two countries over the past five centuries – an exercise, Alain Colignon has noted, "inspired by gratitude" more than "objective historical analysis." Indeed, at the end of that same year, even when writing for an American audience, a high-ranking Belgian foreign affairs official concluded that Belgium would seek security from Britain, continental neighbors, and the UN, but omitted to mention the US.[97]

All this did not, however, prevent Belgian public opinion from realizing fairly shortly after the liberation that the war had made Britain's hegemony less rather than more pronounced. Commenting on the British elections early in July 1945, *Vooruit* said these remained an important event, even though it was true that "the power of Great Britain no longer stands in relation to that of the US and Russia as it did before the war." The same newspaper on numerous occasions also observed that rationing in Britain had reached "draconian" proportions and was in effect much worse than

[97] Struye, "Sentiment public," 215. Spaak is quoted in Grosbois, "Relations diplomatiques," 178. On Anglo-Belgian relations after the war, see vanden Berghe, "België en het buitenland," 200–7; and Deloge, "Belgique et Grande-Bretagne." The archivist is Joseph Lefèvre, *L'Angleterre et la Belgique à travers les cinq derniers siècles* (Brussels, 1946). Colignon, "Résistance," 30. The official is Fernand Van Langenhove, "Belgium's Role in Europe," in BT, 162–3.

during the war. Indeed, to escape such a harsh economic climate, many British soldiers who had married local girls preferred to stay put on the Continent. Belgians thought it even more telling that several of those who did go home with their brides in the months and years that followed decided to trade life in Britain for what they thought would be a better one on the far side of the Channel.[98]

It was clear that a nation in such dire economic straits would be hard pressed to continue providing leadership in Europe in the face of an even more massive red totalitarianism. American soldiers, encouraged by a booming economy and a GI Bill that promised generous financial and educational benefits, could not wait to go home. Theirs was an economy that appeared more than capable of containing communism and sustaining hegemony even in the furthest corners of the globe. On the very day in August 1945 that news of de Gaulle paying tribute in Washington was splashed across front pages, Belgian newspapers headlined that American General MacArthur had taken up residence in Japan's imperial palace. Barely a month later, readers learned that President Truman had asked the British to allow 100,000 Jews into Palestine, a request hailed by Jews, denounced by Arabs, and protested by Iraq. No wonder then that in November 1945 *Het Volk* approvingly cited Lord Russell's plan to protect the free world against Soviet threats. The idea was, the newspaper explained, to create "a world under American leadership." Peace-loving nations would join a military alliance with the US. They would remain in step with American foreign policy and refuse to undertake war except with the support of the US. And they would promise not to build atomic weapons, a pledge to be verified by on-site inspections. The US in return would commit itself to protecting the members of the alliance against aggression. "If England was to point the way," Lord Russell was purported to have said, "the other nations, with the exception of Russia and its satellites, would probably follow its example."[99]

It was too early for this to happen in 1945. Yet, in less than four years, as Britain's economy worsened and the challenges to its empire mounted, Lord Russell's plan, as relayed by the Belgian Catholic newspaper, in its broad outlines was to be a reality. "In fact," Lundestad has noted, "no country expressed Europe's attitude of inviting, even urging the Americans to abandon their isolationism and play an active part in Europe's affairs as clearly as did Britain." In explaining Belgium's

[98] *Vooruit*, July 4, 1945, 1 and December 14, 1945, 2. For the British soldiers, see De Vos, *Bevrijding*, 91–2; Aelbrecht and Maghe, "Braine," 77; and Roden, *Tessenderlo*, 263–4.

[99] De Gaulle and MacArthur were on the front page of *HBVL*, August 29, 1945. On the US and Palestine, see *Het Volk*, October 3, 1945. Lord Russell's plan is on the front page of *Het Volk*, November 9, 1945.

postwar abandonment of neutrality, Spaak in 1948 said, "The only way to resist a dictatorship is to be as strong as it is." During the war, Spaak had been convinced as Foreign Minister that this could only be done by leaning on Britain. Now, as Belgium's Prime Minister, he knew that there was no other alternative than to look towards the far shore of the Atlantic. The US in 1948 not only seemed less distant to Spaak, but its hegemony, like that of Britain before it, much more tolerant and tolerable than that of the Soviet Union. Before a session of the UN General Assembly that year, the socialist Prime Minister in a famous speech took the Soviet Union to task for its aggressive imperialism. There was only one superpower, Spaak indicted, that had emerged from the war "with the conquest of other territory." And he was unrelenting when he characterized Soviet foreign policy as "more audacious and more ambitious than the policy of the Czars themselves." "The basis of our policy," Spaak was not ashamed to admit, "is fear."[100]

Fear is what made Western European governments embrace the Truman Doctrine, the Marshall Plan, and NATO in rapid succession and with the approval of their populations. These forms of close economic, military, and political cooperation in turn bound Western Europe to the US as never before. And they threw open the floodgates of America's influence. The American presence was symbolized most potently by the continuing presence of military personnel. As soon as NATO came into being in 1949, the number stood at 80,000 and Europeans were unanimous in their support for the beloved Second World War hero Dwight D. Eisenhower as the commander of the new integrated force. The Korean War quickly pushed the number of GIs in Europe to more than 240,000 by 1953. That this did not bring back the currents of discontent that the GIs had stirred up in 1945 had much to do with lessons learned at the time. Truman and Eisenhower remade the image of the "swaggering, sometimes anarchistic" GIs with the help of what historian John Willoughby has called "domesticating reforms." These allowed soldiers to be stationed overseas with their families, brought them together on comfortable bases, and made sure that they remained more radically separated from civilian society.[101]

Despite such separation between troops and the Europeans, however, American influence extended far beyond the insular bases. For

[100] Lundestad, *United States and Western Europe*, 44. Spaak is quoted in vanden Berghe, "België en het buitenland," 189. For the speech on fear, see "Discours de Paul-Henri Spaak à l'Assemblée Générale des Nations Unies (28 septembre 1948)," www.ena.lu/mce.cfm. Last accessed on September 28, 2007.

[101] Lundestad, *United States and Western Europe*, 31 and 52–3; and Willoughby, *Conquering Heroes*, 150–1.

what continued to bind together the Atlantic alliance was not just fear and the craving for protection, but also the insatiable appetite for material prosperity. Europe had seen the first hints of an American-style consumer culture at the turn of the century and even more so after the First World War. But it was in the wake of the mass deprivation of the Second World War and in direct confrontation with the fabulous wealth of America that the Old World embraced the cult of abundance with a vengeance. For the Belgians this embrace started with the frenzied plunder of GI items. It was strengthened by the return from exile of a reformist government that made a decent standard of living for all the centerpiece of its program. And it was solidified through the forging of a close alliance with what Victoria de Grazia has called America's Market Empire. By highlighting the numerous big strikes in 1945, newspaper *Vooruit* might have exposed to its labor readership what at one point it called American capitalism's "system of exploitation." But that did not stop the socialist newspaper from contradicting itself when rejoicing that, because of high labor costs at home, big American companies soon might be relocating to Belgium and boosting employment. And it did so amidst photos of the newest women's fashion from New York and background information on Hollywood's sexiest stars. Belgium gladly shared in the $8.3 billion in economic assistance that the US provided to Western Europe between July 1945 and June 1947 and the $14.1 billion of the four-year Marshall Plan. Belgians in the context of the Marshall Plan also actively participated in an American program of technical assistance whose main aim it was to spread the gospel of productivity. In 1951 Belgium created its own agency for productivity growth and in the next five years hundreds of businessmen, workers, and union delegates traveled to the US "in order to discover," in the words of historian Cécile Hubert, "the secrets of the fascinating American prosperity." The US encouraged all this, of course, because it fitted into its broader strategic and economic design. That it could accomplish this convergence so smoothly, however, had everything to do with Western Europeans considering American hegemony not only tolerable but, in more than one way, appealing.[102]

In the wake of American military bases and production methods inevitably followed all the rest. Western European scientists flocked to the US in what constituted a major brain drain for at least two decades.

[102] On the shared commitment to consumption as a basis for the Atlantic alliance, see de Grazia, *Irresistible Empire*, 5, 11, and 338–43; Berghahn, *Europe*, 5 and 133–9; Nehring, "Westernization," 176–8 and 187–8; and Hoganson, "Stuff It," 579 and 584–5. *Vooruit*, October 31, 1945, 1 and December 27, 1945, 1. Lundestad, *United States and Western Europe*, 47–8; and Hubert, "Campagne de productivité," 197–8.

The number of foreign students enrolled at American colleges and universities jumped from 17,000 in 1947–8 to 26,000 in 1949–50. Of the academic staff at Belgian universities in 1950, one in every five had in one way or another passed through the Belgian American Educational Foundation, although many had already done so before the Second World War. The fascination with American media and culture surpassed the admiration for its science and education. News agencies AP and UPI in 1939 only had 954 customers in all of Europe; by 1949 that number had swelled to 2,551 in Western Europe alone. Hollywood strengthened its position as the world's most influential industry of popular culture. But Europe's elites too caught themselves glancing at America as New York replaced Paris as the center of avant-garde art and abstract expressionism joined jazz as the epitome of freedom and modernity. That this cultural hegemony did not derive solely from European admiration but also from US political, military, and economic domination was demonstrated repeatedly. The CIA, for example, engaged in subtle cultural diplomacy by lending support to the exhibitions of abstract expressionists overseas. The US State Department switched to more muscled tactics by threatening to withhold reconstruction aid from European countries considering protective measures against Hollywood. Whatever the exact mechanisms of American hegemony, it was the same interplay of fascination and domination that immediately after the Second World War had more Austrians study English than French even in the French sector of occupation. And it was through that same combination of soft and hard power that America before the end of the century had made English the lingua franca of the globe.[103]

A third world in the shadows

In 1945 Belgians were well aware of the threat that the Soviet world posed to their security and values. And they clearly saw that the democratic world was bound to rally around the Anglo-Saxons and the Americans in particular. But, if they sensed that the Second World War had brought unmistakable change also to a third world lurking in the shadows, here they failed to understand its full implications. The world of non-whites arrived at the doorstep of Belgium's homogeneous society most vividly in the shape of large numbers of black soldiers from the US. Most Belgians, like the British and French before them, gave the African-Americans a warm and friendly reception. Indeed, in many

[103] Duignan and Gann, *Rebirth*, 615–17; Lundestad, *United States and Western Europe*, 34–5; Bertrams, "Échanges culturels," 5 and 7; and Wagnleitner, *Coca-Colonization*, 100, 160, 238–41, and 295–6.

a case they recoiled from the treatment black liberators were receiving at the hands of white comrades. Instructions posted by American authorities in the Liège area to facilitate cohabitation urged inhabitants immediately to report any colored soldier claiming to be an MP because it was impossible for any of them there to belong to this service. Others learned about the realities of segregation in the American military in ways they thought even more shocking and reprehensible. When white GIs arrived in Eisden and learned that black troops had been stationed there just earlier, they told inhabitants to give toilets an extra cleaning and demanded to know which of the beds had been slept in by "niggers." The people of Hermée, just north of Liège, took much offense too at the behavior of white American soldiers. In the wake of the Battle of the Bulge they had been hosting black GIs for several weeks. The men belonged to the 761st Tank Battalion, one of the rare black combat units that the US army tolerated. They had fought long and hard and had charmed many in the village. All that, however, did not add up to much in the eyes of the white GIs who took their place. They were annoyed to learn that blacks had been there before them and tried hard to convince villagers that these soldiers were like monkeys and had to be avoided at all cost. Soon after, the village witnessed how white troops refused shelter to a black driver whose truck had broken down and forced him to spend the night in the icy cabin. Their attitude certainly did not get the approval of Mrs. Fumal, who earlier had hosted seventeen perfectly well-behaved black GIs. She was surprised by the discrimination, she later remembered, because she had thought the US to be "ahead of the others."[104]

Despite such indignation, however, Belgians could not help sharing many of the prejudices and fears of their white liberators. Colonial propaganda on the Congo had conditioned them to think of blacks as distant, primitive, and powerless in the face of superior white force. Now they were suddenly confronted up close with countless blacks demonstrating that they could handle even the most complex technology in the form of trucks, bulldozers, and on occasion even tanks. What intrigued Belgians more than anything else, however, was the sight of blacks in the streets carrying arms. In sharp contrast to photos taken of white GIs, it appears that civilians regularly asked black soldiers to pose with their weapons clearly displayed, as if wanting to emphasize the novelty and deviant nature of this situation. A most striking example of this is a

[104] On relations with black troops elsewhere in Europe, see Reynolds, *Rich Relations*, 307–8; Torrent, *La France américaine*, 234–5; and Willoughby, *Conquering Heroes*, 60–4. Lognard-Poncin and Michel, *Chaudfontaine*, 45; Kohlbacher, "Eisden," 30; and transcript interview Ms. Fumal, No. 526, AA 1450.

photo taken of three black GIs in a bivouac at Pepinster near Verviers. The photo has clearly been staged and shows one soldier clutching a knife, another aiming a revolver, and still another holding a carbine.[105]

Still, nothing preoccupied the minds of Belgians more than the threat that black soldiers, armed or not, might pose to their women. They showed strong similarities in this regard with Europeans from Britain to Germany. Stereotypical images of primitive sexual appetites combined with a predisposition against miscegenation so that these concerns were aired at an early stage. "Certain, perhaps timorous, souls," the SE reported from Arlon just weeks after the liberation, "regard the arrival of colored troops with dread; they predict that soon these colored soldiers might be seducing women and young girls in the area." When American authorities in Boom near Antwerp in the spring of 1945 decided to organize a dance for the many black quartermaster troops stationed in the area, local girls arrived with their beaux to a chorus of disapproving whistles that forced them to keep their eyes glued to the ground in shame. Historian Fabrice Virgili in a preface to Lilly's work on wartime rape has suggested that in France many more African-Americans were punished for sexual crimes than white GIs not only because of the color prejudice of the US military, but also as a result of "a greater readiness" among the civilian population to report perpetrators who were black. Although much tension arose from relations between Belgian women and Allied troops in general, it is telling that in several peace parades, floats acted out the presence of Americans by showing women in the intimate and compromising company of inhabitants dressed up as *black* GIs.[106]

In the peace parades of 1945 many traditional stereotypes of blacks that had been common in theater plays and colonial parades before the war resurfaced without much change. Blacks were primitives who wore straw skirts, engaged in wild dances, and lived in huts among monkeys. Alternatively, they could just as well be cute little children with happy smiles and not a care in the world. In Beringen's peace parade, a single child with a blackened face and a clownish suit rode by on a festooned bicycle. A sign simply identified him as "American Boy," shamelessly repeating the hated epithet for a black man in the US. In the same parade, more than a dozen American sailors and soldiers were represented by inhabitants whose hands and faces were painted pitch-black. All of the roles, including that of the black soldier bearing the American

[105] *Pepinster*, 66. For examples of other photos, see Lecerf, *Libération*, 328; and Vandenbroucke, *Andenne*, 137.

[106] SE Arlon, WR October 7, 1944, Folder 993, AA 1311; Van de Velde, *Boom*, 301; and Lilly, *Taken by Force*, xvii. For a good example of such a parade float, see photo No. 7122, CEGESOMA.

flag, but with the notable exception of the defeated German, were played by children from one of the local schools. Meanwhile, where there were blacks in a parade, actors dressed up as missionaries and nurses in white robes and uniforms could be counted on to be following close behind, ready and eager to provide much needed enlightenment and tutelage. In discussing the wonders of radar that same summer, *Het Volk* rejoiced that the West, through its manifold creations and inventions during the war, had demonstrated its unassailable superiority in technology, science, and human thought. That these included the V1s and V2s that had terrorized the Belgian population until half a year ago appeared to be of little consequence in a racialized vision of the world, because *Het Volk* made a point of specifically mentioning Germany's wartime technology too. Indeed, what was most important, the Catholic newspaper exulted, was that the Atlantic world had remained ahead of Russia and Japan and that "civilization" had ultimately been saved.[107]

No wonder then that such a circumscribed understanding of civilization prevented many from questioning empire as practiced outside Europe. It is true that the Belgian communist press agitated against the continuation of colonialism. *Le Drapeau Rouge*, for example, early in October 1945 condemned the secret transport of weapons from ports in Australia and Belgium that it claimed were intended to help suppress the Indonesian struggle for independence. And it called on dockers to remain vigilant and, if necessary, to join their party comrades in Sydney who, the paper said, had gone on strike to show solidarity with the Indonesians. Such appeals did nothing, however, to prevent Belgian peace parades from expressing unabashed gratitude not only to Churchill and the British people, but also to the British empire. Nor did they stop Belgian women who had shown exemplary courage in resisting the imperial ambitions of Nazi Germany from accepting the Order of the British Empire in November 1945. Meanwhile, the mainstream press, both Catholic and socialist, showed little enthusiasm for the movements of independence that were being reported from Indonesia to Algeria. *Vooruit* quoted British Labor Prime Minister Attlee without comment when he announced that he regarded the UN charter as key to the security of Britain *and* its empire. The same newspaper some weeks later published a photo of children in West Africa receiving what it called

[107] For photos of blacks as primitives see, for example, image No. 104378, CEGESOMA; and Henry, *Aywaille*, 122. The Koersel photos are located in the Provinciaal Archief en Documentatiecentrum in Hasselt, Belgium, and also show depictions of blacks as wild men. For the central role of the missionary see, for example, a photo of a float in Celis *et al.*, *Zepperen*, 308. "De 'Radar' heeft de beschaving gered!" *Het Volk*, August 21, 1945, 1.

a fine education in art under British guidance. The general tone in the Belgian press was that to shatter such benevolent imperialism abruptly and with violence was highly irresponsible and that calm and diplomacy would eventually see differences reconciled.[108]

Such a dose of wishful thinking was needed also, of course, if Belgians were to remain optimistic about their own future in Africa. No matter how much Belgians had suffered from German exploitation, the war appeared to have shown them that to continue their own occupation of the Congo was more important than ever. The press in 1945 believed that with much of Belgium and Europe in ruins, many young people would be forced to look for opportunities elsewhere. White Anglo-Saxon settlement countries were cited as the most likely destinations. But newspapers plugged the Congo too as an ideal place for youthful energy to be absorbed. It was one of the richest colonies of the African continent, *Le Soir* noted, and was in dire need of more white brains and hands. Just as importantly, by fully developing a colony so rich in raw materials, the new colonists would help still the insatiable appetite for material goods. The war had made Belgians realize how dependent they were on the Congo for many of the things they had taken for granted until then. Belgian authorities in the colony had cooperated with the British early on to give morale in the motherland a much needed boost. The initiative had already led British aircraft in 1942 to drop thousands of small packs of ground coffee over occupied Belgium. Bilingual labels attached to the luxury had read, "Belgian Congo has not forgotten you. Distributed by the RAF. Long live Belgium!" And there was more than coffee to remind Belgians of their colony. Just days after the liberation, for example, the press announced that 9,000 tons of soap lay waiting to be shipped from the colony. Only the lack of shipping space prevented such scarce goods from arriving in Belgium without delay. "Why," one newspaper lamented at the end of the harsh winter in February 1945, "is it not made possible for our Colony to provide us with goods that have been piled up there for so long and that would much benefit the Belgian population: oils, coffee, rice, cotton, rubber, copper, and so on?"[109]

It seemed that if, next to democracy, Belgians wanted to be assured also of prosperity, the Congo would have a crucial role to play. That this meant

[108] The communist article appeared on October 2, 1945, and was attached to a report in SE Folder 1489, AA 1311, on the port of Ostend. For a tribute to the British empire, see De Roey and Van Hee, *Bevrijding*, 30. "Belgische vrouwen aan de eer," *Het Volk*, November 5, 1945, 2. *Vooruit*, October 12, 1945, 1 and December 27, 1945, 2.

[109] Roger Motz, "L'Avenir du Congo Belge," *Le Soir*, February 21, 1945, 1. For the coffee drops, see Vints, *Kongo*, 90; and Maleux, "Propagande," 75. *HBVL*, September 17, 1944, 1 and "Nieuws uit Congo," February 27, 1945, 1.

that the Congolese would have to abandon any aspirations they might be entertaining about democracy and human liberties few in Belgium seemed to find inconsistent with the lofty ideals for which the Allies had professed to fight the war. Belgian media chose to remain silent about the bloody repression of the repeated strikes that Congolese workers had engaged in from as early as 1943 to protest the pressures of the war effort. In an article on the UN written at the end of 1945, a high-ranking foreign affairs official was keen to assure his American audience that "Belgium frankly adhered to the intention of the Charter which proclaimed the great fundamental principle of the paramount interest of the natives of the colonial territories." But he also hastened to add that his government was "desirous of putting into effect as soon as possible the system of trusteeship." That, of course, would assure continued Belgian control of the former mandates Ruanda and Burundi. For Belgium's jewel in the crown, meanwhile, not much change seemed to be in the offing at all. To mark the anniversary of the Congo colony early in July 1945, various representatives of colonial organizations, joined by numerous schoolchildren, assembled in Brussels' famous Grand Place. They hoisted a Belgian flag as well as pennants reminding spectators of the various African campaigns. Then, to the tune of the national anthem, they marched across town, concluding the ceremony with a tribute to King Leopold II, the country's imperial lion. A week later, fourteen Belgians boarded an American Lockheed in the Congo's capital. They were the first colonials to arrive in Brussels by air and were greeted by the Minister of Colonies himself. The minister expressed the hope that this would be the first of many aircraft providing an intensive connection between "colonies and the motherland." The war's enormous advances in aircraft technology, *Het Volk* mused, might at last make possible what many Belgians had been wishing to see, namely for the Congo to become "a true tenth province."[110]

A modern liberation

Historians

To say that the trauma of war, the humiliation of occupation, and the exhilaration of liberation had a major impact on Belgian society is to state the obvious. Still, to ask the question if and to what extent the Second World War represented a turning point in the country's history is to invite

[110] For the strikes, see Vints, *Kongo*, 89–90; and Stéphany, *1945*, 269. Walter Loridan, "Belgium and the United Nations," in BT, 169. "Koloniale dag te Brussel," *Het Volk*, July 3, 1945, 2. For the air connection, see *Het Volk*, July 11, 1945, 2; July 12, 1945, 3; and "Kongo, een tiende provincie?" July 25, 1945, 1.

discussion and controversy. In terms of its political history, for example, a growing revisionist interpretation in the 1990s claimed that, rather than bringing firm restoration, the end of the war had landed Belgium somewhere between continuity and change. Yet, as late as 1996, Martin Conway was emphasizing that "the period of the Liberation served ultimately to reveal the resilience of the existing social and political order," while four years later Pieter Lagrou lent additional weight to the revisionist thesis by highlighting how occupation and liberation had "deepened notions of democracy and citizenship" in Belgium and across Western Europe. Matters tend to be even more complex, and at times more heated, when the watershed question is approached from the perspective of women's history. Discussing the international debate that raged over whether the war's gains had been merely temporary or truly transformative for women, Joan Scott in 1987 called the debate "ultimately unresolvable." It took a Belgian journal a decade later more than twenty pages to present a digest of the historiography on that same theme.[111]

Historians cannot provide a brief and simple judgment in the case of continuity/restoration versus change/renewal. This is so because of three fundamental issues that complicate the analysis of the effects of the Second World War. First, much of what changed as a result of the war was not entirely new, but rather an acceleration of trends already in existence before 1940. The process of cultural Americanization in Europe, for example, started in the interwar years and not during the liberation. This, in turn, was a contributing factor to the gradual emergence of the consumer society that Fabrice Maerten has pointed to as an explanation for major transformations among Belgian youth taking shape as early as the end of the First World War.

Second, historians have to avoid teleological positions for, as Jay Winter has noted in his seminal work on the collective remembrance of the Great War, "To array the past in such a way is to invite distortion by losing a sense of its messiness, its non-linearity, its vigorous and stubbornly visible incompatibilities." Many of the effects of the Second World War certainly were messy and non-linear too. What David Reynolds has observed with respect to Great Britain, for example, namely that Americanization might not have taken the shape of such a continuous process had it not been for the Cold War following so closely on the heels of the Second World War, applies to much of Western Europe. Indeed, Cold War pressures also combined with the trauma of the Second World War to create a conformist climate emphasizing the traditional family

[111] For the revisionist thesis, see van Doorslaer, "Oorlog," 23–6. Conway, "Liberation," 134–5; Lagrou, *Legacy*, 306; and Scott, "Rewriting History," 25. The historiographical article is Thébaud, "Deuxième guerre."

of marriage and manifold children as well as a retreat into the private sphere with its concurrent female domesticity. Many historians agree that the Cold War's male-instigated domestic containment does much to explain why, after the bright promise of the liberation and initial political progress, the road to women's rights suddenly became winding, hobbled, and at times cut off where it concerned further legal, economic, and social rights.[112]

Finally, that it took women until the 1960s to get back on track with their demands demonstrates not only the non-linearity of their emancipation after the Second World War. It also highlights the usefulness of the concept of "long liberation" that Karen Adler has developed in her history of France at the end of the Second World War. Adler points to the "protracted process of imagining, hoping for and planning liberation," which started during the war and lasted until long after France's physical liberation in 1944–5. Indeed, among "a variety of cut-off dates for this liberationism," May 1968 is one that she suggests. This is when, as Mark Mazower has observed, a younger and numerically stronger generation of males and females in a more urban and wealthy Europe "became conscious of the vast social changes which had taken place since the war, and demanded that politics and the law catch up." From the perspective of a less Eurocentric understanding, on the other hand, Adler also strongly suggests 1962, the year in which the Algerian war came to an end, as a symbolic hinge. If for Belgium 1968 is as valid a cut-off date for its long liberation as it is for France, then 1960 in its case has to be substituted for 1962. This is when Belgians woke up to realize not only that they had failed to make the Congo a tenth province, but that they had lost an empire. It was a crucial moment in the long and tortuous process of Belgium confronting its own racial problems and facing the undeniable truth that liberty and democracy were human and not just white rights, a process in which the Second World War had served as a powerful catalyst.[113]

Witnesses

Yet, if historians owe it to themselves and their profession to identify the complexities and nuances of the impact of the Second World War, Belgians who have looked back on their own war experience tend to classify it more firmly and simply as a watershed in their lives. This

[112] Winter, *Sites of Memory*, 4–5. Reynolds, *Rich Relations*, 436–7. For the Cold War's domestic containment see, for example, Mazower, *Dark Continent*, 228, 295, 318, and 322.

[113] Adler, *Liberation France*, 4–5; and Mazower, *Dark Continent*, 316–17 and 199–200.

Plate 7.5 Belgians act out the modern liberation. Oneux, 22 July 1945. (Collection Lemaire, CEGESOMA, Brussels, picture number 104379)

goes a long way towards explaining how they have been able to imbue even a third generation in the twenty-first century with an automatic understanding of what it means to say that something or another happened before or after "the war." A synthesis of a large number of oral testimonies on the liberation of Walloon Brabant, a Belgian province that hailed British as well as American troops in 1944, concludes that, although interviewees agreed there was little immediate improvement in terms of their material existence, they nevertheless "perceived that something fundamental had changed at that time." One can argue that in such an historical exercise forty years after the facts, witnesses may retroactively have assigned meaning to events that these did not possess at the time. Even then, however, the historian is forced to contemplate where the conviction has come from that motivates them to do so and obliged to acknowledge that it is significant that they themselves present this interpretation.[114]

It is altogether much harder, of course, to argue with evidence suggesting that people were well aware of fundamental changes taking

[114] Maerten, "Brabant Wallon," 160.

place even while the events were unfolding. Inhabitants of the village of Oneux near Comblain, in their peace parade on July 22, 1945, offered perhaps the most incisive synthesis of what the liberation meant to them. In one particular group, three villagers were dressed like GIs, who could easily be understood to stand for the new world order in which American power, hard and soft, had moved center stage. That they had chosen to be black soldiers to represent the US and that another actor had painted his face half-black and half-white sent out clear signals of changes in racial relations and the challenges this posed in terms of imperial future and national identity. That the other two actors in this group were young women was equally revealing. They simply played themselves. But by showing themselves provocatively intimate with the black Americans and defiantly in control of the steering wheel of the vehicle transporting the group, they demonstrated that it was not just white dominance, but male authority too that might never again be what it had been before. The vehicle itself was a horse-drawn, canvas replica of a jeep, symbol of the imaginative power of science and technology, but even more so of a cult of abundance promising to smother painful memories of an era of sacrifice. This truly was, bright letters summed up on the driver's side, a "modern liberation."[115]

115 Image No. 104379, CEGESOMA.

Bibliography

PRIMARY SOURCES

ARCHIVAL MATERIALS

Centre d'Études et de Documentation Guerre et Sociétés Contemporaines (CEGES) – Studie- en Documentatiecentrum Oorlog en Hedendaagse Maatschappij (SOMA) Brussels, Belgium

AA 77: Gemeentebestuur Vilvoorde

Folder: "Diverse documenten betreffende bezetting en bevrijding, 1940–1945."

AA 82: Radiodiffusion Nationale Belge Namur

Transcripts of broadcasts September 5, 1944–October 22, 1944

AA 525: Directives from Oberfeldkommandantur 520 (Mons)

AA 608/22: Archives Émile Clersy

Documents regarding the liberation and purging of Courcelles

Folder III: "Après-guerre."

AA 1230: Fortnightly reports and other documents from the SHAEF Mission to Belgium and Luxembourg, 1944–1945

WO 202/554: Minutes of meetings of the Four-Party Supply Committee (Belgium)

WO 202/681–701: Fortnightly reports, October 3, 1944–June 26, 1945

WO 219: Administrative memoranda

AA 1311: Archives Haut Commissariat à la Sécurité de l'État–Hoog Commissariaat voor 's Lands Veiligheid

Agriculture

499: Marché noir

503: Direction générale de la mobilisation des produits agricoles

Dossiers concernant les armées alliées

526: Relations entre population et troupes alliées: État d'esprit

527: Incidents entre militaires alliés et population belge

528: Infractions commises par armées alliées: Comportement

536: Infractions commises au préjudice des armées alliées

537: Claims and Hirings Commission: Secteur anglais/Secteur américain

572: Civil Affairs: Généralités

575: Civil Affairs: Controle circulation automobile

576: Civil Affairs: Repression infractions commises au préjudice des armées alliées
578: Civil Affairs: Divers
579: Civil Affairs: Infractions commises par militaires alliés ayant porté préjudice à la population civile (procès-verbaux)

Rapports des officiers généraux

889: Anvers; 890: Brabant; 891: Flandre Orientale; 892: Flandre Occidentale; 893: Hainaut; 894: Liège; 895: Limbourg; 896: Namur et Luxembourg

Situation des provinces

939: Anvers: Administration-Police
944: Anvers: Renseignements généraux
947: Brabant: Gendarmerie
951: Brabant: Renseignements généraux
958: Flandre Occidentale: Renseignements généraux
960: Flandre Orientale: Administration-Police
968: Hainaut: Gendarmerie
972: Hainaut: Renseignements généraux
973: Hainaut: Travail
979: Liège: Renseignements généraux
980: Liège: Travail
981: Limbourg: Administration-Police
986: Limbourg: Renseignements généraux
993: Luxembourg: Renseignements généraux
1000: Namur: Renseignements généraux

Situation des communes

1004: Anvers; 1005: Arlon; 1006: Athus; 1014: Blankenberge; 1017: Bruges; 1018: Bruxelles; 1020: Charleroi; 1025: Courtrai; 1027: Denderleeuw; 1035: Gand; 1044: Hasselt; 1047: Houthulst; 1048: Huy; 1054: La Louvière; 1057: Liège; 1062: Lot; 1063: Louvain; 1066: Malines; 1075: Namur; 1076: Neerpelt; 1078: Nieuwpoort; 1079: Nivelles; 1082: Ostende; 1084: Perwez; 1085: Philippeville; 1088: Renaix; 1090: Roelers; 1094: Saint Nicolas; 1095: Saint Trond; 1098: Soignies; 1099: Spa; 1100: Termonde; 1101: Theux; 1102: Tirlemont; 1103: Tongres; 1104: Tournai; 1106: Turnhout; 1107: Verviers; 1109: Visé; 1110: Vilvorde; 1111: Virton; 1118: Zaventhem; 1119: Zotteghem

Courrier auditorats militaires

1170: Flandre Orientale
1172: Liège
1176: Cour militaire

Maintien de l'ordre

1184: Comité ministériel restreint

Internements

1194: Situation d'internés – Évasion – Enlèvement par autorités alliées

Justice

1331: Vols au préjudice des armées alliées: Anvers

1335: Vols au préjudice des armées alliées: Limbourg
1336: Vols et recels de combustibles

Mission militaire belge
1371: Officiers et gradés en service auprès des armées alliées
1392: Divers

Manifestations-réunions-tracts-affiches
1458: Union des Femmes
1470: Universitaires de Gand

Sécurité-Coordination des Ports
1486: Réunion du 15 juin 1945
1487: Port de Gand
1489: Port d'Ostende

Ports
1491: Main d'œuvre dans les ports
1493: Divers

Travail
1634: Brasseries
1635: Distilleries

AA 1341: Circulars and memoranda from the Office of Mutual Aid to the municipalities regarding requisitioning and employment by the Allied armies, 1944–1948
Folder: "Verschillende onderrichtingen van het OAM aan de burgemeesters betreffende de tewerkstelling van Belgen door de geallieerde legers, 1944–1948."
AA 1450: Collection "Jours de guerre" RTBF Charleroi
Interviews No. 118: Felix Facq; No. 414: Marie-Claire Dandois; No. 427: Roger Laroche; No. 517: Angèle Eeckhaut; and No. 526: Ms. Fumal and Ms Nelissen
AA 1593: Collection "Jours de guerre" RTBF Mons-Radio
Interviews M348-9: Georges Brausch; M357: Jacques Gondry; M359: André Grégoire; and MS421: Jacques Wynants
AA 1798/9: Research collection José Gotovitch
Fortnightly reports from the SHAEF Mission to Belgium and Luxembourg, 1944–1945: "Final Report No. 21. For period September, 1944 – July, 1945."
AA 1882: Archives Auditorat-Général – Auditoraat-Generaal
C4-1: Faits commis par un militaire allié au préjudice d'un membre de la population
C4-2: Accidents de la circulation dans lesquels sont impliqués des militaires des armées alliées
C4-4: Circulaire No. 1075 du 8 janvier 1945
C5: Infractions commises au préjudice des armées alliées:
C5-0: Divers
C5-2-3-1: Contrôle des permis de circulation

C5-2-5: Vols et recels d'essence: Correspondance avec le Major Général Erskine
C5-3: Rapports vols ou recels d'essence
C5-4: Condamnations prononcées par les Conseils de Guerre
C5-10: Avis à la population avertissant des peines en cas de vols
C5-15-0: Recours en grâce
C5-15-1: Recours en grâce
C5-15-2: Correspondance avec le Ministre de la Justice
C5-15-3: Recours en grâce
C5-16-1: Visites domiciliaires
C5-16-3: Perquisitions faites par la police militaire américaine
C5-16-5-1: Correspondance avec les autorités militaires alliées
C5-16-5-2: Visites domiciliaires opérées par la police militaire alliée
C5-17-3: Réponses des Auditeurs Militaires à la dépêche secrète du 16/2/1945
C5-17-5: Incidents survenus au port d'Anvers
C5-17-6: Incidents survenus à Quaregnon
C5-21: Vols commis au préjudice des dépôts de munitions de l'armée britannique
C5-23: Circulaire No. 1306 du 7.6.1945: Infractions contre les armées alliées
Z34-10-6-0-3: Activité de la justice militaire

AB 81
Gemeentebestuur Mechelen. "De oorlog 1940–1944 in de stad Mechelen: verslag, mei 1940 – februari 1945."

AB 89
Dejardin, Georges. "Journal personnel, 1938–1945."

AB 122
Schilders, Angèle. "Het wegtrekken van de Duitsers uit Duffel: mémoires, 1944."

AB 680
Brock, R. "Bevrijdingsdag van Antwerpen: Dagboek, 4/9/1944."

AB 711
De Zusters van Vorselaar. "Dagboek, 10/5/1940–1/10/1944."

AB 712
Banneux, Paule. "Souvenirs sur 1940 et la libération."

AB 1298
Boulet, René. "Journal, 14/5/1940–11/5/1945."

AB 1380
Gossiaux, V. "Deuxième guerre mondiale, 1939–1945."

AB 1381
Challe, Jean-Pierre. "Florennes: Chronique d'une ville durant la Seconde Guerre Mondiale."

AB 1591: Eyewitness reports on the final year of the war collected by *Gazet van Antwerpen* in 1995:
D. Aerts, Juul Blondé, Alfons Claes, Jim Daponte, Lydie Degueldre, Paul De Strooper, Germaine Dierckx, Jeannine Haesen, Guido Kips, Lily Klockaerts, G. Lhermitte, M. Matheussen, Maria Selderslaghs, Leo Serroyen, Jérôme Storme, Emiel Thiron, G. Van Aerschot, Irène Van Cleemput, F. Van de

Vloed, Gabij Van de Wiele, Hildegonde Van Gils, Theo Van Oosterwyck, Wilfried Verleyen, J. Vinck, Lucienne Vleugels, and Liliane Wolters

AB 1734

De Tollenaere, Alberic. "Oorlogsdagboek van een 13-jarige: Wereldoorlog II."

AB 2166

Greeve, Theo. "Oorlogsdagboek, 1940–1945."

AB 2240

Debroux, Désiré. "Histoire d'un gamin (1939–1945): Ottignies-Limelette."

Published materials

Commissie voor Oorlogsmisdaden. *De oorlogsmisdaden bedreven gedurende de bevrijding van het Belgisch grondgebied: Het gebied van Oost- en West-Vlaanderen*. Liège: Georges Thone, 1947.

Commissie voor Oorlogsmisdaden. *De oorlogsmisdaden gepleegd tijdens de bevrijding van 's lands grondgebied, september 1944: Gewest Hoei-Namen*. Liège: Georges Thone, 1949.

De Corte, Marcel. *Du fond de l'abîme: Essai sur la situation morale de notre pays au lendemain de la libération*. Bruges: Desclée-De Brouwer, 1945.

Gheude, Charles. *La Libération (de juillet 1943 au 8 mai 1945)*. Brussels: Emile Bruylant, 1949.

Institut d'Éducation et de Documentation Nationales. *Chronique de la vie nationale, 1944–1945*. Antwerp: Egmont, 1946.

Libération: Ayant comme but de rendre un vibrant hommage aux libérateurs de notre chère Patrie. Brussels: Revue Militaire Belge, s.d.

Ministerie Van Financiën. *Rondschrijven betreffende de door de gemeentebesturen te treffen voorloopige maatregelen om aan de opeischingen der geallieerde legers te voldoen*. Charleroi, 1944.

La Réparation par l'Office d'Aide Mutuelle – Service de Conciliation des dommages causés en Belgique par les armées alliées. Les accords et la législation "claims." Rapport sur les activités à la date du 31 décembre 1954. S.l., 1955.

Simpson, Smith, ed. "Belgium in Transition." *The Annals of the American Academy of Political and Social Science*, 247, special issue (September 1946).

SECONDARY SOURCES

Local histories

Absil, Christian. *Gilly et la libération*. Gilly: privately published, 1975.

Aerts, Kristof *et al. Leuven: De bevrijding, 1944–1945*. Stad Leuven, 1994.

Ameeuw, Jozef *et al. Koksijde, Sint-Idesbald, Oostduinkerke, Wulpen: Herinneringen aan 60 jaar bevrijding wereldoorlog '40–'44*. Koksijde: Gemeentelijke Archiefcommissie, 2004.

Auquier, André. *Souvenirs de guerre et libération de Quaregnon et d'ailleurs*. Wasmes: privately published, 1994.

Bijdragen tot de geschiedenis en de folklore van Zulte. Zulte: Geschied- en Heemkundige Kring, 1995.

Boffin, Wim. *Wij waren jong maar...: Getuigenissen over de Tweede Wereldoorlog in Zuid-West Limburg*. Volume II. Sint-Truiden: privately published, 2000.

Bosse, Jean and Charles Van Gucht. *Braine-l'Alleud: La Libération, Septembre 1944*. Association du Musée de Braine-l'Alleud, 1995.

Bours, Gerard. *Limburg, mei 1940 – september 1944*. Genk: privately published, 2002.

Buchet, Eugène. "La Libération en province de Liège." In *La Mémoire*. Edited by Francis Balace *et al.* Liège: Province de Liège/Service des Affaires Culturelles, 1994.

Caudron, André. *La Libération: Nord Pas-de-Calais. Belgique*. Strasbourg: La Nuée Bleue and Roubaix: Nord Éclair, 1994.

Celis, Jozef *et al. Zepperen in twee grote oorlogen*. Zepperen: Remacluskring, 1994.

Chapelle, J. "La Libération de Marchin." Marchin: Le FNC de Marchin, 1994.

Coenegrachts, Colette. *Hasselt: Oorlog en bevrijding*. Cultuur en Toerisme Hasselt, 1994.

Dechaineux, Maurice. "La Libération de Herve." In *1940–1945 au Pays de Herve*. Société d'Archéologie et d'Histoire du Plateau de Herve, 1995.

Decuypere, Dirk. "La Libération de la région de Comines-Warneton." *Mémoires de la Société d'Histoire de Comines-Warneton et de la région*, XVI (1986): 531–6.

De Roey, Johan and Maryse Van Hee. *Hun kleine bevrijding*. Brussels: Elsevier, 1984.

De Sany-Norro, Gisèle. *Forest-Vorst, 1944–1994*. Forest: Administration Communale, 1994.

Deseyne, André. *Zonnebeke bezet en bevrijd*. Zonnebeke: De Zonnebeekse Heemvrienden, 1996.

Devolder, Eddy, ed. *Libération de la ville de Tournai*. Académie des Beaux-Arts de la Ville de Tournai, 1994.

Deweer, J.-P. *Marlborough kwam terug: De bevrijding van Oudenaarde in september 1944*. Oudenaarde: Vereniging voor Vreemdelingenverkeer en Monumentenzorg, 1987.

De Zaeger, Piet. *Lier, bezet en bevrijd*. Leuven and Amersfoort: Acco, 1995.

D'hont, André. *Knokke onder de oorlog, 1939–1945*. Knokke: Heemkring "Cnoc is ier," 1987.

Gorsele, Luc, ed. *Antwerpen 50 jaar bevrijd*. Stadhuis Antwerpen, 1994.

"Des habitants racontent la Libération et les 'robots.' " *Seraing, Ougrée, Jemappe au passé*, no. 3, special issue (1994).

Hasquin, René-Pierre. *Les Villes libérées: Charleroi*. Montigny-le-Tilleul: Éditions Scaillet, 1984.

Henry, René. *Dis, raconte-moi: La Guerre et la libération d'Aywaille*. Liège-Bressoux: Éditions Dricot, 1993.

Herstal 1944. Herstal: Musée Communal, 1994.

Janssen, Pierre *et al.* "De bevrijding van het Limburgse Maasland." Geschied- en Heemkundige Kring Eisden 21, no. 3, special issue (2004).

Janssens, Antoine and Frans Van Maldeghem. *Nevele, 1944–1994*. Nevele: Gemeentebestuur, 1994.

Jour, Jean. *Les Villes libérées: Liège*. Montigny-le-Tilleul: Éditions Scaillet, 1984.
La Libération de Liège. Brussels: Éditions Libro-Sciences, 1990.
Kohlbacher, Jan. "Kroniek van 'n oorlog, 1945: Het unieke Amerikaanse Rest- en Recreation Center in het verkeerde Eisden." *Geschied- en Heemkundige Kring Eisden* 18, no. 1 (2001): 29–38.
Laakdalse Werkgroep voor Geschiedenis en Heemkunde. *50 jaar bevrijding*. Laakdal: Gemeentebestuur, 1994.
Laby, Hubert. *Waremme, août–septembre 1944*. Faimes: privately published, 1993.
Lambiet, Thomas. "La Libération d'Aubel." In *1940–1945 au Pays de Herve*. Société d'Archéologie et d'Histoire du Plateau de Herve, 1995.
Lejeune, B. "C'était il y a cinquante ans: La Libération de Nalinnes." *Le Marloyat* no. 109 (September 1994): 1–14.
La Libération à Marchin. Le FNC de Marchin, 1994.
Lognard-Poncin, Bernadette and Fernand Michel. *Chaudfontaine. Il y a 50 ans*. Chaudfontaine: privately published, 1994.
Marchal, Jean-Paul. *Gent september '44*. Ghent: Julien Verbeke, 1992.
Meunier, Pierre. *La Libération des communes de Dison et d'Andrimont*. Dison: privately published, 1994.
Neufort, André. *Il y a trente ans: La Libération de Charleroi*. Manage: Éditions Dufour, 1974.
Neys, R. *et al. 50 jaar bevrijding Kalmthout*. Kalmthout, 1995.
Offergeld, Jacques. *Les Villes libérées: Bruxelles*. Montigny-le-Tilleul: Éditions Scaillet, 1984.
Les Villes libérées: Namur, Luxembourg et régions. Montigny-le-Tilleul: Éditions Scaillet, 1984.
Oorlog en bevrijding te Kontich-Waarloos. Kontich: Gemeentebestuur, 1994.
Patteet, René. *Heist en zijn dorpen tijdens de Tweede Wereldoorlog*. Heist-op-den-Berg: Koninklijke Heemkring Die Swane, 2001.
Pepinster et la libération, 40–45. Pepinster: Éditions C. C. J., 1984.
Pied, Robert. *Wavre, septembre 1944*. Syndicat d'initiative de la Ville de Wavre, 1994.
Quaghebeur, Roger and Roger V. Verbeke. *Ze zijn daar! De bevrijding van Ieper en het Westland in september 44*. Veurne: De Klaproos, 1994.
Ravyts, Kurt and Peter Struyve. *Het Tieltse, 1940–1945*. Tielt: Heemkundige Kring De Roede, 1995.
Rijmen, Carl. *De Bevrijding van Ham*. Heemkunde Ham, 1995.
Roba, J.L. and J. Leotard. 1944–1945. Volume III of *La Région de Walcourt-Beaumont pendant la Seconde Guerre Mondiale*. Cercle d'Histoire de l'Entité de Walcourt, 1994.
Roden, Dimitri. *Tessenderlo, bezet en bevrijd*. Tessenderlo: Boerenbelang, 2006.
Roeselare Bevrijd. Roeselare: Stadsbestuur, 1994.
Rogister, Henri. *Chênée survit: Chênée espère, Chênée se libère*. Chênée: privately published, 1994.
Rutten, Mathieu. *De bevrijding van Tongeren, 8 september 1944*. Tongeren, s.d.
Ruwet, Armand. *Vues d'une occupation et d'une libération: Verviers, 1940–1945*. Andrimont-Dison: Éditions Irezumi, 1994.
Sabus, Pierre. *1944: Enfin la libération*. Virton: C. Baudoin, 1994.

Triffaux, Gaston and Jean-Marie. *La Libération d'Arlon*. Arlon: privately published, 1984.

Vanbossele, José. *De bevrijding van het Kortrijkse*. Volume IV of Kortrijk tijdens de Tweede Wereldoorlog. Kortrijk: Groeninghe, 1994.

Van Bouchaute, Piet and Patty De Meester. *Bezet en bevrijd: Sint-Niklaas tijdens de Tweede Wereldoorlog*. Sint-Niklaas: Stadsbestuur, 2004.

Van Braeckel, Bert. *De bevrijding van de Barrier*. S.l., 1994.

Van Cauwenbergh, George. *Ze zijn d'er! September 1944, bevrijding van Antwerpen*. Brugge: Marc Van de Wiele, 1984.

Vandenbroucke, Jacques. *Andenne, Landenne, Maizeret, Namêche, Samson, Sclayn, Seilles, Thon, Vezin, 1940–1945*. Andenne: privately published, 1995.

Van Der Straeten, Erna. *Stad Oudenaarde: De Tweede Wereldoorlog volgens de notulenboeken*. Oudenaarde: Stadsbestuur, 1994.

Van de Velde, Marc. *De bruggen van Boom: Kroniek van de oorlogsjaren 1939–1945*. Boom: Studiecentrum voor Oorlogsgeschiedenis, 1994.

Van Gorp, Hendrik. *Doei en despotie: Arendonk in oorlog en bevrijding*. Edegem: privately published, 1991.

Vanstreels, Frank. *De bevrijding van Hasselt*. Erpe: De Krijger, 2002.

Vermaesen, Maurice. *Londerzeel tijdens Wereldoorlog II*. S.l., 1995.

Vierstraete, Albert *et al.* "La Libération de la région de Comines-Warneton." *Mémoires de la Société d'Histoire de Comines Warneton* XVI (1986): 491–530.

Vierstraete, P. *et al. Les Fourons libérés*. Centre Sportif et Culturel des Fourons, 1994.

Warnier, Bob. *Brugge bevrijd*. Brugge: Uitgaven West-Vlaamse Gidsenkring, 1995.

ed. *Brugge en september '44*. 2 vols. Brugge: Uitgaven West-Vlaamse Gidsenkring, 2002.

Waterval, Maryse and Jean-Pierre Lensen, eds. *1940–1945: La Basse-Meuse dans la guerre*. Société Archéo-Historique de Visé, 1990.

Wollants, Arthur and Jos Bouveroux, *Russische partizanen: WOII-Limburg*. Leuven: Davidsfonds, 1994.

Wynants, Jacques. *Verviers libéré de l'allégresse à l'inquiétude*. Verviers: Librairie Dérive, 1984.

GENERAL LITERATURE

Adler, Karen. "No Words to Say It? Women and the Expectation of Liberation." In *The Liberation of France: Image and Event*. Edited by H. R. Kedward and Nancy Wood. Oxford and Washington, DC: Berg Publishers, 1995.

Jews and Gender in Liberation France. Cambridge: Cambridge University Press, 2003.

Balace, Francis. "Charleroi-Namur, la bataille des ponts." In *Jours libérés II*. Edited by Francis Balace. Volume XX of *Jours de guerre*. Brussels: Crédit Communal, 1995.

"Les hoquets de la liberté." In *Jours libérés II*. Edited by Francis Balace. Volume XIX of *Jours de guerre*. Brussels: Crédit Communal, 1995.

"La Nuit la plus courte ... La libération de Bruxelles." In *Jours libérés I*. Edited by Francis Balace. Volume XIX of *Jours de guerre*. Brussels: Crédit Communal, 1995.

Beck, Earl R. "The Anti-Nazi 'Swing Youth,' 1942–1945." *Journal of Popular Culture* 19, no. 3 (1985): 45–53.

Beevor, Antony and Artemis Cooper. *Paris: After the Liberation, 1944–1949*. London: Penguin Books, 2004.

Berghahn, Volker R. *Europe in the Era of Two World Wars: From Militarism and Genocide to Civil Society, 1900–1950*. Princeton: Princeton University Press, 2006.

Beyen, Marnix. "Nostalgie naar een nieuwe tijd: De Tweede Wereldoorlog en de roep van de traditie. België en Nederland, 1940–1945." *Revue Belge de Philologie et d'Histoire* 79, no. 2 (2001): 465–506.

Oorlog en verleden: Nationale geschiedenis in België en Nederland, 1938–1947. Amsterdam University Press, 2002.

Braybon, Gail and Penny Summerfield. *Out of the Cage: Women's Experiences in Two World Wars*. London and New York: Pandora, 1987.

Brossat, Alain. *Libération, fête folle, 6 juin 44–8 mai 45: Mythes et rites ou le grand théâtre des passions populaires*. Paris: Autrement, 1994.

Campbell, D'Ann. "Servicewomen of World War II." *Armed Forces and Society* 16, no. 2 (1990): 251–70.

Coates, Ken and W. R. Morrison. "The American Rampant: Reflections on the Impact of United States Troops in Allied Countries during World War II." *Journal of World History* 2, no. 2 (1991): 201–21.

Coles, Harry L. and Albert K. Weinberg. *Civil Affairs: Soldiers Become Governors*. Washington, DC: Office of the Chief of Military History, 1964.

Colignon, Alain. "La Résistance en Belgique francophone: Une anglophilie par défaut." In *La Résistance et les Européens du Nord*. Volume I. Brussels: CREHSGM, 1994.

"Leurs adieux de Fontainebleau." In *Jours libérés I*. Edited by Francis Balace. Volume XIX of *Jours de guerre*. Brussels: Crédit Communal, 1995.

"Une libération diférée: 'Nos prisonniers,' un enjeu politique." In *Jours libérés II*. Edited by Francis Balace. Volume XIX of *Jours de guerre*. Brussels: Crédit Communal, 1995.

Colignon, Alain and José Gotovitch. "Du sang, de la sueur, de l'encre." In *Jours de Paix*. Edited by Renaud Gahide. Volumes XXII–XXIV of *Jours de guerre*. Brussels: Dexia, 2001.

Conway, Martin. "The Liberation of Belgium, 1944–1945." In *The End of the War in Europe, 1945*. Edited by Gill Bennett. London: HMSO, 1996.

"Justice in Post-War Belgium." *Cahiers d'Histoire du Temps Présent* No. 2 (1997): 7–34.

Crombois, Jean-François, "Les Milieux d'affaires et le gouvernment belge de Londres." In *Jours de Londres*. Edited by Francis Balace. Volumes XVI–XVIII of *Jours de guerre*. Brussels: Dexia, 2000.

De Grazia, Victoria. *Irresistible Empire: America's Advance through Twentieth-Century Europe*. Cambridge, MA and London: The Belknap Press of Harvard University Press, 2005.

Delarue, Thomas. "Aspects de la vie quotidienne sous l'occupation." In *La Mémoire*. Edited by Francis Balace *et al.* Liège: Province de Liège/Service des Affaires Culturelles, 1994.

Delbrück, Jost. "International Law and Military Forces Abroad: US Military Presence in Europe, 1945–1965." In *US Military Forces in Europe*. Edited by Simon W. Duke and Wolfgang Krieger. Boulder, CO and Oxford: Westview Press, 1993.

Deloge, Pascal. "Belgique et Grande-Bretagne en quête de sécurité." In *Jours libérés II*. Edited by Francis Balace. Volume XX of *Jours de guerre*. Brussels: Crédit Communal, 1995.

Deneckere, Gita. "Jeugd, beweging en regeneratie: Een inleiding." *Cahiers d'Histoire du Temps Présent* No. 8 (2001): 7–17.

De Pinchart, Henry. *Historique de l'Office d'Aide Mutuelle (O.M.A.) en Belgique 1944–1955*. Brussels, 1973.

De Vos, Luc. "US Forces in Belgium since 1944." In *US Military Forces in Europe*. Edited by Simon W. Duke and Wolfgang Krieger. Boulder, CO and Oxford: Westview Press, 1993.

De bevrijding: Van Normandië tot de Ardennen. Leuven: Davidsfonds, 1994.

Diamond, Hanna. "Women's Aspirations, 1943–47: An Oral Enquiry in Toulouse." In *The Liberation of France: Image and Event*. Edited by H.R. Kedward and Nancy Wood. Oxford and Washington, DC: Berg Publishers, 1995.

Domenico, Roy Palmer. "'For the Cause of Christ Here in Italy': America's Protestant Challenge in Italy and the Cultural Ambiguity of the Cold War." *Diplomatic History* 29, no. 4 (2005): 625–54.

Donnison, F.S.V. *Civil Affairs and Military Government: North-West Europe, 1944–1946*. London: HMSO, 1961.

Duignan, Peter and L.H. Gann. *The Rebirth of the West: The Americanization of the Democratic World, 1945–1958*. London and Lanham, MD: Rowman and Littlefield, 1996.

Duportail, Patrick. "De oorlog tussen heden en verleden: Beeldvorming over de Tweede Wereldoorlog in de Oost-Vlaamse plattelandsgemeente Bottelare." *Cahiers d'Histoire du Temps Présent* No. 2 (1997): 129–54.

Fehrenbach, Heide and Uta G. Poiger. "Americanization Reconsidered." In *Transactions, Transgressions, Transformations: American Culture in Western Europe and Japan*. Edited by Heide Fehrenbach and Uta G. Poiger. New York: Berghahn Books, 2000.

Gaier, Claude. "Réflexions sur les changements de l'après-guerre." In *La Mémoire*. Edited by Francis Balace *et al.* Liège: Province de Liège/Service des Affaires Culturelles, 1994.

Gerard, Emmanuel. "Les Partis et les organisations de pilier: du neuf et de l'ancien." In *Jours libérés II*. Edited by Francis Balace. Volume XX of *Jours de guerre*. Brussels: Crédit Communal, 1995.

Gérard, Jo. *La Libération, 1944–1945*. Brussels: Meddens, 1984.

Gotovitch, José. "Communistes et résistants: Les (en)jeux de dupes d'une libération." In *Jours libérés II*. Edited by Francis Balace. Volume XX of Jours de guerre. Brussels: Crédit Communal, 1995.

Gourvish, T. R. and N. Tiratsoo, eds. *Missionaries and Managers: American Influences on European Management Education, 1945–60*. Manchester University Press, 1998.

Grosbois, Thierry. "Les Relations diplomatiques entre le gouvernement belge de Londres et les États-Unis (1940–1944)." *Guerres mondiales et conflits contemporains* 51, no. 202–203 (2001): 167–87.

Hardenne, Christel. "Entre les Belges et leurs libérateurs: Des relations tendues." In *Jours libérés II*. Edited by Francis Balace. Volume XX of *Jours de guerre*. Brussels: Crédit Communal, 1995.

Henau, Brigitte. "Shaping a New Belgium: The CEPAG – The Belgian Commission for the Study of Post-War Problems, 1941–44." In *Making the New Europe: European Unity and the Second World War*. Edited by M. L. Smith and Peter M. R. Stirk. London and New York: Pinter, 1990.

Higonnet, Margaret R. and Patrice L.-R. Higonnet. "The Double Helix." In *Behind the Lines: Gender and the Two World Wars*. Edited by Margaret R. Higonnet *et al*. New Haven and London: Yale University Press, 1987.

Hoganson, Kristin. "Stuff It: Consumption and the Americanization of the World Paradigm." *Diplomatic History* 30, no. 4 (2006): 571–94.

Horn, Michiel. "More than Cigarettes, Sex, and Chocolate: The Canadian Army in the Netherlands, 1944–1945." *Journal of Canadian Studies/Revue d'Études Canadiennes* 16, nos. 3–4 (1981): 156–73.

Hubert, Cécile. "La Campagne de productivité en Belgique: Modernisation autour du modèle américain." In *Milieux économiques et intégration européenne en Europe Occidentale au XXe siècle*. Edited by Eric Bussière and Michel Dumoulin. Arras: Artois Presses Université, 1998.

Huet, Henri. "La 'Poche de Mons.' " In *Jours libérés I*. Edited by Francis Balace. Volume XIX of *Jours de guerre*. Brussels: Crédit Communal, 1995.

Huyse Luc and Kris Hoflack, eds. *De democratie heruitgevonden: Oud en nieuw in politiek België, 1944–1950*. Leuven: Van Halewyck, 1995.

Jacquemyns, Guillaume. "La Société belge sous l'Occupation allemande (1940–1944)". In *La Belgique sous l'Occupation allemande (1940–1944)*. Edited by José Gotovitch. Brussels: Éditions Complexe, 2002.

Kaspi, André. *Le Temps des Américains: Le Concours américain à la France en 1917–1918*. Paris: Publications de la Sorbonne, 1976.

La Libération de la France, juin 1944–janvier 1946. Paris: Perrin, 1995.

Kelly, Michael. "The Reconstruction of Masculinity at the Liberation." In *The Liberation of France: Image and Event*. Edited by H. R. Kedward and Nancy Wood. Oxford and Washington, DC: Berg Publishers, 1995.

Kramer, Steven Philip. "La Crise économique de la libération." *Revue d'Histoire de la Deuxième Guerre Mondiale* 28, no. 111 (1978): 25–44.

Kroes, Rob. "European Anti-Americanism: What's New?" *Journal of American History* 93, no. 2 (2006): 417–31.

Lagrou, Pieter. "La Résistance et la politique d'après-guerre." In *Jours libérés II*. Edited by Francis Balace. Volume XX of *Jours de guerre*. Brussels: Crédit Communal, 1995.

"US Politics of Stabilization in Liberated Europe: The View from the American Embassy in Brussels, 1944–6." *European History Quarterly* 25, no. 2 (1995): 209–46.
"Een oorlog achter de rug, een oorlog voor de boeg, 1944–1965." In *Oost West West Best: België onder de Koude Oorlog, 1947–1989*. Edited by Mark Van Den Wijngaert and Lieve Beullens. Tielt: Lannoo, 1997.
The Legacy of Nazi Occupation: Patriotic Memory and National Recovery in Western Europe, 1945–1965. Cambridge: Cambridge University Press, 2000.
Lake, Marilyn. "Female Desires: The Meaning of World War II." *Australian Historical Studies* 24, no. 95 (1990): 267–84.
Laurens, Corran. "'La Femme au Turban': Les Femmes tondues." In *The Liberation of France: Image and Event*. Edited by H. R. Kedward and Nancy Wood. Oxford and Washington, DC: Berg Publishers, 1995.
Laureys, Eric. "Le Personnel du HCSE: Un profil socioprofessionnel." In *Jours de Londres*. Edited by Francis Balace. Volumes XVI–XVIII of *Jours de guerre*. Brussels: Dexia, 2000.
Lecerf, Maurice, ed. *La Libération*. Seraing: Département Production de Supports Pédagogiques, 1994.
Lilly, J. Robert. *Taken by Force: Rape and American GIs in Europe during World War II*. New York and Basingstoke: PalgraveMacmillan, 2007.
Lilly, J. Robert and François Le Roy. "L'armée américaine et les viols en France, juin 1944–mai 1945." *Vingtième Siècle* No. 75 (2002): 109–21.
Lundestad, Geir. *The United States and Western Europe since 1945: From 'Empire' by Invitation to Transatlantic Drift*. Oxford: Oxford University Press, 2003.
Maerten, Fabrice. "Aspects de la libération dans le Brabant Wallon (septembre 1944–début février 1945." *Cahiers-Bijdragen* 11 (1988): 121–60.
"La Résistance, facteur d'émancipation des femmes? Le cas du Hainaut." *Cahiers d'Histoire du Temps Présent* No. 4 (1998): 173–206.
"Jeunesse et résistance. Entre mythe et réalité: Le Cas du Hainaut, 1940–1944." *Cahiers d'Histoire du Temps Présent* no. 8 (2001): 257–305.
Marquet, Victor. "La Sauvegarde du port d'Anvers." *Cahiers-Bijdragen* 13 (1990): 149–217.
Marquet, Victor. "La Tuerie de Forêt-Trooz." In *Jours libérés I*. Edited by Francis Balace. Volume XIX of *Jours de guerre*. Brussels: Crédit Communal, 1995.
Marwick, Arthur. *War and Social Change in the Twentieth Century*. London and Basingstoke: Macmillan, 1978.
Mazower, Mark. *Dark Continent: Europe's Twentieth Century*. London: Penguin Books, 1999.
Neckers, Jan. *De Bevrijding*. Antwerp and Amsterdam: De Nederlandsche Boekhandel, 1984.
Nehring, Holger. " 'Westernization': A New Paradigm for Interpreting West European History in a Cold War Context." *Cold War History* 4, no. 2 (2004): 175–91.
Newman, Victoria Beck. "'The Triumph of Pan': Picasso and the Liberation." *Zeitschrift für Kunstgeschichte* 62, no. 1 (1999): 106–22.

Pauwels, Jacques R. *De Canadezen en de bevrijding van België*. Berchem: EPO, 2004.

Plumet, Philippe. *La Presse quotidienne belge de la libération (4 septembre 1944–31 décembre 1945)*. Leuven and Brussels: Éditions Nauwelaerts, 1985.

Poiger, Uta G. *Jazz, Rock, and Rebels: Cold War Politics and American Culture in a Divided Germany*. Berkeley and Los Angeles: University of California Press, 2000.

Reynolds, David. *Rich Relations: The American Occupation of Britain, 1942–1945*. New York: Random House, 1995.

"Churchill and Allied Grand Strategy in Europe, 1944–1945: The Erosion of British Influence." In *World War II in Europe: The Final Year*. Edited by Charles F. Brower. New York: St. Martin's Press, 1998.

Rosenberg, Emily S. *Spreading the American Dream: American Economic and Cultural Expansion, 1890–1945*. New York: Hill and Wang, 1982.

Saler, Michael, "Modernity and Enchantment: A Historiographic Review." *American Historical Review* 111 (June 2006): 692–716.

Schrijvers, Peter. *The Crash of Ruin: American Combat Soldiers in Europe during World War II*. New York: New York University Press, 1998.

The GI War against Japan: American Soldiers in Asia and the Pacific during World War II. New York: New York University Press, 2002.

The Unknown Dead: Civilians in the Battle of the Bulge. Lexington: University Press of Kentucky, 2005.

Schulten, C. M. "Commentary on the Liberation of the Netherlands." In *World War II in Europe: The Final Year*. Edited by Charles F. Brower. New York: St. Martin's Press, 1998.

Scott, Joan W. "Rewriting History." In *Behind the Lines: Gender and the Two World Wars*. Edited by Margaret R. Higonnet *et al.* New Haven and London: Yale University Press, 1987.

Shukert, Elfrieda B. and Barbara S. Scibetta. *War Brides of World War II*. Novato, CA: Presidio Press, 1988.

Sottiau, Françoise. "La Libération des prisonniers de guerre et le retour au pays." In *Jours Libérés II*. Edited by Francis Balace. Volume XX of *Jours de guerre*. Brussels: Crédit Communal, 1995.

Stacey, C. P. and Barbara M. Wilson. *The Half-Million: The Canadians in Britain, 1939–1946*. Toronto: University of Toronto Press, 1987.

Stengers, Jean. "L'Attitude des Belges à l'égard de la Grande-Bretagne avant la guerre." In *Jours de Londres*. Edited by Francis Balace. Volume XVI–XVIII of *Jours de guerre*. Brussels: Dexia, 2000.

Stéphany, Pierre. "Comment la Belgique entra dans l'après-guerre." In *Jours libérés II*. Edited by Francis Balace. Volume XX of *Jours de guerre*. Brussels: Crédit Communal, 1995.

1945: L'Année de la fin du cauchemar et du commencement de l'après-guerre. Brussels: Le Livre, 1995.

Stirk, Peter M. R. "Anti-Americanism in National Socialist Propaganda during the Second World War." In *Making the New Europe: European Unity and the Second World War*. Edited by M. L. Smith and Peter M. R. Stirk. London and New York: Pinter, 1990.

Struye, Paul. "L'Évolution du sentiment public en Belgique sous l'Occupation allemande." In *La Belgique sous l'Occupation allemande (1940–1944)*. Edited by José Gotovitch. Brussels: Éditions Complexe, 2002.

Taghon, Peter. *België 44: De bevrijding*. Tielt: Lannoo, 1993.

Thébaud, Françoise. "Deuxième guerre, femmes et rapports de sexe: essai d'historiographie." *Cahiers d'Histoire du Temps Présent* No. 4 (1998): 227–48.

Torrent, Régine. "L'Image du soldat américain en France, de 1943 à 1945." In *Les Américains et la France (1917–1947): Engagements et représentations*. Edited by François Cochet et al. Paris: Maisonneuve et Larose, 1999.

La France américaine: Controverses de la Libération. Brussels: Éditions Racine, 2004.

Ugeux, William. "Aspects divers de la psychologie du résistant belge, 1940–1945." *Revue Internationale d'Histoire Militaire* 29 (1970): 963–74.

Vanden Berghe, Yvan. "België en het buitenland." In *De democratie heruitgevonden: Oud en nieuw in politiek België, 1944–1950*. Edited by Luc Huyse and Kris Hoflack. Leuven: Van Halewyck, 1995.

Van den Wijngaert, Mark *et al. België tijdens de Tweede Wereldoorlog*. Antwerp: Standaard Uitgeverij, 2004.

"De buitenlandse en militaire politiek van België in een gebipolariseerde wereld." In *Oost West West Best: België onder de Koude Oorlog, 1947–1989*. Edited by Mark Van den Wijngaert and Lieve Beullens. Tielt: Lannoo, 1997.

Van der Wee, Herman and Monique Verbreyt. *Oorlog en monetaire politiek: De Nationale Bank van Belgie, de Emissiebank te Brussel en de Belgische regering, 1939–1945*. Volume I of *De Nationale Bank van België*. Brussels: Nationale Bank van België, 2005.

Van de Velde, Marc. "La Surprenante Libération d'Anvers." In *Jours libérés I*. Edited by Francis Balace. Volume XIX of *Jours de guerre*. Brussels: Crédit Communal, 1995.

Van de Vijver, Herman. *Het cultureel leven tijdens de bezetting*. Volume VIII of *België in de Tweede Wereldoorlog*. Kapellen: DNB/Pelckmans, 1990.

Van Doorslaer, Rudi. "De oorlog tussen continuïteit en verandering: Vragen en problemen." In *De democratie heruitgevonden: Oud en nieuw in politiek België, 1944–1950*. Edited by Luc Huyse and Kris Hoflack. Leuven: Van Halewyck, 1995.

Van Goethem, Herman. "Le Prince Charles, régent de Belgique: La Question Royale, la démocratie, les alliés." In *Jours libérés II*. Edited by Francis Balace. Volume XX of *Jours de guerre*. Brussels: Crédit Communal, 1995.

Van Poucke, Guy. "Pour votre liberté et la nôtre." In *Jours libérés II*. Edited by Francis Balace. Volume XX of *Jours de guerre*. Brussels: Crédit Communal, 1995.

Vanwelkenhuyzen, Jean. "La Libération de la Belgique: Quelques aspects des opérations militaires." *Revue Belge d'Histoire Militaire* (December 1984): 725–58.

Veraghtert, Karel. "De naoorlogse economie en het Marshallplan, 1944–1960." In *Oost West West Best: België onder de Koude Oorlog, 1947–1989*. Edited by Mark Van den Wijngaert and Lieve Beullens. Tielt: Lannoo, 1997.

Verbeeck, Georgi. "In de spiegel van de internationale politiek: Belgie en het 'Duitse vraagstuk.'" In *Oost West West Best: België onder de Koude Oorlog, 1947–1989*. Edited by Mark Van den Wijngaert and Lieve Beullens. Tielt: Lannoo, 1997.

Vints, Luc. *Kongo made in Belgium: Beeld van een kolonie in film en propaganda*. Leuven: Kritak, 1984.

Virgili, Fabrice. *La France "virile": Des femmes tondues à la Libération*. Paris: Payot, 2000.

Wagnleitner, Reinhold. *Coca-Colonization and the Cold War: The Cultural Mission of the United States in Austria after the Second World War*. Chapel Hill and London: University of North Carolina Press, 1994.

Willett, Ralph. *The Americanization of Germany, 1945–1949*. London: Routledge, 1989.

Willoughby, John. "The Sexual Behavior of American GIs during the Early Years of the Occupation of Germany." *Journal of Military History* 62, no. 1 (1998): 155–74.

Remaking the Conquering Heroes: The Social and Geopolitical Impact of the Postwar American Occupation of Germany. New York and Basingstoke: Palgrave, 2001.

Wils, Lode. "De naoorlog in historisch perspectief." In *De democratie heruitgevonden: Oud en nieuw in politiek België, 1944–1950*. Edited by Luc Huyse and Kris Hoflack. Leuven: Van Halewyck, 1995.

Winter, Jay. *Sites of Memory, Sites of Mowning: The Great War in European History*. Cambridge: Cambridge University Press, 1995.

Witte, Els *et al.* *Politieke Geschiedenis van België van 1830 tot heden*. Antwerp: Standaard Uitgeverij, 2005.

Woods, Randall Bennett. *A Changing of the Guard: Anglo-American Relations, 1941–1946*. Chapel Hill and London: University of North Carolina Press, 1990.

Wouters, Nico. "Hetzelfde en toch verschillend: Oorlog en oorlogsherinnering in twee aangrenzende dorpen, Essen (België) en Wouw (Nederland)." *Cahiers d'Histoire du Temps Présent* No. 5 (1998): 133–70.

"New Order and Good Government: Municipal Administration in Belgium, 1938–1946." *Contemporary European History* 13, no. 4 (2004): 389–407.

Wynants, Jacques. "La Libération de Verviers." In *Jours libérés II*. Edited by Francis Balace. Volume XX of *Jours de guerre*. Brussels: Crédit Communal, 1995.

THESES AND SEMINAR WORKS FROM THE CEGESOMA COLLECTION

Aelbrecht, Vincent. "Les Églises et les mouvements de pensée en Belgique à la Libération." Université Catholique de Louvain, 1985.

Aelbrecht, Vincent and Alain Maghe. "La Libération de Braine-le-Château et de Braine-l'Alleud." Université Catholique de Louvain, 1985.

Bertrams, Kenneth. "Échanges culturels, campagne de productivité et importation des sciences de la gestion: Quelques aspects des relations belgo-américaines d'après-guerre (1945–1960)." Université Libre de Bruxelles, 1999.

Blanco-Rincon, Mariana and Xavier Pierre Dusausoit. "La Libération et ses conséquences à Nivelles." Université Catholique de Louvain, 1985.

Brigode, F. "Les Commémorations patriotiques dans l'agglomération bruxelloise du 5 septembre au 31 décembre 1944." Université Catholique de Louvain, 1985.

Brigode, F. "La Commune de Grez-Doiceau à la libération." Université Catholique de Louvain, 1985.

Catoire, Philippe and Diane de Bellefroid. "La Libération de Waterloo." 2 vols. Université Catholique de Louvain, 1985.

Combaluzier, Jean-Pierre and Eric Lepage. "La Libération de la commune de Villers-la-Ville." Université Catholique de Louvain, 1985.

Duchenne, Pascal. "Les Théâtres et les spectacles de variétés à Bruxelles de septembre à décembre 1944." Université Catholique de Louvain, 1985.

Hogge, Thibaut. "La Propagande alliée en Belgique (1940–1944)." Université Catholique de Louvain, 1994.

Kaiser, Alain. "La Croix-Rouge en sept–oct 44." Université Catholique de Louvain, 1985.

Leblon, Muriel. "Américanophilie et anglophilie dans les comportements quotidiens en Belgique à la Libération." Université Catholique de Louvain, 1985.

Maleux, Nathalie. "La Propagande parachutée d'Angleterre sur la Belgique occupée." Université Libre de Bruxelles, 1995.

Malevez, Marc. "Aspects démographiques de la libération." Université Catholique de Louvain, 1985.

Marechal, Cécile. "Le Cinéma et le jazz à Bruxelles à la Libération." 3 vols. Université Catholique de Louvain, 1985.

Plumet, Philippe. "La Presse quotidienne belge de la libération." Université Catholique de Louvain, 1978.

Sulbout, Pierre. "Les Troupes américaines à Liège (septembre 1944–décembre 1945): De l'enthousiasme aux réalités." Université de Liège, 1989.

UNPUBLISHED RESEARCH REPORTS FROM THE CEGESOMA COLLECTION

Dauphin, Frédéric. "La Belgique libérée, septembre 1944–novembre 1945: Faits, opinions et représentations."

Laureys, Eric. "Het bevrijde België: Feiten, opinies en voorstellingen."

"L'enjeu du maintien de l'ordre: L'intervention du Haut Commissariat à la Sécurité de l'État en territoire libéré (septembre 1944–novembre 1946)."

Van Ypersele, Laurence. "La Belgique libérée (septembre 1944–novembre 1945): Faits, opinions et représentations. Résultat de recherches."

Index

Studies in the Social and Cultural History of Modern Warfare

Titles in the series:

1 *Sites of Memory, Sites of Mourning: The Great War in European Cultural History*
Jay Winter

2 *Capital Cities at War: Paris, London, Berlin 1914–1919*
Jay Winter and Jean-Louis Robert

3 *State, Society and Mobilization in Europe during the First World War*
Edited by John Horne

4 *A Time of Silence: Civil War and the Culture of Repression in Franco's Spain, 1936–1945*
Michael Richards

5 *War and Remembrance in the Twentieth Century*
Edited by Jay Winter and Emmanuel Sivan

6 *European Culture in the Great War: The Arts, Entertainment and Propaganda, 1914–1918*
Edited by Aviel Roshwald and Richard Stites

7 *The Labour of Loss: Mourning, Memory and Wartime Bereavement in Australia*
Joy Damousi

8 *The Legacy of Nazi Occupation: Patriotic Memory and National Recovery in Western Europe, 1945–1965*
Pieter Lagrou

9 *War Land on the Eastern Front: Culture, National Identity and German Occupation in World War I*
Vejas Gabriel Liulevicius

10 *The Spirit of 1914: Militarism, Myth and Mobilization in Germany*
Jeffrey Verhey

11 *German Anglophobia and the Great War, 1914–1918*
Matthew Stibbe

12 *Life between Memory and Hope: The Survivors of the Holocaust in Occupied Germany*
Zee W. Mankowitz

13 *Commemorating the Irish Civil War: History and Memory, 1923–2000*
Anne Dolan

14 *Jews and Gender in Liberation France*
Karen H. Adler

15 *America and the Armenian Genocide of 1915*
Jay Winter (ed.)

16 *Fighting Different Wars: Experience, Memory and the First World War in Britain*
Janet S. K. Watson

17 *Vienna and the Fall of the Habsburg Empire: Total War and Everyday Life in World War I*
Maureen Healy

18 *The Moral Disarmament of France: Education, Pacifism, and Patriotism, 1914–1940*
Mona L. Siegel

19 *National Cleansing: Retribution against Nazi Collaborators in Post-War Czechoslovakia*
Benjamin Frommer

20 *China and the Great War: China's Pursuit of a New National Identity and Internationalization*
Xu Guoqi

21 *The Great War: Historical Debates, 1914 to the Present*
Antoine Prost and Jay Winter

22 *Citizen Soldiers: The Liverpool Territorials in the First World War*
Helen B. McCartney

23 *The Great War and Medieval Memory: War, Remembrance and Medievalism in Britain and Germany, 1914–1940*
Stefan Goebel

24 *The Great War and Urban Life in Germany: Freiburg, 1914–1918*
Roger Chickering

25 *Capital Cities at War: Paris, London, Berlin 1914–1919. Volume 2: A Cultural History*
Jay Winter and Jean-Louis Robert

26 *The Great Naval Game: Britain and Germany in the Age of Empire*
Jan Rüger

27 *Ghosts of War in Vietnam*
Heonik Kwon

28 *Japanese Society at War: Death, Memory and the Russo-Japanese War*
Naoko Shimazu

29 *The Legacy of the French Revolutionary Wars: The Nation-in-Arms in French Republican Memory*
Alan Forrest

30 *The Final Battle: Soldiers of the Western Front and the German Revolution of 1918*
Scott Stephenson

31 *Liberators: The Allies and Belgian Society, 1944–1945*
Peter Schrijvers

CW00731193

AQUAPONICS

A Beginners guide to Start Growing Herbs, Fruits, Vegetables and Fish at Home Without Soil. Build A DIY Perfect and Inexpensive Hydroponic Growing Gardening System

Copyright © 2020 [Nick Brown]

All rights reserved. No part of this guide may be reproduced in any form without permission in writing from the publisher except in the case of brief quotations embodied in critical articles or reviews.

Legal & Disclaimer

The information contained in this book and its contents is not designed to replace or take the place of any form of medical or professional advice; and is not meant to replace the need for independent medical, financial, legal or other professional advice or services, as may be required. The content and information in this book have been provided for educational and entertainment purposes only.

The content and information contained in this book have been compiled from sources deemed reliable, and it is accurate to the best of the Author's knowledge, information, and belief. However, the author cannot guarantee its accuracy and validity and cannot be held liable for any errors and/or omissions. Further, changes are periodically made to this book as and when needed. Where appropriate and/or necessary, you must consult a professional (including but not limited to your doctor, attorney, financial advisor or such other professional advisor) before using any of the suggested remedies, techniques, or information in this book.

Upon using the contents and information contained in this book, you agree to hold harmless the Author from and against any damages, costs, and expenses, including any legal fees potentially resulting from the application of any of the information provided by this book. This disclaimer applies to any loss, damages or injury caused by the use and application, whether directly or indirectly, of any advice or information presented, whether for breach of contract, tort, negligence, personal injury, criminal intent, or under any other cause of action.

You agree to accept all risks of using the information presented inside this book.

You agree that by continuing to read this book, where appropriate and/or necessary, you shall consult a professional (including but not limited to your doctor, attorney, or financial advisor or such other advisor as needed) before using any of the suggested remedies, techniques, or information in this book.

Table of Contents

What is aquaponic

Aquaponics is a combo of aquaculture, that keeps growing fish and other aquatic creatures, and hydroponics that can be growing plants without dirt. Aquaponics employs both at a hierarchical mix by which plants have been fed with the aquatic creatures' release or waste. In turn, the veggies wash out the water, which extends straight back into fish. Together side the fish along with their waste, microbes play a major function in the nutrition of their plants. These beneficial bacteria accumulate in the distances between the origins of this plant also transforms the fish waste and also the solids to compounds the plants could use to cultivate. The outcome is the perfect cooperation between aquaculture and gardening.

Aquaponics is a significant expectation for renewable organic crop production, aquaculture, and water ingestion. The fish waste is recycled and used for plant growth rather than throwing it at sea. The water can be inserted into a closed system diminishing the ingestion of this particular resource.

Kinds of methods:

Since aquaponics uses precisely the exact approaches as hydroponics, there are few gaps in the way the strategy works, with the exception of the extra fish from the water tank(s). Drip irrigation, flood and drain, profound water or culture underwater roots, and also nutrient film processes are highly harmonious and flexible to unite with fish.

Fish and other aquatic creatures you can develop in aquaponics:

Fish would be the people feeding on your plants. The fish utilized inside this kind of aquaculture are freshwater fish, popular being tilapia and barramundi only because they endure better diverse water requirements and so they grow fast. Trout may be used, especially for lower water temperatures. Other aquatic creatures, it's possible to grow, are snails and shrimps.

You're able to feed the fish special food; it is possible to get within a creature shop or alternative foods such as plain water lettuce along with duckweed.

Aquaponics

Aquaponics utilizes the very best of each of growing techniques, using the waste of 1 element to reap a second mimicking a natural ecosystem. It's really a video game changer

Waist-high aquaponic gardening eliminates weeds back strain and modest creature usage of an own garden.

Aquaponics depends upon the recycling of nutrient-rich water constantly. In aquaponics, there isn't any toxic runoff from hydroponics or aquaculture.

Aquaponics uses 1/10th of their water of soil-based gardening and less water compared to hydroponics or recirculating aquaculture.

No harmful petrochemicals, pesticides, or compost may be utilized. It's an all-natural ecosystem.

Gardening errands are cut dramatically or eradicated. The aquaponics grower can concentrate on the enjoyable activities of feeding on the fish and adapting to and harvesting plants.

Aquaponic approaches can be placed anywhere, rely on them out, at a greenhouse, on your cellar, or even in your living room. By employing grow-lighting, space and distance could turn into a garden.

Aquaponic systems are all scalable. They could fit many budgets and sizes, out of small counter-top herb systems into garden gardens, to full-scale farms, so aquaponics may get it done.

And the very best part -- you have to harvest both fish and plants from the own garden. Truly increasing your whole meal on your garden

Rather than using hazardous or dirt chemical methods to build plants, aquaponics uses exceptionally wholesome fish noodles, which contains all of the needed nutrients for optimum plant growth. Rather than releasing water, then aquaponics uses the plants, naturally occurring bacteria, and also the press from that they grow inside to wash and purify the atmosphere; after that, it's returned into the tank for your fish. This water could be reused forever and may just have to become topped-off if it's lost through transpiration in the plants and evaporation.

There are a couple of main procedures of aquaponic growing broadly in usage now:

Deep-water civilization (dwc) or raft established growing utilizes a polyurethane raft that's floating into a station full of fish effluent water that's been filtered to eliminate solid wastes. Plants are set in holes at the raft along with also the origins dangle freely in the water.

This system is the most right for growing salad greens along with some other fast-paced, relatively low-nutrient plants. It's also most widely utilized in larger commercial-scale techniques.

Media-based aquaponics media are growing calls for growing plants from inert planting media like expanded clay pellets or shale. The press provides the biological filter (conversion of ammonia into nitrates) and mechanical filter (removal of solid wastes) at precisely the exact same system. Media-based systems are fantastic for hobby and home-scale systems, and that means that you may grow a broad array of plants. Specifically, big metropolitan plants perform well along with leafy greens, greens, and other forms. Cases of media-based systems would be the harmony (envisioned), the aqua urban 60-gallon system, as well as the abundance method

Nutrient film technique (nft) nft systems operate by flowing soapy water by way of a narrow trough, like a PVC pipe. Plants are set in holes drilled inside this pipe, and also the origins dangle openly within this flow of drinking water. This way of growing works well for plants that need little aid, like berries (envisioned) and different herbaceous plants. NFT can be a wonderful solution to use unused space since they are able to be suspended from ceilings above additional thriving areas.

Vertical aquaponics, some of the most significant areas of aquaponics, is the way it can cultivate an amazing quantity of food at a really compact location. No method does that a lot better than perpendicular aquaponics. Plants are piled on top of one another in tower systems like the aquavertica. Water leaks through the surface of the tower, also flow via a weatherproof material that the plants' roots absorb nutrients and water out of. The water then drops to a trough or into the tank for your fish. This sort of agriculture gets the maximum of each square foot of distance, also works well with leafy greens, greens, along with other plants which don't demand aid to cultivate.

What veggies you can increase in aquaponics:

In a modest aquaponic established garden you may grow veggies which do not require heavy nutrient enter. Lettuce, kale, watercress, arugula, cosmetic flowers, peppermint, herbs, okras, spring onions and leek, radishes, spinach, and other smallish veggies. Cabbageberries, cucumbers, beans, broccoli, and cauliflower may take more nourishment and also a well-stocked or much more complex

Aquaponic system. Stay clear of growing plants which need alkaline or acidic water, because all those degrees of ph. can absolutely harm fish.

Great things about aquaponics:

1) Aquaponics is a way to cultivate your fish and vegetables in precisely the exact same moment. You feed the fish, and the fish can nourish your plants throughout their waste output.

2) There isn't any requirement to make use of fertilizers since the fish provide rich nutrients to plants.

3) In aquaponics, less water can be useful for its plants. Studies have revealed that aquaponic gardens use 1/10th of this water you'd use for dirt garden.

4) Routine gardening dyes or other compounds cannot be used since they'd harm fish.

5) This also leads to healthy and organic veggies.

6) You won't experience any dirt bore diseases within aquaponics since there isn't any soil.

7) You are able to build plants in a very compact distance, also have a fantastic harvest.

8) Plants grow fast since they get very wholesome chemicals from fish waste.

9) fish and algae production might be accomplished in a controlled temperature setting.

10) Water can be found in a closed system and circulated effortlessly, reducing the consumption and the water invoices.

Guidelines in an aquaponic backyard setup:

1) Now, you can make your personal aquaponics strategy, and here is a very simple and complete lead you'll be able to use to create. Start small; see whether or not it's very good for you to feel free to move larger.

Two) Put another power source for being a backup. It's crucial to maintain the water flowing and also the air pumps.

3) Be sure that you feed the fish and allow them to flourish. The depletion of fish stock creates such a farming hopeless.

4) Maintain food inputs persistent to your fish and which is going to end in routine fish waste; it is possible to use to nourish your plants.

5) Make sure that your fish and plants together with great aeration. Maybe not just the plants want their own origins to become oxygenated, but in addition, the fish and the bacteria want the water to become empty. Whilst the fish grow bigger, their oxygen demands increase, and you also may want to correct so.

6) If you select what plants that you would like to cultivate, decide on those who have similar water illness demands whilst the fish, and also you may have greater success.

7) Eliminate some surplus fish waste if necessary. Too much may harm the overall health of the fish.

8) Maintain your eye on the degree of ph., as shown previously; it's vital for the lawn.

9) Fish tanks need to be made from glass or plastic.

10) Prevent making use of any pesticide aside from organic, or every other chemical that may and can harm the fish or perhaps the great bacteria (vinegar, citric and/or lactic acid).

Ways aquaponics improves on hydroponics

Nutritional elements

Now you know how much you invest in nutritional supplement solutions each year. Now think about this scenario: at our aqua urban aquaponics system, a 60-gallon tank forces 7.5 sq. feet of growing space. Because space, you may grow 6 -- 7 indeterminate tomato plants and roughly 10 tilapia. The single inputs to the machine are 15 g of power to get your pump (let us imagine that's comparable to hydroponics), water on fill up the tank (significantly less than in hydroponics as you won't ever release and then exchange the nutrient solution) and fish food.

Tilapia develop from fingerling point to plate-sized (1.5 pounds) inside a yr. Tilapia convert feed into bodyweight for an efficient 1.2 -- 1.5 pounds of fillets for each pound of feed. This usually means you may desire (10 * 1.5 * 1.5) = 22.5 pounds of fish feed annually to elevate your own 10 tilapia. Fish feed costs about $1/lb. predicated on feed grade, shipping expenses, bulk prices, etc...

What exactly is aquaponics for the health and your market

I want to consume food that is organic, because of this consistently generally seems to have high quality and far superior taste. It's likewise friendlier for types. It's roughly 30 percent higher-priced with organic food that class is a drawback for individuals with ordinary-sized pockets. The nutrient value can also be decreasing on the veggies we all buy compared to the hottest 50 to 100 decades.

Therefore, less nourishment and greater costs, how can you deal with this. I actually don't know if veggies increased in an aquaponics system are high in nutrition than conventionally grown veggies, what I understand is that, from the aquaponics system, you consistently have adequate nutrition for your plants.

When cultivating soil, it's not unusual to see a growing number of depletion of crucial minerals and vitamins from the ground. Which path may be your main reason for decreasing nutritional significance. Healthful eating and becoming green really are crucial to everybody else's future, along with also your aquaponics garden will reveal to you just how to a more sustainable and more economical method of living.

A growing number of people are eating organic produce, which is likely to make it simpler for one to earn money selling the plants and fish you've remaining after using exactly what you require.

An aquaponics backyard is not just a way of healthy organic fish and vegetables to your loved ones; however, it may also signify an additional income for you personally. It's really a certain no lousy circumstance.

Many folks can manage to buy organic brand new fruits and veggies. If you believe this does work for you personally, you can always begin growing your own fish and vegetables using this aquaponic farming procedure.

The interesting thing is that you can place your own aquaponics system nearly anywhere, in your home, in your garage, in your garden and in your flat. Only be sure that there's enough lighting for those plants.

This may make you independent, freedom from rising independence, and prices out of over-priced under grade veggies you'll discover in the supports. You'll have freedom day daily.

Together with your aquaponic platform you won't just save yourself a bit of fund to your little delights of life that you've stalled, however, you'll also have fresh organic food in your desk, and your loved ones should have the ability to eat a wholesome, yummy meal.

Just starting to earn money with your business could be both a daunting and quite a departing undertaking. But, there's 1 business that needs the absolute minimum investment pays in under annually. It's the aquaponics platform also it can alter your life permanently. Even in the event that you don t create any profit, you are going to live more economical since you take in healthier, and also a profit and stored cent is really an earned penny.

Advantages of aquaponic

An aquaponics strategy is a food manufacturing system that combines traditional agricultural techniques of planting aquatic creatures in tanks and the growth of plants in water lacking dirt. Unions are frequently noticed in good lighting, 'two heads are better than one'. The marriage of aquaculture and hydroponics is the same. There is an abundance of advantages that derive from this marriage. These are a few of the main advantages of an aquaponics system:-

Rich food manufacturing

Aquaponics systems have the assurance of plentiful food creation. Considering one set an efficient aquaponics system, bountiful harvests can lead to. The fantastic idea is that businesses like e co-constructed offer pre-fab aquaponics systems alongside a wealth of recommendations for people that don't need to think of this full aquaponics system from scratch. Using an aquaponics system, you're assured of an eclectic selection of foods out of sumptuous fish into green cabbages. This prosperity makes many owners of all aquaponics strategies sell their manufacture for a king's ransom.

Up to 75 percent more energy-efficiency

Traditional farming techniques are accepted by many to be the sole methods of planting animals and nurturing vegetables and plants. When these clinics are inspected, they show gaping inefficiencies that promote the international food deficit. Aquaponics systems are designed with energy efficiency in your mind. Therefore, they offer up to 75 percent more energy efficacy in contrast to traditional farming techniques. Even the aquaponics system can be itself sustaining a system that's consistently in motion because of using pumps in regions where gravity can't perform the secret.

Conservation up to 90 percent of water

Aquaponics systems re-circulate and bottled water quite effortlessly as compared to the majority of traditional farming techniques that exchange or discharge water leading to heavy water declines. The water that's inserted from the aquaponics systems is merely the minimal amount necessary in substituting minimal water loss by evaporation from water, absorption, and transpiration from plants, flow brought on by excess rain or displacement of water throughout removing items from the tanks. Together with aquaponics systems, you're assured of saving up to 90 percent of the water that you'll have normally consumed when using the traditional farming strategies.

Definitely no usage of chemical fertilizers

Chemical fertilizers are a bane to the majority of nutritionists and health experts who care against their use as a result of the side effects of compounds on both individual and other styles of life. Aquaponics systems utilize definitely no compound fertilizers while still permitting the creation of copious quantities of food.

The decline of labor time

Aquaponics systems will lessen the labor time required under normal farming techniques by half an hour. That is due to its self-improvement character. Nobody is going to be asked to always water plants, to boil fishtanks, and also to remove fleas. Therefore, labor time is reduced from 50 percent.

Complete elimination of parasitic life

The character of aquaponics systems causes it to be reverted to parasites. Parasites that could torment farmers with conventional farming techniques from assaulting aquatic creatures and plants are, for that reason, nonexistent within an aquaponics method.

All-year-round farming solutions despite climate

Aquaponics systems do not count on nonsteroidal elements within the environment like climate, such as prosperity. They're self-evident energy source that ensures a continuous stream of drinking water and maintenance of ambient temperature. They consequently offer you all year round farming methods for farmers irrespective of climatic conditions which arise in their place.

Cheap

The self-evident temperament of aquaponics systems which makes it very economical in contrast to conventional farming approaches. They considerably decrease the time, money, and labor spent throughout all stages of the production.

No soil necessary

Aquaponics systems solve the numerous issues farmers face brought on by a deficiency of abundant soil. No dirt is expected from aquaponics systems. This doesn't negate the creation of plants that are abundant and veggies, which could cause those made out of abundant soil light in contrast.

Savior to endangered species

Aquaponics systems additionally have come to assist in plant and animal species that are aquatic. That is due to curative farming.

For research (an exemplary tool for teachers!):

In case you have children in work or school with a school, make them understand aquaponics can be actually a fantastic teaching tool (yes, still another benefit!)! We love dealing together with schools, and so they love dealing together with us! It's almost as though aquaponics has been supposed to help stem (science, technology, engineering, and math) teachers and teachers generally bring an intriguing multi-faceted tool right into schools to hold children engaged while still learning!

The Nutritional Advantages of Aquaponics

When a lot of people believe in why is healthy foods we are predisposed to think in comparative terms--for example, an apple is much far better than a donut. We seldom go as far as to look at any particular 1 apple cider may be a lot better compared to just another apple, and now we have a tendency to believe less about the expanding process that made them away. But quite a few studies are revealing that conclusions about food growth procedures have a great deal more of an effect the health than we imagined.

Agriculture is an industry exactly as with any other. It probably won't come as a jolt that largescale growers regularly head for pretty extreme measures to maintain their returns high and also their plants healthy. Regrettably, it's also not really that surprising that the healthiness of the harvest can be kept at the cost of the medical value of their food that is produced. What's shocking is that growers are still keeping their plants healthy through processes having the capability to produce users very sick.

Insects are people's number one opponents for food on earth. Insect ingestion can induce individual agricultural production with a shocking amount, as one swarm of locusts could eat over 400 million pounds of plant material each day. The frequent type of thinking is that rugs would be the very first and best line of defense against the ravenous horde. Poisoning our very own food to maintain different species out of eating it, but has been demonstrated to be somewhat shortsighted.

Pesticide exposure has been connected to all forms of acute human disorders, including cancer, Parkinson's disease, child mortality, and birth defects, and low male potency. Pesticide residue may remain in foods after they're peeled and cleaned, although u.s. food & drug administration has put strict limits to the forms and levels of pesticides, which can be still tolerable; you can find certainly a couple of different elements that enter in to play in regards to your meal.

Old pesticides which are no more users can have quite a very long time for you to break and will be within growing soil years once they have been prohibited. Even the FDA recommendations also don't take into consideration the dangers of exposure to multiple pesticides, but mostly because such data will not exist. By way of instance, eating an apple that's been confronted with brand substance and after it with a pear infected with new y pesticide might potentially have accumulative consequences.

If spraying pesticides on your own food still sound yummy, imagine should the food you ate actually generated its own toxin? That really is really what genetically modified foods (GMO's) perform, even though pesticides normally undergo extended trials to ascertain a decent health hazard, GMOs have become production with hardly any research done in their consequences on the body. Even worse, they're currently beginning to kill critters.

The proof against genetically modified foods (GMOs) is accumulating. New breeds of corn and cotton are designed for producing a version of a widely used natural pesticide named bt. Like a pesticide spray, bt was demonstrated to cause flu-like symptoms in humans. The bt immersion present within GMO plants is higher than at the spray material, and as the plant generates, the compound can't simply be removed off. Bt cotton and corn have been associated with the deaths of many grazing animals in India, Germany, and the Philippines.

Certainly, one of the strangest risks of GMOs appears just like it was torn from the pages of a sci-fi book. From the recently published study by which the person has been fed GMO's to identify any potential health threats, it had been detected that the genetic alterations really moved out of the foods into the microbes residing within the gut. The enzymes which were inserted into the foods to make sure they are insect-resistant were found to become earnestly operating in bacteria in the intestine. It's some frightening consequences, namely that ingestion GMO's may turn your intestines to some living pesticide mill. Additionally, it has been recorded in animal evaluations that swallowing GMO food caused absolute sterility by another production.

Advantages of aquaponics over ground-based gardening

There have been many improvements in the field of agriculture within the years. A lot of individuals think agriculture to be truly a ground established form of food that is growing. But now's tech will permit one to cultivate your organic food. This may be completed on your home. Growing food at a water established garden is referred to as gallop. A correlated system is called aquaponics.

In case you grow the meal in plain water. Aquaponics unites hydroponics with aquaculture to make a more maintenance-free system of food production than hydroponics. Both approaches have similar benefits over earth dependent agriculture.

Within an aquaponics and also a hydroponics system backyard, you remove the means of weeding. The weeding process might be quite labor-intensive. However, this procedure has to be done since the weeds will probably limit the rise of your own food-producing plants.

With all these water established systems, fertilization of one's own plant is simplified. The procedure for menstruation gets automatic after all of the aspects of aquaponics are functioning at the necessary degrees of efficacy.

There'll not be longer dirt insects. This means you'll no more need to apply toxic compounds to food-producing plants. The vegetables and fruits that you grow will undoubtedly be far fitter and safe to consume.

Yet another thing to think about is that crops increase in those water established systems much quicker than at a dirt dependent system. Plants like lettuce may grow up to twice as fast.

Deciding to develop meals in these approaches will require a strategy and a few aquaponics just how to. There'll undoubtedly be a learning curve. Nevertheless, as soon as you've learned how to construct one's body and also have it running, you'll reap the advantages.

Reasons for Trying Out Aquaponic Farming

Together with many scam company strategies and plans encouraging one to address all of your difficulties with minimal work and investment, even putting your fantasies into the following, new activity looks unfeasible. Some folks are somewhat less inclined to use new things, such as fear of never getting scammed. But this brand new aquaponic system can be rather simple and profitable because it appears! Once you've tried this form of farming, you'd not desire to visit the industry again! However, before that, below are several of the reason why you ought to begin your miniature aquaponic farm.

1. It doesn't require a lot of money or period - that fundamentally means you have nearly nothing to eliminate. What you need is just a couple of containers for vegetables and fish and oxygenized to get a fish tank along with some other few substances to finish the device construction, all relatively affordable. Additionally, the care timing is low - several minutes each daily. You merely need to feed the fish, put the seeds, and wait for them to raise and harvest your plants.

2. The machine is easy to set up and maybe placed anywhere inside your home or garage provided; you might have enough lighting to your plants to grow normally. You certainly can take action yourself by the

start till the end; therefore, there will not be any expenses related to the installation.

3. You can plant just about all kinds of plants, meaning irrespective of what vegetables you would like for dinner, then you can crop them onto the area, from the aquaponic garden, with no hassle. The ideal thing is they all are organic, natural plants that'll taste better and be much more affordable than the people out of the industry.

4. Last but not least, you may no longer cover fortunes to cook up your meal together with ingredients that are organic. You'll have all of them at your fingertips, without paying each time that the oil price is uncontrollable. You're going to be financially separate, and as the machine will likely probably pay off no less than a calendar year, the plants and bass you are going to receive will probably be merely a profit. You are able to use it to get you, or you may even promote the plants and earn a little additional cash. Does not this seem great!

Importance of All Aquaponics

Aquaponics is a very important way for all individuals to cultivate food today and for future generations. Aquaponics can grow an enormous sum of food, having a small percent of the water that's ordinarily utilized inland agriculture.

Aquaponics - some food source for your future which conserves water and resources

Developing sustainable food resources to fit the requirements of an increasing population can be a struggle. The access to freshwater can be limited, particularly in towns, together with resources and land, such as producing meat and crops. In Australia, as an instance, water restrictions are imposed in the majority of elements of the nation that forbid people from using a conventional garden to boost vegetables that are seasonal.

What is your answer?

Most people today believe that it really is aquaponics, as well as particularly, a scaled-down kind of aquaponics that may be practiced in your rear yard.

"Aquaponics" is an expression describing a brand new technology, mixing aquaculture, the farming of fish, and hydroponics, and water-based farming of crops. As notable as it sounds, this brand new technology lets both fish and vegetables to be produced exceptionally effectively in a scale which may fit a normal backyard. The cornerstone for aquaponics is that the symbiotic relationship between plants and fish, which makes it possible for both to be raised together in an all pure balance.

Here is how it works.

Fish live in tiny fish, and ponds waste provides nutritional elements for veggies or different plants. The plants filter out the water where the fish live. Both may be chosen frequently providing both vegetables and protein for humans.

Based on Charlie Price, creator of aquaponics UK, a non-profit organization that conducts an aquaponics farm at Moffat, Scotland, the technique creates an unusually simple closed-loop to get food creation. A kg (2.2 lb.) of fish food produces at least 50 kilograms (110 lb.) of veggies and 0.8 kilograms (approximately 2 pounds) of fish.) the plants increase carbon dioxide out of the air and sun utilizing photosynthesis and so are bathed by fish waste. The plants also filter out the water from the pond since they put it to use, keeping it clear to that fish to live in. Cuttings from plants have been composted to make food for earthworms, which then provide food to fish. The strategy is all but entirely self-evident. Aquaponics uses about 80-90percent less water than normal growing techniques

Aquaponics remains very much a philosophical tech; however, the possibility for aquaponics is huge. Perhaps the furthest and also a metropolitan farm place up near Milwaukee, Wisconsin, within an older mill. Called sweet water organics, the plantation now creates yellow sands with leafy vegetables. Right now, the manufacturing scale is roughly 150 lbs. of veggies each week; however, plans will scale the functioning to approximately 900 lbs. of greens each week, which may likewise yield approximately 1820 lbs. of fish on a per-day basis.

Aquaponics systems that may be installed on your rear yard are getting to be available, even though the field is still very much in its own infancy. Estimates are that we now have 800 1200 systems in homes in America and the other 1, 000 based in schools. Back-yard aquaponics sells roughly 300 systems annually from Perth, Australia.

Aquaponics is a system of producing numerous plants together side a nutritious protein source having minimum requirements for water as well as other resources. Launched on your rear yard, aquaponics put up has got the capacity to extend a family group with renewable, chemical-free fish and vegetables, which may counter a sizable part of its food funding. I expect essential contributions out of this exceptionally sustainable tech since it continues to grow.

You may grow vegetables and plants instantly almost anywhere using an easy aquaponic system

The latest gardening and anger is aquaponics. It's a lot like hydroponics on steroids. A newcomer with a rather modest distance may establish a straightforward aquaponic system, or an extremely expert gardener with a great deal of acreage may utilize an aquaponic program.

Why is it appealing isn't merely its simplicity; however, accelerated plant growth too. The system may be installed having a relatively lower cost. It's quite cost-effective to keep up as it's indeed efficient.

Why purchase products from the supermarket that's covered in harmful compounds, pesticides, and even GMOs. There are lots of studies that have shown exactly how detrimental that will be into the body and especially for kids. It is possible to grow your own products only and readily having an efficient aquaponic system that takes advantage of not one of those harmful products.

An aquaponic program is fairly easy to place up. Once you receive it, the chemistry is 100 percent automated. No hauling dirt, manures, composting, or cracking up your spine weeding all of the time. That you never have water and you also receive all the advantages of eating healthy food!

In case you did not consider aquaponics or even gardening, I'd advise you to give it a go. It's straightforward, takes hardly any time, and hardly any distance. For those who have kids or acquaintances, it's a great, rewarding, and enlightening experience for these at the same time. An excellent job to work together. In reality, I see these appear in lots of school rooms to get their educational value. Therefore give it a go; you truly don't have anything to lose and too much to profit!

Starting your personal backyard aquaponics

If you're wondering exactly what aquaponics is and what its advantages are, then you're one of many as it's a fresh farming technology. Essentially, aquaponics can be something that combines hydroponic or expanding nitric crops and aquaculture or expanding fish to a clinic. An entirely natural method uses hardly any water and also benefits the atmosphere. Aquaponics makes it feasible for farmers to develop fresh veggies or back fish from dry regions. Besides commercial use, the machine has turned into a widespread training aid on incorporated bio systems with senior school diploma programs and vocational agriculture classes. Aquaponics utilizes an extremely intricate technology that needs the capability to handle the creation and earnings of 2 individual services and products at precisely the exact same moment.

For those who want to exercise this method but possess a restricted distance, they are able to clinic back-yard aquaponics. Yes, it's likely to begin your aquaponics system right in your own garden. It's not hard, plus you don't require a great deal of expertise to establish. The system only includes the Invention of a system that's ecologically feasible to cultivate both fish and vegetables in the home. One begins with the fish and the aquarium. Compounds are utilized to divide waste material out of fish to nutrition for plants. One then takes advantage of the water to irrigate plants. It requires approximately a month until the machine can set itself. The plants use the nutrients up and also maintain the water fresh for fish.

The thing you want to begin

1. A tiny aquarium to maintain your fish

2. A little pump which has a timer which may utilize to circulate the water

3. A watertight electric cable to your pump

4. A container that's flat at the base for growing veggies

5. Water-pipes which can go into the aquaponics bed

6. An irrigation power that is over the bed to disperse water evenly

7. Gravel to function like a bedding moderate

Piecing together the garden aquaponics system

1. Set the fish jar onto a marginally lower level compared to the aquaponics bed.

2. Use water that has not been chlorinated since chlorine will kill the ecosystem fish and germs

3. The bed should float the aquarium, secured to an incline that's marginal to the tank for your fish.

4. Drill a couple of holes near the bed's underside, where it moves the fish container.

5. Fill out the dirt right into the bed

6. Set the pump at the aquarium firmly and mend it

7. Fit the irrigation section of this bed

8. Join the irrigation pipes into the irrigation grid out of the pump

9. Time the pump to operate fifteen minutes of every hour

10. Activate the pump and also make sure that everything operates

Valuable information around aquaponics

What's aquaponics? It's a mix of two words "aquaculture" (increasing aquatic creatures such as fish in tanks) and also "hydroponics" (care of plants from water). Formally, it's thought of as a fresh farming technology that employs the symbiotic connection between creatures and plants. It's just a sustainable food production system that's being successfully embraced in these times. Basically, that really is invisible because the waste substances of these plants are fed into the fish, while at the exact same period, the waste of this fish is found in fertilizing the vegetables and plants.

To begin your aquaponics platform, you absolutely won't have to be a specialist or even a genius- you simply should be familiar with fundamental things linked to it just like the simple requirements of the fish, and also the simple requirements of the plant life.

Standard demand for your plant: by the biology class in senior high school, you're able to understand that plants need oxygen, light, nutrients, and also most well - water. Each one these have to be shown at only the optimal / adequate amounts; also, it could be natural or artificial. Bearing this in mind that you will ostensibly feel your aquaponics machine ought to own the correct water, oxygen source (usually synthetic, through battery-powered ones), and so on. Obviously, looking into this, how the plant may be confused about the way that it is able to absorb both oxygen and water? This includes the roster of this flood valve. You want this to allow oxygen to be consumed by the roots, also to allow the roots perhaps not to be bombarded by water. The straightforward notion of a flooding valve prevents the hassle of presenting digital elements on your systems, such as timers or pc controller.

Standard requirements of the fish: in the event you're fond of possessing an aquarium once you had been a youngster, you'll surely understand the living demands of a bass. Alone using plants, they want water that's packed with oxygen so they can breathe correctly throughout their gills. Additionally, a few fish are somewhat temperature sensitive, and therefore you want to watch it also.

Last, the fish demands food. You want to realize that these demands are all supplied at the ideal level to steer clear of dangers of overfeeding that induces cloudy water and frequently oxygen deprivation. To address that, you want to set a filter in your own installation. 1 essential thing to discover, and an all pure index of one's aquaponics environment could be your smell. When the smell isn't good, instantly clean and replaces your own body - it only tells and shows you that there might be potential germs and microbes living in the water.

Simple, right? In addition to this, a fundamental knowledge of a few of the procedures that inherently occur between such as nitrification can genuinely help you.

In terms of the price, aquaponics isn't high priced. You may always figure out ways to earn your installation simple and manageable. Certainly, one of the significant things would be to continue to keep it healthy and clean. Ultimately, you're able to love the attractiveness with the self-sustaining atmosphere.

The New Age of Gardening - Aquaponics

Now from the 21st century, conventional farming is altering every single day - folks have enough time, less distance, and sometimes fewer funds.

But despite those hardships, you can still possess a booming garden, literally climbing anything you desire if you like, where you would like.

Imagine if I told you that after putting up a very straightforward system, you'd not need to execute one thing while the plants were climbing until they're ready for harvest? Imagine if I told you at precisely the exact same time it's possible to raise your favorite type of fish? Imagine if I told you kids, adults, and seniors may cherish participate in the?

That really is what you receive with aquaponics. In other words, aquaponics keeps growing a garden, increasing fish, also feeding on the garden with water that the fish are now living in. This creates a full freezer, throughout the year, and a lot of fun. Children enjoy watching the plants and fish grow together; they like feeding on the fish, plus they'll surely delight in researching the relationship entailed.

Now you are able to try that anywhere, at just about any volume. We had systems in which we climbed your plant with one particular fish, and we had approaches where we now increased 300 fish and one million baskets of lettuce. It's all your choice!

Listed below are a couple of reasons why aquaponics will be fast turning into one of the primary trends, and it really is advisable afterward hydroponics.

Together with hydroponics, you need to provide your plants with a variety of compounds to mimic what they'd profit from the dirt and also sunlight. This leaves them invulnerable, and of course, taste different. Trust me; you're able to taste the change. We did research with seven volunteers. Each was handed a pineapple, a banana, a cherry, and a couple of legumes - double. 1 negative was increased at a hydroponics system, and also one other was improved within an aquaponics program. All of 7 volunteers consented, without knowing what was the produce grown from the aquaponics system believed better. All 7 additionally stated that produce increased in the hydroponics system only tasted watered down.

The motive aquaponics is significantly more valuable is simple. The fish eat all sorts of things - candy corn, poultry, lettuce, bugs, bugs, minnows - that they afterward create waste. This remains in the water, which is subsequently pumped into the plants. This is exactly the reason you won't ever observe that a “feeble" appearing Lilly mat!

The selection is straightforward. You and your loved ones simply take the children to school, work regular occupations, have extracurricular activities - you do not also have enough opportunity to cultivate tomatoes or lettuce inside. Until now. Together with all the aquaponics system, it is possible to literally place this and forget it. Well, besides feeding fish!

Ph.'s significance in aquaponic

Certainly, one of the essential elements in keeping a healthy, functioning aquaponics system is suitably managing ph. degrees.

Fish, plants, and bacteria have their particular ideal ph. range, and also finding a happy medium is essential in the accomplishment of an aquaponics method.

Together with lots of aspects which could cause changes in ph., it may be rather hard to retain a frequent balance your fish, plants, and bacteria may flourish in.

What's ph.?

Ph., or even power of hydrogen, can be just a logarithmic scale used to quantify how acidic or basic a solution relies upon the hydrogen ion (h+) concentration. The concentration of hydrogen ions in an answer determines the acidity or alkalinity of a solution. In acidic solutions, the concentration of hydrogen ions is significantly more than the concentration of hydroxide ions, whereas, in alkaline solutions, the concentration of hydrogen ions is significantly lower compared to the concentration of hydroxide ions.

The Arrhenius theory of bases and acids introduced in 1884 is just a very simple theory that explains the number of substances as bases or acids depending on the type of ions generated when included with water. It says that if acid is put into water, then it also provokes a hydrogen ion (h+) to water to create h3o+. The greater the concentration of h3o+ (or h+) in a way, the more acidic the answer. By comparison, a base substance creates oh- ions. The greater the concentration of hydroxide ions (oh-) in a way, the simpler the answer is. This formula is applied to ascertain the ph. value dependent on the concentration of the hydrogen ions.

Ph. = -log[h+]

The ph. scale ranges from 0 to 14. Even a ph. value less than 7 indicates a solution is more acidic, a ph. value adds up to 7 is neutral, and a ph. value higher than 7 signals that a remedy is basic. The lower the ph., the stronger the acidity, and the higher the ph., the sturdier the alkalinity.

You will find three chief techniques to assess the ph. amount of an answer.

1. A newspaper strip coated at a ph. suggesting dye could also be utilized having a ph. color graph

2. A ph. testing kit may be used for fluids with a ph. color graph

3. An electronic digital ph. meter enables you to automatically acquire the ph. level of their clear answer. It's also the very precise

How ph. affects plant nutrient absorption, compounds, and fish

Managing that the ph. level is essential in aquaponics to the wellness of the whole system, like hydroponics and soil gardening. But, managing the ph. level is harder with aquaponic ecosystems as it represents three major surviving organisms -- fish, plants, and bacteria, most of which may have different ph. level preferences.

Whilst the ph. of the soil affects the dispersal of several plant enzymes, it greatly impacts the availability of nutrients to plants and also the nutrient absorption from plants. Ergo, soil ph. also affects plant development. Most plant nutritional supplements are available over the product range 6.5 to 7.5; therefore, the perfect soil ph. is near neutral. Extreme soil ph. levels might be damaging to plant survival.

In very acidic dirt, micronutrients like zinc and aluminum might turn out to be chemically inaccessible. In rather acidic dirt, micronutrients like magnesium, calcium, and potassium aren't consumed as the accessibility declines. Ergo, it's very important to keep a ph. level over the best selection.

Optimum ph. range

The best ph. range for fish is based upon the kind of fish used for your own aquaponic program. While saltwater fish prefer an alkaline ph. of 8.0 or freshwater bass flourish in a slightly acidic ph. varying from 5.5 to 7.5. Ergo, the best ph. range for bass is regarded as 6.5 to 9.0. Outside this optimal ph. range, when the ph. is too much or too low, then the fish may get stressed, and there's a heightened probability of dying. The ph. of this water may also affect how toxic and soluble compounds and heavy metals that the water is that could significantly impact the wellbeing of fish.

Compounds are very adaptive, generally speaking. But, every microorganism has the best ph. value for growth. The best ph. range for the majority of bacteria increase is 6.5 to 7.0. But some bacteria can flourish in very acidic conditions; some bacteria might have the ability to endure ph. values as little as 1. Though these bacteria can flourish in very acidic conditions, their internal ph. is quite a bit closer to impartial.

As plants generally favor a slightly acidic setting, whilst germs and fish like a slightly acidic state, a ph. within an array of 6.5 - 7.5 is usually kept in systems that are stored.

Carbonate buffer and water hardness

The ph. level of this water from the aquaponic system is influenced by the water hardness that determines that the buffering capacity of drinking water. The flowing capacity describes the capacity of the water to keep a well-balanced ph. despite minor changes like the inclusion of acids or bases. If you aren't using distilled water, then there'll more than likely be a few dissolved mineral salts found that'll affect the ph. level of this water. The expression water hardness can be utilized to refer to the concentration of those dissolved nutrient salts from water. The greater the concentration of these minerals, the tougher the water is and vice-versa.

KH and GH

There are two chief kinds of water hardness -- carbonate hardness (KH) and overall hardness (GH). Carbonate hardness denotes the water's buffering capacity or alkalinity, whereas the overall hardness denotes the concentration of magnesium and calcium ions.

The carbonate hardness plays a larger role in fixing the buffer capacity for this aquaponic system to stabilize the human ph. Buffers are important to protect against a striking or sudden shift in the ph. level, which is fatal to the fish from the computer system. Buffers also play an integral part in keeping the wellness of bacteria inside the computer system. An extremely lower carbonate hardness could lead to a very low ph. that can kill most bacteria.

To get the aquaponic system, the perfect kh degree is something above 4.0 that helps to ensure that a top rotational possible is preserved to get an even far more stabilized ph. Even the kh degree of an aquaponic system might be quantified with a stipulated water evaluation kit.

To increase the kh amount of a machine in case it drops below the best degree of 4.0 dkh, you may add potassium bicarbonate into the machine at an interest rate of two 1/2 tsp per 100 gallons of water to rise the dkh degree.

What causes ph. from aquaponic systems into fluctuating

It's important to be alert to those things which lead from the fluctuation of the ph. of one's own body to keep up a near-neutral grade. There are many outside factors that may possibly bring about an increase or decline from the ph. amount of an aquaponic program.

An increase in the ph. will be usually because of carbonate buildup from the machine, which might be a result of the water used being harder. The grow media getting used might also contribute, in addition to the substances used to create the beds or take, for example, concrete and limestone. Even though a superior ph. is not uncommon through the initial beginning of this device, a well-established bacteria colony may finally decrease the ph. by avoiding the buildup of carbonate via the nitrification procedure. A quite large ph. could lead to poor plant development and bad fresh fruit and blossom development.

A decline from the ph. is often a result of the nitrification process of converting fish waste to plant food, which increases the acidity of the water from the computer system. A decline in ph. can additionally as a result of material employed to create the aquaponic system and also the kind of plants being increased. A minimal ph. ought to be increased to prevent issues with the germs and fish in the computer system.

How to correct ph. from aquaponic systems?

A buffer may help assess the ph. of this water at the aquaponic system, but you might need to interfere once the ph. level gets too much or too low.

After the ph. is too low, then you are going to need to raise the alkalinity of the water to elevate your ph. stage. This is sometimes accomplished by mixing calcium carbonate and potassium carbonate in equal quantities and also adding the mix to the drinking water. Carbonates are preferred since they're not caustic and can bring strength to this carbonate buffer. You might even add simple hydroxides like sodium hydroxide to increase the ph. level of their water.

When the ph. is too high, so you might need to boost the acidity of their water to decrease the ph. stage. This is sometimes accomplished with the addition of phosphoric acid that will be safe and effective. Additionally, this adds phosphate to the device that may further help the plants concerning nutritional elements. Reverse osmosis (RO) filter may even be utilized to preserve the ph. from becoming too large. Ro filters can eliminate the carbonates from the water, leading in very pristine, carbonate-free water using a diminished the ph.

Fixing ph. from aquaponic systems

Managing ph. is equally as significant in aquaponics since it's in hydroponics and dirt gardening; however, it's trickier in aquaponics since you can find just three surviving constituencies to take into account within an aquaponic ecosystem: fish, plants, and bacteria.

Even though the crops usually prefer a marginally acidic ph. (at the low sixes to upper fives), both the germs and fish would rather have a slightly alkaline ph. (from the top sevens to non-eights). For that reason, ph. direction in aquaponics can be an exercise in compromise involving both ranges. The perfect target can be really a ph. of 6.8 to seven.

Ph. on the life span of one's aquaponics system

Most water comes from the tap ph. levels over a 7 as municipalities are worried about the long-term harmful effects of water in order that they correct so. If your machine's water originates out of the good, you'll probably uncover exactly the exact same task, however in this event; it's the mineral content of this water that's maintaining your ph. quite high.

Excellent news--a marginally higher ph. is generally not an issue because whenever you begin a brand new siphoned system, it. The cycling method is intended to encourage beneficial nitrifying bacteria to take up residence on the human body. This course of action is entirely centered on the bacteria and also the fish, which prefer a greater ph. This usually means that water somewhat above a ph. of 7 helps to acquire your system invisibly.

Once the nitrogen cycle is totally created, and you've added plants into your own body, you'll often understand the ph. of one's own body diminish as time passes. Why? As the nitrogen cycle really creates nitric oxide, which may naturally make your ph. to really go down.

However, there'll be instances, particularly if your own system is still young, once you need to behave to push on the ph. down. And in the very long term, you will regularly raise your ph. We'll talk about just how to do so safely within aquaponics.

How to produce a buffer on your aquaponic system

Here's what I recommend to make a buffer on your aquaponic system:

Receive an API GH and kh test kit and also discover what your carbonate degrees are.

If you're preceding 4 dkh, then you then ought to be ok for today, but make sure you retest per week in one's typical testing regimen. Bear in mind that since one's body evolves, it is going to create increasingly more nitric oxide, which means that your kh degrees will drop over time.

When you plan a dkh of lower or 4, I suggest adding potassium bicarbonate to your own body at an interest rate of two 1/2 tsp. 100 gal. Of system water to get each dkh amount, you want to move up.

The value of an aquaponic buffer

The majority of people have an additional buffer to our own aquaponic systems sooner or later, but a lot of individuals are conscious about how frequently they try so and exactly what they utilize to buffer their approaches together with, believing when their fish are still living, what is alright. While this report emphasizes, adding buffer (the ideal kind) into an aquaponic system can be really a critical process which has to be carried out regularly (ideally on a regular basis) rather than merely when your ph. is at risk of moving off the shade graph! Adding buffer regularly helps prevent substantial swings in ph., stay away from stressing or damaging your fish (irrespective of how resilient they will be to ph. changes) and empower your body to perform economically and efficiently.

Since you're likely aware, ph. is a step of this acidity/alkalinity of an answer. Various organisms want different ph. levels, such as growth. Compounds will be the easiest going, inhabiting a broad ph. range (~6.0 -- 8.0); plants prefer acidic conditions (~4.5 -- 7.0); whereas fish flourish in marginally more basic states (~6.5 -- 8.0) [1]. Pros do disagree ever-so-slightly to the specific top and lower parameters that an optimal ph. range for aquaponic systems needs to collapse between (since they perform in specifying the above best ph. ranges for various organisms). The overall consensus, however, is the fact that the perfect ph. range for aquaponics is located within this area, at which 3 best ranges for plants fish and plants overlap each other.

Assuming that the hardware on your own body is inert, and also the water perhaps not too hard or alkaline, the ph. of a balanced and established aquaponic system generally has a tendency to maneuver within inevitable downward management as time passes. That is basically on account of the nitrification process since the conversion of ammonia into nitrate contributes to the discharge of hydrogen ions that make the water acidic[2]. Therefore, even though a persistent, continuous drop in ph. is still an indication of a healthier aquaponic system, even if it's left unattended without a buffer is inserted, this drop may stress your fish. To be honest, many growers are not aware that there's an issue using their ph. degree because fish are elastic animals that do not necessarily exhibit any bodily signs of these worries, especially when the ph. level changes gradually as time passes.

Humans can endure a broad temperature array between the reverted extremes of arctic Australia into arctic-Esque temperatures below, but this does not mean we'd gladly and amenably decide to introduce ourselves to those extremes, nor can we try so to the pets -- for instance leaving our dogs while in the vehicle in a heatwave! At a similar way even though your fish could possibly be capable of carrying out an extensive ph.-range it's crucial to be an accountable aquaponics and where possible make an effort to maintain them optimally, or as near to optimal ph. requirements as you can (especially due to the fact since ph. works to a logarithmic scale each unit reduction represents a ten-fold growth in acidity). The best range is really where they have been happiest and certainly will nourish and work normally.

It's important to utilize buffers that are beneficial to fish, plants, and humans. Because of this, the usage of fish-only (aquaculture) buffers isn't recommended as these frequently contain sodium (e.g., sodium bicarbonate buffer), which plants dislike. There's mixed opinion seeing natural buffers (e.g., eggshells or seashells) simply because they require a very long time and energy to kick and provide you fewer hands in balancing your own body [2]. More optimal are buffers composed of potassium or calcium (just two of those three nourishment fish foods do not supply that crops need) [5]. The issue with excess calcium, though, is it may decrease phosphate utilization from plants; therefore, a perfect balance can be reached by including a calcium-dependent buffer six times per week, and calcium established daily weekly.

Thus the precise potassium and also calcium-based buffers you employ are more inclined to be an issue of preference. The absolute most significant issue is to put in tether frequently, enough to protect against the down drop created by nitrification, however, perhaps not really much in which the ph. begins shooting upward from the opposite way.

Because of the significance of optimal ph. degrees, it's surprising why several aquaponic manufacturers are negligent in regards to tracking and adjusting their own ph., or just do this if their machine is in a crisis point.

In aquaponics, it might be tempting to fail ph. changes and just add markup into a procedure once the ph. level works well and truly outside from this system optimal range, i.e., when fish start to expire plant or plant growth will be clearly influenced. The fact remains that like anything else in life, prevention is much far better than cure.

Tilapia is an ideal illustration of the. They're adapted to a broad ph. range (3.7 into 11.0), and really could endure in such a variety; however, they flourish at a neutral to slightly simple scope (7.0 -- 9.0) [6]. Due to tilapia's adaptability to this large ph. range, it'd not likely disturb many people when the ph. amount in this aquaponic system dropped below 6.5. But, acidic water was demonstrated to impede the development of tilapia, a sign of stress[7], for example, plant expansion, and also, the growth of the aquaponic system may also be influenced. But losing profits really should not be the sole concern if ph. amounts payable. More crucial may be the dilemma of animal welfare!

Looking subsequent to the organisms inside your aquaponic system can be an email that ethical aquaponics like doctor Lennard has strived to urge for, and also yet another of the ways we are able to try it would be to 1) quantify our ph. each day -- to inspect the ph. is moving in the natural downward way it must be moving; two) buffer the technique regularly (ideally everyday) earlier this downward tug gets an opportunity to descend out of these systems best selection. Frequent ph. analyzing and buffering may help to maintain the ph. level relatively stable (irrespective of the minimal, alternating downward and up ph. changes caused by nitrification and the inclusion of buffer). Hence your fish who do not enjoy abrupt, large changes in ph. -- will probably be much more joyful.

Again there's mixed information in regards to the kind of potassium and calcium established buffers to utilize, as every barrier has its own advantages and disadvantages. Bernstein implies any one of these is right: calcium hydroxide, calcium carbonate, potassium carbonate, potassium bicarbonate, or potassium hydroxide[2]. Lennard and Rakoczy alike favor calcium hydroxide; nevertheless, Lennard utilizes potassium carbonate because of his strategies, whereas rakocy decided potassium hydroxide because of his uvi setup.

In outline, healthful fish help creates a healthy strategy, therefore when it concerns the employment of buffer, a preventative, as opposed to reactive strategy, is recommended in modulating ph. grades. Not only can your fish like for this, however it is going to help make the body more manageable and reliable.

Therefore, what can you do in case you want to get the ph. down or up on your aquaponic process? To reduce ph., I would urge certain acids, such as nitric oxide, muriatic, and so forth.

My taste is phosphoric as it is the most powerful of these amino acids (it really is a component in cola drinks) plus additionally adds a few phosphates in one's body, which the plants will probably require to. Nevertheless, phosphates can exacerbate a present algae problem; therefore, if that's the case, you might need to make use of one of those additional types.

You ought to avoid uric acid as it's anti-bacterial. Additionally, avoid vinegar since it's too feeble --you might possibly be pickling your fish until you find the ph. results you're searching for.

To increase ph., I suggest utilizing calcium carbonate and potassium carbonate and alternating between them, adding equal quantities of each at exactly the exact same moment. I like to utilize those carbonate chemicals rather than hydroxide chemicals (calcium hydroxide and potassium hydroxide) for all factors. (watch ph. up and ph. down for much more info)

Raising and lowering ph. from aquaponic systems

They increase the potency of this buffer. Secondly, they're perhaps not caustic and won't burn skin just like the hydroxides will. Third, they have been available on the organic materials review institute (omri) set of additives for certified production.

While critical, ph. control in aquaponic systems is, in fact, simple. The ph. of your own system will not cause one to a severe problem so long as you be certain that you keep up a buffer of 4 dkh or longer, and which you simply assess and fix your ph. once every week as essential.

The way to safely decrease ph. from aquaponics information to lower ph. from aquaponics

High-ph. is a frequent concern among intermediate and beginning aquaponic growers, that need a quick cure to make down it.

My doctrine about decreasing the ph. at a method with large ph. is simple.

In case you are considering using a compound or acid to reduce your own ph., do not. You are only going to get your life more complicated and costly than it must be.

Substantial system ph. is almost always brought on by carbonate buildup in the machine (if it is not carbonated at the sort of limestone grow bed press, concrete from the aquarium, etc.).

Whether it's carbonate buildup from the machine, your ph. has been "buffered," or kept unnaturally high by the carbonate cycle of one's own water.

Carbonates can be a complicated issue; therefore, I am not planning overly complicated here. The one thing to bear in mind is the fact that carbonates have the capability to split into the solution and precipitate out of solution.

How they do this preserves ph. at a very particular high range until a day, you are adding an acid just like you do, and also your ph. crashes. Bottoms out. Drops just like a stone.

When this occurs this fast from large ph. techniques, the very first matter that takes place is nitrification ceases - that most of us know is quite a poor thing.

The way to safely decrease ph.

Therefore what exactly are you really likely to perform?

If your water is not too hard (large carbonates), you can finally secure your nitrification into the idea at which your acidification out of nitrification outstrips the carbonates penetrating your own body, resulting in a naturally minimal ph.

Once done properly and gradually, the nitrifying bacteria will correct, and there isn't any shock. Once you accomplish this candy spot on your body's wellbeing and life span, it's an excellent thing.

Now you've got control of your own body ph. Where would you desire it? It's completely your decision.

The easiest way to maintain ph. from becoming out of hands will be the RO filter

Ro filtered water is a simple substance.

You can let nitrification to push ph. down, or you can insert simple hydroxides into raise ph. (and nutritional supplements) without long-term ph. effects.

Ro filters may charge a few hundred bucks, however in my experience, a number of individuals who spend weeks fighting using ph., and trying to cut back it reached the stage whereby return, they wish they had simply installed an RO filter and then avoided the value and frustration of fighting with the fundamental chemistry in this machine.

Do not overlook biological surface-area

Therefore that it is. You've got two options - be individual or fall some cash within an RO filter.

Should you choose to wait, " I really do advocate employing an increasing method that leads a lot of biological surface place into the machine.

This increases the possible number of nitrifying biomass on your system in addition to the consequent efficiency in nitrification. This could cause faster nitrification established carbonate ingestion.

Additional recommendations

1. To lower the ph., not utilize vinegar, that can be overly feeble, or lactic acid that is antibacterial and behaves as an herbicide.

2. Always monitor and correct the ph. level to make sure your aquaponic system consistently works precisely

3. Be certain to create any alterations to the ph. degree gradually to prevent shocking any living aspects of one's system

Managing proper ph. is essential in maintaining a well-functioning aquaponics system. Every living thing from the device, if the fish, the plants, or even the germs, or has their particular ideal ph. range, however a candy area of 6.5 - 7.5 should do the job just fine. Maintain proper kh in 4.0 and put in potassium bicarbonate if needed.

The way to style your own aquaponic system in your home (step by step);

In a nutshell, aquaponics enables you to develop both plants and fish at exactly the same time, saving loads of water from the course of action, at a hierarchical method by which plants prey the aquatic creatures' release or waste, during yield, the veggies as well as different plants clean the water which extends right back into fish.

Aquaponics is, consequently, a type of renewable food sourcing; also, it can have small dimensions or perhaps a large one. From an economic sustainability perspective, aquaponics can be really a plan for its long run to employ in metropolitan regions to help men and women grow their own food at an affordable, safe, ecofriendly, and lasting method.

First, the questions regarding construction aquaponics

In case you wish to know just how to create an aquaponics system step-by-step in your home, you must answer the next questions:

Why? -- can you design an aquaponics system for your own enjoyment or it as scientific experimentation for the youngsters, or are you currently attempting to cultivate your food to conserve a bit of money on the supermarket bills?

Where? -- according to the place you would like to put the machine, the positioning will decide how big and design of this system.

When? -- you have to select attentively your season because a few plants don't grow well in winter months, a few providers don't sell fish at certain cold months, even whereas bacteria will show better at a warmer temperature.

Who? -- before you begin construction, you have to ascertain who will care for the technique. Kiddies could be too small to be in a position to deal with the machine, and that means you have to keep elevation in your mind. Furthermore, in the event you and your relatives travel regularly and also leave the device to do on its own, then you need to think about copy aeration along with different design elements to donate to the machine's durability and very low maintenance as time passes.

In case you possess the answers to each of these questions, now is the time to understand how to create an aquaponics system detail by detail up the convenience of your home!

1. Opt for the positioning

Now you can set your aquaponics system anywhere you would like. But, based upon your own preference, you'll need to correct the plan and variable in many elements.

Out-door location: if you wish to set the aquaponics system at the garden, for example, you've got to think about the weather locally, hours of lighting daily, temperatures, and the default pollution, decent system's insulating material, sturdiness, access and security against injuries, and a lot more.

In-door location: if you wish to construct your aquaponics system within (garage), then you want to look at the quantity of lighting, heat, and also access too. If you don't need big enough windows along with your house doesn't have lots of pure lighting; for example, you need to think about adding an excess supply of artificial light.

2. Hardware

When we discuss the hardware of an aquaponics system, we suggest that the aquarium, the plants' increase bed, and also the pipes (pipes, pumps, etc.). Here's what you want to learn about the hardware:

Tank for your fish: if you would like to view how things proceed, you ought to pick a conventional aquarium made from glass. Ensure that it will hold enough to catch those plants that you would like to cultivate.

Grow taller: greater it's, the plants you're going to have the ability to cultivate, but guarantee the aquarium and also the dining table may do the job together. The grow bed ought to be at least 1-2 inches deep.

Note: the proper grow bed size guarantees that the filter and retains the aquarium balanced. Generally, you might design a 52-53 g fish-tank to improve fish into 10 12 inches in total. You ought to start with this 1:1 ratio of one's own grow bed to fish-tank volume. Whenever your aquaponics system begins devoting over four to six weeks, you're able to raise its ratio to 2:1.

Service: you'll want to encourage the grow bed having a solid base. It's preferable to purchase pre-made eyeglasses; however, you might also utilize concrete cubes or timber (for exterior aquaponics at the least).

Water heater: when selecting a water heater, make certain you obtain yourself a dependable and trustworthy one. Read reviews prior to purchasing it. Magnetic driveway (mag-drive) pumps will be most useful as the engine has its own different compartment, that will be sealed, and it shouldn't ever flow any oil into the tank for your fish. Put the submersible pump at 1 corner of this aquarium that takes up the water into the bed.

Air vacuum: this may pump oxygen in your aquarium. Ensure that you purchase the one which includes a standing and strong technician specs.

Grow bed media: gravel is economical but based upon the stone foundation, it could impact the ph. ranges in water. You might even use clay beans, which can be ph. neutral and hold moisture well.

Bell siphon: this really is a rather effective process of slowly flooding the grow bed and draining it fast. The bell siphon accomplishes this goal by having a no mechanical activity and doesn't have moving parts to break. If you purchase pre-made bell siphons, be certain that they are of good.

Pipes: the previous part is linking the machine with each other to carry it into life. You'll need a press shield with your bell and certainly will continue to keep the grow bed press out of this bell siphon, allowing water to enter.

3. Computing software

Today that you have all of the substances, you have to consider the computer software. You've got any components to think about here, since they are those maintaining your aquaponics system living, healthy, and flourishing:

The range of bass to cultivate: based on aquaponics system pros, you need to utilize the ratio principle: 1718 ounce. Catch 0.330 square feet of this grow bed. Remember that you just base your ratio over the 1 2 inches deep bed.

Water temperature at the tank: this depends upon plenty on the sort of fish that you wish to cultivate. Should they want warmer temperatures, then you also can find an aquarium water heater. Warmer temperatures help bacteria to flourish.

Establish the water ph.: once we discussed in the former essay, you should resolve a wholesome ph. approximately 6.8 to 7.0 within an aquaponics method. You may likely have to correct the ph. from the tank, therefore make sure you try the levels on your aquaponics system weekly approximately three to four days to be able to be certain it remains within the permitted limits.

Pick the fish: the ideal fish to get aquaponics approaches are omnivore fish. You are able to enjoy a vast choice of aquaponics fish, pros advocating the next: rainbow trout, tilapia, grass carp, white bass, crappies, and much more.

The modern home organic garden - the easy way using an aquaponics system

Now there's a climbing tendency to consume organic food; it's getting to be a famous actuality that organic food is far better because of wellbeing. Though many farmers have been still leaning towards growing food, still organic food is somewhat more costly than ordinary food. It's possible to devote a great deal of income on food that's promised to be organic; however, you are actually getting food that's of lesser grade compared to regular food-growing with additives and other compounds. The only real method to really recognize the grade of the food that you're eating and be sure that you're eating organic foods would be to cultivate the meals.

The handiest and straightforward means to cultivate organic food is aquaponics. This sort of farming is relatively fresh and extremely simple to prepare and maintain, employing the machine is extremely handy and profitable. As a way to prepare your brand-new system, you simply require a couple of things, and they're quite cheap to purchase, and that means you may not need to spend luck on the gear.

In addition to mounting your aquaponic system can be a simple matter to accomplish when you comprehend the fundamental principles of how a strategy works, you'll just require a short while to put it within a couple of days you should get your septic system prepared, and you'll have the ability to set the fish from the tank.

The fish at the aquaponics system is playing with a fantastic role, and also you ought to be certain you are taking excellent care of these; therefore, they remain happy and healthy. The fish can produce bio-nutrients to your crops, even whenever you will find enough wholesome chemicals from the water, which is going to be a very good time to get started planting the seeds and then await them to cultivate, whereas the fish continue to generate more food for those plants.

Now, it is becoming better together with time! Once you put up the device and it's balanced, then you don't have to manually wash out the aquarium since here really is actually the plant's endeavor the origins of these plants collecting each of the staff that's essential due to their growth by the water and also leave the water sterile to that fish to make use again. Perhaps not exactly that it leaves growing organic plants easy; however, it's perhaps not tricky to improve fish in this manner, simpler than aquaculture procedure.

Certainly, one of the maximum advantages of aquaponics will be that it is really simple to build and disassemble. This fact alone has been turning this system among the very elastic farming techniques there's. You are able to almost set it anywhere on your home or garage plus it's really easy to maneuver, if you're moving to some other house, harvest all of your plants until you disassemble your brand-new system, even once you disassemble the device that you will lose each of plants. Then only take the device with one to a home. Be certain that you position it at a suitable location, which has lots of lighting for the plants.

Growing your organic food hasn't been simpler; together with aquaponics, you are able to get your very own abundant organic farm at home and revel in fresh fruits and veggies in your desk daily.

Benefits of home aquaponics

For those who do not understand anything about aquaponics that I only want to quickly explain exactly what home aquaponics is. Aquaponics is ostensibly growing plants by employing fish. It works wonders since the nutrition which fish naturally put from the water that they live in is what the plants will need to cultivate. The gap between ordinary ways of growing veggies, like placing them at the earth, is massive. You're able to grow more plants faster than ever before.

So today, you can imagine the great things about dwelling aquaponics. And the fantastic thing is that aquaponics is quite simple to come up with and do not use up much space. Aquaponics systems vary in size; however that you do not require sufficient space to start out your own personal home aquaponics system. All these are a couple of the advantages of dwelling aquaponics that allow anybody to begin growing their own vegetables and fruits. And what's amazing is a simple fact that the food that you grow doesn't grow quickly; however, in addition, it tastes far greater than any product you should purchase out of the supermarket.

If you enjoy growing plants and food and sell that which you grow, then using aquaponics, you're able to grow a gigantic return by 50 percent the time. Not only are you able to earn more money in selling your products; however, but you'll also likely be providing some fantastic tasting food for the clients and your own family members. Another benefit could be raised in profits from the plants. And what's amazing is aquaponics systems require almost no power to operate, and also the time that it requires to keep up one's body is tiny in the event that you place up the system in the very first location.

I've just been utilizing aquaponics to get a couple of years, but I would not ever return again to grow my plants and vegetables on the floor. There are a number of tools that will assist you in making your home aquaponics system. The greatest could be found on the web. But expect in me once you begin having the gains of one's aquaponics system, you may not return again. You may even begin selling or eating the fish which you employ on the body.

Thus that the advantages of dwelling aquaponics are worth using for the tiny cost it takes to place up the system. You are able to purchase aquaponics systems, but I would advise that you know to establish your system. As you're able to customize your system to that which you really would like to do using it. Additionally, purchased systems have a tendency to get repaired, and that means that you cannot make changes in their mind without even affecting how they work.

DIY aquaponic plans you can build

A lot of people desire their aquaponic system nowadays, and it's not any wonder. Imagine having the capability to grow both plants along with fish at a tidy, closed system using hardly any job.

Insert the pleasure along with the pleasure of increasing fish and your favorite hydroponic plants by employing an all pure cycle, and also, the prevalence of home-scale aquaponics becomes evident.

But pre-made, professional aquaponic systems might be quite high priced. That's the reason why a lot of enthusiasts have resorted to creating their very own aquaponics setup. The outcome is extremely creative and diverse.

1. The simplest DIY in-door aquaponic system

Not all aquaponic setups are created completely from scratch. Lots of folks already possess a tank for your fish and want to get an easy method to upgrade it into an aquaponic program.

The aquaculture element is an aquarium containing four gold-fish. The corner pump attracts up the water into the plant bed - a more frequent window elongated kettle comprising the hydro ton moderate.

The intriguing spin is that the develop bed input is wholly snuggled to a typical aquarium filter cleaner , which functions like a filter (the writer also claims there are wiggler worms living inside it, even though they're perhaps not shown), also ensures the gentle flow of this bed.

The machine is outfitted with a timer that makes it possible for the water to flood the grow bed every quarter-hour. The water has been emptied back in the tank for your fish.

The machine utilizes additional turbo for both the plant bed, along with an abysmal aluminum foil light-box for greater plant development. Because of this, it's perfect and designed for places with no or low organic lighting, i.e., that your garage.

2. Fifty dollars table-top aquaponics from garden thrifty

The other tank-upgrade method - that an aquarium of just 10 g is a home for the bass, and also an easy fitting PVC pipe with end covers plays the use of a hydroponic plant bed.

Because it's indeed simple, economical, and cheap, it generates a great very first take to at aquaponic and also a fantastic chance to coach kids at a house in your own class in regards to the pure nutritional cycles.

Remember that little tanks (and therefore the whole aquaponic systems) tend to be more compound instability, which could endanger both plants and fish. This endeavor was up and functioning for two weeks ahead of your site had been written; therefore, despite the chance, it's passed. First evaluation of functionality.

How to make a profit from aquaponics

There are several aquaponics farms all across the entire world producing vegetables and different plants with aquaponics and attempting to sell their own manufacture for profits. Aquaponics is quite a bit more profitable compared to the standard means of farming since it uses less water so that you never require many liquid nutritional elements as well as different supplements, it develops more veggies at precisely the exact same space and also the vegetables grow faster too.

Overall, it is a “win-win-win" situation. It will not get much better than that.

Understanding how to set up your aquaponics business will demand one to complete a little bit of research. The absolute most crucial issue is that you simply decide to try out it to a modest scale initially and see whether you should be capable of it. You may see the ideas and tricks of this transaction just by being on the job.

What's more economical on an inferior scale along with also your mistakes won't be high priced. After getting the hang of this, the expansion won't be a challenge, and also you are able to scale your system quite readily.

It'd be fantastic for those who can know just as much about aquaponics as possible until you start because learning today is much superior to cope with mistakes.

Research it on the internet for a couple of aquaponics books, and also an online aquaponics class is likely to soon be quite beneficial in teaching you. Knowledge is essential to your results.

See a profitable aquaponics farm

First thing you will want to perform is always checkout exactly what additional aquaponics farms seem of course, when you've got one in just several hours of your geographical area, it'll be worth your driveway check it out -- only call to make sure they'll accept you as a guest. You may be amazed by how hot, helpful, and friendly lots of those water fountains could be.

Do your study and version yourself after the ones that are successful. Seek an expert comment and decide to try to consult with the proprietors of their different farms and request advice. Attempt to locate farms away from yours in the order they usually do not be concerned about rivalry unless you are simply creating as a pastime, or small scale to nourish your family members.

Produce a set of needed aquaponic equipment

Next, you'll need to get a listing of all of the gear you may need and also see whether your budget allows it. Always enable some leeway. Don't overstretch yourself. There'll always be several unexpected costs; therefore, you'll want to get ready.

Draft a “profit with aquaponics" business program

In case you want you, employ a professional to draft a comprehensive business strategy for you personally with estimations on cash flow, fixed and variable expenses, and projected earnings announcements. This helps greatly in the event that you would like to procure financing in the future.

Pick the positioning of one's aquaponics farm

Locate the right site. That really is essential and may not be underestimated. The place of one's aquaponics farm will determine how powerful you're. Several aquaponics farms also have gone bankrupt only because they picked the incorrect site. Exactly enjoy a storefront; the location is critically crucial.

Your farm has to be within a place with the adequate sun for your plants to photosynthesize. Temperatures should really be stable and never change wildly. There needs to be sufficient distance enclosing your farm only in the event you want to enlarge in the future. It is sometimes a large heartache in the future should you would like to enlarge your farm; however, you're restricted by structures that cannot be transferred, thereby limiting your capacity for expansion.

Locate a dependable provider with great rates

Next up, you'll need to supply for and purchase your equipment, gear, and anything else you require. Look for probably the most reliable providers that could also offer decent pricing and prices. You want to use homework because quality and costs could fluctuate greatly from place to place.

If your strategy would be to function commercially, you may even have to enroll your possessions, receive all the needed requirements and blessings, perform the whole IRS item and conform to tax conditions to prevent future legal difficulties. Employing a lawyer is a fantastic idea.

Last, you'll need to advertise your own services and products. That really is beyond the scope of the guide; however, once the time arrives to scale your performance, whatever you have to do is find someone experienced that will assist you along with your own marketing.

That is a fundamental variant of the best way to earn cash with aquaponics. Whether you are taking a look at aquaponic farming being a profitable company or perhaps a means to diminish and eliminate your family food expenses, it's benefit in any event.

There is a lot more which you will detect and know while you go along. The ideal thing that you can do today would be to know just as much as possible before starting and maintain learning as you proceed, and you may succeed.

Is commercial aquaponics sustainable & profitable?

Aquaponics is a combination of hydroponics (growing plants in plain water) and aquaculture (increasing fish). This really is a fresh and “innovative" idea but has been in existence for years and years. It's fixing within our modern environment and bringing lots of men and women.

Plus, a few of those larger concerns can also be rising with an increase in reputation. Whether or maybe aquaponics will be profitable enough to support a family group?

This really is among the most frequent question asked by individuals listen to aquaponics. Even though it's far better than farming in a lot of ways, it's perhaps not just a viable venture for the majority of growers, whether or not it isn't financially viable.

In accordance with the Chicago Tribune, the second tide of ecopreneurs expects to locate the secret to earning aquaponics profitable. As it includes attractive non-monetary added benefits, also it can prevent agricultural threats such as tornadoes, storms, floods, and droughts.

Before we move farther, we must place our goal and scalability. The monetary expectations vary greatly on the farmers. Many are simply hoping to break and intend to use on a charitable foundation. The others are predicting substantial returns having a large agricultural firm as a primary measure; it's essential to recognize your aims when assessing sustainability. On scalability, aquaponics can be divided into three classes

Commercial aquaponics

Backyard/DIY aquaponics

Small goldfish /betta aquaponics tanks

We'll only discuss commercial aquaponics here!

Is commercial-scale aquaponics economically viable?

When it comes to a garden strategy, you might be doing this like a hobby or to encourage the family members or maybe simply to create some salad and berries to the table.

However, on the industrial scale, even the aquaponics farm is assumed to raise profits and capital.

To assess the economic backbone of aquaponic farms, we will need to dip into:

1.Capital/investment cost (construction the device, installation of the performance logistics, etc...)

2.Operational cost

3.The profitability of this performance

4. Aquaponics is profitable if it's done to some particular scale.

5. Investment price is high that can be the most important drawback of aquaponics.

6. In usable cost, more power can be employed compared to conventional aquaponics. But, labor cost, for example, fleas and archiving, are paid down. Water is preserved that can be the principal ingestion in agriculture. Recurring expenditures, overall, are lower when compared with conventional agriculture.

7. Furthermore, every performance differs concerning machine layout, species selection scale. Nobody can make authoritative claims

concerning the sustainability of aquaponics without researching the demographics of their neighborhood market and specifications relating to this aquaponics greenhouse.

8. Here are some numbers of research on aquaponics farms to give you a thought

A 2014 research from researched 257 industrial aquaponics growers located inside the USA. It reasoned that their usable metrics and fiscal success. A number of important findings:

The normal size of these surgeries is .03 acres (1,307 sq. ft.). Approximately 40 percent of surgeries are backyard/home-based; others were on the agricultural or commercial territory.

Though most manufacturers used a combo of two or even more aquaponics systems (press, wicking beds, rafts, nft (and perpendicular towers), both the rafts and press beds would be the most frequently experienced.

Just 31 percent of growers have been rewarding.

The 55% anticipated to become profitable over the following 1-2 weeks, and 75% targeted to become more profitable from another 3-6 weeks.

The industrial aquaponics performance wasn't the key revenue stream for 70 percent of owners.

Perhaps not one farm managed to earn fish production profitable.

Is fish only a nutrient resource for your plant? Or, how can fish become described as a profitable venture of this system? None the less, the fish increase rate must grow to the bass enterprise to afford the benefit.

Total investment cost

The labor and materials required to build the system would be the important cost parts. You're going to require plenty of money to build only a greenhouse.

Any industrial installation could be significantly costlier and will require no less than a dam.

Hydroponic rainwater could be more costly due to some variables. You're going to require a huge concentration of water-mixed nutrition to nourish the plants, and also capacity to pump which water, run both fans and detectors.

Commercial aquaponics isn't just a secure bet or an assuredly profitable industry, as just about 1/3 of surgeries are profitable. Some crucial things we must consider concerning the analysis:

The analysis failed to think about the intention/goals of growers. As nearly all growers don't make aquaponics their principal livelihood, we are able to stipulate the poll comprises some business growers that probably do not need or should make substantial profits.

Most operations continue to be in the original period, using a normal period at the company of roughly 4 years during the time of this analysis.

When we assess just those who left living out of their commercial aquaponics greenhouse, profitability numbers may probably change.

Resources of revenue: just how can aquaponics farms generate income?

Besides fascinating recycling, saving, and saving, everybody else would like to understand the way the techniques to earn by the aquaponics return. Let us dive into to obtain different ways aquaponics farms earning money.

That can be essential since it shows you various procedures that may be appropriate to your future or current plan.

The primary ways comprise:

Selling plants

Aquaponics classes

Selling fish

Selling system

There can be other procedures, but these would be the most frequent ones.

Like every organization, you want to experience or want to involve somebody who gets the business acumen to successfully conduct an industrial aquaponics. Being an interested grower and becoming excited with the coolness of aquaponics will perhaps not guarantee victory, hardheaded organization decisions based on knowledge and experience performing. A whole lot of beginners without firm experience view their vegetable fish and growing ingestion but do not get they truly are slowly pushing the amount of money down the drain.

The way to make aquaponics more profitable

Grow the crops which are more expensive in your area to counter-balance the expenses of resources and energy. You have to perform proper research at the seasonal prices while in the area, you are likely to construct your process. It's possible for you to yield make money from berries and specialty plants such as yellow peppers and ginger as well as other herbs, which encourage this kind of greenhouse. However, you need any limit as you can't grow any grain plants, such as corn and wheat, better fitted to an open discipline.

You can grow more food in less distance as crops require space while growing quite near to each other in aquaponics/hydroponic greenhouses.

Additional tips regarding the fish in aquaponics really are

Boost edible fish rather than goldfish/koi

Take into account the fish into food ratio

Greatest fish to boost in aquaponics could be your indigenous and local the one that is going to prosper with the climatic states and each other

The blend of plants that are pricey and much more food at an inferior area helps alleviate the pain from the very first price of this greenhouse with the capacity for a higher benefit. Alas, the price tag isn't the only real dilemma for farmers.

Aquaponics is for town dwellers who wish to:

Eat refreshing organic food

Buy locally-made products

Start a company

Love food safety that does not need stockpiling canned green beans

Contribute to neighborhood enhancement

Benefit from dealing with crops

Inspire future generations

The way to make a commercial aquaponics system into a profitable business

Starting your aquaponics to gain business isn't difficult to complete. Based upon how big is your own aquaponics system launch costs might be, maintenance and small minimal. Organic food can be really a significant business with several folks attempting to eat foods that are wholesome. These varieties of foods can be exceedingly costly to purchase the shop. Together with your aquaponics business, you're going to have the ability to supply premium quality foods that are healthy at a sensible price providing you with a steady source of clients. Below are a few things you want to bear in mind so as to possess a powerful aquaponics system.

Location: where you can put your own aquaponic system will considerably determine how well your fish perform and also how fast your plants grow. Keep away from temperature extremes and be certain that there is certainly enough beneficial light for your plants to cultivate. Avoid areas where compounds are found. Additionally, for those who own a garden, aquaponics ensure end isn't one variable.

Fish: the most aquaponics fish species that you utilize is a private preference. Many kinds of fish will probably get the job done. A number of popular choices include crappie, channel catfish, tilapia, smallmouth bass, and bluegill. Ensure that on your choice of fish which you simply combine species that adapt well to one another. Your own choice of fish may even be based on where you are and local legislation regulating the increase of fish. Be certain that the water that you put your fish is correctly ventilated.

Plant selection: you'll have the ability to develop a wide array of aquaponic vegetables and plants to offer. Individuals who buy from you'll be stunned at just how well your tastes. Food stated within an aquaponics system features a far more economical, cleaner taste than that which can be bought from the stores. A number of the food items you'll be in a position to produce include berries, oranges, oranges, melons plus a whole lot more. Leafy vegetables, in addition to herbs, may be grown successfully on your aquaponics for benefit enterprise.

Aquaponics will still continue to develop as a company chance in the forthcoming years as people find wholesome food in a less high price. Not only are you able to earn money by fulfilling this requirement, but you might also decrease your food bill and, at the exact same time, eat a fitter too. An aquaponics for benefit company can supply you with the monetary stability you want and help you live a wholesome life.

This really is an opportunity for you to help cure the earth by producing food that's in harmony with how nature intended it to become.

The aquaponics business scheme

The aquaponics company is really a pragmatic method of making money via a straightforward yet effective farming system where farmers could afford and promote both vegetable and fish products at a higher speed.

There are many important items to be conscious of how to start out your own aquaponics business:

1. Execute a study on aquaponics business and collect info about what best to prepare and control a business enterprise. Seek qualified tips about the best way best to use aquaponics farming.

2. Start looking for a professional adviser in preparing the comprehensive business strategy for that aquaponics farm. The master plan should contain a fiscal statement involving a cash flow, estimated start-up, and earnings announcement.

3. Start looking for a place at which you want to prepare the farm. Select a location where temperatures aren't that much or too low. Make sure that the region doesn't have any damaging compounds as it is going to damage and kill the fish along with also the plants. Moreover, make certain plants get sufficient or enough light to guarantee they have the ability to do photosynthesis, and also a very important process from the creation of this food.

4. Get all of the required substances necessary to get aquaponics farming, for example, fish tanks, water pumps, and growing medium for the plants, and also growing beds from which plants will have increased.

5. Register your own aquaponics farm to acquire the mandatory business license and permits from the internal revenue service to acquire employer identification number and also to adhere to federal tax conditions. That is imperative to prevent legal problems because you proceed together with your own aquaponics business.

Understanding how to build and run a commercial aquaponics system is made up of three core purposes.

O advertising

O operations

O finance

Marketing is the main role because running an organization; nothing happens until somebody sells something.

An aquaponics company relies heavily on the tech used from the aquaponics farming procedure. Because Oahu is the cheapest and efficient method to build fish and plants. Fantastic quality, attracting more prospective prospects, is easier in contrast to classic farming. We are all aware that in this generation, all of the things are conducted on top technology we are utilized to. This is the reason why aquaponics farmers hunt professional guidance to direct them on how best to effectively and economically manage their plantation and collect recent improvements from aquaponics.

The others may be cynical and have thoughts-boggling questions at heart. Has anybody successfully handled a profitable industrial aquaponics firm? The solution is yes. That is true since the years' pass; the company system has enhanced -- traders are becoming smarter, and folks are getting to be more business interested, discovering better methods to boost how to manage their small business. And bear in mind, success is dependent upon the patience and love of the company.

We have to face the fact that of-times economics is much more critical than whatever else. We now have to reveal that our wisdom and sustainability in the financial sector will reveal interest within our enterprise market. Additionally, this is the opportunity for one to help restore the healthful condition of types from producing food in a far safer manner -- free of harmful compounds and toxic elements.

Developing a sustainable food supply during aquaponics

Aquaponics is much more effective than conventional backyard gardening methods and creates better harvest yields with less expenditure and energy. Most plants that may be grown in property established vegetable gardens may be generated through aquaponics. Fruits may be increased in aquaponic systems but generally need a greater fish density to offer extra nourishment. As mentioned previously, fish employed in aquaponics might be increased as an additional supply of food as pets. Tilapia, fish, fish, crappie, crayfish, and prawns are good possibilities for fish, which can be finally eaten. Ornamental fish like koi and goldfish are good choices for pets.

This is the way that aquaponics uses the partnership involving fish and plants. Because they grow and eat, fish produce odor, which adds ammonia into the water. At relatively lower concentrations, ammonia is dead to fish. During a natural process called the nitrogen cycle, ammonia in fish waste has been transformed by bacteria that are valuable to nitrites, which can be transformed by different bacteria to nitrates. While nitrites will also be detrimental to fish at low levels, nitrates aren't. But, elevated amounts of nitrates from the water could result in excess algae growth and also are detrimental to fish. Luckily, nitrates provide nutrients that are crucial for the plant. By swallowing the nitrates, the plants filter out the water and also maintain a vibrant aquatic environment to fish. Thus by growing and eating, the fish provide crucial nourishment to your plants, and from growing and eating, the plants deliver safe water to fish. Aquaponics is your ideal answer for bass enthusiasts the need to dump excess nitrates, in addition to hydroponic gardeners, will need to nourish nutrients with their plants.

Just as a growing number of individuals live in metropolitan areas that they've less and less info regarding lunar agriculture development and food manufacturing companies.

People don't know modern farming methods that assist folks in eating up wholesome meals, live healthy lifestyles, and add to the environment at precisely the exact same moment.

But, there's still a great deal of space for advanced farmers to secure their location and also share with this market. With the accessibility of advice and the world wide web, embracing new technologies and advanced solutions has become easier than ever before.

CONCLUSION

Aquaponics is a method of generating Quality produce in a sustainable and effective fashion and has existed for several decades. It's much faster and more effective compared to other alternatives like waste management. For meals waste management to generate progress, the present attitudes and customs of western states must change entirely. This is a pretty large inquire and might take years and years to set a method where people don't waste food. In this way, food waste management could definitely be a fantastic remedy to global food safety, as we require a solution that's going to be extremely powerful and gains immediate support from the western as well as third world nations, and we want this alternative quickly; otherwise, the planet will enter a crisis. However, since aquaponics does not require people to modify their lifestyle on a mass scale, they're a lot more likely to acquire support from people, meaning it may be established far faster and help to keep food safe, and consequently making aquaponics the very best alternative.

Aquaponics is effective sustainable and above most of the very best solution to nourish the entire world. It's easy to conduct and utilizes Less water than conventional farming and genetically modified goods, and Will permit us to visit the demands of food safety at a quicker rate than that which a Solution like food waste management could. Food generated within Aquaponic Systems are full of nourishment, and unlike genetic modification have no Potential dangers to the health of the environment or people consuming the produce. Aquaponics now have a Few of flaws, although they're Minor and with additional study and analysis could be easily overcome.

In Conclusion, it's essential that we, as a society, start to check toward greater meals Generating methods. If society continues to neglect our present situation and proceeds On using unsustainable and ineffective procedures, the future of our environment and agricultural sector may see a downfall. There are lots of various techniques to repair the dilemma of food safety; however, realistically, aquaponics is the most environmentally friendly and Efficient method of farming, which may easily fulfill the requirements of people, and Match all climates across the globe.

CPSIA information can be obtained
at www.ICGtesting.com
Printed in the USA
BVHW060054200321
603031BV00005B/762

9 781801 689342